AN ANTHOLOGY OF
LIVING
RELIGIONS

MARY PAT FISHER
LEE W. BAILEY

PRENTICE HALL
Upper Saddle River, N.J. 07458

Prentice Hall
Upper Saddle River, N.J. 07458

10 9 8 7 6 5 4 3 2 1

ISBN 0–13–015657–4

This book was designed and produced by
CALMANN AND KING LTD., LONDON

Project manager: Richard Mason
Designer: Sara Robin
Typeset by Fakenham Photosetting, Norfolk

Printed in China

Cover: Chase, Michael (living artist),
Greek Dancers, Hosios Lukas Country, detail (Delphi)
Private Collection/Bridgeman Art Library, London

CONTENTS

CHAPTER FOUR

JAINISM
page 92

CHAPTER FIVE
BUDDHISM
page 111

CHAPTER EIGHT
JUDAISM
page 184

CHAPTER NINE

CHRISTIANITY
page 218

CHAPTER TEN
ISLAM
page 254

CHAPTER THIRTEEN

THE INTERFAITH MOVEMENT

page 334

PREFACE

Religious points of view underlie the thinking and behavior of the majority of the world's citizens. As we enter the twenty–first century, a deeper understanding of these perspectives is a necessity in our increasingly interwoven, pluralistic cultures. To enhance understanding and perhaps appreciation of each religion, we offer here a selection of interesting and significant texts explaining each religion from the inside, as its founders and practitioners have explained it and as people are trying to live by its precepts today. Our book gives the major world religions—as well as a sampling of local and new religions—the opportunity to explain themselves in their own terms.

We have tried to open many windows to understanding. We offer excerpts from each religion's original inspired writings or oral traditions, exemplary stories about the founders, significant later elaborations of the teachings, and recent articles showing each religion grappling with contemporary issues These include environmental decay, women's issues, social injustice, the relation between religion and politics, and tensions between fundamentalist and liberal interpretations of the faith. We have included women's voices and histories throughout the anthology. We believe that these excerpts old and new illustrate that religions are dynamic and relevant in today's world.

To guide readers through this wealth of material, we first introduce the founder, history, and basic principles of each faith. Each excerpt or group of excerpts is also preceded by a brief introduction to the context and significance of the material. Unfamiliar terms are defined in a glossary at the end of each chapter as well. For each religion, we also offer historical outlines, questions for study and discussion, and lists of further resources, such as books, periodicals, and Internet websites. Although this anthology thus stands on its own, it follows the organization of Mary Pat Fisher's bestselling textbook, *Living Religions*, and can be used with the text for deeper understanding.

In selecting and pulling together this treasure-trove of old and new religious texts, we have been aided by many people around the world. Working from the Gobind Sadan Institute for Advanced Studies in Comparative Religion, New Delhi, Mary Pat Fisher would like to express her deep gratitude to Dr. Jeffrey Adams, Professor of the Psychology of Religion, St. Michael's College, Vermont, for suggestions pertaining to Chapter 1, "The Religious Response"; Dr. Jacob Olupona, Chair of Afro-American Studies, University of California, Davis, for suggestions on indigenous religions; Swami Dharamananda, Jain Adhyatma Sadhana Kendra, New Delhi, for Jain materials; Dr. Chatsumarn Kabilsingh, Director of Indian Studies Centre, Thammasat University, Bangkok, for Buddhist materials; Dr. Xingzhong Yao, Deputy Head of the Department of Religious Studies, University of Wales, for extensive input on Taoism and Confucianism; Dr. Judith Plaskow of Manhattan College for help with Jewish materials; Dr. Durwood Foster, Professor Emeritus of Christian Theology, Pacific School of Religion, Berkeley, for suggestions on Christian texts; Dr. Mehmet S. Aydin, Professor of Philosophy and Dean of the Faculty of Divinity, Dokuz Eylul University, Izmir,

Turkey, for suggestions pertaining to Islamic texts; Dr. Jodh Singh, Dean of Faculty of Humanities and Religious Studies, Punjabi University, Patiala, India, for aid with Sikh materials; and Dr. David Craig, formerly Director of Religious Broadcasting for BBC World Service and now Visiting Professor in the Multi-Faith Department, University of Middlesex, U.K., for advice on new religions and interfaith materials. She would also like to gratefully thank Rev. Marcus Braybrooke, Director of the International Interfaith Centre, Oxford, and Rev. Martin Forward, Academic Dean of Wesley House, Cambridge University, for their help in providing and locating interfaith materials; and Dr. G. S. Anand of the Bhai Vir Singh Sahitya Sadan Library, Bhai Kirpal Singh of the Gobind Sadan Institute, Novin Doostdar, Publisher of Oneworld Publications, and Edward G. Fisher for their assistance in tracking down many significant texts.

Working from the other side of the world at Ithaca College in New York State, Dr. Lee Bailey expresses his grateful thanks to Dr. Karen Bergmann, Dr. Brian Karafin, Dr. Richard Creel, and Dr. Lynn Schweber, of Ithaca College's Department of Philosophy and Religion, for very important input on Buddhism, Christianity, and Judaism; to Ruth Mas at the University of Toronto's Centre for the Study of Religion for most essential counsel on Islam; to Peter Fortunato, a poet of skillful ways, formerly of Ithaca College's Writing Program, for careful readings, critical feedback, and advice on several chapters; to Dr. José Barriero of Cornell University's American Indian Program and Editor of "Native Americas" Magazine, for valued input on Indigenous Sacred Ways, to Dr. Asma Barlas, of Ithaca College's Politics Department, for much appreciated guidance on Islam; to Michael Faber, Jewish Chaplain at Ithaca College, for very helpful guidance on Judaism.

The authors and publisher would like to thank the following reviewers for their comments on the manuscript: Dr. James Robinson, University of Northern Iowa; Dr. Nancy Hardesty, Clemson University; Dr. Douglas Evans, University of Central Florida; Dr. Philip C. Schmitz, Eastern Michigan University.

Professor Bailey also expresses his special thanks to the many thoughtful students, devoted collegial scholars, professors, clergy, friends, spiritual seekers, retreat guides, and conference presenters who have contributed to this vision of living world religions. For Mary Pat Fisher, its preparation has been particularly inspired by His Holiness Baba Virsa Singh, patron of the Gobind Sadan Institute for Advanced Studies in Comparative Religion, who generously shares his profound appreciation and understanding of the world's sacred scriptures with people of all faiths. May our readers also grow in understanding and appreciation, for the sake of us all.

Mary Pat Fisher, Gobind Sadan Institute for Advanced Studies in Comparative Religion, New Delhi, 1999

Dr. Lee W. Bailey, Department of Philosophy and Religion, Ithaca College, New York, 1999

CHAPTER 1
THE RELIGIOUS RESPONSE

Religious observances have been, and continue to be, salient around the world in all cultures. Global religions and new religious movements are vibrant in many regions, often playing a significant role in public events as well as people's personal lives. For great numbers of people around the world, religion is a central aspect of life's patterns and meanings. Religious experiences may inspire courage, patience, tolerance, charity, morality, acts of extreme altruism, and selfless love. They may have a healing, transformative effect. They may reveal unseen dimensions of existence. Religious experiences and training may also frighten, oppress, and breed violence and hatred of others, if the teachings have been misunderstood or distorted by religious "authorities" acting in their own self-interest.

There is no one pattern which can be universally termed "religion." Many prophets have appeared, offering what is understood by their followers as enlightened wisdom. Institutions have been built around their teachings and, with them, somewhat different understandings of life and different methods of approaching the truth of existence. To many people, "religion" refers to reverence for and communication with the supernatural, but certain "religions" such as branches of Buddhism refer only to the material world and liberation from worldly sufferings, without explicit reference to deity.

In subsequent chapters, we will offer a wealth of primary source material giving intimate glimpses into each world of faith as the faithful understand it. However, before doing so, in this chapter we will approach religions from a distance, trying to gain a critical basis for understanding the many perspectives from which religious phenomena have been studied.

Some readers coming to the study of world religions from a traditional religious background may react with discomfort as they encounter new ideas and new religions. Others more skeptical or critical of traditional religions may be uncomfortable with certain practices, such as some authors' use of the masculine pronouns or expressions such as "man" meant to include both genders. We hope that readers will maintain both a sympathetic respect and a critical eye, and strive to understand the historical background and personal diversity for the colorful variety of human religious expressions. The best reasons for maintaining or changing religious practices come from understanding them.

The comparative study of religion

As modern technologies accelerate the globalization of culture, believers of the world's religions have come into contact with each other and compared their experiences of the **sacred**. As a consequence, the "comparative" study of religion has blossomed. It has become difficult for an educated person to assume that their religion has the privilege of being the single absolutely valid religion. Interpretation, experience, and participation are now combined with a neutral, non-judgmental, respectful stance toward the richness of the world's spiritual traditions.

Interpreting the Sacred
by William E. Paden

Professor William E. Paden of the University of Vermont explains the contemporary realization that, due to science and global culture, religion is being studied not simply as fixed absolute, literal truths, but as a way of interpreting reality. The sacred reality at the heart of spiritual traditions thus requires new interpretations.

Traditional cultures and religions naturally assumed their own points of view to be absolute. They did not understand their standpoints to be *versions* of the world alongside others. One's own religious beliefs seemed so widely accepted and self-evidently true that they were taken not as one of several descriptions of reality, but simply as the description of reality itself. Every culture socialized its members into these scripts, into religious programs which presented fixed, incontrovertible images of the world and its foundations. Every culture saw itself as the center of the universe, creating geographies and calendars which ordered all space and time around its own sacred absolutes, its own all-satisfying spiritual orders. What could not be seen—so cohesive and authoritative were these traditional worldviews, and so innocent of genuine cross-cultural perspective—was that this "language/reality" frame was one interpretation of the world among hundreds of different ones. . . .

Stepping Back and Studying the Frames Themselves   The capacity to see one's view of the world *as* a view is a mark of contemporary thinking. Such awareness creates a basis for understanding the plurality of standpoints. The moment in which the views of others come into focus arises partly through the contemplative act of stepping back from one's own perspective and recognizing that it, too, is situated. Not just perceiving the world, but perceiving *how* we perceive the world, is in some ways becoming second nature to a pluralistic, self-conscious culture.

A new world of social and cultural diversity has formed the historical setting for this self-reflective moment. The move toward pluralistic thinking is partly an effect of contact with and respect for people who have different worldviews within the same society—the city being now the image of this diversity as the town once was an image of homogeneity. The increasing awareness of global cultures has also helped create consciousness of the positioned nature of our own views, though this realization comes more slowly. Educationally, the multitude of scientific, social scientific, and humanistic ways of construing the world gives students diverse models by which to describe their existence. It is becoming more difficult to imagine any single image of the world as having a privileged, absolute status.

The idea of interpreting religion as a modern subject matter for study alongside other human sciences was a nineteenth-century creation, made possible primarily by the emergent knowledge of Asian religions. In the 1860s the German-born Oxford scholar F. Max Müller began calling for a "science of religion" that would approach the subject not in the previous fashion of speculative theories, but on the basis of accurate information about non-Western traditions and evenhanded comparisons between all types of religions. Because it was grounded in an impartial, unbiased attitude toward the data, he likened it to the new study of geology and other sciences that were now to be inductively accountable to facts rather than based on deductions from a particular religious ideology. Religion was to become a subject that could be examined and generalized about independently of the churches, and no longer used just to illustrate preconceived philosophies that had no sense of religion's global history. The science of religion was to be based on sound comparative study of all religions, and Müller's claim became, "He who knows one, knows none." If we only know one, we do not know what it has in common with the others, and therefore we do not know what is different about it. . . .

The typical modern representative of the comparative viewpoint is Mircea Eliade (1907–86), a Romanian scholar who taught in the United States and whose works and terminology became highly influential. . . .

The Language of Religion   Religion has its own forms of expression, and it is these forms that make it religion rather than science or government. Part of Eliade's contribution was to draw attention to the way religion expresses itself through the languages of myth, symbol, and ritual.

Religious language in its primary sense is participatory and invocative rather than **empirical** and detached. It is language which grounds human action in images about the nature of the world and which is exemplified in scriptures or their oral equivalents. Unlike scientific language, which by its nature is nonsubjective and nonparticipatory, religious language connects individuals with a moral order, offering stories, teachings, and images about the meaning or purpose of life, and giving guidelines for behavior that correspond to them. Religious language is not just an explanation of the world—science does that too—but a way, for its adherents, of *inhabiting* the world. This habitative function means that religious people see the world through the lens of **mythic** or scriptural vocabularies and regulate their lives according to the models and injunctions set forth in such traditions. They rest on the Sabbath because God did, exercise love and compassion because Jesus or the Buddha did, observe the Ten Commandments because people were enjoined to do so in the great time of the Mount Sinai revelation, or practice selfless action because Krishna so taught in the immortal words of the Bhagavad Gita.

Here is language endowed with the prestige of primal, divine status and origins, with the power of creation, the memory of founding ancestors, and the wisdom of great beings like Buddha, Christ, or Confucius. Religious words are of such sacred authority that followers live and die by them.

Religion is therefore an entirely different system of language than science, and the two systems clearly describe different parts of the human universe. . . .

Religion and the Sacred   For comparativists like Eliade, religion is about *the sacred*, just as for Durkheimians[1] it is about society, and for Jungians[2] it is about the psyche. What does it mean to say that religion is a system of language and practices which organizes the world around what is deemed sacred?

In this context *the sacred* refers to those focal objects which to the insider seem endowed with superhuman power and authority. Depending on the culture, it could be a scripture, a great person or high religious leader, a god, an ancestor, an institution like the Catholic Church, an aspect of nature such as a mountain or river, a path of discipline taught by a Buddha, or a sacred rite. . . . Other expressions, like "experience of the supernatural," "encounter with the holy," "feeling of the **numinous**," or "sense of the **transcendent**" have also been used. . . .

Because sacredness is always embodied in particular forms, students of comparative religion are expected to see that it is not the literal, surface aspect of the forms or objects that are revered, but the transhuman force or sacredness felt *in* them. . . .

---

[1] Durkheimians—followers of Emile Durkheim (1858–1917), the French sociologist who argued that religion is only the collective images produced by society to codify the sacred and the profane for social solidarity.
[2] Jungians—followers of Carl G. Jung (1875–1961), the Swiss psychologist who developed archetypal psychology, which sees religious images as meaningful expressions of the psyche.

Suspension of Judgment As a descriptive enterprise, the comparative study of religion tries to proceed without the interpretive bias of any particular religious or antireligious position. Rather than looking at religion as something right or wrong, it looks as it as a *type* of experience, behavior, and symbol system. Religion is therefore seen as a *phenomenon.* . . .

To the comparativist, religious beliefs are first of all expressions of someone's worldview rather than propositions to be argued in terms of their independent truth.

The comparative attitude therefore calls for a dispassionate capacity to comprehend and explain other people's experience of their worlds without interjecting one's own preferences. One must "bracket off"[3] one's own concepts of how the world ought to be organized in order to listen to how others configure it, and temporarily set aside what the world means to oneself in order to gain access to what the world means to others.

SOURCE: William E. Paden, *Interpreting the Sacred: Ways of Viewing Religion.* Boston, MA: Beacon Press, 1992, pp. 2–74

The phenomenology of religions

Many contemporary scholars of religion are attempting to understand the meanings of sacred behaviors and beliefs as their own practitioners understand them, and through cross-cultural phenomena such as myth, ritual, and the sacred/profane distinction, rather than imposing norms from a particular culture.

The Sacredness of Nature and Cosmic Religion
by Mircea Eliade

Professor Mircea Eliade (1907–86) of the University of Chicagos was a pioneer in the phenomenological approach to the study of religion. The Encyclopedia of Religion, *which he edited, is now a standard research tool in the discipline of world religions. He blended two major methods in his approach: first, the history of religions, in order to clarify the factual side of religions, such as the dates, places, historical contexts, and texts; and second, the* **phenomenology** *of religions, in order to reflect intuitively and symbolically on the essence of religion by comparing archetypal themes such as the sacred and the* **profane** *in space, time, nature, and human existence. He was a major contributor to a renewed understanding of myth and ritual as worldwide religious phenomena, highly symbolic and meaningful. Eliade's multi-cultural analysis of the "sky gods" from his classic 1957 book* The Sacred and the Profane *is an example of this approach.*

---

[3] Bracket off—to hold one's evaluation of a religious element in suspension while studying it neutrally; an aspect of phenomenology.

For religious man, nature is never only "natural"; it is always fraught with a religious value. This is easy to understand, for the cosmos is a divine creation; coming from the hands of the gods, the world is impregnated with sacredness. It is not simply a sacrality *communicated* by the gods, as is the case, for example, with a place or an object consecrated by the divine presence. The gods did more; *they manifested the different modalities of the sacred in the very structure of the world and of cosmic phenomena.*

The world stands displayed in such a manner that, in contemplating it, religious man discovers the many modalities of the sacred, and hence of being. Above all, the world exists, it is there, and it has a structure; it is not a chaos but a cosmos, hence it presents itself as creation, as work of the gods. This divine work always preserves its quality of transparency, that is, it spontaneously reveals the many aspects of the sacred. The sky directly, "naturally," reveals the infinite distance, the transcendence of the deity. The earth too is transparent; it presents itself as universal mother and nurse. The cosmic rhythms manifest order, harmony, permanence, fecundity. The cosmos as a whole is an organism at once *real*, *living*, and *sacred*; it simultaneously reveals the modalities of being and of sacrality. Ontophany[4] and hierophany[5] meet.

In this chapter we shall try to understand how the world presents itself to the eyes of religious man—or, more precisely, how sacrality is revealed through the very structures of the world. We must not forget that for religious man the supernatural is indissolubly connected with the natural, that nature always expresses something that transcends it. As we said earlier: a sacred stone is venerated because it is *sacred*, not because it is a *stone*; it is the sacrality *manifested through the mode of being of the stone* that reveals its true essence. This is why we cannot speak of naturism or of natural religion in the sense that the nineteenth century gave to those terms; for it is "supernature" that the religious man apprehends through the natural aspects of the world.

The Celestial Sacred and the Uranian Gods   Simple contemplation of the celestial vault already provokes a religious experience. The sky shows itself to be infinite, transcendent. It is pre-eminently the "wholly other" than the little represented by man and his environment. Transcendence is revealed by simple awareness of infinite height. "Most high" spontaneously becomes an attribute of divinity. The higher regions inaccessible to man, the sidereal zones, acquire the momentousness of the transcendent, of absolute reality, of eternity. There dwell the gods; there a few privileged mortals make their way by rites of ascent; there, in the conception of certain religions, mount the souls of the dead. The "most high" is a dimension inaccessible to man as

---

[4] Ontophany—a manifestation of being or sacred ultimate reality.
[5] Hierophany—a manifestation of the sacred in a limited earthly form.

man; it belongs to superhuman forces and beings. He who ascends by mounting the steps of a sanctuary or the ritual ladder that leads to the sky ceases to be a man; in one way or another, he shares in the divine condition.

All this is not arrived at by a logical, rational operation. The transcendental category of height, of the superterrestrial, of the infinite, is revealed to the whole man, to his intelligence and his soul. It is a total awareness on man's part; beholding the sky, he simultaneously discovers the divine incommensurability and his own situation in the cosmos. For the sky, *by its own mode of being*, reveals transcendence, force, eternity. It *exists absolutely* because it is *high, infinite, eternal, powerful*.

This is the true significance of the statement made above—that the gods manifested the different modalities of the sacred in the very structure of the world. In other words, the cosmos—paradigmatic work of the gods—is so constructed that a religious sense of the divine transcendence is aroused by the very existence of the sky. And since the sky *exists* absolutely, many of the supreme gods of primitive peoples are called by names designating height, the celestial vault, meteorological phenomena, or simply Owner of the Sky or Sky Dweller.

The supreme divinity of the Maori is named Iho; *iho* means elevated, high up. Uwoluwu, the supreme god of the Akposo Negroes, signifies what is on high, the upper regions. Among the Selk'nam of Tierra del Fuego God is called Dweller in the Sky or He Who is in the Sky. Puluga, the supreme being of the Andaman Islanders, dwells in the sky; the thunder is his voice, wind his breath, the storm is the sign of his anger, for with his lightning he punishes those who break his commandments.

SOURCE: Mircea Eliade, *The Sacred and the Profane: The Nature of Religion*, trans. W. R. Trask. New York and London: Harcourt Brace Jovanovich, 1959, pp. 116–20

Materialistic perspectives on religion

In recent centuries, the point of view of people of faith has often given way to a more materialistic point of view, which suggests that only the quantifiable material world is real and the sacred reality which most people have not seen is just a figment of human imagination. The following three excerpts give Freud's and Marx's interpretations that humans invented religion and then Nietzsche's charge that "God is dead."

The Future of an Illusion
by Sigmund Freud

Sigmund Freud (1856–1939), a Viennese physician, founded the widely influential psychoanalytic movement. He demonstrated, through the interpretation of dreams, errors, and physical symptoms, the reality and meaningfulness of the unconscious mind. He saw sexuality and distorted relationships with one's parents as the central dynamic of the unconscious. He saw religion as an infantile illusion, an unconscious search for security in a father figure, projected into the heavens.

When the growing individual finds that he is destined to remain a child forever, that he can never do without protection against strange superior powers, he lends these powers the features belonging to the figure of his father; he creates for himself the gods whom he dreads, whom he seeks to propitiate, and whom he nevertheless entrusts with his own protection. Thus his longing for a father is a motive identical with his need for protection against the consequences of his human weakness. . . .

Religious ideas . . . are not precipitates of experience or end-results of thinking: they are illusions, fulfillments of the oldest, strongest and most urgent wishes of mankind. The secret of their strength lies in the strength of those wishes. As we already know, the terrifying impression of helplessness in childhood aroused the need for protection—for protection through love— which was provided by the father; and the recognition that this helplessness lasts throughout life made it necessary to cling to the existence of a father, but this time a more powerful one. Thus the benevolent rule of a divine Providence[6] allays our fear of the dangers of life; the establishment of a moral world-order ensures the fulfillment of the demands of justice, which have so often remained unfulfilled in human civilization; and the promulgation of earthly existence in a future life provides the local and temporal framework in which these wish-fulfillments shall take place. Answers to the riddles that tempt the curiosity of man, such as how the universe began or what the relation is between body and mind, are developing in conformity with the underlying assumptions of this system. It is an enormous relief to the individual psyche if the conflicts of its childhood arising from the father-complex—conflicts which it has never wholly overcome—are removed from it and brought to a solution which is universally accepted.

An Illusion is not the same thing as an error. . . . What is characteristic of illusions is that they are derived from human wishes. In this respect they come near to psychiatric delusions . . . For instance, a middle-class girl may have the illusions that a prince will come and marry her. This is possible; and a few such cases have occurred. That the Messiah will come and found a golden age is much less likely . . . Thus we call a belief an illusion when a wish-fulfillment is a prominent factor in its motivation, and in so doing we disregard its relations to reality, just as the illusion sets no store by verification.

SOURCE: Sigmund Freud, *The Future of an Illusion.* New York: Doubleday, 1961, pp. 35–49

---

[6] Providence—God's care and guidance through inward inspiration and outer events.

Religion as the Opium of the People
by Karl Marx

Karl Marx (1818–83) was a German philosopher who founded Communism. With Friedrich Engels (1820–95), he developed the theory that class struggle is the primary mover of history, and posited that the working class would lead society from democratic bourgeois capitalism to a socialist, then a communist state. His analyses of the alienation of workers from industrialism and of the unjust and destructive effects of capitalism still influence many thinkers. Marx proclaimed "dialectical materialism"—the material interchange between human economic arrangements and the natural world—to be the guiding force in history. His view of religion is similar to that of Ludwig Feuerbach (1804–72), who in 1841 charged that religion is an illusory psychological projection of human emotions into the heavens. Marx added that this process is more social than psychological, with religion sanctioning and blessing the unjust status quo.

For Germany the *criticism of religion* is in the main complete, and criticism of religion is the premise of all criticism.

The *profane* existence of error is discredited after its *heavenly* speech for the altars and hearths has been rejected. Man, who looked for a superman in the fantastic reality of heaven and found nothing there but the *reflexion* of himself, will no longer be disposed to find but the *semblance* of himself, the non-human where he seeks and must seek his true reality.

The basis of irreligious criticism is: *Man makes religion*, religion does not make man. In other words, religion is the self-consciousness and self-feeling of man who has either not yet found himself or has already lost himself again. But *man* is no abstract being squatting outside the world. Man is *the world of man*, the state, society. This state, this society, produce religion, *a reversed world-consciousness*, because they are a *reversed* world. Religion is the general theory of that world, its encyclopaedic compendium, its logic in a popular form, its spiritualistic point of honor, its enthusiasm, its moral sanction, its solemn completion, its universal ground for consolation and justification. It is *the fantastic realization* of the human essence, because the *human essence* has no true reality. The struggle against religion is therefore mediately the fight against *the other world* of which religion is the spiritual *aroma*.

Religious distress is at the same time the *expression* of real distress and the *protest* against real distress. Religion is the sigh of the oppressed creature, the heart of a heartless world, just as it is the spirit of a spiritless situation. It is the *opium* of the people.

The abolition of religion as the *illusory* happiness of the people is required for their real happiness. The demand to give up the illusions about its condition is the *demand to give up the condition which needs illusions*. The criticism of religion is therefore in embryo the criticism of the vale of woe, the halo of which is religion. . . . Religion is only the illusory sun which revolves round man as long as he does not revolve round himself.

SOURCE: Karl Marx and Friedrich Engels, *On Religion*. Moscow: Foreign Languages Publishing House, 1955, pp. 41–2

God is Dead
by Friedrich Nietzsche

The maverick German intellectual Friedrich Nietzsche (1844–1900) was one of the most influential of modern thinkers. Highly iconoclastic, he challenged many social and intellectual conventions. He said: "Morality is nothing else . . . than obedience to customs." He took the implications of industrial culture a step further than many dared, charging that "God is dead," thereby strengthening modern atheism and clearing the way for science. Nietzsche also foreshadowed other important themes of the twentieth century, such as the Will to Power, soon unleashed in new wars of unimagined destruction, and in technologies applied with minimal ethical restraint. But Nietzsche did not cling to consistency. He was skeptical about the certainty of accepted truths, so his madman's proclamation of the death of God, reproduced below, also expresses his fear of the consequences.

The Madman. Have you not heard of the madman who lit a lantern in the bright morning hours, ran to the market-place and cried incessantly: "I seek God! I seek God!"—As many of those who did not believe in God were standing around just then, he provoked much laughter. Why, did he get lost? said one. Did he lose his way away like a child? said another. Or is he hiding? Is he afraid of us? Has he gone on a voyage? or emigrated?—Thus they yelled and laughed. The madman jumped into their midst and pierced them with his glances.

"Whither is God?" he cried. "I shall tell you! *We have killed him,*—you and I. We are all his murderers! But how have we done this? How were we able to drink up the sea? Who gave us the sponge to wipe away the entire horizon? What did we do when we unchained this earth from its sun? Whither is it moving now? Whither are we moving now? Away from all suns? Are we not plunging continually? Backward, sideward, forward, in all directions? Is there any up or down left? Are we not straying as through an infinite nothing? Do we not feel the breath of empty space? Has it not become colder? Is not night and more night coming on all the while? Must not lanterns be lit in the morning? Do we not hear anything yet of the noise of the gravediggers who are burying God? Do we not smell anything yet of God's decomposition? Gods too decompose. God is Dead. God remains dead. And we have killed him. How shall we, the murderers of all murderers, comfort ourselves? What was holiest and most powerful of all that the world has yet owned has bled to death under our knives. Who will wipe this blood off us? . . . Must we not ourselves become gods simply to seem worthy of it?

SOURCE: Friedrich Nietzsche, *The Gay Science*, repr. in *The Portable Nietzsche*, ed. Walter Kaufmann. New York: Viking Press, 1968, pp. 95–96

Religious points of view

Even the faithful do not necessarily share the same point of view. In the following three extracts, we see contemporary statements of faith in the monotheistic oneness of divinity, in the polytheistic plurality of divinities, and in no-divinity, concentrating instead upon human consciousness as part of the ground of being.

The Oneness of the Divine
by Abraham Heschel

Abraham Heschel (1907–72) was born into the Jewish mystical tradition of Hassidism in Warsaw, and educated in the mysticism of the Kabbalah. He studied in Berlin, but in 1938 he was forced out of Germany and escaped to England, then to New York, where he taught for many years at New York's Jewish Theological Seminary and wrote several influential books, including Man is not Alone *and* The Prophets. *He spoke for civil rights and interfaith co-operation. He blends the traditional Hassidic yearning for spirituality with the modern taste for free inquiry and impartial truth.*

How do we identify the divine? . . . The notion of God as a perfect being is not of Biblical extraction. It is the product not of prophetic religion but of Greek philosophy; a postulate of reason rather than a direct, compelling, initial answer of man to His reality.[7] In the Decalogue,[8] God does not speak of His being perfect but of His having made free men out of slaves. Signifying a state of being without defect and lack, perfection is a term of praise which we may utter in pouring forth our emotion; yet for man to utter it as a name for His essence would mean to evaluate and to endorse Him.

There is, however, one idea that carries our thoughts beyond the horizon of our island; an idea which addresses itself to all minds and is tacitly accepted as an axiom by science and as a dogma by **monotheistic** religion. It is the idea of the one. All knowledge and understanding rest upon its validity. In spite of the profound differences in what it describes and means in the various realms of human thought, there is much that is common and much that is of mutual importance.

The perspective on which we depend in science and philosophy, notwithstanding all specialization and meticulousness in studying the details, is a view of the whole, without which our knowledge would be like a book

---

[7] Heschel presented his position in a traditionally masculine voice. Jewish feminists (including Heschel's daughter, later in this book) have subsequently presented another view.
[8] Decalogue—the Ten Commandments.

composed exclusively of iotas. Accordingly, all sciences and philosophies have one axiom in common—the axiom of *unity* of all that is, was and will be. They all assume that things are not entirely divorced from and indifferent to each other, but subject to universal laws, and that they form, by their interaction with one another or, as Lotze put it, by their "sympathetic rapport," a universe. However, the possibility of their interaction with each other is conditioned upon a unity that pervades all of them. The world could not exist at all except as one; deprived of unity, it would not be a cosmos but chaos, an agglomeration of countless possibilities....

Knowledge is at all possible because of the kinship of the knower and the known, because man's intelligence seems to correspond to the world's intelligibility. But over and above that there is another kinship: the kinship of being. We are all—men, stars, flowers, birds—assigned to the same cast, rehearsing for the same inexplicable drama. We all have a mystery in common—the mystery of being.

SOURCE: Abraham Heschel, *Between God and Man: An Interpretation of Judaism*. New York and London: Simon Schuster, 1998, pp. 98–100

The New Polytheism
by David Miller

David Miller is a comparative mythologist at Syracuse University whose 1974 book The New Polytheism *showed the growing impact of the study of world religions. He argued that monotheism—a belief in only one Deity—may suffer from industrial culture's critique, but under the surface,* **polytheism**—*belief in a plurality of deities—has always been at work.*

The death of God was in fact the demise of a monotheistic way of thinking and speaking about God and a monotheistic way of thinking and speaking about human meaning and being generally. The announcement of the death of God was the obituary of a useless single-minded and one-dimensional norm of a civilization that has been predominantly monotheistic, not only in its religion, but also in its politics, its history, its social order, its ethics, and its psychology. When released from the tyrannical imperialism of monotheism by the death of God, man has the opportunity of discovering new dimensions hidden in the depths of reality's history. He may discover a new freedom to acknowledge variousness and many-sidedness. He may find, as if for the first time, a new potency to create imaginatively his hopes and desires, his laws and pleasures....

The death of God gives rise to the rebirth of the Gods. We are polytheists.

Polytheism is the name given to a specific religious situation. The situation is characterized by plurality, a plurality that manifests itself in many forms.

Socially, polytheism is a situation in which there are various values, patterns of social organization, and principles by which man governs his political life. These values, patterns, and principles sometimes mesh harmoniously, but more often they war with one another to be elevated as the single center of normal social order. Such a situation would be sheer anarchy and chaos were it not possible to identify the many orders as each containing a coherence of its own. Socially understood, polytheism is eternally in unresolvable conflict with social monotheism, which in its worst form is fascism and in its less destructive forms is imperialism, capitalism, feudalism and monarchy. There is an incipient polytheism always lurking in democracy. This polytheism will surface during the history of democracies if the civilization does not first succumb to anarchy. In calling our time polytheist, we are saying something about the state of democracy in our time.

Polytheism is not only a social reality; it is also a philosophical condition. It is that reality, experienced by men and women when Truth with a capital "T" cannot be articulated reflectively according to a single grammar, a single logic, or a single symbol-system. It is a situation that exists when metaphors, stories, anecdotes, aphorisms, puns, dramas, and movies, with all their mysterious ambiguity, seem more compelling than the rhetoric of political, religious, and philosophical systems. They seem more compelling than tightly argued and logically coherent explanations of self and society because they allow for multiple meanings to exist simultaneously, as if Truth, Goodness, and Beauty can never be contained in a logic that allows for only one of the following: good versus evil, light versus dark, truth versus fiction, reality versus illusion, being versus becoming. In a philosophically polytheistic situation the "new science" of the time will break forth with principles of relativism, indeterminacy, plural logic systems, irrational numbers; substances that do not have substance, such as quarks; double explanations for light; and black holes in the middle of actual realities....

Religiously, polytheism is the worship of many Gods and Goddesses. Though monotheism in its exclusive forms—say, in Christianity, Judaism, and Islam—rules out the possibility of polytheism in religion, polytheism, in a curious way, includes a monotheism of sorts. The great polythesist cultures—Greek, Hindu, Egyptian, Mesopotamian, American Indian—have in actual practice been composed of communities of men and women who worship one God or Goddess, or at least they worship one at a time—Athena, Vishnu, Ra, Baal, Wakan Tanka. The *theologies* of these peoples, however, affirm the reality and the worship of many. This implies that a polytheistic religion is actually a polytheistic theology, a system of symbolizing reality in a plural way in order to account for all experience, but that the religious practice is composed of consecutive monotheisms. Similarly, it would seem possible that one might profess a monotheistic faith, but need a polytheistic theology to account for all of one's experiences in the life-context of that faith....

What does this mean about theological explanations, about the nature of the Gods and Goddesses? It means that the Gods and Goddesses are the names of powers, of forces, which have autonomy and are not conditioned or affected by social and historical events, by human will or reason, or by personal and individual factors. This is one meaning of our use of the word "Immortal" as it is applied to divinities. The Gods are not contingent upon the conditions of mortality. Insofar as they manifest themselves in life they are felt to be informing powers that give shape to social, intellectual, and personal behavior. The Gods and Goddesses are the names of the plural patterns of our existence. Their stories are the paradigms[9] and symbols that allow us to account for, to express, and to celebrate those multiple aspects of our reality that otherwise would seem fragmented and anarchic.

SOURCE: David L. Miller, *The New Polytheism: Rebirth of the Gods and Goddesses*. New York and London: Harper and Row, 1974, pp. 3–7

The Ground of Being
by Tarthang Tulku

Religion can also exist without reference to any deity, as it does in some forms of Buddhism. Here the object of contemplation is consciousness itself. Tarthang Tulku is a contemporary Buddhist teacher in California, one of the first refugees from Tibet who began to explain to Westerners the insights of Tibetan Buddhism. In this selection from his 1978 book Openness Mind, *he discusses meditation as a process of discovering various levels of the workings of the mind in search of peace, the resolution of conflicting emotions, and, ultimately, the* **ground of being**. *Is this "open ground" that which monotheists call God? This question is much debated today.*

All of us are part of being; we *are* being. Our total life experience is this being, this ground, which embraces all of existence. Nirvana[10] and samsara[11] are both manifested within this ground level. The more we understand this, the more life becomes rich and fulfilling. We see that this ground of being is totally open; everything is manifest there. Nothing can destroy this openness.

Meditation enables us to remain at this ground state for long periods of time. Because it is a very peaceful state, free from desires and conflicting emotions, some of the Buddha's disciples stayed on this level for hundreds of years. However, this ground level is only an initial stage; nothing can actually be realized there. The mind naturally moves from this ground level to a second stage, which is a more conscious level, similar to recognition. This second stage is not actually sense perception, but rather an intuitive,

---

[9] Paradigm—a model of reality, such as the materialistic or idealistic model.
[10] Nirvana—in Buddhism, the cessation of suffering, attained through spiritual awakening.
[11] Samsara—the endless round of bodily reincarnations in this world, with all its illusions.

seeing quality, a lightness and clarity. By very sensitively developing our awareness, we touch this intuitive second level directly.

The first stage of experience is like touching the ground, the second stage is like looking around, and then the third stage occurs, which is like surveying the horizon—observing with more precision and perceptivity. What we usually refer to as "experience" is produced on the second and third levels. We can learn to recognize these three levels of experience in each thought: first, the ground state; then we recognize the quality of the experience; finally we learn to extend the experience as long as possible.

As we become more familiar with the distinctions and qualities of each of these levels of experience, we are able to appreciate the subtle complexities and the more inward workings of the mind. Until our perception has developed in this way, we are like someone who has never eaten an apricot: we cannot imagine the taste. But once we are skilled at perceiving the arising and flowing of thought, we are able to go beyond this level of perception, to experience a level that is similar to the fresh perception of childhood. We are able to directly experience mind as a process. When we can soar, when we can transmute the quality of the mind, then we approach genuine freedom.

SOURCE: Tarthang Tulku, *Openness Mind*. Berkeley, CA: Dharma Publishing, 1978, pp. 92–4

Scientific perspectives on religion

Since the eighteenth-century Enlightenment, science and religion seemed to have gone separate ways. Scientists placed their faith in that which could be observed and quantified, so leaving out explanations of reality which rest on the unseen and unquantifiable. However, twentieth-century scientific advances revealed that the universe is not as it appears on the surface, and that the tiny components of any apparently solid object seem to be racing through space behaving somewhat like energy and somewhat like matter. Probing the limits of human reason and mechanical measurements, some scientists have admitted the possibility that what religions are indicating is actually real. In the following two passages, the so-called *anthropic principle* and research into near-death experiences are examples of the growing closeness between scientific research and religious belief.

A Not-So-Random Universe
by Patrick Glynn

Patrick Glynn is a writer who explores the **anthropic principle** *in his 1997 book* God: The Evidence. *This theory is based on the mathematical analyses by scientists of the basic constants of the physical structure of the universe, from atoms to gravity.*

Were they ever so slightly different, the universe might be only dark, lifeless clouds of hydrogen or helium. This raises religious questions such as: is the universe a brutally absurd, meaningless chance accident, or a meaningful, even a caring spiritual structure?

The anthropic principle says that all the seemingly arbitrary and unrelated constants in physics have one strange thing in common—these are precisely the values you need if you want to have a universe capable of producing life.

This discovery, already percolating among physicists in the early 1970s, came as something of a surprise, to put it mildly. For centuries, scientific exploration seemed to be taking us down precisely the opposite road—toward an ever more mechanistic, impersonal, and random view of the cosmos. Twentieth-century intellectuals had commonly spoken of the "random universe." The predominant view of modern philosophers and intellectuals was that human life had come about essentially by accident, the by-product of brute, material forces randomly churning over the eons. The conclusion seemed to follow naturally from the two great scientific revolutions of the modern era, the Copernican and the Darwinian. . . .

The philosophical, cultural, and emotional impact of this conclusion could hardly be overstated. It explained the tone of despair and angst that came to characterize modern culture, the desperate feeling that humankind was alone and without moorings, and above all without God. It was this random universe cosmology that underpinned all the atheistic modern philosophies—from Russell's own **positivism**, to **existentialism**, Marxism, even Freudianism.

But then the unexpected occurred. Beginning in the 1960s, scientists began to notice a strange connection among a number of otherwise unexplained coincidences in physics. It turns out that many mysterious values and relationships in physics could be explained by one overriding fact: Such values had been necessary for the creation of life. . . .

The Cambridge astrophysicist Bandon Carter presented some of these points in his 1973 lecture. Any tinkering with the gravitational constant in relation to electromagnetism, he pointed out, would have resulted in a universe with no middling stars like our sun, but only cooler "red" or hotter "blue" ones—incapable of sustaining life's evolution. Any weakening of the nuclear "strong" force would have resulted in a universe consisting of hydrogen and not a single other element. That would mean no oxygen, no water, nothing but hydrogen. . . .

Even the most minor tinkering with the value of the fundamental forces of physics—gravity, electromagnetism, the nuclear strong force, or the nuclear weak force—would have resulted in an unrecognizable universe: a universe consisting entirely of helium, a universe without protons or atoms, a universe without stars, or a universe that collapsed back in upon itself before the first moments of its existence were up. Changing the precise ratios of the masses of subatomic particles in relation to one another would have similar effects. Even such basics of life as carbon and water depend upon uncanny "fine-tuning" at the subatomic level, strange coincidences in values for which physicists had no other explanation.

To take just a few examples:

- Gravity is roughly 10^{39} times weaker than electromagnetism. If gravity had been 10^{33} times weaker than electromagnetism, "stars would be a billion times less massive and would burn a million times faster."
- The nuclear weak force is 10^{28} times the strength of gravity. Had the weak force been slightly weaker, all the hydrogen in the universe would have been turned to helium (making water impossible, for example).
- A stronger nuclear strong force (by as little as 2 percent) would have prevented the formation of protons —yielding a universe without atoms. Decreasing it by 5 percent would have given us a universe without stars.
- If the difference in mass between a proton and a neutron were not exactly as it is— -roughly twice the mass of an electron—then all neutrons would have become protons or vice versa. Say good-bye to chemistry as we know it—and to life.
- The very nature of water—so vital to life—is something of a mystery. . . . Unique among the molecules, water is lighter in its solid than liquid form: Ice floats. If it did not, the oceans would freeze from the bottom up and earth would now be covered with solid ice. This property in turn is traceable to unique properties of the hydrogen atom.
- The synthesis of carbon— the vital core of all organic molecules—on a significant scale involves what scientists view as an "astonishing" coincidence in the ratio of the strong force to electromagnetism. This ratio makes it possible for carbon-12 to reach an excited state of exactly 7.65 MeV at the temperature typical of the center of stars, which creates a resonance involving helium-4, beryllium-8, and carbon-12—allowing the necessary binding to take place during a tiny window of opportunity 10^{-17} seconds long.

The list goes on. A comprehensive compilation of these coincidences can be found in John Leslie's book *Universes*.

The depth of the mystery involved here has been captured best by astronomer Fred Hoyle, the former proponent of the steady state theory:

All that we see in the universe of observation and fact, as opposed to the mental stage of scenario and supposition, remains unexplained. And even in its supposedly first second the universe itself is acausal. That is to say, the universe has to know in advance what it is going to be before it knows how to start itself. For in accordance with the Big Bang Theory, for instance, at a time of 10^{-43} seconds the universe has to know how many types of neutrino there are going to be at a time of 1 second. This is so in order that it starts off expanding at the right rate to fit the eventual number of neutrino types.

Hoyle's notion of the universe needing to "know in advance" later outcomes captures the depth of the mystery. The fine-tuning of seemingly heterogeneous values and ratios necessary to get from the big bang to life as we know it involves intricate coordination over vast differences in scale—from the galactic level down to the subatomic one—and across multi-billion-year tracts of time. Hoyle, who coined the term "big bang," has questioned the very legitimacy of the metaphor of an initial "explosion." "An explosion in a junkyard does not lead to sundry bits of metal being assembled into a useful working machine," he writes. The more physicists have learned about the universe, the more it looks like a put-up job. . . .

The great modern era—spanning the nearly 350 years between the trial of Galileo and the 500th birthday of Copernicus—is at an end. It is truly justifiable to speak of our current period as the "postmodern age." And there is every reason to suppose that this postmodern age will also be postsecular, since the original philosophical assumptions underpinning the modern secular worldview have been shattered—ironically enough, by science itself. . . .

The barrier that modern science appeared to erect to faith has fallen. Of course, the anthropic principle tells us nothing about the Person of God or the existence of an afterlife; it has nothing to say about such issues as right or wrong or the "problem of evil." But it does offer as strong an indication as reason and science alone could be expected to provide that God exists.

SOURCE: Patrick Glynn, *God: The Evidence*. Rocklin, CA: Prima Publishing, 1997, pp. 21–55

Near-Death Experiences: Light in the Shadow of Death
by Lee W. Bailey

In 1975 a physician/philosopher published a study of over a hundred people who had been considered dead but had come back to life; he named these strange events "near-death experiences." Subsequent research has shown this phenomenon to be ancient and global. NDEs raise many religious questions about death, life, afterlife, and consciousness.

I know a man who entered the borderland of death and came back. In 1982 a young artist in North Carolina, extremely discouraged about nuclear and environmental crises, died of brain cancer. He was dead, his hospice volunteer said, for at least an hour and a half. During that time, he reports, he rose up out of his body and encountered a cosmic Light. He asked it many questions, during which the Light kept changing into figures, like Jesus, Buddha, Krishna, and other archetypal[12] symbols. The Light took him on an incredible tour of the universe, he said, through the Big Bang, into the Void before creation that some religions point to, full of creative energy. He returned brimming with remarkable insights. His brain cancer disappeared, and he invented a healing light system.

This is a near-death experience (NDE), one of an increasing number of mystical experiences that are being reported since Raymond Moody published the first breakthrough book *Life After Life* in 1975. He described the typical elements that appear in various NDEs: an ineffable experience beyond words, hearing the news of your own death, feelings of peace and quiet, noises, a dark tunnel, out of body experiences, meeting others who have died, experiencing the Being of Light who is full of love and accepting wisdom, a review of one's life, a border between life and the next world, difficulty returning to earthly life and telling others, a new sense of life's precious value, and loss of the fear of death.

Research shows that NDEs have been reported in history—Plato's *Republic*, *The Tibetan Book of the Dead*, European medieval texts, and the vision of the Lakota shaman Black Elk, for example, all include accounts that contain such elements. They are worldwide, surfacing in Europe, Africa, China, Japan, the U.S., and the South Pacific. 1982 and 1990 Gallup Polls found that at least 8 million people in the United States alone have had a brush with death accompanied by a mystical event. Anyone is a candidate for a NDE, including children. Most NDEs are peaceful and blissful, but a tiny percentage involve dark experiences. Most report a self-evaluation, not an external judgment, and a focus on loving and learning in the Light.

Most survivors of NDEs return with a new spiritual vision, as the psychologist Kenneth Ring reports. Many change boldly, giving up alcoholism or drug abuse, for example, feeling an increased confidence, compassion, empathy, tolerance, inward prayer, and a universal spiritual faith. Life is considered such a precious gift that suicide, even for those who almost died of suicide, is never again considered. Not all life's problems are automatically solved, but they are approached with far more peace and equanimity.

How are NDEs interpreted? The biological interpretation suggests that brain chemistry such as pain-killing endorphins can explain NDEs. Psychological theories suggest denial of death, wish fulfillment, and archetypal death, rebirth and enlightenment patterns. The philosophical interpretations range from empiricist skepticism to phenomenological

---

[12] Archetypal—relating to an unconscious, collective psychological instinct or pattern.

analysis of global patterns such as the Being of Light. Religious interpretations of NDEs range from rejection of experiences not found in one's scripture to mystics who see NDEs as a type of mystical experience.

Such powerful NDE experiences clearly challenge the conventional views of religions that are largely based on ancient history as recorded in a holy book, or based on the authority of an institution. They press us to ask not only "what is death?" but "what is life?", "what is religion?", and "what is consciousness?". NDEs strongly suggest that consciousness is far larger that our ordinary ego or subjectivity, and that the nature and boundaries of existence can hardly be drawn by narrow human declarations. As William James[13] concluded: "No account of the universe in its totality can be final which leaves these other forms of consciousness quite disregarded."

SOURCE: Lee Bailey and Jenny Yates, *The Near-Death Experience: A Reader*. New York: Routledge, 1996, pp. 39–52

Worship, symbol, and myth

Whereas some branches of every religion have interpreted their faith's stories, scriptures and rituals as literally true, others have embraced them as symbols and metaphors for spiritual realities that cannot be described in worldly terms. Two leading figures in the study of religions from the latter point of view have been Carl Jung and Joseph Campbell.

Mandalas: Deity Unfolding in the World
by Carl G. Jung

Carl Jung (1875–1961) was a Swiss psychologist who developed archetypal psychology, which is the psychology most open to religious understanding. Jung built on Freud's demonstration of the meaningfulness of the unconscious psyche, while rejecting his views on the centrality of sex and the illusoriness of religion. Jung saw images from all religions as meaningful expressions of the "collective unconscious" of humanity. He spoke of archetypes, *meaning unconscious, collective psychological instincts or patterns. The "Self" for Jung is the central, regulating archetype, the "God within" that guides and heals. It may be symbolized in many ways, not just as a heavenly old man on a throne. In dreams and myths, rituals and theologies, the ineffable depth called "God" may appear as a crystal, a goddess, a star, a tree, an animal, or even a geometric form, most notably the "mandala," a circular design focusing on the "center": the center of the universe, the center of one's life.*

---

[13] William James—the psychologist/philosopher author of *The Varieties of Religious Experience* (1902).

The Sanskrit word *mandala* means "circle" in the ordinary sense of the word. In the sphere of religious practices and in psychology it denotes circular images, which are drawn, painted, modelled, or danced. Plastic structures of this kind are to be found, for instance, in Tibetan Buddhism, and as dance figures these circular patterns occur also in Dervish monasteries. As psychological phenomena they appear spontaneously in dreams, in certain states of conflict, and in cases of schizophrenia. Very frequently they contain a quaternity or a multiple of four, in the form of a cross, a star, a square, an octagon, etc. . . .

In Tibetan Buddhism the figure has the significance of a **ritual** instrument (*yantra*), whose purpose is to assist meditation and concentration. . . . Its spontaneous occurrence in modern individuals enables psychological research to make a closer investigation into its functional meaning. As a rule a mandala occurs in conditions of psychic dissociation or disorientation, for instance in the case of children between the ages of eight and eleven whose parents are about to be divorced, or in adults who, as the result of a neurosis[14] and its treatment, are confronted with the problem of opposites in human nature and are consequently disoriented; or again in schizophrenics whose view of the world has become confused, owing to the invasion of incomprehensible contents from the unconscious. In such cases it is easy to see how the severe pattern imposed by a circular image of this kind compensates the disorder and confusion of the psychic state—namely, through the construction of a central point to which everything is related, or by a concentric arrangement of the disordered multiplicity and of contradictory and irreconcilable elements. This is evidently an *attempt at self-healing* on the part of Nature, which does not spring from conscious reflection but from an instinctive impulse. Here, as comparative research has shown, a fundamental schema is made use of, an archetype which, so to speak, occurs everywhere and by no means owes its individual existence to tradition, any more than the instincts would need to be transmitted in that way. Instincts are given in the case of every newborn individual and belong to the inalienable stock of those qualities which characterize a species. What psychology designates as archetype is really a particular, frequently occurring, formal aspect of instinct, and is just as much an *a priori* factor as the latter. Therefore, despite external differences, we find a fundamental conformity in mandalas regardless of their origin in time and space.

The "squaring of the circle" is one of the many archetypal motifs which form the basic patterns of our dreams and fantasies. But it is distinguished by the fact that it is one of the most important of them from the functional point of view. Indeed, it could even be called the *archetype of wholeness*. Because of this significance, the "quaternity of the One" is the schema for all

---

[14] Neurosis—a mild form of mental illness.

images of God, as depicted in the visions of Ezekiel, Daniel, and Enoch, and as the representation of Horus[15] with his four sons also shows. The latter suggests an interesting differentiation, inasmuch as there are occasionally representations in which three of the sons have animals' heads and only one a human head, in keeping with the Old Testament visions as well as with the emblems of the seraphim which were transferred to the evangelists, and—last but not least—with the nature of the Gospels themselves: three of which are synoptic and one "Gnostic.". . .

As is to be expected, individual mandalas display an enormous variety. The overwhelming majority are characterized by the circle and the quaternity. In a few, however, the three or the five predominates, for which there are usually special reasons.

Whereas ritual mandalas always display a definite style and a limited number of typical motifs as their content, individual mandalas make use of a well-nigh unlimited wealth of motifs and symbolic allusions, from which it can easily be seen that they are endeavouring to express either the totality of the individual in his inner or outer experience of the world, or its essential point of reference. Their object is the *self* in contradistinction to the *ego*, which is only the point of reference for consciousness, whereas the self comprises the totality of the psyche altogether, i.e., conscious *and* unconscious. It is therefore not unusual for individual mandalas to display a division into a light and a dark half, together with their typical symbols. An historical example of this kind is Jakob Böhme's mandala, in his treatise *XL Questions concerning the Soule*. It is at the same time an image of God and is designated as such. This is not a matter of chance, for Indian philosophy, which developed the idea of the self, Atman or Purusha, to the highest degree, makes no distinction in principle between the human essence and the divine. Correspondingly, in the Western mandala, the *scintilla* or soul-spark, the innermost divine essence of man, is characterized by symbols which can just as well express a God-image, namely the image of Deity unfolding in the world, in nature, and in man.

The fact that images of this kind have under certain circumstances a considerable therapeutic effect on their authors is empirically proved and also readily understandable, in that they often represent very bold attempts to see and put together apparently irreconcilable opposites and bridge over apparently hopeless splits.

SOURCE: Carl G. Jung, "Mandalas," in *The Archetypes and the Collective Unconscious*, vol. 9, part 1 of *The Collected Works of C. G. Jung*. Princeton: Princeton University Press, 2nd edn 1968, pp. 387–90

---

[15] Horus—the ancient Egyptian sun-god.

The Hero with a Thousand Faces
by Joseph Campbell

Joseph Campbell (1904–87), at Sarah Lawrence College, expanded Jung's archetypal theory of myth as a meaningful story, rather than a fictional error. He proposed a theory of the "monomyth," a pattern found, sometimes fragmentarily, in myths worldwide. The pattern follows the hero's journey into the mystical underworld where various powers are met for struggles and learning. After the re-ascent to ordinary life, the hero can use the new powers to aid his or her people. As Campbell developed his theory of myth, he integrated more anthropological and historical themes.

Myth is the secret opening through which the inexhaustible energies of the cosmos pour into human cultural manifestation. Religions, philosophies, arts, the social forms of primitive and historic man, prime discoveries in science and technology, the very dreams that blister sleep, boil up from the basic, magic ring of myth. . . .

The bold and truly epoch-making writings of the psychoanalysts are indispensable to the student of mythology; for, whatever may be thought of the detailed and sometimes contradictory interpretations of specific cases and problems, Freud, Jung, and their followers have demonstrated irrefutably that the logic, the heroes, and the deeds of myth survive into modern times. In the absence of an effective general mythology, each of us has his private, unrecognized, rudimentary, yet secretly potent pantheon of dream.[16] The latest incarnation of Oedipus, the continued romance of Beauty and the Beast, stand this afternoon on the corner of Forty-second Street and Fifth Avenue[17] waiting for the traffic light to change. . . .

The unconscious sends all sorts of vapors, odd beings, terrors, and deluding images up into the mind—whether in dream, broad daylight, or insanity; for the human kingdom, beneath the floor of the comparatively neat little dwelling that we call our consciousness, goes down into unsuspected Aladdin caves. There not only jewels but also dangerous jinn abide: the inconvenient or resisted psychological powers that we have not thought or dared to integrate into our lives. And they remain unsuspected, or, on the other hand, some chance word, the smell of a landscape, the taste of a cup of tea, or the glance of an eye may touch a magic spring, and then dangerous messengers begin to appear in the brain. These are dangerous because they threaten the fabric of the security into which we have built ourselves and our family. But they are fiendishly fascinating too, for they carry keys that open the whole realm of the desired and feared adventure of the discovery of the self. Destruction of the world that we have built and in

---

[16] Campbell's 1940's masculine view has stimulated feminist versions of his theory of myth. See Maureen Murdock's *The Heroine's Journey*. Boston: Shambhala, 1990. Also, see Clyde Ford's *The Hero With an African Face*. New York: Bantam, 1999.
[17] Forty-second Street and Fifth Avenue in New York City.

which we live, and of ourselves within it; but then a wonderful reconstruction, of the bolder, cleaner, more spacious, and fully human life— that is the lure, the promise and terror, of these disturbing night visitants from the mythological realm that we carry within. . . .

It has always been the prime function of mythology and rite to supply the symbols that carry the human spirit forward, in counteraction to those other constant human fantasies that tend to tie it back. In fact, it may well be that the very high incidence of neuroticism among ourselves follows from the decline among us of such effective spiritual aid. We remain fixated to the unexorcised images of our infancy, and hence disinclined to the necessary passages of our adulthood. . . .

The first work of the hero is to retreat from the world scene of secondary effects to those causal zones of the psyche where the difficulties really reside, and there to clarify the difficulties, eradicate them in his own case (i.e., give battle to the nursery demons of his local culture) and break through to the undistorted, direct experience and assimilation of what C. G. Jung has called "the archetypal images." This is the process known to Hindu and Buddhist philosophy as *viveka*, "discrimination."

The archetypes to be discovered and assimilated are precisely those that have inspired, throughout the annals of human culture, the basic images of ritual, mythology, and vision.

Dream is the personalized myth, myth the depersonalized dream; both myth and dream are symbolic in the same general way of the dynamics of the psyche. But in the dream the forms are quirked by the peculiar troubles of the dreamer, whereas in myth the problems and solutions shown are directly valid for all mankind.

The hero, therefore, is the man or woman who has been able to battle past his personal and local historical limitations to the generally valid, normally human forms. Such a one's visions, ideas, and inspirations come pristine from the primary springs of human life and thought. Hence they are eloquent, not of the present, disintegrating society and psyche, but of the unquenched source through which society is reborn. The hero has died as a modern man; but as eternal man—perfected, unspecific, universal man—he has been reborn. His second solemn task and deed therefore . . . is to return then to us, transfigured, and teach the lesson he has learned of life renewed. . . .

Furthermore, we have not even to risk the adventure alone; for the heroes of all time have gone before us; the labyrinth is thoroughly known; we have only to follow the thread of the hero-path. And where we had thought to find an abomination, we shall find a god; where we had thought to slay another, we shall slay ourselves; where we had thought to travel outward, we shall come to the center of our own existence; where we had thought to be alone, we shall be with all the world. . . .

The standard path of the mythological adventure of the hero is a magnification of the formula represented in the rites of passage: *separation—initiation—return*: which might be named the nuclear unit of the monomyth.

> A hero ventures forth from the world of common day into a region of supernatural wonder: fabulous forces are there encountered and a decisive victory is won: the hero comes back from this mysterious adventure with the power to bestow boons on his fellow man.

Aeneas[18] went down into the underworld, crossed the dreadful river of the dead, threw a sop to the three-headed watchdog Cerberus, and conversed, at last, with the shade of his dead father. All things were unfolded to him: the destiny of souls, the destiny of Rome, which he was about to found, "and in what wise he might avoid or endure every burden." He returned through the ivory gate to his work in the world. . . .

A comparable vision is described in the apocryphal[19] Gospel of Eve. "I stood on a lofty mountain and saw a gigantic man and another a dwarf; and I heard as it were a voice of thunder, and drew nigh for to hear; and He spake unto me and said: I am thou, and thou art I; and wheresoever thou mayest be I am there. In all am I scattered, and whensoever thou willest, thou gatherest Me; and gathering Me, thou gatherest Thyself."

The two—the hero and his ultimate god, the seeker and the found—are thus understood as the outside and inside of a single, self-mirrored mystery, which is identical with the mystery of the manifest world. The great deed of the supreme hero is to come to the knowledge of this unity in multiplicity and then to make it known.

SOURCE: Joseph Campbell, *The Hero with a Thousand Faces* Princeton: Princeton University Press, 2nd edn 1968, pp. 3–40

Women and the feminine in religion

The twentieth century also saw many attempts to research and restore women's place in religion. Some of the research pertains to the theory that worship of the Goddess preceded patriarchal God-worship in many parts of the world.

When God Was a Woman
by Merlin Stone

Merlin Stone is a writer who did early research about the age, diversity, and widespread appearance of the ancient Goddess. She criticizes the patriarchal bias that

---

[18] Aeneas—legendary founder of the Roman race, whose journey is described by Virgil in the *Aeneid*.

[19] Apocryphal—relating to unofficial, uncanonical ancient texts considered sacred by some.

ignores or reduces the Ancient Near Eastern Goddess to a mere "fertility" figure. Stone shows that the goddess had wider functions, such as the Egyptian goddess Maat, who represented the order and truth of the universe. She points out that the surviving statuettes of Paleolithic goddesses far outnumber surviving male symbols, suggesting the great age of the Goddess, and that she preceded the rise of patriarchal gods, such as Zeus in Greece, whose social patterns later came to dominate European culture.

In the beginning, people prayed to the Creatress of Life, the Mistress of Heaven. At the very dawn of religion, God was a woman. Do you remember?...

In most archaeological texts the female religion is referred to as a "fertility cult," perhaps revealing the attitudes towards sexuality held by the various contemporary religions that may have influenced the writers. But archaeological and mythological evidence of the veneration of the female deity as creator and law-maker of the universe, prophetess, provider of human destinies, inventor, healer, hunter and valiant leader in battle suggests that the title "fertility cult" may be a gross oversimplification of a complex theological structure.

I am not suggesting a return or revival of the ancient female religion. As Sheila Collins writes, "As women our hope for fulfilment lies in the present and future and not in some mythical golden past ..." I do hold the hope, however, that a contemporary consciousness of the once-widespread veneration of the female deity as the wise Creatress of the Universe and all life and civilization may be used to cut through the many oppressive and falsely founded patriarchal images, stereotypes, customs and laws that were developed as direct reactions to Goddess worship by the leaders of the later male-worshiping religions.

I had somewhere assimilated the idea that the earth was invariably identified as female, Mother Earth, the one who passively accepts the seed, while heaven was naturally and inherently male, its intangibility symbolic of the supposedly exclusive male ability to think in abstract concepts. This too I had accepted without question—until I learned that nearly all the female deities of the Near and Middle East were titled Queen of Heaven, and in Egypt not only was the ancient Goddess Nut known as the heavens, but her brother-husband Geb was symbolized as the earth.

Most astonishing of all was the discovery of numerous accounts of the female Creators of all existence, divinities who were credited with bringing forth not only the first people but the entire earth and the heavens above. There were records of such Goddesses in Sumer, Babylon, Egypt, Africa, Australia and China.

In India the Goddess Sarasvati was honored as the inventor of the original alphabet, while in Celtic Ireland the Goddess Brigit was esteemed as the patron deity of language. Texts revealed that it was the Goddess Nidaba in Sumer who was paid honor as the one who initially invented clay tablets and the art of writing. She appeared in that position earlier than any of the male deities who later replaced Her. The official scribe of the Sumerian heaven was a woman. But most significant was the archaeological evidence of the earliest examples of written language so far discovered; these were also located in Sumer, at the temple of the Queen of Heaven in Erech, written there over five thousand years ago. Though writing is most often said to have been invented by *man*, however that may be defined, the combination of the above factors presents a most convincing argument that it may have actually been woman who pressed those first meaningful marks into wet clay.

In agreement with the generally accepted theory that women were responsible for the development of agriculture, as an extension of their food-gathering activities, there were female deities everywhere who were credited with this gift to civilization. In Mesopotamia, where some of the earliest evidences of agricultural development have been found, the Goddess Ninlil was revered for having provided Her people with an understanding of planting and harvesting methods. In nearly all areas of the world, female deities were extolled as healers, dispensers of curative herbs, roots, plants and other medical aids, casting the priestesses who attended the shrines into the role of physicians of those who worshiped there.

Some legends described the Goddess as a powerful, courageous warrior, a leader in battle. The worship of the Goddess as valiant warrior seems to have been responsible for the numerous reports of female soldiers, later referred to by the classical Greeks as the Amazons. More thoroughly examining the accounts of the esteem the Amazons paid to the female deity, it became evident that women who worshiped a warrior Goddess hunted and fought in the lands of Libya, Anatolia, Bulgaria, Greece, Armenia and Russia and were far from the mythical fantasy so many writers of today would have us believe.

I could not help noticing how far removed from contemporary images were the prehistoric and most ancient historic attitudes toward the thinking capacities and intellect of woman, for nearly everywhere the Goddess was revered as wise counselor and prophetess. The Celtic Cerridwen was the Goddess of Intelligence and Knowledge in the pre-Christian legends of Ireland, the priestesses of the Goddess Gaia provided the wisdom of divine revelation at pre-Greek sanctuaries, while the Greek Demeter and the Egyptian Isis were both invoked as law-givers and sage dispensers of righteous wisdom, counsel and justice. The Egyptian Goddess Maat represented the very order, rhythm and truth of the Universe. Ishtar of Mesopotamia was referred to as the Directress of People, the Prophetess, the Lady of Vision, while the archaeological records of the city of Nimrud, where Ishtar was worshiped, revealed that women served as judges and magistrates in the courts of law....

The worship of female deities appeared in every area of the world, presenting an image of woman that I had never before encountered. As a result, I began to ponder upon the power of myth and eventually to perceive these legends as more than the innocent childlike fables they first appeared to be. They were tales with a most specific point of view.

Myths present ideas that guide perception, conditioning us to think and even perceive in a particular way, especially when we are young and impressionable. Often they portray the actions of people who are rewarded or punished for their behavior, and we are encouraged to view these as examples to emulate or avoid. So many of the stories told to us from the time we are just old enough to understand deeply affect our attitudes and comprehension of the world about us and ourselves. Our ethics, morals, conduct, values, sense of duty and even sense of humor are often developed from simple childhood parables and fables. From them we learn what is socially acceptable in the society from which they come. They define good and bad, right and wrong, what is natural and what is unnatural among the people who hold the myths as meaningful. It was quite apparent that the myths and legends that grew from, and were propagated by, a religion in which the deity was female, and revered as wise, valiant, powerful and just, provided very different images of womanhood from those which we are offered by the male-oriented religions of today.

Ashtoreth, the despised "pagan" deity of the Old Testament, was (despite the efforts of biblical scribes to disguise her identity by repeatedly using the masculine gender) actually Astarte—the Great Goddess, as She was known in Canaan, the Near Eastern Queen of Heaven. Those heathen idol worshipers of the Bible had been praying to a woman god—elsewhere known as Innin, Inanna, Nana, Nut, Anat, Anahita, Istar, Isis, Au Set, Ishara, Asherah, Ashtart, Attoret, Attar and Hathor—the many-named Divine Ancestress. Yet each name denoted, in the various languages and dialects of those who revered Her, The Great Goddess. Was it merely coincidence that during all those years of Sunday School I never learned that Ashtoreth was female?

Even more astonishing was the archaeological evidence which provided that Her religion had existed and flourished in the Near and Middle East for thousands of years before the arrival of the patriarchal Abraham, first prophet of the male deity Yahweh. Archaeologists had traced the worship of the Goddess back to the Neolithic communities of about 7000 BC, some to the Upper Paleolithic cultures of about 25,000 BC. From the time of its Neolithic origins, its existence was repeatedly attested to until well into Roman times. Yet Bible scholars agreed that it was as late as somewhere between 1800 and 1550 BC that Abraham had lived in Canaan (Palestine).

SOURCE: Merlin Stone, *When God was a Woman*, New York and London: Harcourt Brace & Co., 1976, pp. 1–10

The need for religion today

At the dawn of the twenty-first century, many thoughtful people are asserting that religion is a necessity today, not just an historical artifact. However, they are redefining that is meant by "religion." The extract which follows, from Paul Tillich, is an example of fresh ways of thinking about religion and its place in modern life.

The Lost Dimension in Religion
by Paul Tillich

Paul Tillich (1886–1965) was a German Protestant theologian who emigrated to the United States. He developed many fresh themes for twentieth-century religions, such as "ultimate concern" as a definition of religion, "the ground of Being" as a way of discussing "God," and "the new being" as a new way of viewing Christ. Religious institutions, he envisioned, are "emergency" institutions, only made necessary by our forgetfulness of Being. He urged industrial culture to overcome its anxiety and despair due to its estrangement from the depths, from the ground of Being.

Being religious means asking passionately the questions of the meaning of our existence and being willing to receive answers, even if the answers hurt. Such an idea of religion makes religion universally human, but it certainly differs from what is usually called religion. It does not describe religion as the belief in the existence of gods or one God, and as a set of activities and institutions for the sake of relating oneself to these beings in thought, devotion and obedience. No one can deny that the religions which have appeared in history are religions in this sense. Nevertheless, religion in its innermost nature is more than religion in this narrower sense. It is the state of being concerned about one's own being and being universally.

There are many people who are ultimately concerned in this way who feel far removed, however, from religion in the narrower sense, and therefore from every historical religion. It often happens that such people take the question of the meaning of their life infinitely seriously and reject any historical religion just for this reason. They feel that the concrete religions fail to express their profound concern adequately. They are religious while rejecting the religions. . . .

If we define religion as the state of being grasped by an infinite concern we must say: Man in our time has lost such infinite concern. And the resurgence of religion is nothing but a desperate and mostly futile attempt to regain what has been lost.

How did the dimension of depth become lost?. . .

Modern man is neither more pious nor more impious than man in any other period. The loss of the dimension of depth is caused by the relation of man to his world and to himself in our period, the period in which nature is being subjected scientifically and technically to the control of man. In this period, life in the dimension of depth is replaced by life in the horizontal dimension. The driving forces of the industrial society of which we are a part go ahead horizontally and not vertically. In popular terms this is expressed in phrases like "better and better," "bigger and bigger," "more and more." One should not disparage the feeling which lies behind such speech. Man is right in feeling that he is able to know and transform the world he encounters without a foreseeable limit. He can go ahead in all directions without a definite boundary. . . .

The predominance of the horizontal dimension over the dimension of depth has been immensely increased by the opening of the space beyond the space of earth.

If we now ask what does man do and seek if he goes ahead in the horizontal dimension, the answer is difficult. Sometimes one is inclined to say that the mere movement ahead without an end, the intoxication with speeding forward without limits, is what satisfies him. But this answer is by no means sufficient. . . . He transforms everything he encounters into a tool; and in doing so he himself becomes a tool. But if he asks, a tool for what, there is no answer.

One does not need to look far beyond everyone's daily experience in order to find examples to describe this predicament. Indeed our daily life in office and home, in cars and airplanes, at parties and conferences, while reading magazines and watching television, while looking at advertisements and hearing radio, are in themselves continuous examples of a life which has lost the dimension of depth. It runs ahead, every moment is filled with something which must be done or seen or said or planned. But no one can experience depth without stopping and becoming aware of himself. Only if he has moments in which he does not care about what comes next can he experience the meaning of this moment here and now and ask himself about the meaning of his life. As long as the preliminary, transitory concerns are not silenced, no matter how interesting and valuable and important they may be, the voice of the ultimate concern cannot be heard. This is the deepest root of the loss of the dimension of depth in our period—the loss of religion in its basic and universal meaning.

When in this way man has deprived himself of the dimension of depth and the symbols expressing it, he then becomes a part of the horizontal plane. He loses his self and becomes a thing among things. He becomes an element in the process of manipulated production and manipulated consumption. This is now a matter of public knowledge. We have become aware of the degree to which everyone in our social structure is managed, even if one knows it and even if one belongs himself to the managing group. The influence of the gang mentality on adolescents, of the corporation's demands on the executives, of the conditioning of everyone by public communication, by propaganda and advertising under the guidance of motivation research, et cetera, have all been described in many books and articles.

Under these pressures, man can hardly escape the fate of becoming a thing among the things he produces, a bundle of conditioned reflexes without a free, deciding and responsible self. The immense mechanism, set up by man to produce objects for his use, transforms man himself into an object used by the same mechanism of production and consumption.

But man has not ceased to be man. He resists this fate anxiously, desperately, courageously. He asks the question, for what? And he realizes that there is no answer. He becomes aware of the emptiness which is covered by the continuous movement ahead and the production of means for ends which become means again without an ultimate end. Without knowing what has happened to him, he feels that he has lost the meaning of life, the dimension of depth. . . .

What we need above all—and partly have—is the radical realization of our predicament, without trying to cover it up by secular or religious ideologies. The revival of religious interest would be a creative power in our culture if it would develop into a movement of search for the lost dimension of depth.

This does not mean that the traditional religious symbols should be dismissed. They certainly have lost their meaning in the literalistic form into which they have been distorted, thus producing the critical reaction against them. But they have not lost their genuine meaning, namely, of answering the question which is implied in man's very existence in powerful, revealing and saving symbols. If the resurgence of religion would produce a new understanding of the symbols of the past and their relevance for our situation, instead of premature and deceptive answers, it would become a creative factor in our culture and a saving factor for many who live in estrangement, anxiety and despair. The religious answer has always the character of "in spite of." In spite of the loss of dimension of depth, its power is present, and most present in those who are aware of the loss and are striving to regain it with ultimate seriousness.

SOURCE: Paul Tillich, "The Lost Dimension in Religion," in *The Essential Tillich*, ed. F. Forrester Church. New York: Macmillan, 1987, pp. 1–8

GLOSSARY

Anthropic principle The new scientific hypothesis that the structure of the universe is so precise that its origin could not have been random.

Empiricism Philosophical view that experience, especially of the senses, is the only valid source of knowledge.

Existentialism A disparate mid-twentieth-century philosophical movement emphasizing issues such as death, experience, and life's meaning.

Ground of being An image of ultimate reality used by Paul Tillich.

Monotheism Belief in only one god, contrasted with polytheism.

Myth A religious and literary language expressing not factual error, but symbolic images of psychological and transcendent meanings.

Numinous From the Latin "numen," the uniquely religious experience of awesome mystery, tremendous and fascinating, beyond reason, goodness and beauty.

Phenomenology Study of appearances of religious manifestations, seeking the "essence" of religion, and focusing on themes such as myth, ritual, shamanism, and the sacred/profane.

Polytheism Belief in many gods, contrasted with monotheism.

Positivism Philosophical doctrine limiting truth to sensory and logical data.

Profane Opposite of sacred, literally "outside the temple," whatever is considered impure or rejected by a community's sense of the sacred.

Ritual Repeated actions with symbolic significance, such as religious services (Roman Catholic Mass, Buddhist meditation) or social drama (football as refined combat).

Sacred Opposite of profane, the realm of ultimate reality, the appearance of the infinite.

Transcendence Rising above common thought; exalted, mystical, ultimate.

REVIEW QUESTIONS

1   What are the effects on the study of religions when the world's diverse cultures come in closer contact with each other?

2   To what extent can one be neutral and non-judgmental in studying world religions?

3   Can nature be sacred without being supernatural? Give examples.

4   Does Freud's view of religion as an illusion pose a threat to religion?

5   Why do you think Marx saw the happiness gained from religion as an opiate?

6   Do gods cease to exist when people no longer have faith in them?

7   Does Heschel's view of unity and an imperfect God go beyond reason?

8   Could a culture be psychologically or socially polytheistic and also religiously monotheistic? Give examples.

9   Why does Buddhism teach that it is important to be at a "ground level" instead of just at a conscious level? How would one seek that state?

10   What effect would acceptance of the anthropic principle have on the relationship between science and religion?

11   How do near-death experiences challenge traditional views of life after death? How do they support them?

12   What do mandalas symbolize? Give examples.

13   How do we understand myth and ritual in the comparative study of religion? Give examples.

14   What evidence do we have about the ancient goddess? Name five goddesses. What effect does this information have on biblical faiths?

15   How has the "ultimate concern" of religion been affected by industrial society?

INFORMATION RESOURCES

Bolle, Kees, "Myth," in *The Encyclopedia of Religion*, ed. Mircea Eliade, vol. 10, pp. 261–85. New York: Macmillan, 1987.

Bowker, John, ed. *Oxford Dictionary of World Religions*. Oxford: Oxford University Press, 1997.

Eliade, Mircea, ed. *The Encyclopedia of Religion*, 16 vols. New York: Macmillan, 1987.

Insight Media, 2162 Broadway, New York, NY, 10024–0621. An excellent source of videos on world religions. www.insight-media.com/religion-html

Stull, Andrew, and Eric Hiatt, *Religion on the Internet*. Upper Saddle River, NJ: Prentice Hall, 1999.

Walker, Barbara, *The Women's Encyclopedia of Myths and Secrets*. San Francisco: Harper and Row, 1983.

Young, Serinity, ed. *Encyclopedia of Women and World Religion*. New York: Macmillan, 1999.

CHAPTER 2

INDIGENOUS SACRED WAYS

In pockets of the world remote from modern industrial culture, traditional small-scale societies still exist. Although they are increasingly being drawn into the global economy, some have managed to maintain at least part of their traditional religious ways. In these **indigenous** religions, the sacred and the profane are not separate; religious understanding pervades everyday life and every aspect of the local environment.

Despite great differences from one indigenous culture to the next, certain common themes can be found. One is the concept of sacred relationship to all that exists. One's individuality is of less importance than one's kinship with the whole natural system. All beings are interrelated, and shaking the cosmic web at any point affects all things. Such relationships are often described metaphorically in myths and symbols.

Another common indigenous belief is that the natural world is pervaded by living, thinking presences, which should not be ignored even if one cannot see them. There are spirits in trees, in rocks, in rivers, in mountains, in the elements, and one should stay in proper spiritual relationship with them. The appropriate human attitude toward these spirits may be a certain fear or awe, and it may be necessary to make offerings to the spirits or carry out certain **divinations** or other rituals to keep them happy. Often these spirits are seen as the souls of dead **ancestors**. In addition to a plurality of spiritual beings, there may also be a belief in an underlying cosmic force which creates and sustains the natural world.

Although such awarenesses are incumbent on everyone in traditional indigenous cultures, there are also specialists who deal with the spirit worlds. By enduring great hardships, they develop communication with the spirits and thus can act as go-betweens on behalf of the people.

These ancient spiritual ways have typically been handed down and added to orally over the millennia within the local communities. But now that these small-scale societies have been marginalized, oppressed, or brought into industrial society, there are few people left to carry on the rituals and retell the stories. However, people both within and outside these ancient ways are learning to cherish them again as containing valuable instructions for living in harmony with the cosmos.

African sacred ways

Sub-Saharan Africa is home to at least 742 tribes, each with its own religious patterns and understandings. However, some patterns, such as worship of ancestors, are widespread. The incursions of Christianity and Islam have stimulated new thinking within the indigenous religions, particularly with regard to the belief in a single High God. Initiation, drumming, and prayer are dramatic ceremonies that give an African flavour to universal themes, such as ritual awakening to the spiritual realm, celebrating it, and seeking its blessings.

Of Water and the Spirit: An African Boy's Initiation
by Malidoma Patrice Somé

Malidoma Somé, born in Burkina Faso, West Africa, is an initiated **shaman** *in his Dagara culture. He also holds three master's degrees and two doctorates. This selection from his 1994 book* Of Water and Spirit *tells of his initiation into his tribal wisdom, after several years in a French missionary school. It describes the ritually altered states of consciousness through which he grasped the transcendent mysteries of his ancient people's traditions.*

"So my initiation begins tomorrow—and I am not the least prepared for it."

"Your not knowing is your being prepared.". . .

I walked out of my room into the inner yard, where Father was waiting for me. He held ash in one hand and a bowl of water in the other. He handed me the water and I followed him into the medicine room.

We knelt down and he began. "*Walai!*" he said, saluting the spirits. "To the rising of the sun, to the powers of life. To you who established the directives and the meaning of crossing the bridge from nonperson to person through the hard road of knowledge. Here is another one who leaves his warm home and comes to you seeking the path of memory. The road is dangerous, the process uncertain, but with your protection, upon which we rely, he will return to us a man. Let him come back alive."

Father motioned to me to hand him the water, which he sprinkled onto the spirits, the statues of the male and female ancestors. He had already done the same with the ash in his hands. Then he continued, "Take this ash and give him the power of his ancestors. Take this water to seal the contract between us that he will return from his journey with a heart turned toward his tribe and a soul toward his ancestors."

He then turned to me and said, "The time has come. I will not have much to say to you again until . . . I may never say anything to you again unless you come back. I have done what a father should do, the rest is in your hands. Please come back to us."

The whole family was outside watching. When I followed Father out into the compound, everybody looked at me with sympathy. My younger brothers were staring at me as if I were going on a long journey with no specific time of return. I had no idea how long I was going to be absent. We all walked away from the house toward the outskirts of the village. As we neared the bush, more and more people joined us. There was a large group of young adolescents, maybe thirteen, maybe fourteen years old packed together at the end of the bush. They looked so young that I felt out of place. They were all naked.

Nakedness is very common in the tribe. It is not a shameful thing; it is an expression of one's relationship with the spirit of nature. To be naked is to be open-hearted. Normally, kids stay naked until puberty and even beyond. It was only with the introduction of cheap cloth from the West, through Goodwill and other Christian organizations, that nakedness began to be associated with shame.

The naked kids were singing. As I came closer I could hear their words.

My little family I leave today.
My great Family I meet tomorrow.
Father, don't worry, I shall come back,
Mother, don't cry, I am a man.

As the sun rises and the sun sets
My body into them shall melt,
And one with you and them
Forever and ever I shall be . . .

As the candidates for initiation passed through the crowd, they took off their shirts and shorts. Their families embraced them. Some family members grabbed their hands and sobbed with them; perhaps they were saying goodbye for the last time. There were so many young men that I could not count them all. Many of them were strangers to me. My father asked me to take my clothes off. I obeyed him, but I felt ashamed. No one paid any attention to my nakedness, however. In the village clothing attracts more attention than nakedness. My sister was weeping . . .

We sang as we walked into the belly of the bush, swallowed by the trees. . . .

In the middle of the circle that we had instinctively formed, the coach was directing the singing. The song got inside of you, burning your heart like fire. I was quickly caught up with its rhythms, words, melody. We held each other's hands and swayed in cadence. It was intoxicating to sing in the middle of the bush at night—even on an empty stomach . . .

The elders chose this time to make a dramatic entrance. They looked like living skeletons, half naked and covered with white lines painted on their faces, necks, bellies, and backs. Each elder wore ritual cotton shorts. They were voluminous and looked from afar like bags. Their thin black bodies were not visible in the dark, just the white, almost phosphorescent lines painted on them. In addition each elder was carrying his **medicine** bag, made of feline skin. They walked in a line; slowly, quietly, and imperturbably. When shrouded in the darkness, far away from the fire, their bodies were luminescent, but as they came closer, into the light, the luminescence disappeared.

Their presence intensified the song. We sang more furiously as if the force of the elders, suddenly available, were a gift that flowed from the power of being old. Our teachers walked around the fireplace in the center of the circle—three times clockwise and three times counterclockwise. They did not sing with us. When they stopped their procession the song stopped as if by enchantment. Nobody asked us to stop singing—we simply lost the song. It departed from us as if a force had removed it from our lips as a calabash of water is removed from the thirsty lips of its drinker. The silence that followed was as thick as the darkness behind us in the bush.

One of the elders pulled something out of his bag, a pouch with an end like a tail. One could see long, mysterious, stiff hairs sprouting from the pouch as if they grew there. He brought the thing to his mouth and said something silently. Only his lips moved. Then he directed the tail end of the pouch toward the fire and uttered something in primal language. The color of the fire changed to violet and increased its roar. We still held each other's hands. The elder moved close to the fire, speaking again in primal tongue. With each of his movements, the fire grew taller and taller until the violet flame stood almost six meters in the air. From then on I heard nothing and thought nothing. . . .

The fifth elder, the one responsible for the initial experience, still stood in the middle of the circle next to the fireplace. Walking slowly around the circle, he spoke incessantly and breathlessly . . .

What he said was this: The place where he was standing was the center. Each one of us possessed a center that he had grown away from after birth. To be born was to lose contact with our center, and to grow from childhood to adulthood was to walk away from it.

"The center is both within and without. It is everywhere. But we must realize it exists, find it, and be with it, for without the center we cannot tell who we are, where we come from, and where we are going."

He explained that the purpose of Baor[1] was to find our center. . . .

All around me and underneath me I could feel life pulsating, down to

---

[1] Baor—a boys' initiation into manhood ritual for the West African Dagora people.

the smallest piece of dirt on the ground. The way this life expressed itself was otherworldly: sounds were blue or green, colors were loud. I saw incandescent visions and apparitions, breathing color and persistent immobility. Everything seemed alive with meaning. Even the stonelike circle of people partook of the same cacophony of meaning. Each person was like the sum total of all the emanations taking place. The people, however, were not in charge of the operation of the universe around them—they were dependent on it and they were useful to it as well.

The elder in the center of the circle was the most intriguing to watch. He looked like an impalpable being in fusion, an amalgamation of colors, sounds of varying pitch, and innumerable forms. All of his smallest constituent parts—his cells and bacteria in his body, even the tiniest atomic particles of his being—had come alive. He was not moving, but the colors, the sounds, and the life forms were. Without being able to put it into words, I understood what was happening, for at that stage of consciousness there is no difference between meaning and being. Things had become their meaning and I knew that was the lesson for the evening. I also understood that this was the kind of knowledge I was going to become gradually acquainted with—not by going outside of myself, but by looking within myself and a few others. For now, all I could do was to feel and honor the effects of the subtle invisible world breaking through my own blindness and preempting my perceptions. How acquiescent one becomes when face to face with the pure universal energy! . . .

I thought about the hardships of the day—the baking heat of the sun and my sweat falling into my eyes and burning them like pepper. I had lost all sense of chronology. I told myself that this is what the world looked like when one had first expired. I felt as if I were being quite reasonable. I could still think and respond to sensations around me, but I was no longer experiencing the biting heat of the sun or my restless mind trying to keep busy or ignoring my assignment. Where I was now was just plain real.

When I looked once more at the yila, I became aware that it was not a tree at all. How had I ever seen it as such? I do not know how this transformation occurred. Things were not happening logically, but as if this were a dream. Out of nowhere, in the place where the tree had stood, appeared a tall woman dressed in black from head to foot. She resembled a nun, although her outfit did not seem religious. Her tunic was silky and black as the night. She wore a veil over her face, but I could tell that behind this veil was an extremely beautiful and powerful entity. I could sense the intensity emanating from her, and that intensity exercised an irresistible magnetic pull. To give in to that pull was like drinking water after a day of wandering in the desert.

My body felt like it was floating, as if I were a small child being lulled by a nurturing presence that was trying to calm me by singing soothing lullabies and rocking me rhythmically. I felt as if I were floating weightless in a small body of water. My eyes locked on to the lady in the veil, and the feeling of being drawn toward her increased. For a moment I was overcome with shyness, uneasiness, and a feeling of inappropriateness, and I had to lower my eyes. When I looked again, she had lifted her veil, revealing an unearthly face. She was green, light green. Even her eyes were green, though very small and luminescent. She was smiling and her teeth were the color of violet and had light emanating from them. The greenness in her had nothing to do with the color of her skin. She was green from the inside out, as if her body was filled with green fluid. I do not know how I knew this, but this green was the expression of immeasurable love.

Never before had I felt so much love. I felt as if I had missed her all my life and was grateful to heaven for having finally released her back to me. We knew each other, but at the time I could not tell why, when, or how. I also could not tell the nature of our love. It was not romantic or filial; it was a love that surpassed any known classifications. Like two loved ones who had been apart for an unduly long period of time, we dashed toward each other and flung ourself into each other's arms.

The sensation of embracing her body blew my body into countless pieces, which became millions of conscious cells, all longing to reunite with the whole that was her. If they could not unite with her, it felt as if they could not live. Each one was adrift and in need of her to anchor itself back in place. There are no words to paint what it felt like to be in the hands of the green lady in the black veil. We exploded into each other in a cosmic contact that sent us floating adrift in the ether in countless intertwined forms. In the course of this baffling experience, I felt as if I were moving backward in time and forward in space.

While she held me in her embrace, the green lady spoke to me for a long time in the softest voice that ever was. She was so much taller than I was that I felt like a small boy in her powerful arms. She placed her lips close to my left ear and she spoke so softly and tenderly to me that nothing escaped my attention. I cried abundantly the whole time, not because what she told me was sad, but because every word produced an indescribable sensation of nostalgia and longing in me.

Human beings are often unable to receive because we do not know what to ask for. We are sometimes unable to get what we need because we do not know what we want. If this was happiness that I felt, then no human could sustain this amount of well-being for even a day. You would have to be dead or changed into a something capable of handling these unearthly feelings in order to live with them. The part in us that yearns for these kinds of feelings and experiences is not human. It does not know that it lives in a body that can withstand only a certain amount of this kind of experience at a time. If humans were to feel this way all the time, they would probably not be able to do anything other than shed tears of happiness for the rest of their lives—which, in that case, would be very short.

Human beings never feel that they have enough of anything. Ofttimes what we say we want is real in words only. If we ever understood the genuine desires of our hearts at any given moment, we might reconsider the things we waste our energy pining for. If we could always get what we thought we wanted, we would quickly exhaust our weak arsenal of petty desires and discover with shame that all along we had been cheating ourselves.

Love consumes its object voraciously. Consequently, we can only experience its shadow. Happiness does not last forever because we do not have the power to contain it. It has the appetite of a ferocious carnivore that has been starved for a long time—this is how much love and bliss and happiness there is in nature, in the place that was there before we existed in it.

I cannot repeat the speech of the green lady. It lives in me because it enjoys the privilege of secrecy. For me to disclose it would be to dishonor and diminish it. The power of nature exists in its silence. Human words cannot encode meaning because human language has access only to the shadow of meaning. The speech of the green lady was intended to stay alive in silence, so let it be.

I loosened my grip, lifted my wet face up to hers, and read departure in her eyes. I did not know where she was returning to, but wherever it was I did not want her to go without me. My feelings for her were so strong I felt that I would be able to brave anything to stay with her, nor did I think there was any reason we should part after having been separated for so long. Her face, however, said I could not go where she was going and that this was one of those imperatives that one had to respond to without negotiation. Things had to stay as they were. In despair I clung harder to her soft body, unable to do anything else. My eyes closed as my grip tightened, and the soft body under my hands became rough.

When I opened my eyes I realized I was desperately hugging the yila tree. It was the same as it had been before. Meanwhile, the elders had moved closer to me, obviously watching everything I had been doing. I heard one of them say, "They are always like this. First they resist and play dumb when there are a lot of things waiting to be done, and then when it happens, they won't let go either. Children are so full of contradictions. The very experience you rejected before with lies, you are now accepting without apology."

This seemed to have been directed at me. I looked up at the elder who spoke. He met my eyes, and I felt no further need to be holding on to the tree.

"Go find something to eat, and make your bed for the night," he said gently.

It was then that I noticed that the sun had set. My experience had lasted several hours, but the time had felt so short!

When I arrived back at the camping circle, the students were almost done making up their sleeping places. Nyangoli in his faithfulness was discreetly waiting for me. He looked relieved when I appeared, so relieved that, for the first time since we had arrived at the camp, he spoke to me first. "You're still alive! *Walai.*"...

Nature looks the way it looks because of the way we are. We could not live our whole lives on the ecstatic level of the sacred. Our senses would soon become exhausted and the daily business of living would never get done. There does, however, come a time when one must learn to move between the two ways of "seeing" reality in order to become a whole person.

Traditional education consists of three parts: enlargement of one's ability to see, destabilization of the body's habit of being bound to one plane of being, and the ability to voyage transdimensionally and return. Enlarging one's vision and abilities has nothing supernatural about it, rather it is "natural" to be a part of nature and to **participate** in a wider understanding of reality.

SOURCE: Malidoma Patrice Somé, *Of Water and Spirit: Ritual, Magic, and Initiation in the Life of an African Shaman*. New York: Penguin, 1994, pp. 192–226

Women and Prayers in African Religion
by John Mbiti

John Mbiti is a Kenyan, formerly Professor of Religious Studies at Makere University, Uganda, East Africa. He published several studies of African religions, including African Religions and Philosophy *(1969). He later became the director of an ecumenical institute, then a parish minister in Switzerland. He describes the unique spiritual roles of African women as priestesses, healers, and prayer-senders. A new baby, for example, is dedicated to God by lifting it skyward with prayers.*

A beautiful picture of women in African society is presented in a proverb from Ghana, which says: "A woman is a flower in a garden; her husband is the fence around it!" In this paper I wish to examine the place and the role of women according to African Religion....

In traditional African life the women play a significant role in the religious activities of society. One of the areas where this role is prominent is in offering prayers for their families in particular and their communities in general. In many areas there were (and still are) women priests (priestesses). Almost everywhere in Africa the mediums (who are so important in traditional medical practice) are nearly always women. In most cases it is also the women who experience spirit possession. Traditional healing is a profession of both men and women, but it is more often the women practitioners who handle children's and other women's medical needs. In this paper we have space for only a few prayers which illustrate how actively involved the women are in the spirituality of African religion. The examples are cited out of my own book: *The Prayers of African Religion*, 1975.

A woman's morning prayer runs: "Morning has risen. God, take away from us every pain, every ill, every mishap. God, let us come safely home" (*Mbiti*, II, 31). In this prayer the woman (mother) brings before God her family and hands it over to God, believing that he will keep away all evil. It is a prayer from the Pygmies of Zaire.

The Aro women of Sierra Leone pray in a litany for a sick child. They address it specially to the departed members of the family who are taught to participate in the healing process by conveying the request to God. The mother prays: "O spirits of the past, this little one I hold is my child; she is your child also, therefore be gracious unto her." The other women chant: "She has come into a world of trouble: sickness is in the world, and cold and pain; the pain you knew, the sickness with which you were familiar." The mother prays on: "Let her sleep in peace, for there is healing in sleep. Let none among you be angry with me or with my child." The other women take up their chanting: "Let her grow, let her become strong. Let her become full-grown. Then will she offer such a sacrifice to you that will delight your heart" (*ibidem*, 50). In this prayer we see how close to the spirit world the women feel. They enter into it, they solicit help from it. The physical and spiritual worlds mingle here in a harmony of "going" and "coming." The women depict here a deep sensitivity towards the invisible and spiritual realities.

A woman whose husband is away fighting in war prays for his protection and safe return. She prays not just for him alone, but for others who are with him. Like all similar prayers all over the world, this is one-sided, favoring one's own side. It comes from the Banyarwanda and pleads: "Let him be saved with those who went with him! Let him stand firm with them. Let him return from the battle with them..." (*op. cit.*, 83). In this way the women participate in fighting on the side of their husbands. The husbands would be encouraged to get this form of spiritual support from their wives.

Recognizing that menstruation is intimately linked to the passing on of life, many African peoples perform a ceremony to mark the first menstruation. At one such ceremony in Ghana, the Ashanti mother of the concerned girl prays that she may grow to full maturity and bear children. This is the wish of every mother for her children. "Nyankonpon Tweaduapon Nyame (Supreme Sky God, Who alone is great), upon whom men lean and do not fall, receive this wine and drink. Earth Goddess, whose day of worship is Thursday, receive this wine and drink. This girl child whom God has given to me, today the Bara state has come upon her.... Do not come and take her away, and do not have permitted her to menstruate only to die" (*op. cit.*, 96).

In many parts of Africa it does not always rain enough. Rainmaking ceremonies are performed at which sacrifices, offerings, and prayers are made to God, beseeching Him to give more rain or to let it rain if the rain has delayed. Here is one such prayer made by the Maasai women of Kenya and Tanzania. The woman leader intones one part while other people who are present for the occasion sing or recite the other part:

Leader: "We need herbs on the earth's back!"
Others: "Hie! Wae! Almighty God."
Leader: "The father of Nasira has conquered, has conquered."
Others: "The highlands and also the lowlands of our vast country which belongs to thee, O God."
Leader: "May this be our year, ours in plenty (when you grant us rain!)."
Others: "O messenger of Mbatian's son" (*op. cit.*, 113).

This prayer is for the welfare of people, animals, and nature at large, since all depend on water for their survival.

Women express gratitude to God after childbirth. Then they know that life comes ultimately from Him and is sustained by Him. The following prayer is said by Pygmy women in a ceremony dedicating a baby to God. The mother and father lift the baby towards the sky and pray:

"To Thee, the Creator, to Thee, the Powerful, I offer this fresh bud, new fruit of the ancient tree. Thou art the Master, we Thy children. To Thee, the Creator, to Thee, the Powerful: Khmvoum (God), Khmvoum, I offer this new plant" (*op. cit.*, 124).

The sorrows of being childless go very deep in the wife. There are many prayers for help in such situations. From an affected woman of the Barundi we get the following prayer, in which we feel with her the agony of her spirit:

"O Imana (God) of Urundi, if only you would help me! O Imana of pity, Imana of my father's home, if only you would help me!. . . O Imana, if only you would give me a homestead and children! I prostrate myself before you, Imana of Urundi. I cry to you: Give me offspring, give me as you give to others! Imana, what shall I do, where shall I go? I am in distress: where is there room for me? O Merciful, O Imana of mercy, help this once!" (*op. cit.*, 86).

Death also brings with it its own sorrows and problems, and many prayers are offered in such times. The following prayer pours out desperation with the same forcefulness as the previous prayer:

"My husband, you have abandoned me. My master is gone and will never return. I am lost. I have no hope. For you used to fetch water and collect firewood for me. You used to clothe and feed me with good things. . . . Where shall I go?" (*op. cit.*, 99).

This prayer comes from the Basoga of Uganda, but its echoes can be heard all over Africa.

It is clear that women both participate in the religious activities of society and make their own contributions for the spiritual welfare of their lives, their families, and of society in general. Through prayer women express themselves as self-determining. The prayers are a small window that opens into their spirituality which indeed is the spirituality of all human beings. As the women share with God in the great mysteries of passing on life, so they share also in giving human life a spiritual orientation. They are truly flowers in the garden. They give beauty, scent, and seed to life.

SOURCE: John S. Mbiti, "Flowers in the Garden: The Role of Women in African Religion," in *African Traditional Religions in Contemporary Society*, ed. Jacob Olupona. New York: Paragon House, 1991, pp. 59–71

The Talking Drum: African Sacred Liturgy
by Georges Niangoran-Bouah

Georges Niangoran-Bouah, Professor at the University of Abidjan in Ivory Coast, West Africa, brings to life the deeper meanings of the African drum's sacred messages. The drums' ancient poetry, carrying in rhythm far across African plains, praises God the Creator, Goddess Earth, and beautiful Moon. This primal discourse carries the sacred consciousness of ancient ways, he says, much as holy books do for other faiths.

Generally speaking, the outsider who comes to Africa for the first time is surprised by the omnipresence of the drum in both religious and profane ceremonies. The drum is an instrument that everybody hears and sees; it is the instrument of kings. . . .

The Sacred   According to religious anthropology, the Sacred is that which is connected to religion and that which inspires respect and deep veneration. The Sacred is whatever goes beyond man and inspires his respect, his admiration. From the Sacred generally emanates a particular fervor, coupled with an element of fear of an absolute power and an element of mystery. The sacred being or object enjoys a fascinating power, often presented as being the locus of energy able to manifest itself at any moment and anywhere.

For the traditional African, the Sacred is an organized and hierarchized universe filled with invisible beings which include God, spirits, the spirits of the ancestors, myths, legends, ceremonies, elaborate rituals, and cult objects.

It is this universe of absolute power, of mystery, of fascinating might, that we are trying to reconstitute through what the African drums say.

The texts chosen to illustrate the point in this paper will not be followed by commentaries, in order to allow the reader to find for himself their philosophical, religious, or theological importance. The poet is not wrong in saying:

> Contemporary drum
> Of founding ancestors,
> Messenger coming
> From the beginning of time;
> Drum, wherever you are
> And whatever your state,
> Drum word,
> Memory of the Ancients,
> We implore you, speak,
> Talk to us in the African way
> Of immemorial times,
> Speak, speak to us
> Of deep Africa
> Of true Africa!

In black Africa, the talking drum is in fact a precious element of communication. In the highlands, with a favorable direction of the wind, the language of a drum can be heard at a distance of forty kilometers.

For the Akan, the drummed documentation is serious; it is sacred and respected by the whole population. This is the reason that it is the preferred method of communication with gods, the spirits, and the ancestors. . . .

Among the Akan in Côte d'Ivoire and Ghana, the drum defines its origin itself by saying:

> God in creating the world
> Has suffered to create.
> What did he create?
> He created the Drum.
> Divine Drum,
> Wherever you are
> In nature,
> We call upon you,
> Come.
> *(Abron² drum text)*

---

² Abron—West African tribe in Ghana and Ivory Coast.

The drum is an animated being. In this chapter, the drum is no longer only perceived as a material object of human conception and fabrication but also as an animated being endowed with a vital force and spiritual principle.

While organizing the world,
God-the-Creator
Has suffered to create.
What did He create?
He has created the Word
And the Word-carrier,
Has created the drum and
The drummer. . . .
Divine drum,
Wherever you be
In nature,
We call upon you, come!
Divine drum,
We shall wake you up
And make you heard.
(Abron drum text)
I am coming from my dream
And find myself
In the hands
Of the drummer.
(Abron drum)

The Creation according to the drum
God-the-Creator
Has created Heaven,
And he has created the Earth.
He has created the night,
And has created the day,
Alone
Absolutely alone.
God has created the water
And has created the crocodile.
(Agni[3] drum)

Attitude and behavior of humans towards the Eternal One
Great God
Infinitely mighty

---

[3] Agni—West African tribe in Ivory Coast.

You who give us life
We glorify you,
Bless us!
(Agni drum)

Goddess Earth

Oh you good earth
Who nourishes us
The year has come to its end.
We glorify you,
Bless us!
(Agni drum)

Goddess Moon

Beautiful moon
Who brings together
The joyful troupes
Give me the strength
To sing to you all the years!
(Agni drum)

Conclusion It is customary when talking of the religious thoughts of the ancient people of the Middle East to refer to the Bible or the Quran. In the same way the Akan refer themselves to the talking drum in order to quote any discourse related to the sacred. Bible, Quran, and Drum have the same vocation; these are fundamental sacred "books" venerated by their respective peoples. They are monuments of the human spirit because they are timeless. The drum is a tool and an appropriate instrument of knowledge which for a long time was considered as not being accessible to the universe of African traditional beliefs. The discourse of the drum, unchangeable and conventional, is not a discourse of an isolated wise man, but a real ideology of several thousand years which the memory of a whole people preserves with piety from generation to generation.

SOURCE: Georges Niangoran-Bouah, "The Talking Drum: A Traditional African Instrument of Liturgy and of Mediation with the Sacred," in *African Traditional Religions in Contemporary Society*, ed. Jacob Olupona. New York: Paragon House, 1991, pp. 81–92

Native North American sacred ways

The Americas have been home to a great variety of ancient indigenous ways. In North America alone, there were at least 2,000 different languages being spoken before the European settlers arrived. Many aspects of the indigenous religions are specific to the local environment, but some are now spreading throughout the region, such as the **sacred pipe**, **sweat lodge** and **vision quest**. After centuries of oppression by people of European origin, the remaining indigenous tradition-carriers are being carefully studied and valued for their spiritual wisdom and ecological example.

That Mountain Has Spirit
by Southwest Indigenous Peoples

You go out and get a certain piece of rock. It's not just a rock. It's got energy forces in it; it's a living thing, too. . . .

You look at that mountain, that mountain has spirit, that mountain has holiness. There's a quiet there and yet there's a fervor there. And if you've ever seen clouds there you see that mountain like a hand grasping those clouds. There's life up there. That's why it's sacred. . . .

Before you go hunting the important thing is that you are going to have a little prayer . . . to the Mother Nature, the nature of the sky, and then the animal, and then you more or less cry a little bit, and ask Mother Nature to spare you some meat. When you went into that forest, you had to be that deer. . . .

We must try and worship the land, the ground and the stars and the skies, for they are the ones that have spirit. They are the mighty spirits which guide and direct us, which help us to survive.

SOURCE: Stephen Trimble, ed., *Our Voices, Our Land*. Flagstaff, AZ: The Heard Museum, Northland Press, 1986, pp. 24–47

The Great Vision
by Black Elk, Lakota Shaman

In the Plains area around the Black Hills (in what is now called South Dakota), a nine-year-old Lakota (Sioux) boy with virtually no contact with European culture had an unsought visionary experience. He fell deathly ill and had an intense vision in which he was carried up to a sky full of horses and a cloud tepee with a rainbow door. Entering the sky lodge, he sat with six cosmic Grandfathers who gave him powers to understand and to heal. He grieved for his nation's suffering at the hands of the oncoming invasion of European immigrants. He sought strength from the Great Mystery behind his vision, called **Wakan Tanka**, *the spiritual power present in all the world: in blood, thunder, birds, and buffalo, saying: "I was seeing in a sacred manner the shapes of all things in the spirit." This boy grew up to become Black Elk (1862–1950), a medicine man, or shaman. Later Black Elk told his life story to John Neihardt, a poet, who in 1932 edited it, condensed it, and added a few poetic elabo-rations. The resulting book,* Black Elk Speaks, *has become a classic. In 1984*

Raymond DeMallie published the original manuscripts of Neihardt's interviews as The Sixth Grandfather *with editorial notes, from which the following extract is taken.*

We stopped at a creek to get a drink. When I got off my horse I crumbled down, helpless, and I couldn't walk. The boys helped me up and when the camp camped again, I was very sick. . . . Both my legs and arms were swollen badly and even my face. This all came suddenly. . . .

As I lay in the tipi[4] I could see through the tipi the same two men whom I saw before and they were coming from the clouds. . . . They came and stood off aways from me and stopped, saying: "Hurry up, your grandfather is calling you." When they started back I got up and started to follow them. Just as I got out of the tipi I could see the two men going back into the clouds and there was a small cloud coming down toward me at the same time, which stood before me. I got on top of the cloud and was raised up, following the two men, and when I looked back, I saw my father and mother looking at me. When I looked back I felt sorry that I was leaving them. . . .

I followed those men on up into the clouds and they showed me a vision of a bay horse standing there in the middle of the clouds. . . .

I looked over there and saw twelve black horses toward the west, where the sun goes down. All the horses had on their necks necklaces of buffalo hoofs. . . . I was very scared of those twelve head of horses because I could see the light[ning] and thunder around them. . . .

When I had seen it all, the bay horse said to me: "Your grandfathers are having a council, these shall take you; so take courage." . . .

I followed the bay horse and it took me to a place on a cloud under a rainbow gate and there were sitting my six grandfathers, sitting inside of a rainbow door, and the horses stopped behind me. . . .

One of the grandfathers said to me: "Do not fear, come right in" (through the rainbow door). So I went in and stood before them. The horses in the four quarters of the earth all neighed to cheer me as I entered the rainbow door.

The grandfather representing where the sun goes down said: "Your grandfathers all over the world and the earth are having a council and there you were called, so here you are. Behold then, those where the sun goes down; from thence they shall come, you shall see. From them you shall know the willpower of myself, for they shall take you to the center of the earth, and the nations of all kinds shall tremble. Behold where the sun continually shines, for they shall take you there."

The first grandfather then showed me a wooden cup with water, turning it toward me. He said: "Take courage and be not afraid, for you will know

---

[4] Tipi—Native American conical tent of animal skins.

him. And furthermore, behold him, whom you shall represent. By representing him, you shall be very powerful on earth in medicines and all powers. He is your spirit and you are his body and his name is Eagle Wing Stretches."

When I looked up I saw flames going up from the rainbow. The first grandfather gave me a cup of water and also a bow and arrow and said: "Behold them, what I give you shall depend on, for you shall go against our enemies and you shall be a great warrior." Then he gave me that cup of water and said: "Behold, take this, and with this you shall be great." (This means that I should kill all sickness on earth with this water.)

After this he got up and started to run toward where the sun goes down and as he ran he changed into a black horse as he faced me. The five men left said: "Behold him." And this black horse changed into a poor [emaciated] horse.

The second grandfather rose and said: "Take this and make haste." So I took an herb out of the second grandfather's hand. And as [*I turned to the dying horse*] I held it toward the black horse [*and this holy herb*] cured the black horse, making him strong and fat once again.

The second grandfather represented the north. He said: "Behold the mother earth, for you shall create a nation." (This means that I am going to cure lots of sickness with this herb—bring children back to life.) The bay horse stood with the black horse and said to me: "Father, paint me, for I shall make a nation on the earth." [The] second grandfather of the north said again: "Take courage and behold, for you shall represent the wing of the great giant that lives." The second grandfather stood up and ran toward the north and as he turned around he changed himself again into a white goose. I looked toward where the black horses were and they were thunders and the northern white horses turned into white geese. The second grandfather said: "Behold then, your grandfather, for they shall fly in circles from one end of the earth to the other." [*Through this power of the north I will make everybody cry as geese do when they go north in the spring because the hardship is over.*]

First grandfather's song:

> They are appearing, may you behold.
> They are appearing, may you behold.
> The thunder nation is appearing, may you behold.

Second grandfather's song:

> They are appearing, may you behold.
> They are appearing, may you behold.
> The white geese nation is appearing, may you behold.

The third grandfather, where the sun continually shines, says: "Younger brother, take courage, for across the earth they shall take you. Behold them" (pointing to the morning star and below the star there were two men flying), "from them you shall have power. All the fowls of the universe, these he has wakened and also he has wakened the beings on the earth" (animals, people, etc.). As the third grandfather said this, he held in his hand a peace pipe, which had a spotted eagle outstretched on the handle of the pipe; apparently the eagle was alive for it was moving. He said: "Behold this, for with this you shall walk across the earth. Behold this, for with this whatever is sick on this earth you shall make well."

Then the third grandfather pointed to a man who was solid red in color and said: "Behold him." Then the red man lay down and changed into a buffalo before he got up. When he was standing up, the third grandfather said "Behold him" again. The buffalo ran back to the east and when he looked at the horses in this direction they all turned into buffalo.

The fourth grandfather said to me: "Younger brother, behold me; a nation's center of the earth I shall give you with the power of the four quarters. With the power of the four quarters like relatives you shall walk. Behold the four quarters." And after he said this I looked and saw that at each of the four quarters there was a chief. . . .

The fifth grandfather represented the Great Spirit above. He said: "Boy, I sent for you and you came. Behold me, my power you shall see." He stretched his hands out and turned into a spotted eagle. Then he said: "Behold them; they, the fowls of the universe, shall come to you. Things in the skies shall be like relatives" (meaning stars) "They shall take you across the earth with my power. Your grandfathers shall attack an enemy and be unable to destroy him, but you will have the power to destroy. You shall go with courage. This is all." Then the eagle flew up over my head and I saw the animals and birds all coming toward me to perform a duty.

Then the sixth grandfather said: "Boy, take courage, you wanted my power on earth, so you shall know me. You shall have my power in going back to the earth. Your nation on earth shall have great difficulties. There you shall go. Behold me, for I will depart." (The sixth grandfather was a very old man with very white hair.) I saw him go out the rainbow gate. I followed him out the rainbow gate. I was on the bay horse now that had talked to me at the first. I stopped and took a good look at the sixth grandfather and it seemed that I recognized him. I stood there for awhile very scared and then as I looked at him longer I knew it was myself as a young man. At the first he was an old man, but he got younger and younger until he was a little boy nine years old. This old man had in his hand a spear.

I remembered that the grandfather of the west had given me a wooden cup of water and a bow and arrow and with this bow and arrow I was going to destroy the enemy with the power of the fearful road. With the wooden cup of water I was to save mankind. This water was clear and with it I was to raise a nation (like medicine). . . .

I could see nothing but dust flying on the four quarters of the earth. I looked up and could see right above me a spotted eagle hovering over me and this was evidently who had told me to look back. I started back to the camp with the eagle guarding me. No one was with me then but the eagle, but I knew that I was coming back to the center of the nation's hoop by myself. I could see the people following me. Soon I saw my own tipi at home and I walked fast to get there. As I entered the tipi I saw a boy lying there dying and I stood there awhile and finally found out that it was myself.

The next thing I heard was somebody saying: "The boy is feeling better now, you had better give him some water." I looked up and saw it was my mother and father stooping over me. They were giving me some medicine but it was not that that cured me—it was my vision that cured me. The first thought that came to me was that I had been traveling and my father and mother didn't seem to know that I had been gone and they didn't look glad. I felt very sad over this.

SOURCE: Raymond J. DeMallie, ed., *The Sixth Grandfather: Black Elk's Teachings Given to John G. Neihardt*. Lincoln: University of Nebraska Press, 1984, pp. 111–42

Basic Call to Consciousness
by the Hau De No Sau Nee (Iroquois) Nation

Basic Call to Consciousness *is a collective statement written by the northeastern Hau De No Sau Nee (Iroquois) Nation for a United Nations conference in Geneva. It was published in 1978. This passage expresses the powerful indigenous way of participation in the spirit in every living thing, and respecting it.*

The Hau de no sau nee, or the Six Nations Iroquois Confederacy, has existed on this land since the beginning of human memory. Our culture is among the most ancient continuously existing cultures in the world. We still remember the earliest doings of human beings. We remember the original instructions of the Creators of Life on this place we call Etenoha—Mother Earth. We are the spiritual guardians of this place. We are the Ongwhehonwhe—the Real People

In the beginning, we were told that the human beings who walk about on the Earth have been provided with all the things necessary for life. We were instructed to carry a love for one another, and to show a great respect for all the beings of this Earth. We are shown that our life exists with the tree life, that our well-being depends on the well-being of the Vegetable Life, that we are close relatives of the four-legged beings. In our ways, spiritual consciousness is the highest form of politics.

Ours is a Way of Life. We believe that all living things are spiritual beings. Spirits can be expressed as energy forms manifested in matter. A blade of grass is an energy form manifested in matter—grass matter. The spirit of the grass is that unseen force which produces the species of grass, and it is manifest to us in the form of real grass.

All things of the world are real, material things. The Creation is a true, material phenomenon, and the Creation manifests itself to us through reality. The spiritual universe, then, is manifest to Man as the Creation, the Creation which supports life. We believe that man is real, a part of the Creation, and that his duty is to support Life in conjunction with the other beings. That is why we call ourselves Ongwhehonwhe—Real People.

The original instructions direct that we who walk about on the Earth are to express a great respect, an affection, and a gratitude toward all the spirits which create and support Life. We give a greeting and thanksgiving to the many supporters of our own lives—the corn, beans, squash, the winds, the sun. When people cease to respect and express gratitude for these many things, then all life will be destroyed, and human life on the planet will come to an end.

Our roots are deep in the lands where we live. We have a great love for our country, for our birthplace is there. The soil is rich from the bones of thousands of our generations. Each of us were created in those lands, and it is our duty to take great care of them, because from these lands will spring the future generations of the Ongwhehonwhe. We walk about with a great respect, for the Earth is a very sacred place.

We are not a people who demand, or ask anything of the Creators of Life, but instead, we give greetings and thanksgiving that all the forces of Life are still at work. We deeply understand our relationship to all living things. To this day, the territories we still hold are filled with trees, animals, and the other gifts of the Creation. In these places we still receive nourishment from our Mother Earth.

We have seen that not all people of the Earth show the same kind of respect for this world and its beings. The Indo-European people who have colonized our lands have shown very little respect for the things that create and support Life. We believe that these people ceased their respect for the world a long time ago. Many thousands of years ago, all the people of the world believed in the same Way of Life, that of harmony with the universe. All lived according to the Natural Ways.

SOURCE: Iroquois Nation (Han De No Sau Nee), "Basic Call to Consciousness," ed. *Akwesasne Notes*. Via Rooseveltown, NY: Mohawk Nation, 1978, pp. 71–3

The Essence of Cosmic Man
by Tlakaelel (Mexica-Tolteca)

Tlakaelel is a Mexica-Tolteca elder, from near Mexico City. He is a teacher, heir and guardian of the oral tradition, and spiritual guide. He explores the meanings of his ancestors' monumental pyramids and hidden caverns, and wrote the book Nahui Mitl: The Journey of the Four Arrows. *He says: "Brethren: Mexicayotl (the essence of cosmic man) will never die." But to keep this essence in our hearts, we must come closer to the Creator.*

How can we come closer to the Creator? For us Indigenous People, communication is not only realized through the use of our five senses. There also exists the sense of direction, of balance, of time, of panic, and many more. For us to communicate with the different people, we must bond with their different sensitivities.

To communicate with the Creator, we have various ceremonies like the ceremony of initiation, which is done when we are born. This ceremony opens our road to life. With it, we receive the sensibility that with time develops as it is impulsed by our teachers.

When one of our children is born, we dedicate him to the sun. We raise him up over our head and offer him to the sun by saying, "You gave the energy so that this child would reach the world. Give him strength, continue giving him life, nourish him." Then we present him to the south. We ask that *"Omeyotl,"* the great spirit of the south, *Ketzalkoatl*, take possession of his body and participate in his knowledge, and grant him the universal wisdom, the cosmic knowledge that is manifested through movement. Then we turn him to the place where the sun sets, and we invoke the forces that one day gave life to our ancestors. We present him to our ancestors, the ones who formed this world, the ones who with their existence and their work, have made this moment and the existence of this new being possible. We thank them and ask them that wherever they are and whatever form they now have, they manifest their love and give their strength to this new child. And we continue turning towards the north where a great force exists. This is the synthesis of all the forces. This is death, this is *"Miktlan,"* the place where all the forces that exist converge. All that was, is, and will be rests here. We come to this place to participate with the forces that are here at that moment of creation. We call for rest here, so that later, we can resurge in a more energetic way.

Death signifies the union of the dual energy of the principal Creator. We will know that when we exhale for the last time, we have an internal force that maintains our lives within our bodies. We will know that we are no longer in this body, that we leave this place to return to the place from where we came to integrate ourselves to the "all." Because we are part of the energy of the Great Spirit, we will be in the west where the sun sets, in the red place.

When we leave the earth, our bones will be clean, they will become ashes. But we will continue having a consciousness and we will go where the Great Spirit is. This is the place where black, white, red, and yellow are concentrated. This is where the four cardinal points are reunited. We will realize that we are a bird, a tree, a star, a cloud, and that we are free. We will find that we are the spirit and that we will continue the great work of the Creator.

This ceremony of the life/death cycle is a petition to all of the creative forces so that the new being, the new child, this new balance, be in equilibrium with life and death. When the child grows, he is taught to share everything, respect everything, and to create and be happy creating. The child learns to pray in sweat lodges (*temazcales*), in the mountains, and during the night, while gazing at the stars. He is taught to pray for every act of his life. He is taught to give thanks to the Creator for the favors that were granted to us. There are more ceremonies such as: the acquisition of a sacred pipe (*chanupa*), vision quests, and the culmination: the Sun Dance.

SOURCE: Tlakaelel, *Nahui Mitl: The Journey of the Four Arrows*. Chaplin, CT: Mexicayotl Productions, 1998, pp. 144–45

Seeing with a Native Eye
by Barre Toelken

Barre Toelken, an anthropologist at Utah State University, lived with the southwestern Navajo people for two years, during which his "adopted Navajo father" helped him how to see with a native eye, rather than with the eye of industrial culture. The immense gap between cultures and religious attitudes becomes evident in their discussion of a tall building, a jet bomber, and springtime.

In Western culture, religion seems to occupy a niche reserved for the unreal, the Otherworld, a reference point that is reached only upon death or through the agency of the priest. Many native American tribes see religious experience as something that surrounds man all the time. In fact, my friends the Navajos would say that there is probably *nothing* that can be called nonreligious. To them, almost anything anyone is likely to do has some sort of religious significance, and many other tribes concur. Procedurally, then, our problem is how to learn to talk about religion, even in preliminary ways, knowing perfectly well that in one society what is considered art may in another be considered religion, or that what is considered as health in one culture may be religion in another. Before we can proceed, in other words, we need to reexamine our categories, our "pigeonholes," in order to "see" things through someone else's set of patterns. This is the reason for the odd title: "Seeing with a Native Eye."

Through our study of linguistics and anthropology we have learned that different groups of people not only think in different ways, but that they often "see" things in different ways. Good scientific experiments can be provided, for example, to prove that if certain ideas are offered to people in patterns which they have not been taught to recognize, not only will they not understand them, they often will not even see them. We see things in "programmed" ways. . . .

If we talk about native American religions using the categories of Western religions, we are simply going to see what *we* already know is there. We will recognize certain kinds of experiences as religious, and we will cancel out others. To us, for example, dance may be an art form, or it may be a certain kind of kinesis. With certain native American tribes, dance may be the most religious act a person can perform. . . .

We might consider the Pueblo view that in the springtime Mother Earth is pregnant, and one does not mistreat her any more than one might mistreat a pregnant woman. When our technologists go and try to get Pueblo farmers to use steel plows in the spring, they are usually rebuffed. For us it is a technical idea—"Why don't you just use plows? You plow, and you get 'x' results from doing so." For the Pueblos this is meddling with a formal religious idea. Using a plow, to borrow the Navajo phrase, "doesn't hold any sheep." In other words, it does not make sense in the way in which the world operates. It is against the way things really go. Some Pueblo folks still take the heels off their shoes, and sometimes the shoes off their horses, during the spring. I once asked a Hopi whom I met in that country, "Do you mean to say, then, that if I kick the ground with my foot, it will botch everything up, so nothing will grow?" He said, "Well, I don't know whether that would happen or not, but it would just really show what kind of person you are."

One learns slowly that in many of these native religions, religion is viewed as embodying the reciprocal relationships between people and the sacred *processes* going on in the world. It may not involve a "god." It may not be signified by praying or asking for favors, or doing what may "look" religious to people in our culture.

SOURCE: Barre Toelken, "Seeing with a Native Eye: How Many Sheep Will it Hold?" in *Seeing with a Native Eye*, ed. Walter H. Capps. New York: Harper and Row, 1976, pp. 11–14

GLOSSARY

Ancestors Indigenous ancestors, who created the world and founded clans, need to be fed and honored. They continue to give guidance through divination and are reborn in new bodies.

Indigenous Native to or occurring naturally in a region.

Medicine Since indigenous cultures participate fully in the environment, healing partakes of several factors: physiological, astronomical, behavioral, and spiritual. Good medicine may include herbal mixtures, songs to ancestors or divinities, art, good social co-operation, family counseling, or sacrificial offerings.

Oral tradition Oral storytelling and singing are the vehicles for teaching and passing on sacred knowledge among indigenous peoples with no books.

Participation Indigenous people cultivate a deep sense of integration with a dependence upon the powers of the environment, and this is central to indigenous sacred ways. Any star, plant, or animal could be a cosmic or natural power, or a deceased ancestor who must be honored.

Shaman An indigenous people's medicine healer and leader of sacred ways; an inspired, ecstatic and charismatic man or woman with the power to control spirits, often by incarnating them or making out-of-body journeys.

Vision quest Visions, whether during sleep or awake, are revelations of ultimate reality for indigenous people. Some come unsought, as Black Elk's, others are sought in a vision quest.

Wakan tanka For the Lakota Sioux, the ultimate power of the universe present in all the world, "the center of everything."

TYPICAL INDIGENOUS HOLY DAYS

Corroboree An Australian Aborigine dance festival held at special ceremonial grounds to celebrate events such as the gathering of clans, a battle victory, marriages, and initiations.

Divination An indigenous ritual for uncovering the spiritual cause of a problem and how to solve it, by indicators such as dreams, ordeals, reading bones, or animal behavior.

Kwanzaa An African-American and Pan-African holiday for family, community, and culture. Celebrated from 26 December through 1 January, its origins are in the first harvest celebrations of Africa. The name Kwanzaa is derived from the phrase "*matunda ya kwanza*" which means "first fruits" in Swahili, the most widely spoken African language. Kwanzaa was created by an African-American to introduce and reinforce the Nguzo Saba (the Seven Principles): *Umoja* (unity), *Kujichagulia* (self-determination), *Ujima* (collective work and responsibility), *Ujamaa* (cooperative economics), *Nia* (purpose), *Kuumba* (creativity), and *Imani* (faith). Kwanzaa is a cultural holiday, not a religious one, thus available to and practiced by Africans of all religious faiths.

Sacred Pipe A ceremonial, long, wood-stemmed pipe with a bowl made of pipestone, common in North American Plains tribes. As the pipe is filled with sacred tobacco, all the world, including the ceremony's participants, identify with it as their own center and the center of the universe. Its smoke is an offering to the powers of the universe.

Sun Dance A Lakota Sioux summer full-moon ceremony where men pierce their chest or back skin and dance around a central sacred tree or drag buffalo skulls until the skin rips, as an offering to the great sacred power, Wakan Tanka.

Sweat Lodge A purification ceremony in a domed lodge of skins; a group of participants sit inside, while a central hole is filled with hot rocks and water is poured over them, making steam; prayers are offered to the powers of the universe present in the earth, stone, water, and all beings.

HISTORICAL OUTLINE

c. 5 million BCE—evolution of human ancestors in Africa

c. 200,000 BCE—*Homo Sapiens* appears in Africa

c. 22,000 BCE—possible date for migration of Native Americans across the Bering Strait from Asia

c. 1st century CE—hunting-gathering Bantu people start migration to central and southern Africa

5th century CE—empire of Ghana in Africa established; lasts until Islamic civilization arrives in 12th century

1100–1400 CE—empire of Mali in West Aftica

1300–1600 CE—empire of Songhay in West Africa

REVIEW QUESTIONS

1   What do you think was meant by the Dagara song: "My little family I leave today / My great Family I meet tomorrow"?
2   What role in African society do the women's prayers indicate?
3   How does African drumming compare with Western drumming and with religious organ music?
4   Who were the six grandfathers and what powers did they give Black Elk?
5   How does the Hau De No Sau Nee view of nature differ from that of industrial society?
6   What is Tlakaelel's view of life, death, and ancestor spirits?
7   Why do some traditional Pueblo people walk more carefully in spring?

INFORMATION RESOURCES

AFRICAN SACRED WAYS

De Heusch, Luc, "Southern African Religions," in *The Encyclopedia of Religion*, ed. Mircea Eliade, vol. 13, pp. 530–46. New York: Macmillan, 1987.

Isizoh, Chidi Denis, ed. "African Traditional Religions."
<http://users.iol.it/cdi>

Karenga, Maulana, ed. "Kwanzaa." 1 January 1999.
<http://www.OfficialKwanzaaWebsite.org>

Lawson, E. Thomas, *Religions of Africa: Traditions in Transformation*, Prospect Hts, IL: Waveland Press, 1985.

Mbiti, John S. *African Religions and Philosophy*, New York: Praeger, 1969.

Mbiti, John S. "Flowers in the Garden: The Role of Women in African Religion," in *African Traditional Religions in Contemporary Society*, ed. Jacob Olupona. New York: Paragon House, 1991.

Middleton, John, ed. *Encyclopedia of Africa South of the Sahara*, 4 vols. New York: Scribner's, 1987.

Murray, Larry, et al., eds. *Encyclopedia of African American Religions*. New York: Garland, 1993.

Niangoran-Bouah, Georges, "The Talking Drum: A Traditional African Instrument of Liturgy and of Mediation with the Sacred," in *African Traditional Religions in Contemporary Society*, ed. Jacob Olupona. New York: Paragon House, 1991.

Ray, Ben C. et al., eds. "African Religions," in *The Encyclopedia of Religion*, ed. Mircea Eliade, vol. 1, pp. 61–96. New York: Macmillan, 1987.

Zahan, Dominique, *The Religion, Spirituality and Thought of Traditional Africa*. Chicago: University of Chicago Press, 1979.

Zuesse, Evan M. *Ritual Cosmos: The Sanctification of Life in African Religions*. Athens, OH: Ohio University Press, 1979.

NATIVE AMERICAN SACRED WAYS

<http://www.nativeweb.org>
<http://www.indians.org>

Beck, Peggy, et al., eds. *The Sacred: Ways of Knowledge, Sources of Life*. Tsaile, AZ: Navajo Community College Press, 1992.

Black Elk, as told through John G Neihardt. *Black Elk Speaks*. Lincoln: University of Nebraska Press, 1932.

Black Elk, as told through Joseph Epes Brown. *The Sacred Pipe: Black Elk's Account of the Seven Rites of the Oglala Sioux*. Norman and London: University of Oklahoma Press, 1953.

Campbell, Joseph, *Historical Atlas of World Mythology*. San Francisco: Harper and Row, 1983.

Chapman, Abraham, *Literature of the American Indians*. New York: Signet New American Library, 1975.

DeMallie, Raymond, ed. *The Sixth Grandfather: Black Elk's Teachings Given to John G. Neihardt*. Lincoln: University of Nebraska Press, 1984.

Drury, Nevill, *Shamanism*. Shaftesbury, Dorset, UK: Element Books, 1996.

Eliade, Mircea, *Shamanism: Archaic Techniques of Ecstasy*. Princeton, NJ: Princeton University Press, 1951, 1964.

Fogelson, Raymond, et al., eds. "North American Religions," in *The Encyclopedia of Religion*, ed. Mircea Eliade, vol. 10, pp 469–550. New York: Macmillan, 1987.

Gill, Sam D. *Native American Religions*. Belmont, CA: Wadsworth Inc., 1982.

Halifax, Joan, *Shamanic Voices: A Survey of Visionary Narratives*. New York: Viking Penguin Arkana, 1979.

Hirschfelder, Arlene, and Paulette

Molin, *Encyclopedia of Native American Religions.* New York: Facts on File, 1992.

Hoxie, Frederick, *Encyclopedia of North American Indians.* Boston: Houghton Mifflin, 1996.

Iroquois Nation (Hau De No Sau Nee), "Basic Call to Consciousness," *Akwesasne Notes.* Via Rooseveltown, NY: Mohawk Nation, 1978.

Kehoe, Alice, *North American Indians: A Comprehensive Account*, Englewood Cliffs, NJ: Prentice Hall, 1981

Mails, Thomas E. *The Mystic Warriors of the Plains.* Garden City, NY: Doubleday, 1972.

Malinowski, Sharon, *et al.*, eds. *Encyclopedia of Native American Tribes.* Detroit: Gale Research, 1988.

Native Peoples Magazine, Media Concepts Group, 5333 N. Seventh St., Suite C-224, Phoenix, AZ 85014–2804.

Native Americans, *Akwe:kon's Journal of Indigenous Issues*, Akwe:kon Press, 300 Caldwell Hall, Cornell University, Ithaca, NY 14853.

Sacred Ways, 3-volume videotape set, 1993. Insight Media, 2162 Broadway, New York 10024–0621.

Sturtenant, William, ed. *Handbook of North American Indians*, 20 vols. Washington, DC: Smithsonian Institute, 1988.

Thorpe, Dagmar, *People of the Seventh Fire: Returning Lifeways of Native America.* Ithaca, NY: Akwe:kon Press, Cornell University American Indian Program, 1996.

Tlakaelel, *Nahui Mitl: The Journey of the Four Arrows.* Chaplin, CT: Mexicayotl Productions, 1998.

Toelken, Barre, "Seeing with a Native Eye: How Many Sheep Will it Hold?" in *Seeing with a Native Eye*, ed. Walter H. Capps. New York: Harper and Row, 1976.

Trimble, Stephen, ed. *Our Voices, Our Land.* Flagstaff, AZ: The Heard Museum, Northland Press, 1986.

Weatherford, Jack, *Native Roots: How the Indians Enriched America.* New York: Fawcett Columbine, 1991.

CHAPTER 3

HINDUISM

The label "Hinduism" has been applied to a great variety of practices, beliefs, and scriptures which seem to have originated in the Indian subcontinent at least five thousand years ago and which are continuing to evolve today. This term is disputed by contemporary scholars, however, who question the idea that "Hindu" refers to any particular institutionalized religion. They prefer the term "**Sanatana Dharma**," meaning the ageless way of moral order, duty, and natural law in the cosmos. At the same time, the term "Hindu-ness" is being waved as a banner by those using "Hindu" identity as a political rallying point.

Sanatana Dharma encompasses ancient mystical texts referring to the formless and transcendent Self, abstract philosophical treatises which disagree with each other about the truth of existence, and a wealth of ascetic meditation practices for realization of the eternal. It also includes a large pantheon of deities, many of whom may be individually worshiped as the totality of divinity and yet may coexist with other deities even in the same temples. Devotees are free to choose their own favorite manifestations of the Divine. Today, as from ancient times, deities are worshiped with offerings of grains and clarified butter placed in sacred fires, with the waving of oil lamps, with fragrances and flowers, and with song and chants. In addition, villagers worship their local goddesses and gods, many of whom are unknown elsewhere.

Despite its great diversity, Sanatana Dharma has certain underlying themes. One is a belief in **reincarnation**: the idea that we are born again and again. Our lives are molded by our **karma**: the positive or negative effects of our previous thoughts and actions. Human life should reflect the order of the cosmos, and thus one has social obligations and a certain social standing defined by one's hereditary **caste**. Through good actions, lofty thoughts, detachment from the illusory and ephemeral material world, and profound meditation on the Absolute or self-surrendering love for any one of its divine manifestations, one may gradually achieve enlightenment, merge with Ultimate Reality, and escape from the karmic wheel of rebirths.

"Hinduism" has spread far beyond India, initially carried by emigrants and more recently by growing Western interest in its ancient wisdom and spiritual practices. It is currently undergoing a vibrant renaissance, with many new temples being built around the world and staffed by a growing number of **brahman pandits** (those of the hereditary priestly caste who are learned in the ancient ways and scriptures). Issues which are being disputed today include the politicizing of "Hindu-ness," the status of women, and the traditional system of castes which is still deeply entrenched in India.

Sruti texts

According to orthodox Hindu scholarship, the ancient sciptures of Sanatana Dharma are divided into two categories. One is the **sruti** texts which were "heard" by ancient **rishis** (enlightened sages) in profound and ascetic meditation, after they had so thoroughly cleansed their minds that they were transparent to eternal truth. The other category is the subsequent **smrti** texts, which explain the hidden meanings of the sruti texts for wider audiences in later, less enlightened ages.

The foundational sruti texts for most forms of Sanatana Dharma are the **Vedas.** Scholars think that they were written down by about 1500 BCE, but represent a much older orally transmitted tradition. According to Hindu belief, the Vedas were heard by the rishis and then written down in 3102 BCE at the beginning of **Kali Yuga**, the current dark age, by the sage Vyasa. The language is terse poetic **Sanskrit**, whose sounds are said to evoke the realities to which they refer but whose deep meanings are not easily translated or fully understood.

Hymn to Agni, God of Fire
from the Rig Vedas

The oldest of the Vedas are the Rig Vedas. They consist largely of invocations of different gods or goddesses, such as Usha, goddess of dawn, or Agni, the god of fire, which have been used since ancient times to carry offerings to the Unseen. These deities have also been understood metaphysically as abstract forces within the oneness of Creation. The extract below, a hymn to Agni, comes from Book 4 of the Rig Vedas.

Your envoy who possesses all, Immortal, bearer of your gifts,
Best worshipper, I woo with song.
He, Mighty, knows the gift of wealth, he knows the deep recess of heaven:
He shall bring hitherward the Gods.
He knows, a God himself, to guide Gods to the righteous in his home:
He gives e'en treasures that we love.
He is the Herald: well-informed, he doth his errand to and fro,
Knowing the deep recess of heaven.
May we be they who gratify Agni with sacrificial gifts,
Who cherish and enkindle him.
Illustrious for wealth are they, and hero deeds, victorious,
Who have served Agni reverently.
So unto us, day after day, may riches craved by many come,
And power and might spring up for us.
That holy Singer in his strength shoots forth his arrows swifter than
The swift shafts of the tribes of men.

Hymn on Creation
from the Rig Vedas

This hymn is from Book 10 of the Rig Vedas. It illustrates the philosophical sophisti-
cation of the realization of ancient rishis. They sat in profound meditation to explore
the mysteries of primordial time before anything existed in the material universe. It is
interesting to compare this passage with the theories of modern science about the ori-
gins of the cosmos.

Then was not non-existent nor existent: there was no realm of air, no sky
    beyond it.
What covered in, and where? and what gave shelter? Was water there,
    unfathomed depth of water?
Death was not then, nor was there aught immortal: no sign was there, the
    day's and night's divider.
That One Thing,[1] breathless, breathed by its own nature: apart from it was
    nothing whatsoever.
Darkness there was: at first concealed in darkness this All was
    indiscriminated chaos.
All that existed then was void and formless: by the great power of Warmth
    was born that Unit.
Thereafter rose Desire in the beginning, Desire, the primal seed and germ of
    Spirit.
Sages who searched with their heart's thought discovered the existent's
    kinship in the non-existent.
Transversely was their severing line[2] extended: what was above it then, and
    what below it?
There were begetters, there were mighty forces, free action here and energy
    up yonder.
Who verily knows and who can here declare it, whence it was born and
    whence comes this creation?
The Gods are later than this world's production. Who knows then whence it
    first came into being?
He, the first origin of this creation, whether he formed it all or did not form
    it,
Whose eye controls this world in highest heaven, he verily knows it, or
    perhaps he knows not.

SOURCE: *The Hymns of the Rgveda*, trans. Ralph T. H. Griffith. Delhi: Motilal
Banarsidass, 1973, pp. 206, 633–4

---

[1] That One Thing—the single primordial substance out of which the universe was made.
[2] Severing line—a line drawn by the rishis to divide the upper world from the lower, to bring
duality out of unity.

You are That
from the *Upanishads*

Probably the latest of the Vedas are the **Upanishads**. *Scholars think that they were recorded perhaps 1000 to 500 BCE. They are profound and haunting reflections on ulti-mate truth as realized by the rishis and transmitted to their students. The extract below is from Book 6 of the Chhandogya Upanishad. Shwetaketu is the student, Uddālaka is his father, a sage. He describes the metaphysical process by which indi-viduals emanate from, and are thus connected to, one formless Being, the* **Brahman**. *This undifferentiated, nonmanifest Being, the essential underlying Reality, subtly manifests as the energy of light or life-force, which thence gives rise to water, which gives rise to food, which sustains the body.*

When a man is dying, his speech merges into mind, his mind into life, his life into light, his light into the one Being.

"That Being is the seed; all else but His expression. He is truth, He is Self, Shwetaketu! You are That."

"Explain once more, Lord!" said Shwetaketu.

"I will explain!" said Uddālaka.

"My son! Bees create honey by gathering the sweet juices from different flowers, and mixing all into a common juice.

"And there is nothing in honey whereby the juice of a particular flower can be identified, so it is with the various creatures who merge in that Being, in deep sleep or in death.

"Whatever they may be, tiger, lion, wolf, bear, worm, moth, gnat, mosquito, they become aware of particular life when they are born into it or awake.

"That Being is the seed; all else but His expression. He is truth, He is Self. Shwetaketu! You are That."

"Explain once more, Lord!" said Shwetaketu.

"I will explain!" said Uddālaka.

"My son! Rivers, flowing east and west, rise from the sea, return to the sea, become the sea itself, forget their identities.

"These creatures do not know that they have risen from that Being, or returned to that Being.

"Whatever they may be, tiger, lion, wolf, boar, worm, moth, gnat, mosquito, they become aware of particular life when they are born into it or awake.

"That Being is the seed; all else but His expression. He is truth, He is Self. Shwetaketu! You are That."

SOURCE: *The Ten Principal Upanishads*, trans. Shree Purohit Swāmi and W. B. Yeats. Calcutta: Rupa, 1992, pp. 90–92

What Is the World but Spirit?
from the *Upanishads*

This extract is from Book 2 of the Mundaka Upanishad. It is a beautiful expression of mystical realization of Ultimate Reality lying hidden within everything that is. Ineffable, eternal, formless, but existing in all forms, its existence can only be grasped through meditation based in devotion and informed by the sacred wisdom of the sages. And only when one's limited personal identity (the self) loses itself like an arrow which strikes and sinks into the target (the all-pervading self) can this essential Spirit be realized.

Shining, yet hidden, Spirit lives in the cavern. Everything that sways, breathes, opens, closes, lives in Spirit; beyond learning, beyond everything, better than anything; living, unliving.

It is the undying blazing Spirit, that seed of all seeds, wherein lay hidden the world and all its creatures. It is life, speech, mind, reality, immortality. It is there to be struck. Strike it, my son!

Take the bow of our sacred knowledge, lay against it the arrow of devotion, pull the string of concentration, strike the target.

Ôm[3] is the bow, the personal self the arrow, impersonal Self the target. Aim accurately, sink therein.

Into His cloak are woven earth, mind, life, the canopy, the Kingdom of Heaven, He is alone and sole; man's bridge to immortality.

Come out of all the schools. Meditate upon Ôm as the Self. Remember He takes many shapes, lives in the hub where the arteries meet; and may His blessing bring you out of the darkness.

He knows all, knows every particular. His glory prevails on earth, in heaven, in His own seat, the holy city of the heart.

He becomes mind and guides body and life. He lives in man's heart and eats man's food. He that knows Him, in finding joy, finds immortality.

He that knows Him as the shaped and the shapeless, cuts through the knot of his heart, solves every doubt, exhausts every action.

In a beautiful golden scabbard hides the stainless, indivisible, luminous Spirit.

Neither sun, moon, star, neither fire nor lightning, lights Him. When He shines, everything begins to shine. Everything in the world reflects His light.

Spirit is everywhere, upon the right, upon the left, above, below, behind, in front. What is the world but Spirit?

SOURCE: *The Ten Principal Upanishads*, trans. Shree Purohit Swāmi and W. B. Yeats. Calcutta: Rupa, 1992, pp. 55–6.

---

[3] Ôm—the primordial sound vibration by which all has been created, recited as a mantra.

Smrti texts

According to classical Hindu thought, the sublime realizations recorded in the Upanishads cannot be understood by the masses. In the current long period of darkest ignorance and irreligion, *Kali Yuga*, more popular scriptures and forms of worship are needed. Thus great epic poems, lengthy descriptions of the gods and goddesses, and codes of moral conduct have been added to the scriptural treasury of Sanatana Dharma.

Devotion to the Lord
from the *Bhagavad Gita*

One of the two greatest Indian narratives is the Mahabharata, *a lengthy semi-historical depiction of events thought to have taken place approximately 1000 BCE, as two rival branches of a great family both laid claims to a kingdom near what is now Delhi. Its 100,000 verses depict all that is noble and ignoble in human nature. They include a major text of Hindu philosophy, the* Bhagavad Gita. *In it, Krishna, incarnation of one of the three main gods of the old Hindu pantheon, gives lofty spiritual instruction to Arjuna, one of the combatants, on the threshold of the great battle. He then goes on to discuss the nature of worship.*

One who works in devotion, who is a pure soul, and who controls his mind and senses is dear to everyone, and everyone is dear to him. Though always working, such a man is never entangled.

A person in the divine consciousness, although engaged in seeing, hearing, touching, smelling, eating, moving about, sleeping and breathing, always knows within himself that he actually does nothing at all. Because while speaking, evacuating, receiving, or opening or closing his eyes, he always knows that only the material senses are engaged with their objects and that he is aloof from them.

One who performs his duty without attachment, surrendering the results unto the Supreme Lord, is unaffected by sinful action, as the lotus leaf is untouched by water.

The yogīs,[4] abandoning attachment, act with body, mind, intelligence and even with the senses, only for the purpose of purification.

The steadily devoted soul attains unadulterated peace because he offers the result of all activities to Me; whereas a person who is not in union with the Divine, who is greedy for the fruits of his labor, becomes entangled. . . .

The Supreme Personality of Godhead said: Those who fix their minds on My personal form and are always engaged in worshiping Me with great and transcendental faith are considered by Me to be most perfect.

But those who fully worship the unmanifested, that which lies beyond

---

[4] Yogīs—those who have mastered yoga, the technique for spiritual realization.

the perception of the senses, the all-pervading, inconceivable, unchanging, fixed and immovable—the impersonal conception of the Absolute Truth—by controlling the various senses and being equally disposed to everyone, such persons, engaged in the welfare of all, at last achieve Me.

For those whose minds are attached to the unmanifested, impersonal feature of the Supreme, advancement is very troublesome. To make progress in that discipline is always difficult for those who are embodied.

But those who worship Me, giving up all their activities unto Me and being devoted to Me without deviation, engaged in devotional service and always meditating upon Me, having fixed their minds upon Me, O son of Prthā—for them I am the swift deliverer from the ocean of birth and death.

Just fix your mind upon Me, the Supreme Personality of Godhead, and engage all your intelligence in Me. Thus you will live in Me always, without a doubt.

SOURCE: *Bhagavad-Gītā As It Is*, trans. A. C. Bhaktivedanta Swami Prabhupāda. Los Angeles: Bhaktivedanta Book Trust, 1989, pp. 613–634

Rama, Sita, and Lakshman Enter the Forest
from the *Ramayana*

The greatest examples of noble human conduct which continue to inspire Hindus today are Lord Rama and his wife Sita. They are central characters in a long epic poem, the Ramayana, *which was compiled in its present form approximately 400 BCE to 200 CE. In brief, Rama, noble son of King Dasaratha by one of his three wives, Kausalya, was about to be crowned king. But instead, Rama was banished to the forest for fourteen years by the king, due to the machinations of his stepmother Kaikeyi's evil friend. Rama's wife Sita and his stepbrother Lakshman, son of Kaikeyi, nobly insisted on accompanying him. During their sojourn in the forest, Sita was kidnapped by the king of the demons. A terrific battle ensued in which Rama was at last victorious, and he and Sita returned to the capital of Ayodhya. In some parts of India, Lord Rama is worshiped as the Lord Incarnate. The following excerpt (from chapter 19 of the* Ramayana), *in which Prince Rama first enters the forest to live as an ascetic, illustrates his exceptionally noble qualities.*

The chariot reached the bank of the Ganga. They proceeded along the bank, admiring the beauty of the river. Finding a spot of surpassing charm, Raama said: "We shall spend the night here."

Untying the horses, they sat under a tree. Guha, the chief of the region, having learnt already from his men that Raama would be coming there, came forward with his retinue to greet Raama and Lakshmana.

He had unbounded love for the Royal family and for Raama. Being the chieftain of the tribes who dwelt on the banks of Ganga, he was a man of great prestige and power. Raama and Lakshmana rose to greet Guha, even while the latter was still at some distance from them. Guha welcomed them with a hearty embrace, saying: "Regard this land as your own. This place is as much yours as is Ayodhya. Who can hope to have a guest like you? It is indeed my good fortune."

Guha had prepared a lavish entertainment. He said "Feel perfectly at home and happy in my kingdom. You may spend all the fourteen years with us here. You will not lack anything, I assure you. Looking after you will be a pleasure and privilege to me. Be gracious enough to accept my hospitality."

Warmly embracing Guha again, Raama said: "Brother, I know how deep is your love for me. Your wish is itself as good as hospitality rendered. I am bound by my vows and must refuse anything more. I have come to dwell in the forest and not to enjoy life as a chieftain's guest. These horses are my dear father's favourites. Pray feed them well. We shall be content with simple food and rest for the night."

They lay under the tree for the night. . . .

Early next morning, Raama told Lakshmana: "We must now cross the river. Ask Guha to make ready a boat big enough for crossing this broad river." Guha ordered his men to get this done and informed Raama.

Sumantra bowed low and stood before Raama seeking his further commands.

Raama understood Sumantra's unuttered grief and, laying his hand on Sumantra's shoulders, said: "Sumantra, return to Ayodhya with all speed and be at the side of the King. Your duty is now to look after him."

"O Raama," exclaimed Sumantra, "rectitude, learning and culture seem to be of no value. You and your brother and Vaidehi are going to live in the forest. What is going to be our lot? How are we going to fare under Kaikeyi's rule?" He now wept like a child.

Wiping the tears from Sumantra's eyes, Raama said: "Our family has known no nobler friend than you. It will be your task to console my father. His heart is riven by grief. Whatever his commands, carry them out dutifully. Do not ask yourself whether he wants a thing for himself or with a view to pleasing Kaikeyi. Avoid giving him any pain of mind. Have no anxiety about us.

"You should say this on my behalf to my aged father who is stricken with a grief he never knew before. Clasp his feet as you have seen me do, and assure him from me that none of us—not I nor Lakshmana, nor Seeta—feel injured or sorry at having been sent away from Ayodhya. We look forward to fourteen years of forest life which will speed on happy wings, and then surely we shall return to his feet for blessings. Give our love to my mother Kausalya, and tell her that protected by her blessings we are well and give a like message to my stepmothers, specially to Kaikeyi, lest she should think we have parted in anger. Tell the Mahaaraaja that it is my earnest prayer that he should hasten with the installation of Bharata, so that he may be a comfort to him in our absence."

But Sumantra, unable to restrain his grief, burst out: "How am I to return and with what words can I give comfort?" And when he looked at the empty chariot, he wept and said: "How shall I drive this chariot that stands desolate without you?"

Once again Raama spoke words of comfort and courage to Sumantra and urged on him the duty of patience, and sent him home.

"Guha," said Raama, "I could indeed spend fourteen years in your kingdom as you desire. But would that be fulfilling my vow? I have left Ayodhya to fulfil my father's pledge. I must therefore lead the life of a *tapasvi*.[5] I must not touch dishes daintily cooked and served. We have to live only on fruits, roots and permissible kinds of meat such as we offer in the sacrificial fire."

Comforting Guha thus, the brothers got their locks matted with the milk of the banyan. They helped Seeta into the boat and then got into it themselves. Guha bade the boatmen to row it across.

The boatmen took them quickly across the river. At midstream Seeta offered a prayer to the goddess of the river: "Devi, help us fulfil our vow and return safe to our homeland."

They talked as they went on. They reached the farther bank of Ganga. And there, for the first time, the three stood alone, unattended by friends!

"Lakshmana, you are my sole armed guard now," said Raama. "You will go first. Seeta will follow. And I shall walk behind you both. We must save Seeta as far as possible from the hardships of forest life. Hereafter there will be none to keep us company and no fun or amusement."

Raama's thoughts went to his mother Kausalya.

"Lakshmana," he said, "should you not go back to Ayodhya and look after mother Kausalya and Sumitra Devi? I shall manage my forest stay somehow."

Lakshmana replied: "Forgive me, brother; I am not going back to Ayodhya." Raama indeed expected no other answer.

SOURCE: *Ramayana*, trans. C. Rajagopalachari. Bombay: Bharatiya Vidya Bhavan, 27th edn, 1990, pp. 86–9

Duties of the Four Castes
from the *Manu smriti*

Hindu legal and social mores are codified in The Laws of Manu, *or* Manu smriti, *compiled into twelve books by 100 to 300 CE. These codes are regarded by some as propaganda by the priestly brahman caste, for they give divine authority for the division of humanity into four castes: the priestly brahmans, the warrior kshatriyas, the merchant vaishyas, and the servant class, shudras. The extract below, from* Manu smriti *chapter 1, describes how the castes were assigned different duties.*

---

[5] Tapasvi—renunciate.

For the sake of the preservation of this entire creation, [Purusha],[6] the exceedingly resplendent one, assigned separate duties to the classes which had sprung from his mouth, arms, thighs, and feet.

Teaching, studying, performing sacrificial rites, so too making others perform sacrificial rites, and giving away and receiving gifts—these he assigned to the brāhmans.

Protection of the people, giving away of wealth, performance of sacrificial rites, study, and nonattachment to sensual pleasures—these are, in short, the duties of a kshatriya.

Tending of cattle, giving away of wealth, performance of sacrificial rites, study, trade and commerce, usury, and agriculture—these are the occupations of a vaishya.

The Lord has prescribed only one occupation for a shūdra, namely, service without malice of even these other three classes.

Man is stated to be purer above the navel than below it; hence his mouth has been declared to be the purest part by the Self-existent One.

On account of his origin from the best limb of the Cosmic Person, on account of his seniority, and on account of the preservation by him of the Veda—the brāhman is in respect of **dharma** the lord of this entire creation. . . .

Of created beings, those which are animate are the best; of the animate, those who subsist by means of their intellect; of the intelligent, men are the best; and of men, the brāhmans are traditionally declared to be the best . . .

The very birth of a brāhman is the eternal incarnation of dharma. For he is born for the sake of dharma and tends toward becoming one with the Brahman. . . .

SOURCE: W. Theodore de Bary, ed., *Sources of Indian Tradition*, vol. 1. New York and London: Columbia University Press, 1958, pp. 220–21

The Faithful Wife
from the *Manu smriti*

Manu smriti *also justifies the subjugation of women to men. In this extract, from* Manu smriti *chapter 5, the virtues of the faithful wife are described.*

The husband who wedded her with sacred texts, always gives happiness to his wife, both in season and out of season, in this world and in the next.

Though destitute of virtue, or seeking pleasure (elsewhere), or devoid of good qualities, (yet) a husband must be constantly worshipped as a god by a faithful wife.

---

[6] Purusha—the Self, Brahman, the all-pervading Supreme Being.

No sacrifice, no vow, no fast must be performed by women apart (from their husbands); if a wife obeys her husband, she will for that (reason alone) be exalted in heaven.

A faithful wife, who desires to dwell (after death) with her husband, must never do anything that might displease him who took her hand, whether he be alive or dead.

At her pleasure let her emaciate her body by (living on) pure flowers, roots, and fruit; but she must never even mention the name of another man after her husband has died.

Until death let her be patient (of hardships), self-controlled, and chaste, and strive (to fulfil) that most excellent duty which (is prescribed) for wives who have one husband only.

SOURCE: Serinity Young, ed., *An Anthology of Sacred Texts by and about Women*. New York: Crossroad, 1995, p. 278

Desire to Know the Brahman
by Sankara

The Vedas also gave rise to a number of different schools of Hindu philosopy, which sought to explain the texts according to human logic. One of the major schools was that of Sankhya, classically attributed to the sage Kapila, who made clear distinctions between spirit and matter. An opposing school is that of Advaita Vedanta, whose greatest teacher was the highly influential Sankara (approximately 788–820 CE or earlier). In his nondualistic philosophy, the absolute ground of being is Brahman, the eternal and unchanging which lies within the world of changing appearances. According to Advaita Vedanta, realization of this eternal undifferentiated Self within oneself is the greatest goal of human life and the means to liberation from illusion. This perspective became predominant in Hindu philosophy.

Superimposition is the seeing of a thing in something which is not that; thus, when son, wife, etc., are all right or not, one considers one's own self as all right or not, one superimposes external attributes on the self even so does one superimpose on the self the attributes of the *body* when one considers that "I am corpulent, I am lean, I am fair, I stand, I go, I jump"; similarly attributes of the *senses* when one says, "I am dumb, one-eyed, impotent, deaf, blind"; and in the same manner the properties of the *internal organs*, e.g., desire, volition, cogitation, and resolution. Even so, man superimposes the self[7] presented in the cognition of "I" on the inner Self which is the witness of all the activities of the internal organ; and that inner Self, the very opposite and the witness of all, on the inner organ.

Thus without beginning or end, existing in the very nature of things, this superimposition which is of the form of a knowledge that is subject to

---

[7] Self—the individual soul, which is ultimately one with the universal Self, or Brahman.

sublation and is responsible for the agency and experience of man, is something which the whole world knows. It is for casting away this superimposition which is the cause of evil and for gaining the knowledge of the oneness of the Self that all the Upanishads are begun. . . .

The Brahman's existence is well known, because it is the Self of all; everyone realizes the existence of the Self, for none says, "I am not"; if the existence of the self is not well known, the whole world of beings would have the notion "*I* do not exist." And the self is the Brahman.

It may be contended that if the Brahman is well known in the world as the Self, it has already been known, and again it becomes something which need not be inquired into. It is not like that, for there are differences of opinion about its particular nature. Ordinary people and the materialists are of the view that the self is just the body qualified by intelligence; others think that it is the intelligent sense-organs themselves that are the self; still others, that it is the mind; some hold it as just the fleeting consciousness of the moment; some others as the void; certain others say that there is some entity, which is different from the body, etc., and which transmigrates,[8] does and enjoys; some consider him as the enjoyer and not as the doer; some that there is, as different from the above entity, the Lord who is omniscient and omnipotent. According to still others, it is the inner Self of the enjoyer. Thus, resorting to reasonings and texts and semblances thereof, there are many who hold divergent views. Hence one who accepts some view without examining it might be prevented from attaining the ultimate good, and might also come to grief. Therefore, by way of setting forth the inquiry into the Brahman, here is begun the discussion of the meaning of the texts of the Upanishads, aided by such ratiocination[9] as is in conformity to Scripture and having for its fruit the Supreme Beatitude. . . .

It is by the examination of the meaning of the scriptural texts and determining it exactly that Brahman-realization is achieved, not by inference and other sources of knowledge.

SOURCE: W. Theodore de Bary, ed., *Sources of Indian Tradition*, vol. 1. New York and London: Columbia University Press, 1958, pp. 313–17

Yoga Sutras
by Patanjali

A third major philosophical system based on the Upanishads is the school of **Yoga**, *traditionally thought to have been given organized form by the sage Patanjali by 200 BCE. The Yogic system combines ancient meditation practices with a philosophy which is similar to that of Sankhya, but asserts the existence of a supreme God. These excerpts*

---

[8] Transmigrates—the soul passes into a different body.
[9] Ratiocination—logical reasoning.

are from Patanjali's Yoga Sutras, *196 sutras or sayings methodically delineating a system for attaining the highest state of consciousness.*

Now Yoga is explained.
Yoga is restraining the activities of the mind.
At that time, the perceiver rests in his own true nature.
When the mind is not concentrated, the perceiver identifies with its modifications.
There are five types of thought waves, some of which are painful and some of which are not.
The five kinds of thought waves are correct knowledge, erroneous understanding, verbal delusion, sleep and memory. . . .
Their control is brought about by practice and non-attachment.
Abhyasa is the continuous effort towards firmly establishing the restraint of thought waves.
Practice becomes firmly grounded on being continued over a long period of time without interruption and with sincere devotion.
Vairagya, or non-attachment, is that state of consciousness in which the cravings for objects both seen and unseen is controlled through mastery of the Will.
The highest state of non-attachment stems from awareness of Purusha; it renounces even the three qualities of nature.
Samprajnata samadhi (*samadhi*[10] with consciousness) is accompanied by reasoning, discrimination, bliss, and an awareness of individuality. . . .
Asamprajnata samadhi (seedless state) is reached when all mental activity ceases and only unmanifested impressions remain in the mind.
Liberation comes quickly when the desire for it is intense. . . .
[Success is swift for those who are] devoted to *Ishwara.*[11]

Ishwara is that particular center of Divine Consciousness that is untouched by misery, Karma, or desires.
In Him lies the seed of omniscience.
Unlimited by time, He is the Teacher of all other teachers, from the most ancient of times.
He manifests in the word OM.
Constant repetition of OM and meditation on its meaning
Lead to enlightening introspection and elimination of all obstacles.
The obstacles to Realization are disease, mental torpor, doubt, indifference, laziness, craving for pleasure, delusion, inability to practice and maintain concentration, and restlessness of mind due to distractions.

10. Samadhi—the superconscious state of spiritual absorption.
11 Ishwara—God with manifest attributes, such as omniscience, mercy, kindness, and love, as opposed to Purusha or Brahman—God as pure, abstract essence.

Mental pain, depression, physical nervousness, and irregular breathing are the symptoms of a distracted state of mind.

In order to remove these obstacles one should meditate on one aspect of Truth.

The mind becomes clear through the cultivation of friendliness, kindness, contentment, and indifference towards happiness, vice and virtue.

[Regulated] expulsion and retention of the breath [also clear the mind].

Steadiness of the mind is easily established when the higher senses come into operation,

Or the state of luminescence which is beyond sorrow,

Or by fixing the mind on one who has transcended human passions and attachments,

Or knowledge gained in dreams or deep sleep,

Or by meditation on what is agreeable.

Mastery extends from the smallest atom to infinity.

For the person who has controlled the waves of the mind through meditation, there is a merging of the perceiver, perceived, and perception, just as a crystal assumes the color of the background.

SOURCE: *Meditation and Mantras*, ed. Swami Vishnu Devananda. New York: Om Lotus Publishing Co., 1975, pp. 133–54

In Praise of Durga
from the *Siva Purana*

Whereas philosophical texts were for the highly learned, a much more widespread form of smrti scriptures are the **Puranas**. *These are Sanskrit poetic texts which were probably set down in written form between 500 and 1500 CE, although they contain material which is much older. This popular devotional literature gives elaborate depictions of various gods and goddesses and their miraculous powers and exploits, as known to their devotees. Excerpted first here is a passage from the* Siva Purana, *in which the powers of the goddess Durga are briefly described. Seated on her lion, she defeated the demons who were threatening to overrun the world. She is also known as the consort and spiritual power of the god Siva.*

I began a continuous laudatory prayer of the Goddess Durgā, the beloved of Śiva, the creator of the universe, of the nature of Vidyā and Avidyā[12] and identical with the pure supreme Brahman.

I salute the Goddess who is omnipresent, eternal, for whom there is no support, who is never distressed, who is the mother of the three deities, who is the grossest of the gross and yet has no form.

O Goddess of the devas,[13] you are Perfect knowledge, Supreme Bliss,

[12] Vidyā and Avidyā—knowledge and ignorance.
[13] Devas—gods.

identical with the supreme Soul. Be pleased. Grant me the fulfilment of my task. Obeisance to you.

O celestial sage, on being thus lauded Candikā,[14] the mystic slumber, appeared before me.

Her complexion had the glossy hue of collyrium. She had comely features. She had four divine arms. She was seated on a lion. She showed the mystic gesture of granting boons by one of her hands, and pearls adorned her dishevelled hair.

Her face shone like the autumnal moon, the crescent moon bedecked her forehead, She had three eyes, looked beautiful and the nails of her lotus-like feet glistened.

O sage, seeing her who was Śiva's Energy herself, directly in front of me, my lofty shoulders bent down with devotion and I eulogized her after due obeisance.

Obeisance, obeisance, to Thee, who art in the form of Pravṛtti (Action) and Nivṛtti (Abstinence); who art in the form of creation and sustenance of the universe. Thou art the eternal Energy of the movable and the immovable beings capable of enchanting everyone.

Thou hast manifested thyself as Śrī, a garland round Keśava's form, who in the form of Earth holdest everything within, who art of yore the great Goddess causing creation and the destruction of the three worlds and art beyond the three Gunas.[15]

Thou art present in everything even in the essential atom and who art charmingly honoured by Yogins;[16] who art perceivable in the hearts of the Yogins purified by restraints, as well as in the path of their meditation.

Thou art the Vidyā of diverse sorts. Thou art endowed with illumination, purity and detachment. Thou assumest Kūṭastha (perpetually immovable), Avyakta (unmanifest) and Ananta (infinite) form and Thou art the eternal time holding all the worlds.

SOURCE: *The Siva Purāna*. Delhi: Motilal Banarsidass Publishers, 1970, pp. 320–21

The Way of Devotion
from the *Bhagavata Purana*

The Puranas also contain instructions for worship of the gods and goddesses, according to the growing **bhakti** *tradition of ecstatic devotion to one's favorite incarnation of the Divine. The feeling is that the Divine takes on human form for the sake of helping humanity, but remains pure in the midst of material life. Most popular of the Puranas is* Bhagavata Purana, *which describes the incarnations of the Lord in forms*

---

[14] Candikā—another name for Durga.
[15] Gunas—the three attributes of material nature (passionate activity; darkness and inertia; and pure intelligence).
[16] Yogins—practitioners of yoga.

such as Krishna, the cowherding boy. This excerpt from the Bhagavata Purana *describes ways of worship which are pleasing to the Lord incarnate.*

One should therefore resort to a teacher, desiring to know what constitutes the supreme welfare. . . . Taking the teacher as the deity, one should learn from him the practices characteristic of the Lord's devotees. . . . First detachment from all undesirable associations, then association with the good souls, compassion, friendliness, and due humility toward all beings, purity, penance, forbearance, silence, study of sacred writings, straightforwardness, continence, nonviolence, equanimity, seeing one's own Self and the Lord everywhere, seeking solitude, freedom from home, wearing clean recluse robes, satisfying oneself with whatever comes to one, faith in the scriptures of devotion and refraining from censure of those of other schools, subjugation of mind, speech, and action, truthfulness, quietude, restraint, listening to accounts of the Lord's advents, exploits, and qualities, singing of the Lord, contemplation of the Lord of wonderful exploits, engaging in acts only for His sake, dedicating unto the Lord everything—the rites one does, gifts, penance, sacred recital, righteous conduct and whatever is dear to one like one's wife, son, house, and one's own life—cultivating friendship with those who consider the Lord as their soul and master, service to the Lord and to the world and especially to the great and good souls, sharing in the company of fellow devotees the sanctifying glory of the Lord, sharing with them one's delight, satisfaction and virtues of restraint, remembering oneself and reminding fellow-worshipers of the Lord who sweeps away all sin; bearing a body thrilled with devotion and ecstatic experience of the Lord, now in tears with some thought of the Lord, now laughing, now rejoicing, now speaking out, now dancing, now singing, now imitating the Lord's acts, and now becoming quiet with the blissful experience of the Supreme—such are the Lord's devotees, who behave like persons not of this world.

SOURCE: W. Theodore de Bary, ed., *Sources of Indian Tradition*, vol. 1. New York and London: Columbia University Press, 1958, pp. 333–4

Songs of the saints

Despite the wealth of ancient Sanskrit scriptures, Jainism and later Buddhism—Indian religions which were not based on the Vedas—gained many adherents. But with the flowering of the bhakti tradition, saintly devotees of the Hindu deities began to sing of their ecstatic realization of the Divine, in their own languages. The tremendous attraction of their songs in the vernacular[17] and the strength of their love, which the common people

---

[17] Vernacular—the language of the people, as opposed to a classical language such as Sanskrit which was not reality understood by everyone.

could understand, brought an upsurge of devotional worship of the Hindu deities. These saints came from all classes and were both women and men, unlike those of the classical Sanskrit tradition, which was controlled by brahman men.

Ravi Das was a fourteenth- to fifteenth-century leatherworker, whose occupation meant that he was considered of extremely low caste. However, his poetry reveals the heights of his realization.

The World of Illusion
by Ravi Das

There is but One God. He is obtained by the True Guru's[18] grace.
When there was egoism in me, Thou wert not with me.
Now that Thou art there, there is no egoism.
As huge waves are raised by the wind in the great ocean, but are only water
    in water.
O Lord of wealth, what should I say about this delusion?
What we deem a thing to be, in reality it is not like that.

It is like a king falling asleep on his throne and becoming a beggar in dream;
His kingdom is intact, but separating from it, he suffers pain. Such indeed,
    has been my condition. . . .
Amidst all, the One Lord has assumed many forms
And He is enjoying within all hearts.
Says Ravi Das, the Lord is nearer to us than our hands and feet.
So let it happen as will naturally happen. . . .

Tell: Of what account are kingly mansion and throne without devotional
    service of the Lord?
Thou has not thought of the relish of the Lord King's Name, a relish in
    which all other relishes are forgotten.
We have become mad, we know not what we ought to know, and consider
    not what we ought to consider.
Like this our days are passing away. . . .

Lord of wealth, if Thou breakest not with me, then I will not break with
    Thee.
For if I break with Thee, with whom else shall I join?
If Thou art an earthen lamp, then I am Thy wick.
If Thou art a place of pilgrimage, then I am Thy pilgrim.
In true love I have joined with Thee, O Lord.

---

[18] True Guru—a perfectly enlightened spiritual teacher who can lead one to God-realisation.

Attaching myself to Thee, I have broken with all others.
Wherever I go, I perform Thy service.
There is no other lord like Thee, O God. . . .

The skeleton is of bones, flesh and veins; within it abides the poor soul bird.
O mortal, what is mine and what is thine?
As a bird perches on a tree, so does the soul in the body.
Thou layest foundations and buildest walls.
Three and a half cubit measure of place is for thee in the end.
Thou beautifully dressest thy hair and wearest slanting turban on thy head,
But this body shall be reduced to a heap of ashes.
Lofty are thy palaces and beauteous thy brides,
But without the Lord's Name, the game is lost.

My caste is low, my lineage is lowly, and mean is my birth.
I have entered Thy sanctuary O my Luminous Lord king, says the cobbler
   Ravi Das.

SOURCE: Rag Sorath, *Guru Granth Sahib*, pp. 657–9, adapted from English
translation of Manmohan Singh. Amritsar: Shiromani Gurdwara Parbandhak
Committee, 3rd edn, 1989, pp. 2157–62

Worship Him in Silence
by Lalla

*Lalla was a mystic of Kashmir, so devoted to Lord Shiva and detached from the world
that she forsook her brahmanic family, her marriage, and her clothing.*

I, Lallā, went out far in search of Shiva, the omnipresent Lord; after
wandering, I, Lallā found Him at last within my own self, abiding in His own
home.

   Temple and image, the two that you have fashioned, are not better than
stone; the Lord is immeasurable and consists of intelligence; what is needed
to realize Him is unified concentration of breath and mind.

   Let them blame me or praise me or adore me with flowers; I become
neither joyous nor depressed, resting in myself and drunk in the nectar of
the knowledge of the pure Lord.

   With the help of the gardeners called Mind and Love, plucking the
flower called Steady Contemplation, offering the water of the flood of the
Self's own bliss, worship the Lord with the sacred formula of silence!

SOURCE: W. Theodore de Bary, ed., *Sources of Indian Tradition*, vol. 1. New York and
London: Columbia University Press, 1958, p. 355

Without Krishna I Cannot Sleep
by Mirabai

Mirabai was a princess of Rajasthan, but she was far more devoted to Lord Krishna than to her husband. When her husband died, she defied her in-laws' desire that she immolate herself along with her husband (i.e. throw herself on his funeral pyre), and instead became a wandering mendicant (beggar).

Without Krishna I cannot sleep.
Tortured by longing, I cannot sleep,
And the fire of love
Drives me to wander hither and thither.
Without the light of the Beloved
My house is dark,
And lamps do not please me.
Without the Beloved my bed is uninviting,
And I pass the nights awake.
When will my Beloved return home?
The frogs are croaking, the peacock's cry
And the cuckoo's song are heard.
Low black clouds are gathering,
Lightning flashes, stirring fear in the heart.
My eyes fill with tears.
What shall I do? Where shall I go?
Who can quench my pain?
My body has been bitten
By the snake of "absence,"
And my life is ebbing away
With every beat of the heart.
Fetch the herb quickly.
Which of my companions
Will come bringing the Beloved to meet me?
My Lord when will you come
To meet your Mīrā?
Manamohan, the Charmer of Hearts,
Fills me with delight. When, my Lord,
Will you come to laugh and talk with me?

SOURCE: *The Devotional Poems of Mīrābāī*, trans. A. J. Alston. Delhi: Motalal Banarsidass, 1980, pp. 64–5

Three Poems
by Kabir

Kabir was a weaver whose hymns are still greatly loved today by Muslims and Sikhs as well as Hindus, for they describe inner experiences which are common to mystics of all religions.

I.13 mo ko kahān ḍhūnṛo bande

O servant, where dost thou seek me?
Lo! I am beside thee.
I am neither in temple nor in mosque: I am neither in Kaaba[19] nor in
   Kailash:[20]
Neither am I in rites and ceremonies, nor in Yoga and renunciation.
If thou art a true seeker, thou shalt at once see Me: thou shalt meet Me in a
   moment of time.
Kabir says, "O Sadhu![21] God is the breath of all breath."

II.61 grah candra tapan jot varat hai

The light of the sun, the moon, and the stars shines bright:
The melody of love swells forth, and the rhythm of love's detachment beats
   the time.
Day and night, the chorus of music fills the heavens; and Kabir says
"My Beloved One gleams like the lightning flash in the sky."

Do you know how the moments perform their adoration?
Waving its row of lamps, the universe sings in worship day and night,
There are the hidden banner and the secret canopy:
There the sound of the unseen bells is heard.
Kabir says: "There adoration never ceases; there the Lord of the Universe
   sitteth on His throne."

The whole world does its works and commits its errors: but few are the
   lovers who know the Beloved.
The devout seeker is he who mingles in his heart the double currents of love
   and detachment, like the mingling of the streams of Ganges and Jumna;
In his heart the sacred water flows day and night; and thus the round of
   births and deaths is brought to an end.

Behold what wonderful rest is in the Supreme Spirit! and he enjoys it, who
   makes himself meet for it.

---

[19] Kaaba—holiest of Muslim shrines, at Mecca.
[20] Kailash—legendary mountain abode of Lord Siva.
[21] Sadhu—Hindu ascetic.

Held by the cords of love, the swing of the Ocean of Joy sways to and fro;
  and a mighty sound breaks forth in song.
See what a lotus blooms there without water! and Kabir says
"My heart's bee drinks its nectar."

What a wonderful lotus it is, that blooms at the heart of the spinning wheel
  of the universe! Only a few pure souls know of its true delight.
Music is all around it, and there the heart partakes of the joy of the Infinite
  Sea.
Kabir says: "Dive thou into that Ocean of sweetness: thus let all errors of life
  and of death flee away."

I.36 sūr parkāś, tanh rain kahā<u>n</u> pāïye

Where is the night, when the sun is shining? If it is night, then the sun
  withdraws its light.
Where knowledge is can ignorance endure? If there be ignorance, then
  knowledge must die.
If there be lust, how can love be there? Where there is love, there is no lust.

Lay hold on your sword, and join in the fight. Fight, O my brother, as long
  as life lasts.
Strike off your enemy's head, and there make an end of him quickly: then
  come, and bow your head at your King's Durbar.[22]
He who is brave, never forsakes the battle: he who flies from it is no true
  fighter.
In the field of this body a great war goes forward, against passion, anger,
  pride, and greed:
It is in the kingdom of truth, contentment and purity, that this battle is
  raging; and the sword that rings forth most loudly is the sword of His
  Name.

Kabir says: "When a brave knight takes the field, a host of cowards is put to
  flight.
It is a hard fight and a weary one, this fight of the truth-seeker: for the vow
  of the truth-seeker is more hard than that of the warrior, or of the
  widowed wife who would follow her husband.
For the warrior fights for a few hours, and the widow's struggle with death
  is soon ended:
But the truth-seeker's battle goes on day and night, as long as life lasts it
  never ceases."

SOURCE: *Songs of Kabir*, trans. Rabindranath Tagore, New York: Samuel Weiser,
1977, pp. 45–86

---

[22] Durbar—court.

Modern texts

Vision of the Mother
by Paramahansa Yogananda

One of the modern saints who has contributed to the global spread of Hindu principles and practices is Paramahansa Yogananda (1893–1952). His Autobiography of a Yogi, *first published in 1946, has awakened keen interest in the miraculous aspects of Sanatana Dharma among people outside India.*

I proceeded alone to the portico that fronts the large temple of Kali (God in the aspect of Mother Nature). Selecting a shady spot near one of the pillars, I sat down and assumed the lotus posture. Although it was only about seven o'clock, the morning sun would soon be oppressive.

The world receded as I became devotionally entranced. My mind was concentrated on Goddess Kali. Her statue in this very temple in Dakshineswar had been the special object of adoration by the great master, Sri Ramakrishna Paramahansa. In answer to his anguished demands, the stone image had often taken a living form and conversed with him.

"Silent Mother of stone," I prayed, "Thou didst become filled with life at the plea of Thy beloved devotee Ramakrishna; why dost Thou not also heed the wails of this yearning son of Thine?"

My aspiring zeal increased boundlessly, accompanied by a divine peace. Yet, when five hours had passed, and the Goddess whom I was inwardly visualizing had made no response, I felt slightly disheartened. Sometimes it is a test by God to delay the fulfilment of prayers. But He eventually appears to the persistent devotee in whatever form he holds dear. A devout Christian sees Jesus; a Hindu beholds Krishna, or the Goddess Kali, or an expanding Light if his worship takes an impersonal turn.

Reluctantly I opened my eyes, and saw that the temple doors were being locked by a priest, in conformance with a noon-hour custom. I rose from my secluded seat on the portico and stepped into the courtyard. Its stone surface was scorched by the midday sun; my bare feet were painfully burned.

"Divine Mother," I silently remonstrated, "Thou didst not come to me in vision, and now Thou art hidden in the temple behind closed doors. I wanted to offer a special prayer to Thee today on behalf of my brother-in-law."

My inward petition was instantly acknowledged. First, a delightful cold wave descended over my back and under my feet, banishing all discomfort. Then, to my amazement, the temple became greatly magnified. Its large door slowly opened, revealing the stone figure of Goddess Kali. Gradually the statue changed into a living form, smilingly nodding in greeting, thrilling me with joy indescribable. As if by a mystic syringe, the breath was withdrawn from my lungs; my body became very still, though not inert.

An ecstatic enlargement of consciousness followed. I could see clearly for several miles over the Ganges River to my left, and beyond the temple into the entire Dakshineswar precincts. The walls of all buildings glimmered transparently; through them I observed people walking to and fro over distant acres.

Though I was breathless and though my body remained in a strangely quiet state, I was able to move my hands and feet freely. For several minutes I experimented in closing and opening my eyes; in either state I saw distinctly the whole Dakshineswar panorama.

Spiritual sight, X-ray-like, penetrates into all matter; the divine eye is centre everywhere, circumference nowhere. I realized anew, standing there in the sunny courtyard, that when a man ceases to be a prodigal child of God, engrossed in a physical world indeed dream, baseless as a bubble, he reinherits his eternal realms. If escapism be a need of man, cramped in his narrow personality, can any other escape compare with that of omnipresence?

SOURCE: Paramahansa Yogananda, *Autobiography of a Yogi*, Bombay: Jaico Publishing House, 2nd edn, 1975, pp. 207–9

Contemporary issues

Santana Dharma has given birth to many reformers who warned against practicing the ancient rituals without inner engagement, or who protested what they regarded as social injustices institutionalized by brahmanic Hinduism. Among these are the deeply embedded caste system and the subordination and abuse of women (which persists side by side with worship of the goddess).

Untouchability
by Mahatma Gandhi

The father of the Indian independence movement, Mahatma Gandhi (1869–1948), was a vehement critic of the caste system, which causes some people to be considered "untouchable" by those of higher castes. He also fought against Hindu exclusivism[23]

---

[23] Exclusivism—belief in the validity of only one religion.

in a country which is home to large numbers of people from other faiths, trying to establish the principle of secularism,[24] meaning that the government would not favor any one religion and would enjoy equal privileges.

There is an ineffaceable blot that Hinduism today carries with it. I have declined to believe that it has been handed down to us from immemorial times. I think that this miserable, wretched, enslaving spirit of "untouchableness" must have come to us when we were at our lowest ebb. This evil has stuck to us and still remains with us. . . .

Untouchability as it is practised in Hinduism today is, in my opinion, a sin against God and man and is, therefore like a poison slowly eating into the very vitals of Hinduism. In my opinion, it has no sanction whatsoever in the Hindu *Shastras*[25] taken as a whole. . . . It has degraded both the untouchables and the touchables. It has stunted the growth of nearly 40 million human beings. They are denied even the ordinary amenities of life. The sooner, therefore, it is ended, the better for Hinduism, the better for India, and perhaps better for mankind in general.

So far as I am concerned with the untouchability question it is one of life and death for Hinduism. As I have said repeatedly, if untouchability lives, Hinduism perishes, and even India perishes; but if untouchability is eradicated from the Hindu heart, root and branch, then Hinduism has a definite message for the world. I have said the first thing to hundreds of audiences but not the latter part. Now that is the utterance of a man who accepts Truth as God. It is therefore no exaggeration. If untouchability is an integral part of Hinduism, the latter is a spent bullet. But untouchability is a hideous untruth. My motive in launching the anti-untouchability campaign is clear. What I am aiming at is not every Hindu touching an "untouchable", but every touchable Hindu driving untouchability from his heart, going through a complete change of heart.

It is bad enough when dictated by selfish motives to consider ourselves high and other people low. But it is not only worse but a double wrong when we tack religion to an evil like untouchability. It, therefore, grieves me when learned pundits come forward and invoke the authority of *Shastras* for a patent evil like untouchability. I have said, and I repeat today, that we, Hindus, are undergoing a period of probation. Whether we desire it or not, untouchability is going. But if during this period of probation we repent for the sin, if we reform and purify ourselves, history will record that one act as a supreme act of purification on the part of the Hindus. But if, through the working of the time spirit, we are compelled to do things against our will and Harijans come into their own, it will be no credit to the Hindus or to

---

[24] Secularism—although usually meaning a non-sacred perspective, in modern India "secularism" means governmental non-preference for any religion.

[25] *Shastras*—Hindu law books, such as *Manu smriti.*

Hinduism. But I go a step further and say that if we fail in this trial, Hinduism and Hindus will perish.

Harijan means "a man of God." All the religions of the world describe God preeminently as the Friend of the friendless, Help of the helpless, and Protector of the weak. The rest of the world apart, in India who can be more friendless, helpless or weaker than the forty million or more Hindus of India who are classified as "untouchables"? If, therefore, any body of people can be fitly described as men of God, they are surely these helpless, friendless and despised people. Hence . . . I have always adopted Harijan as the name signifying "untouchables." Not that the change of name brings about any change of status but one may at least be spared the use of a term which is itself one of reproach. When caste Hindus have of their own inner conviction and, therefore, voluntarily, got rid of the present-day untouchability we shall all be called Harijans for, according to my humble opinion, caste Hindus will then have found favour with God and may, therefore, be fitly described as His men.

SOURCE: Mahatma Gandhi, "For the Well-Being of the Nation," in *The Message of Mahatma Gandhi*, ed. U. S. Mohan Rao. New Delhi: Ministry of Information and Broadcasting, 1968, pp. 90–92

Hindu-ness
by V. D. Savarkar

The exlusivist movement has increased in recent times and has gained considerable political power. A major document encouraging Hindu exclusivism and nationalism was written in 1923 by V. D. Savarkar (1883–1966), who was opposed to harmonious coexistence with Muslims and to Gandhian principles. Many contemporary scholars, however, refute the idea that Sanatana Dharma supports any exclusive claims to truth. They argue that "Hindu-ness" is being used as a political rallying point, for there is no single Hindu religion but rather a multiplicity of ways to the Truth. This essay, Hindutva ("Hindu-ness"), and Savarkar's subsequent ideas have considerably influenced those who have promoted Hinduism as the national tradition of India in opposition to the claims of the non-Hindu minorities in India.

A country, a common home, is the first important essential of stable strong nationality: and as of all countries in the world our country can hardly be surpassed by any in its capacity to afford a soil so specially fitted for the growth of a great nation; we Hindus, whose very first article of faith is the love we bear to the common Fatherland, have in that love the strongest talismanic tie that can bind close and keep a nation firm and enthuse and enable it to accomplish things greater than ever.

The second essential of *Hindutva* puts the estimate of our latent powers of national cohesion and greatness yet higher. No country in the world, with the exception of China again, is peopled by a race so homogeneous, yet so ancient and yet so strong both numerically and vitally.... Mohammedans are no race nor are the Christians. They are a religious unit, yet neither a racial nor a national one. But we Hindus, if possible, are all the three put together and live under our ancient and common roof. The numerical strength of our race is an asset that cannot be too highly prized....

The ideal conditions, therefore, under which a nation can attain perfect solidarity and cohesion would, other things being equal, be found in the case of those people who inhabit the land they adore, the land of whose forefathers is also the land of their Gods and Angels, of Seers and Prophets; the scenes of whose history are also the scenes of their mythology.

The Hindus are about the only people who are blessed with these ideal conditions that are at the same time incentive to national solidarity, cohesion, and greatness....

Thus the actual essentials of *Hindutva* are, as this running sketch reveals, also the ideal essentials of nationality. If we would we can build on this foundation of *Hindutva*, a future greater than what any other people on earth can dream of—greater even than our own past; provided we are able to utilize our opportunities! ...

Thirty crores[26] of people, with India for their basis of operation, for their Fatherland and for their Holyland, with such a history behind them, bound together by ties of a common blood and common culture can dictate their terms to the whole world. A day will come when mankind will have to face the force.

Equally certain it is that whenever the Hindus come to hold such a position whence they could dictate terms to the whole world—those terms cannot be very different from the terms which [the] *Gītā* dictates or the Buddha lays down. A Hindu is most intensely so, when he ceases to be a Hindu; and with a Kabir claims the whole earth for a Benares[27] ... or with a Tukaram[28] exclaims: "My country? Oh brothers, the limits of the Universe—there the frontiers of my country lie."

SOURCE: V. D. Savarkar, *Hindutva* (1923), in S. Hay, ed. *Sources of Indian Tradition*, vol. 2. New York: Columbia University Press, 1988, pp. 292–5

A Paradigm[29] Shift in Religious Cooperation
by Swami Agnivesh

By the end of the twentieth century, the philosophy of Savarkar developed into fanatic exclusivism among some Hindu groups. Leaders of these groups asserted that

---

[26] Crores—10 million.
[27] Benares—Varanasi, a sacred place of pilgrimage.
[28] Tukaram—seventeenth-century Hindu poet who believed in the equality of all humankind.
[29] Paradigm—a model of reality, such as the materialistic or idealistic model.

Christianity and Islam are foreign religions and should be driven out of India. In 1999, escalating violence against Christians reached the point where a mob in Manoharpur, Orissa, burned alive an Australian Christian missionary who had been working for three decades to help lepers, along with his two sons. This act shocked thoughtful Hindus deeply, triggering soul-searching efforts to assert the true spirit of Sanatana Dharma. Swami Agnivesh, a prominent Hindu social activist, wrote these reflections after participating in an inter-religious pilgrimage of support for the missionary's widow, Mrs. Gladys Staines, who won great sympathy for her forgiving attitude in the face of the sectarian hatreds which took the lives of her husband and sons.

In her remarks to the pilgrims, Mrs Staines was emphatic that both in their life of service and in her spirit of forgiveness, the Staines family is empowered by spirituality. For them, religion involves a dynamic engagement with the given human context, addressing the needs especially of the neglected and the discarded. The role of religion is not to make us shun the world of realities. Religion, on the contrary, is the foremost resource we have for transforming human nature and society. But when religions decay and degenerate, this aspect is superseded by religious obscurantism and fanaticism turning religion into a liability rather than a source of light.

The pilgrims to Baripada and Manoharpur returned with the firm conviction that sound religiosity inspired by social spirituality is the foremost need of our country. The politicization of religion, that expresses itself through the cynical abuse and exploitation of religious loyalties to subserve vested interests, has attained epidemic proportions. This is injurious to our social and national health. As a people, we need to condemn and reject this spurious phenomenon. But that is not enough. The positive task is to nurture the people in the practice of true spirituality aimed at social transformation and people's empowerment.

The outbreak of violence in the name of religion and the awakening of the fundamentalist spirit in all religions at present together point to the inadequacy of the secular paradigm. The rise of religious fundamentalism in the Indian context owes a great deal to negative secularism as an anti-religious ideology. This liberated politics from the confines of ethical guidelines. Cynically understood as the art of the possible, politics gradually lost sight of people's welfare as its true goal. The national cause has been pawned to fatten the elite. Since all political parties are unmindful of the welfare of the people, the only way they can secure continued support is by manipulating religious sentiments. The greatest disservice that the people of India can do themselves is to condone this criminality in the name of religion.

The massacre in Manoharpur as well as Mrs Staines' response to it leaves us with some basic questions. What is religion? Is it something that inspires service to people or promotes murder and mayhem? Who represents true religion? People like Mrs Staines who refuse to hate, or the agents of hate who kill the servants of the poor apparently to save their God? What is religion worth if it is not to nurture in us a sense of compassion and fellow feeling that denies us peace unless we practice justice and uphold the truth?

We have been praying for millennia and we continue to pray to be led from "darkness to light, falsehood to truth, and death to immortality." But the forces of darkness, death and deceit are progressively overwhelming us. The fault is not with the prayer. The fault is with us that we do not honor the prayer by acting in its light. No one can say this Vedic prayer honestly without practicing social spirituality, the like of which is exemplified in the Staines family. It is time we realized that true religion involves a fierce commitment to uphold truth, practice justice and to fight forces of evil no matter where they are found. All religions must find their common cause or shared responsibility in this context. When that happens the truth will dawn on us that religions are not each other's enemies, but fellow pilgrims moving towards the shrine of human wellbeing and social health. The tragedy in Manoharpur can be transformed into a national triumph if this paradigm shift in inter-religious cooperation is brought about.

SOURCE: Swami Agnivesh, "Pilgrims' Progress," *The Times of India*, 2 April 1999

GLOSSARY

Bhakti Popular devotion to a god/goddess or guru, with love and adoration.

Brahman The impersonal ultimate principle; also, one of the priestly, aristocratic caste.

Caste A social organization by hierarchy of occupations, sanctified by Hinduism.

Kali Yuga The contemporary era, a dark age, one of many cycles (Yugas) of a vast cosmic time.

Karma The cosmic law of consequences for moral action, leading to reincarnation in a certain caste position.

Pandit One of the hereditary priestly caste learned in ancient texts, customs and rituals.

Puranas Mythological texts of ancient days; popular devotional texts.

Reincarnation After death, rebirth in a new body higher or lower in the caste system, according to one's karma.

Rishi (seer) A poetic sage; Rishis are visionary authors of Vedic hymns heard within in meditation.

Sanatana Dharma The ageless way of moral order, duty, and natural cosmic law.

Sanskrit The ancient language of the holy scriptures.

Smrti texts Great epic poems, descriptions of gods and goddesses, codes of moral conduct, such as the *Mahabharata*.

Sruti texts "Heard" by ancient sages in meditation, mostly the Vedas.

Upanishads Philosophical reflections on ultimate reality, a oneness in which we all participate.

Vedas Foundational scriptures for Hindu tradition, written down *c.* 1500 BCE; oldest are the Rig Vedas.

Yoga (yoking [to divinity]) Techniques for transforming consciousness and attaining liberation; many forms, such as guru yoga, devotion, work, study, asceticism, physical exercises, mantra repetition, visualization, meditation.

HOLY DAYS

Hindu holy days are numerous and varied across India. Times are calculated variously by region, astrological sign, sun, and moon. Most communal religious celebrations are held during the bright half of the lunar months, for the full moon is sacred.

Spring Holi For the lower castes a boisterous celebration, throwing colored powder and water and celebrating Kama, god of sexual desire. Dancing; the past year's evils are symbolically thrown into bonfires. In Bengal, associated with Krishna.

Spring New Year Soon after Holi the New Year is celebrated near the spring equinox, a time of cosmic balance and beginning/ending.

Fall Renewals Gods' birthdays are celebrated as overcoming the hot summer (monsoons included). The birthdays of Krishna, avatar of Vishnu, and Vamana, dwarf avatar of Vishnu, signal a restored, auspicious time of year. The goddess Durga kills a buffalo demon in fall. In some parts of

India New Year in late fall is seen as the time of the awakening of Vishnu, who has been asleep on the cobra Ananta for four months. Divali is a celebration of Lakshmi, the goddess of prosperity, and the victory of gods over evil forces.

Pilgrimages These take place usually in summer, especially to sacred rivers such as the Ganges, where bathing (despite its current physical pollution) is ritually purifying. The dying are taken to Benares to be cremated. Other pilgrimages are taken to temples, for the sake of ancestors and worldly rewards, or for spiritual purification and rebirth in heaven instead of earth.

Domestic Rites Conception, wishing for a son, and birth are surrounded with rituals (*pujas*) with food, fire, and prayers. Between 8 and 12 an upper-caste boy can be initiated into being a "twice-born." At weddings the bride and groom walk around the sacrificial fire in seven stages, solemnizing their union.

HISTORICAL OUTLINE

3500–1500 BCE—Harappan city civilization in Indus valley, now in Pakistan

c. 2000–900 BCE—Aryan invasions of northern India

c. 100–500 BCE—Upanishads systematized by Vyasa

c. 900–700 BCE—Brahmanas recorded

200 BCE—Yoga Sutras organized by Patanjali

400 BCE–200 CE—Ramayana recorded

400 BCE–400 CE—Mahabharata recorded

c. 300 CE—Tantric texts recorded

c. 500–800—Vedanta organized by Sankara

600–1800—Bhakti movement strong

711—Muslim invasions begin

1556–1707—Muslim Mughal Empire

1836–1886—Ramakrishna

1857–1947—British rule in India

1947—Formation of Pakistan and East Pakistan (now Bangladesh)

1948—Assassination of Mahatma Gandhi

REVIEW QUESTIONS

1   Why is the term "Sanatana Dharma" preferred to "Hindu" by scholars?
2   How are reincarnation and caste affected by karma?
3   What are the oldest scriptures?
4   Contrast the Upanishads with the Vedas.
5   What is meant by "Swetaketu! You are That!"?
6   How is a student expected to treat his guru?
7   How would a believer respond to the monotheistic charge of idolatry for worshiping statues?
8   What is Yoga?
9   What is the purpose of meditation?
10 What is "equanimity"?
11 Describe some goddesses.
12 Is the Goddess a better path to divinity for women than a god?
13 What is bhakti yoga?
14 What feelings characterize Krishna devotion? How are they religious?
15 Is Kabir an exclusivist or universalist (believer in the validity of various spiritual paths)? Give quotes.
16 How did Yogananda's meditation "reinherit his eternal realm" at the Temple of the goddess Kali?
17 How did Gandhi argue against untouchability, against Hindu tradition and law? What did he rename untouchables and why?
18 What is "Hindutva"? Is religion used to justify such things in other cultures?
19 What would be a good religious response to Hindu nationalism?

INFORMATION RESOURCES

Alston, A. J. *The Devotional Poems of Mirabai.* Delhi: Motilal Banarsidass Publishers, 1980.

de Bary, Wm. Theodore, *Sources of Indian Tradition.* New York: Columbia University Press, 1958.

Devananda, Vishnu, Swami, *Meditations and Mantras.* New York: Om Lotus Publishing, 1975.

Gandhi, Mahatma, *The Message of Mahatma Gandhi*, ed. U. S. Mohan Rao. New Delhi: Ministry of Information, Government of India, 1990. Hindu Studies <www.rci.rutgers.edu/~religion/links/hindu.html><www.hindunet.org>

Hiltebeitel, Alf, and Marie-Louise

Reiniche, "Hinduism" and "Hindu Religious Year" in *The Encyclopedia of Religion*, ed. Mircea Eliade. New York: Macmillan, 1987.

Hinduism Today, www.hindu.org.

Hinduism Today, 107 Kaholalele Road, Kapaa, Hawaii 96746–9304 U.S.A.

Jayakar, Pupul, *The Earth Mother*, New Delhi and Middlesex: Penguin Books, 1980, 1989.

Kabir, *Songs of Kabir*, trans R. Tagore. New York: Weiser, 1981.

Kinsley, David, *Hindu Goddesses*. Delhi: Motilal Banarsidass, 1986.

Prabhupada, A. C. B., Swami, *Bhagavad-*

Gita As It Is. Los Angeles, London, Bombay: The Bhaktivedanta Book Trust.

Purohit, Shree, Swami, and W. B. Yeats, trans. *The Ten Principal Upanishads.* Calcutta: Rupa Co., 1992.

Rajagopalachari, C., *Mahabharata.* Bombay: Bharatiya Vidya Bhavan, 1994.

— — *Ramayana.* Bombay: Bharatiya Vidya Bhavan, 1990.

—— *The Siva Purana.* Delhi: Motilal Banarsidass, 1990.

Shastri, J. L. ed. *Hymns of the Rigveda,* trans. Ralphy Griffith. Delhi: Motilal Banarsidass, 1986.

Smith, Brian K. *et al.* "Hinduism" in *The New Encyclopedia Britannica,* XX: 519–58, 1997.

Stutley, Margaret and James, *Harper's Dictionary of Hinduism.* New York: Harper and Row, 1977.

Vivekananda, Swami, *Karma-Yoga and Bhakti-Yoga.* New York: Ramakrishna-Vivekananada Center, 1982.

Yogananada, Paramahansa, *Autobiography of a Yogi.* Los Angeles: Self-Realization Fellowship; Bombay: Jaico Publishing House, 1974.

CHAPTER 4

JAINISM

In addition to the Vedic religions of ancient India, another path evolved which is not based on the Vedas. This is Jainism (from **jina**, winner over passions), an extremely ascetic path. Its goal is liberation from the soul-tarnishing negative effects of one's actions, thoughts, and speech—one's **karma**. In Jain teaching, this liberation comes only through one's own strenuous and mindful efforts not to do wrong in any way. Jains reject the Hindu caste system and the idea of a creator God, but, like Hindus and Buddhists, believe in reincarnation.

The teachers of this path are called **Tirthankaras**. According to tradition, there have been twenty-four Tirthankaras during the current era. There is historic evidence of the existence of the last three teachers. The last is the best known: Mahavir (*c.* 559–527 BCE), who had been a prince but renounced his life of pleasure and power at the age of thirty to become a homeless ascetic. His austerities were so extreme that people thought him mad and tormented him. But he endured all hardships with equanimity, achieved perfect liberation, and taught others the way to liberation from karma. In order to increase sensitivity toward non-human life forms, he made detailed studies and gave insights into the categories and qualities of all that exists. A large community of monks, nuns, and laypeople gathered around him, and he gave them minute instructions on how to live without accumulating negative karma.

Today there is renewed interest in this ascetic way of life, for its basic principles arc antidotes to modern problems. For example, Mahatma Gandhi's assertion of the power of non-violent resistance to oppression was strongly influenced by the Jain principle of **ahimsa**, or non-violence, based on reverence for all life. Jain precepts of non-violence, the interdependence of all life forms, compassion, non-acquisitiveness, and relativity are also being invoked as correctives to environmentally destructive modern lifestyles and to conflicts of dogma.

Teachings of Mahavir

The teachings of Mahavir did not necessarily originate with him but are part of a much more ancient tradition. They were carried orally by his followers for several centuries, along with the commentaries of learned teachers. The literature to be remembered was quite vast, and during twelve years of famine about 300 BCE, many monks died who had been carrying the teachings in their memory. Little had been written down, for books were considered possessions and causes for attachment, and were renounced by Jain ascetics like other possessions. At that time, books were written out by hand and were rare in any case.

The compilation of teachings and commentaries formed a canon called the *Agam Sutras*. After the famine, one group of Jain ascetics, the **Svetambara** sect, maintained that they had managed to preserve most of the major texts. They held three conferences to compile and preserve what was available. Another even more ascetic sect, the **Digambara**, claimed that the entire canon had been lost. Today, the sects still disagree about the validity of the Jain Agamic scriptures. The Digambaras use scriptures written by great teachers from 100 to 800 CE which are thought to have been based on the earlier scriptures.

Mahavir's Stoicism
From the *Akaranga Sutra*

Mahavir's own life is cited as a perfect example of the Jain teaching of self-mastery and non-aggressiveness toward all beings. The ideal is to bear both pleasure and pain with equanimity and compassion for other beings. Many stories of the torments endured by Mahavir with great **stoicism** *appear in the classic* Akaranga Sutra, *an excerpt from which is here retold by Shashi Ahluwalia. Before his liberation, Mahavir is referred to by his worldly name, Vardhaman.*

Vardhaman left the palace and started his long journey like an ascetic. He had only a piece of cloth on his body and gave even that to a beggar. He became completely naked—*Digambara*. As Vardhaman was about to start from the Jnatri-sanda park on a wandering career, a Brahman named Soma approached him with a prayer for help. But Vardhaman had hardly anything worthwhile to give. So he shared half of his garment with the beggar and placed the other half on his shoulder.

The Brahman took the garment to a tailor to have the hem bound. The tailor advised him to get the other half, so that the two pieces together, duly repaired, would fetch him a handsome amount in the market. So the Brahman started at once and followed Vardhaman like his shadow, and waiting for a chance to get it. The chance came after 13 months. When Vardhaman was going from South Vacala to the North Vacala the piece on his shoulder was caught in a thorny bush and remained there. It was picked up by Brahman Soma.

At this point, Vardhaman took five resolutions which were "(1) I shall not stay at an uncongenial place; (2) I shall meditate all the time in a statuesque posture; (3) I shall generally maintain silence; (4) I shall use the hollow on my palm as begging bowl; and (5) I shall not humble myself to any householder." These resolutions became his guidelines throughout his life.

The famous "Ohana-Sutra" in the *Akaranga* contains the following account of his soul-stirring sadhana:[1]

Many living beings gathered on his body, crawled about it, and caused pain. Then he meditated, walking with his eye fixed on a square space before him of the length of a man. Many people who were shocked at the sight struck him and cried. He shunned the company of the female sex and of all householders. Asked, he gave no reply. He did not even answer those who saluted him. He was beaten with sticks and struck by sinful people. He wandered about disregarding all slights, not being attracted by any worldly amusement.

For more than a couple of years he went without using cold water. He realized singleness, guarded his body, obtained intuition and became calm. He carefully avoided doing injury to the meanest form of life. He did not use what was specially prepared for him. He used to eat only clean food. He did not use another man's robe, nor did he eat out of another man's vessel. He observed moderation in eating and drinking. He neither rubbed his eyes nor scratched his body.

He sometimes took shelter in workshops, sometimes in factories, sometimes in garden houses, sometimes in a cemetery, in deserted houses, or at the foot of a tree. In such places he sought shelter for thirteen years. He meditated day and night, undisturbed, unperturbed, exerting himself strenuously. He never cared for sleep for the sake of pleasure. He waked up himself and slept only a little, free from cares and desires. Waking up again, going outside for once in a night, he walked about for an hour.

At his resting places, crawling or flying animals attacked him. Bad people, the guard of the village, or lance-bearers attacked him. Well-controlled, he bore all dreadful calamities and different kinds of feelings and he wandered about, speaking but little. Ill-treated he engaged himself in his meditations, free from resentment. He endured all hardships in calmness. Well-guarded, he bore the pains caused by grass, cold, heat, flies and gnats.

He travelled in the pathless country of *Radha*—in *Vajrabhumi* and *Svabhrabhumi*, where he used miserable beds and seats. The rude natives of the place attacked him and set dogs to bite him. But he never used the stick to keep off the dogs. He endured the abusive language of the rustics, being perfectly enlightened. The inhabitants of the place caused him all sorts of tortures. Abandoning the care of his body, he bore pain, free from desire.

---

[1] Sadhana—spiritual practice.

He abstained from indulgence of the flesh, though he was never attacked by diseases. Whether wounded or not, he did not desire medical treatment. In the cold season he meditated in the shade. In summer he exposed himself to the heat. He lived on rough food like rice, pounded jujube, and jujube. Using these three kinds of food, he sustained himself for eight months. Sometimes he did not drink for half a month or even for a month. Sometimes he did not drink for more than two months, or even six months. Sometimes he ate only the sixth meal, or the eighth, the tenth, the twelfth. Sometimes he ate stale food. He committed no sin himself, nor did he induce others to do so, nor did he consent to the sin of others.

He meditated persevering in some posture, without the smallest motion. He meditated in mental concentration on the things above, below, beside. He meditated free from sin and desire, not attached to sounds and colours, and never acted carelessly.

Thus, as a hero at the head of a battle, he bore all hardships, and remaining undisturbed, proceeded on the road to deliverance. Understanding the truth and restraining the impulses for the purification of soul, he was finally liberated.

SOURCE: Shashi Ahluwalia, *Ohana Sutra, Akaranga*, Spiritual Masters from India, Delhi: Manas Publications, 1987, pp. 4–6

Harmlessness

Whatever their historicity, the Jain scriptures comprise a vast body of wisdom. Some of the literature concerns intricate scientific systems for classifying all aspects of living and non-living beings, space, and time. Minute sentient life forms are said to exist in the earth, in fire, in air, and in water, in addition to the more visible plants and "movable beings". Many Jain Sutras concern precepts for doing as little harm as possible to other beings.

"On Non-Violence"

Know other creatures' love for life, for they are like you. Kill them not: save their life from fear and enmity.

All living beings desire happiness, and have revulsion from pain and suffering. They are fond of life, they love to live, long to live, and they feel repulsed at the idea of hurt and injury to or destruction of their life. Hence, no living being should be hurt, injured, or killed.

All things breathing, all things existing, all things living, all beings whatsoever, should not be slain, or treated with violence, or insulted, or tortured, or driven away.

He who hurts living beings himself, or gets them hurt by others, or approves of hurt caused by others, augments the world's hostility toward himself.

He who views all living beings as his own self, and sees them all as being alike, has stopped all influx of karma; he is self-restrained, and incurs no sin.

"On Self-Restraint"

The painful condition of the self is the result of its own action; it has not been brought about by any other cause.

The soul is the maker and the unmaker, the doer and undoer; it is itself responsible for its own happiness and misery, is its own friend and its own foe; it itself decides its own conditions, good or evil.

Wealth and property, movable or immovable, cannot save a person from the sufferings he or she undergoes on account of the fruition of his or her own karma.

Greater is the victory of one who conquers his own self than that of him who conquers thousands of thousands of formidable foes in a valiant fight.

Fight with yourself; why fight with external foes? Happy is he who conquers his self by his self.

Conquer yourself, for difficult it is to conquer the self. If the self is conquered, you shall be happy in this world and hereafter.

All the creatures of the earth look for happiness outside of themselves, but real happiness must be sought inside the depths of their own hearts.

SOURCE: Jain Sutras, trans. Dr. Jyoti Prasad Jain, *Religion and Culture of the Jains*, 3rd edn. New Delhi: Bharatiya Jnanpith, 1983. pp. 187–8.

Respect for Life
from the *Akaranga Sutra*

Earth is afflicted and wretched, it is hard to teach, it has no discrimination. Unenlightened men, who suffer from the effects of past deeds, cause great pain in a world full of pain already, for in earth souls are individually embodied. If, thinking to gain praise, honor, or respect, . . . or to achieve a good rebirth, . . . or to win salvation, or to escape pain, a man sins against earth or causes or permits others to do so, . . . he will not gain joy or wisdom. . . . Injury to the earth is like striking, cutting, maiming, or killing a blind man. . . . Knowing this a man should not sin against earth or cause or permit others to do so. He who understands the nature of sin against earth is called a true sage who understands karma. . . .

And there are many souls embodied in water. Truly water . . . is alive. . . . He who injures the lives in water does not understand the nature of sin or renounce it. . . . Knowing this, a man should not sin against water, or cause or permit others to do so. He who understands the nature of sin against water is called a true sage who understands karma. . . .

By wicked or careless acts one may destroy fire-beings and, moreover, harm other beings by means of fire.... For there are creatures living in earth, grass, leaves, wood, cowdung, or dustheaps, and jumping creatures which . . . fall into a fire if they come near it. If touched by fire, they shrivel up, . . . lose their senses, and die.... He who understands the nature of sin in respect of fire is called a true sage who understands karma.

And just as it is the nature of a man to be born and grow old, so is it the nature of a plant to be born and grow old.... One is endowed with reason, and so is the other; one is sick, if injured, and so is the other; one grows larger, and so does the other; one changes with time, and so does the other. . . . He who understands the nature of sin against plants is called a true sage who understands karma....

All beings with two, three, four, or five senses, . . . in fact all creation, know individually pleasure and displeasure, pain, terror, and sorrow. All are full of fears which come from all directions. And yet there exist people who would cause greater pain to them.... Some kill animals for sacrifice, some for their skin, flesh, blood, . . . feathers, teeth, or tusks; . . . some kill them intentionally and some unintentionally; some kill because they have been previously injured by them, . . . and some because they expect to be injured. He who harms animals has not understood or renounced deeds of sin.... He who understands the nature of sin against animals is called a true sage who understands karma....

A man who is averse from harming even the wind knows the sorrow of all things living.... He who knows what is bad for himself knows what is bad for others, and he who knows what is bad for others knows what is bad for himself. This reciprocity should always be borne in mind. Those whose minds are at peace and who are free from passions do not desire to live [at the expense of others].... He who understands the nature of sin against wind is called a true sage who understands karma.

In short he who understands the nature of sin in respect of all the six types of living beings is called a true sage who understands karma.

SOURCE: Akaranga Sutra, trans. in William Theodore de Bary, ed., *Sources of Indian Tradition*, vol. 1. New York: Columbia University Press, 1958, pp. 59–60.

Perfection of the soul

If one compassionately avoids harming all forms of life, one may gradually free the soul or **jiva** from its karmic accretions and entanglements with material things, thereby achieving perfection and liberation of the *jiva*. The **Five Jain Vows** are made to help achieve this aim.

The Five Great Vows

The first great vow, Sir, runs thus:

I renounce all killing of living beings, whether subtle or gross, whether movable or immovable. Nor shall I myself kill living beings. As long as I live, I confess and blame, repent and exempt myself of these sins, in the thrice threefold way [acting, commanding, consenting, either in the past or the present or the future], in mind, speech, and body.

There are five clauses:

A Nirgrantha[2] is careful in his walk, not careless. The Kevalin[3] assigns as the reason, that a Nirgrantha, careless in his walk, might hurt or displace or injure or kill living beings.

A Nirgrantha searches into his mind. If his mind is sinful, blamable, intent on works, acting on impulses, produces vision and dissension, quarrels, faults, and pains, injures living beings, or kills creatures, he should not employ such a mind in action.

A Nirgrantha searches into his speech; if his speech is sinful, blamable, intent on works, acting on impulses, produces division and dissension, quarrels, faults, and pains, injures living beings, or kills creatures, he should not utter that speech.

A Nirgrantha is careful in laying down his utensils of begging; he is not careless in it. The Kevalin says: A Nirgrantha who is careless in laying down his utensils of begging, might hurt or displace or injure all sorts of living beings.

A Nirgrantha eats and drinks after inspecting his food and drink; he does not eat and drink without inspecting his food and drink. The Kevalin says: If a Nirgrantha would eat and drink without inspecting his food and drink, he might hurt and displace or injure or kill all sorts of living beings.

The second great vow runs thus:

I renounce all vices of lying speech from anger or greed or fear or mirth. I shall neither myself speak lies, nor cause others to speak lies, nor consent to the speaking of lies by others. I confess and blame, repent and exempt myself of these sins in the thrice threefold way, in mind, speech, and body. . . .

The third great vow runs thus:

I renounce all taking of anything not given, either in a village or a town or a wood, either of little or much, of small or great, of living or lifeless things. I shall neither take myself what is not given, nor cause others to take it, nor consent to their taking it. . . .

The fourth great vow runs thus:

I renounce all sexual pleasures, either with gods or men or animals. I shall not give way to sensuality. As long as I live, I confess and blame, repent and exempt myself of these sins, in the thrice threefold way, in mind, speech, and body. . . .

The fifth great vow runs thus:

---

[2] Nirgrantha—a person without attachments, impurities, or possessiveness.
[3] Kevalin—omniscient one.

I renounce all attachments, whether little or much, small or great, living or lifeless; neither shall I myself form such attachments, nor cause others to do so, nor consent to their doing so. As long as I live, I confess and blame, repent and exempt myself of these sins, in the thrice threefold way, in mind, speech, and body.

There are five clauses:

If a creature with ears hears agreeable and disagreeable sounds, it should not be attached to, nor delighted with, nor desiring of, nor infatuated by, nor covetous of, nor disturbed by the agreeable or disagreeable sounds.

If a creature with eyes sees agreeable and disagreeable forms, it should not be attached to, nor delighted with, nor desiring of, nor infatuated by, nor covetous of, nor disturbed by them.

If a creature with an organ of smell smells agreeable or disagreeable smells, it should not be attached to them. . . .

If a creature with a tongue tastes agreeable or disagreeable tastes, it should not be attached to them. . . .

If a creature with an organ of feeling feels agreeable or disagreeable touches, it should not be attached to them. . . .

He who is well provided with these great vows and their twenty-five clauses is really Houseless, if he, according to the sacred lore, the precepts, and the way correctly practices, follows, executes, explains, establishes, and according to the precept, effects them.

SOURCE: Akaranga Sutra, Book II, Lecture 15, trans. Hermann Jacobi. Max Muller, ed., *The Sacred Books of the East*, vol. XXII. Delhi: Motilal Banarsidass, 1964, pp. 202–10 (first published by OUP, 1884)

The principles of Anekantavada and Syadvada

A central Jain principle is that of the multiplicity (**anekantavada**) and relativity (**syadvada**) of all points of view. The total of all perspectives can only be seen by the perfected soul whose clear vision encompasses the entire universe. If we grasp this teaching, we are less likely to fight to defend our own point of view, and thus we will be less violent and more tolerant in our relationships with others. This important teaching is explained elegantly and simply by Dr. L. M. Singhvi, former Ambassador of India to England, as part of a statement about Jain principles presented to His Royal Highness Prince Philip in 1990, marking the entry of the Jain faith into the Network on Conservation and Religion of the World Wide Fund for Nature.

Anekantavada (The Doctrine of Manifold Aspects)
by Dr. L. M. Singhvi

The concept of universal interdependence underpins the Jain theory of knowledge, known as *anekantavada* or the doctrine of manifold aspects.

Anekantavada describes the world as a multifaceted, everchanging reality with an infinity of viewpoints depending on the time, place, nature and state of the one who is the viewer and that which is viewed.

This leads to the doctrine of *syadvada* or relativity, which states that truth is relative to different viewpoints. What is true from one point of view is open to question from another. Absolute truth cannot be grasped from any particular viewpoint alone because absolute truth is the sum total of all the different viewpoints that make up the universe.

Because it is rooted in the doctrines of *anekantavada* and *syadvada*, Jainism does not look upon the universe from an anthropocentric, ethnocentric or egocentric viewpoint. It takes into account the viewpoints of other species, other communities and nations and other human beings.

SOURCE: Dr. L. M. Singhvi, "The Jain Declaration on Nature," pamphlet published privately and presented to His Royal Highness Prince Philip on 23 October 1990, at Buckingham Palace, London

The Blind Men and the Elephant

The principle of relativity of viewpoints is so important to Jain understanding that it is explained by way of numerous fables, such as the traditional Indian story of the blind men and the elephant.

As a joke, a king sent six blind men to feel an elephant and describe its nature. Each approached the elephant from a different direction, seized a different part, and, being blind, assumed that what he perceived was the whole elephant. One grasped the ear and declared, "Elephant is like a large fan." Another grasped a leg and declared, "Elephant is like a great pillar." Another blind man found the trunk, and feeling it, proclaimed, "Elephant is like the branch of a tree." Another grasped the tail and declared, "Elephant is like a rope hanging from the sky." A fifth encountered the side of the elephant and maintained, "Elephant is like a wall." The sixth insisted that the others were all wrong, for he had grasped the tusk. He proclaimed, "Elephant is not any of those; elephant is like a spear." Each being certain of the truth of his own experience, they began to fight.

A person who could see chanced to come by and found them quarreling. After listening to their individual perceptions from their different points of view, he gently explained that there was no need for fighting over the issue, for each was partially right. But to have complete knowledge of the nature of the elephant, he said, one would have to be able to be aware of and combine all the different aspects of the creature.

Renunciation

Another major Jain principle is that of **renunciation**: one should reduce one's desires and keep consumption to a minimum, thus freeing the soul from karmic entanglements with the material world and minimizing one's destruction of the planet. To overconsume, to misuse or pollute natural resources, are considered acts of violence.

There are degrees of harmfulness, corresponding to the karmic density of the soul. An example often used is ways of obtaining fruit. The most densely stained black soul uproots the whole tree to get its fruits. The blue-stained soul cuts the tree down for its fruit. The grey-stained soul cuts off a fruit-bearing branch. These three types of souls are all heavily karmically laden. Three other categories represent successively lighter karmic burdens. The yellow-stained soul cuts off a bunch of fruit. The lotus-pink soul picks ripe fruit from the tree. The sixth and most pure, the luminous white soul, simply picks up ripe fruit which has fallen to the ground.

Today voluntary simplicity and abstinence are being widely hailed as necessary for preservation of the environment. But Jains have always tried to live thus. A Jain fable traditionally used to inculcate this principle follows.

"Forsaking eternal bliss for a drop of honey"

Again and again, the gods and goddesses call out to a person, "Come— leave these earthly attachments and we will show you eternal bliss." At first the person says, "Not yet—let me first get married and raise a family." They call to him again, but he says, "Not yet—let me become financially well-off." And so it goes, year after year, and he remains entangled in worldly life.

One day the man is wandering through the jungle, whereupon a mad elephant begins to charge at him. From another direction, a repulsive demoness brandishes her sword at him with a dreadful cackle. Seeking refuge, he runs to a banyan tree and, unable to climb it, grasps a vine hanging from its branches. Clinging to the vine, he finds that he is suspended over a pit in which five snakes are hissing. Beneath them, a huge python awaits. Two mice, one white and one black, begin gnawing on the vine from above. The enraged elephant grabs the banyan tree with his trunk and shakes it, while the man maintains his perilous hold. As the elephant shakes the tree, a honeycomb on a branch above starts to fall; angry bees swarm out and begin stinging the man as he clings to the vine which is being eaten by the mice, with snakes hissing in the pit below.

The gods appear again, calling to the man that they are ready to free him from his miseries. But at that moment, a drop of honey from the comb falls into his mouth. Tasting its sweetness, he is oblivious to the elephant (death), the demoness (old age), the mice (the diminishing of one's lifespan through the inexorable procession of days and nights), the snakes (the treacherous lure of the five senses), the terrible python (hell that a person who is attached to sensual pleasures will suffer), the pit (human life), and the bees (diseases which torment a person). He says, "Not yet. I long for one more drop of this honey!" If a person were wise and fully aware of the perilous and tenuous nature of his existence, how could he prefer such fleeting pleasures to eternal liberation?

The Renunciate Life of Sādhvi Vicakṣaṇa
by N. Shanta

Although all Jains follow a path of renunciation and austerity, monks and nuns do so to an extreme degree. They have only a few possessions, which they carry with them, including a broom to sweep insects aside before inadvertently treading on them as they walk. Many wear a cloth over their mouth to avoid inadvertently inhaling any minute living beings. In winter they tolerate cold without heavy blankets; Digambara monks in fact never wear any clothing. In summer the monks and nuns tolerate intense heat without fans. This life is so arduous that one might imagine few would undertake it, but in fact there are large communities of Jain monks and nuns in India, even today. Many of them radiate an inner happiness which is the paradoxical result of extreme self-discipline.

The following story of a Jain nun who lived from 1912 to 1980 illustrates the particular difficulties for a woman choosing the path of renunciation, and also the liberating effects of doing so. It is noteworthy that Svetambara Jains have long believed that women are capable of a strict renunciate life, capable of fully understanding the teachings, and capable of helping both men and women to find the way to liberation.

.... The horoscope of the child revealed, so it was said, an unusual degree of courage and predicted that she would become an ascetic of great renown. In the meantime, she was an affectionate, friendly and intelligent child. They called her Dākhi, from *drākṣā*, bunch of grapes. In accordance with the custom of the day, she was affianced in childhood and up to the age of eight she knew the life of a happy family. The sudden death of her father was a terrible shock for her, for not only did she now lack his parental affection, but she began to ask the reason for her father's being so abruptly snatched from her. Life changed for her. Having neither brothers nor sisters, she remained alone with her mother, a young widow who was obliged to yield to the customs of her community. After many enquiries, this latter managed to trace the whereabouts of her cousin Sādhvi Suvarana and, taking Dākhi with her, stayed with her several times. Thus Dākhi came into contact with the sādhvis[4] whom she proceeded to astonish by the liveliness of her intelligence. The mother of Dākhi had decided to receive *dikṣā*[5] when her daughter married the young man to whom she had been betrothed. This, however, was not Dākhi's desire. She felt an attraction for the ascetic life and to fulfil this aspiration, she carried on a tenacious struggle with her paternal

[4] Sādhvi—a Jain nun.
[5] Dikṣā—consecration as a member of an ascetic Jain order.

grandfather, who loved her dearly and refused to give his consent to the *dikṣā*. The young man's family, perturbed and unhappy, also applied pressure. Dākhi struggled alone with a grandfather whom, at the same time, she loved—alone, as neither could her mother or the sādhvis help her in any way, for the grandfather would have accused them of bringing influence to bear upon the child.

Dākhi was kept at home and forbidden to go out to visit the temple or the *upāśrayā*.[6] Dākhi replied that she would obey, that, as she was being forbidden to go to the temple, she would fast. This, then, is what she did. In the evening of the first day of the fast, her grandfather, softened at heart, offered her a cup of milk, but Dākhi refused. Softened still further, the grandfather gave her permission to attend the temple, but re-affirmed stoutly that he would never give his consent to her receiving *dikṣā* and that Dākhi must needs get married. To this she replied that she would not disobey, so, said she, she would wait for *dikṣā* but would never on any account marry! Confrontations of this sort continued for one week. The grandfather, realizing his powerlessness to persuade Dākhi and despairing of the affair, lodged an appeal with the civil authorities. He informed them that the sādhvis had brought pressure to bear upon his thirteen-year-old granddaughter and were desirous of admitting her to *dikṣā* against the will of her guardian (himself); that they should be so good as to help him prevent Dākhi from joining the sādhvis. A *ṭhākura*, a type of magistrate of the district, was appointed to study the case and administer justice.

Here, now, are her chief replies in her dialogue with the magistrate:
Ṭhākura: "Do you really, my child, desire to embrace the ascetic life?"
Dākhi: "Yes, sir."
Ṭhākura: "Why?"
Dākhi: "It is an inner call."
Ṭhākura: "Why do you not wish to marry?"
Dākhi: "I have no desire for it."
Ṭhākura: "Do you know what the ascetic life means?"
Dākhi: "Without a knowledge of the ascetic life it is not possible to experience its attraction. I do know what is meant by both life in the world and by asceticism."
Ṭhākura: "Is not obedience to one's parents also part of the *dharma*?"
Dākhi: "Yes, indeed, but if it is clear that one's parents' demands are an obstacle to the full realization of human life and of the *atman*, respectfully to oppose these demands is not contrary to the *dharma*."
Ṭhākura: "Do you see, my child, what is in front of you?"
Dākhi: "Yes, it is a rifle."
Ṭhākura: (to test her) "Leave aside all these arguments of yours and do as

---

[6] Upāśrayā—community of renunciates.

your grandfather tells you. If not, I'm going to use this rifle."—and with that he grasped the rifle.

Dākhi: "If it is your duty to do so, use the rifle. I have no fear of death; one must die some day. It's all the same, whether I die today from a gunshot or tomorrow from some illness. It is a great thing to die for one's ideal.". . .

Finally, after all these painful contretemps, the mother and her daughter received *dikṣā*; Rūpāmadevi became Sādhvi Vijñāna Śri and Dākhi, Sādhvi Vicakṣaṇa Śri, *vicakṣaṇa* meaning the one who is farsighted, wise, intelligent, who has discernment.

[After the *dikṣā*, the young Sādhvi Vicakṣaṇa] became a disciple of Sādhvi Jatana Śri. Her two first *cāturmāsyas* were spent in Rājasthāna, at Baḍalū and at Javapura where she gave evidence of her capacity for study. Then, to her great joy, she was summoned to Delhi to the side of the *pravartini*,[7] Sādhvi Suvaraṇa. She stayed there until the latter's Great Departure, that is to say, about seven years. These years of training were thus passed under the direction of a remarkable guruni. Sādhvi Suvaraṇa attached prime importance to *dhyāna, svādhyāya* and *adhyayana*.[8] She was herself the example and also the inspiration of her disciples. For her, *dhyāna* did not consist solely in a technique that one followed for a limited time; *dhyāna* was, as it were, the breathing of her whole being. Her depth of contemplation, people say, was most striking. She habitually remained for six to seven hours in deep concentration, in which *japa*[9] alternated with long moments of silence. Whoever her interlocutor might be, she brooked no idle talk. During the last years of her life, her concentration intensified and she was used to remain thus silent and absorbed for about twelve hours.

Viśvamitrā: **The universal Friend**   After the years of training in Delhi, Sādhvi Vicakṣaṇa began her vihāras[10] up and down the country. We find her in the North, in the West, in the Centre and in the South. Her ardour is diminished by no obstacle or difficulty.

They have called her: *jaina kokitā*, the Jaina cuckoo, on account of her melodious voice, the sincerity and convincingness of her words, which, like the cuckoo's song, have enchanted all hearts. Of what does Sādhvi Vicakṣaṇa speak? Why do the crowds flock to hear her? The answer is simple: her language is direct, without pomposity or the slightest affectation; she goes straight to the essentials. It is her deep sincerity, her love for all living beings and the clarity with which she expresses herself that not only

---

[7] Pravartini—spiritual mother.
[8] Dhyāna—mental concentration; svādhyāya—reflective reading of scripture; adhyayana—general studies.
[9] Japa—recitation of a mantra.
[10] Vihāra—movement from one location to another.

captivate all hearts, but transforms them, removing both barriers and prejudices and lessening or even completely obliterating all enmities. . . .

In the presence of Digambaras, Sādhvi Vicakṣaṇa, herself a Śvetāmbara, attacks neither party, but rather seeks that which may unite them. At Hastināpura, a pilgrimage-place venerated by both traditions, but where the Digambaras are more numerous and more firmly entrenched, she broached the subject of the principal causes of dispute between them: can women attain *mokṣa?*[11] Do the *kevalins* take nourishment or not? The Digambaras answer both questions in the negative, the Śvetāmbaras in the affirmative. Addressing the whole assembly, she told them: "Do we not believe, you and I, that the *ātman*[12] is neither male nor female, that it is subject to no change and that male-ness and female-ness are due to the mode of *karman* relative to the body? But is *mokṣā* attained in the *ātman* or in the body?. . ." In the same vein, she said: "Do the *kevalins* take nourishment or not? Does that really affect the state of *kevāla-jñāna*? *Jñāna*[13] appertains to the *ātman*; nourishment is for the body. It is of little concern to us whether the *kevalins* take nourishment or not. Our aim is to believe in the state of being of the *kevalin* and to strive towards it. These useless quarrels are damaging and lead nowhere." Thus she exhorts them all, as disciples of Mahāvira, to drop these scholastic disputes inherited from the past, to come to a brotherly understanding and demonstrate *viśvamaitri*[14] instead of reviling one another.

SOURCE: "The renunciate life of Sādhvi Vicakṣaṇa," in N. Shanta, *The Unknown Pilgrims: The Voice of the Sādhvis: The history, spirituality and life of the Jaina women ascetics*, trans. from French by Mary Rogers. Delhi: Sri Satguru Publications, 1997, pp. 585–96

"The Righteous Path for Laity and Ascetics"
by Acharya Kund-Kund

Acharya Kund-Kund (c. 18 BCE–12 BCE) was a revered ascetic and teacher.

Conduct of laymen is eleven-fold, and of ascetics, ten-fold   Lord Jinendra who enjoys Supreme Bliss ordains an eleven-fold code of conduct for laymen and ten-fold for ascetics. This is based on right perception.

Code for the laity   The stage of the right view, of vows, of attaining equanimity, of fasting on certain holy days, of purity of nourishment, of not consuming food at night, of celibacy or absolute continence, of giving up occupation, of giving up possessions, abstinence from approving household

---

[11] Mokṣa—liberation of the soul from accumulated karma.
[12] Ātman—soul.
[13] Jñāna—knowledge.
[14] Viśvamaitri—universal friendship.

activities, and renunciation of specially prepared food or lodging: These are the eleven stages of the conduct of renunciation for laymen.

The ascetic's code of conduct   Supreme forgiveness, humility, uprightness, truthfulness, purity, restraint, austerity, renunciation, non-attachment, and celibacy: These are the ten forms of righteousness of the ascetics.

Supreme forgiveness   One who does not feel angry in the least, even while there are direct extraneous reasons for provocations to anger, observes the virtue of forgiveness.

Supreme humility   The ascetic who does not in the least feel proud about his ancestry, appearance, birth, wisdom, austerity, scriptural learning, and conduct, observes the virtue of humility.

Supreme uprightness   An ascetic, who abstaining from thoughts of deceit follows the code of conduct with a pure heart, observes the virtue of uprightness as enjoined.

Supreme truthfulness   An ascetic who abstains from speech that torments others and speaks what does good both to oneself and to others observes the fourth virtue of truthfulness.

Supreme purity   An ascetic in the highest stage who has freed himself of desires and conducts himself with aversion for them is endowed with the virtue of purity.

Supreme restraint   An ascetic who gives up the afflictions of mind, speech and body, overcomes all sensual desires and evolves himself by observing the vows and regulations, is endowed with the virtue of restraint.

Supreme austerity   A saint who through meditation and scriptural study realizes the consummation of the subjugation of sensual desires and passions and is devoted to contemplation of self, truly practices the virtue of austerity.

Supreme renunciation   The ascetic who has abjured the desire for all objects and is imbued with the three-fold detachment (from the mundane world, his own body, and pleasures) is endowed with the virtue of renunciation; so have the Jinendras declared.

Supreme non-attachment   The homeless ascetic who has forsaken all possessions, has subdued his thought impulses for pleasure and pain and acts with equanimity, is endowed with the virtue of non-attachment.

Supreme celibacy The ascetic who on seeing all parts of women's body refrains from excitement with passion about them is really able to practice the rigorous virtue of celibacy.
[Explanation: Sex, in fact, has no meaning to a saint who views the physical body as inert and extraneous matter.]

Only those who observe the ascetic's code attain liberation The soul that discontinues the laymen's path to follow the ascetic's righteous path cannot fail to attain emancipation. This ought to be the incessant contemplation on righteousness.

Contemplation of Self with equanimity From the real standpoint, the soul stands distinct from the vows of both the householder and the ascetic. The pure soul should therefore be contemplated upon constantly with equanimity.
[Explanation: With due consideration of practical norms, different codes of conduct have been prescribed for the pious householders and the ascetic. But this distinction is purely conventional.
From the strictly real standpoint, it is the pristine purity of the Soul that is to be contemplated upon. Self-realization is the ultimate goal of the householder and the ascetic alike. The layman in his spiritual quest adopts the ascetic's vows as he advances spiritually. His aim is to liberate himself from the karmic bondage.]

SOURCE: Acharya Kund–Kund, *Barasa Anuvekkha*, Kund Kund Bharati, 18-B, Special Institutional Area, New Delhi 110067, India, 1990, pp. 76–86

Jain ethics today

A globally respected contemporary Jain teacher, Acharya Tulsi, died in 1997 after many years of trying to demonstrate the practical relevance of Jain principles for modern life. He was himself a renowned renunciate. Although his preaching often took him from Rajasthan to other areas, he always walked on foot, according to strict renunciate principles. He placed particular emphasis on interfaith harmony, ending of warfare and nuclear arms, vegetarian lifestyle, meditation, and elimination of caste distinctions. Here he explains the far-reaching significance of *ahimsa*, or non-violence.

Non-violence: A Profile
by Acharya Tulsi

Ordinarily non-violence is taken as negative in meaning. "*Na himsa ahimsa*"—the absence of violence is non-violence. But this is a one-sided definition. In order to understand non-violence fully it is necessary to know both its positive and negative sides. However important avoidance of destroying life may be, much more important than that is the avoidance of any ill-feeling towards a living creature. Untrue thoughts and untrue speech both constitute violence. Behind all lies there is violence. Like untrue thoughts and speech, false behaviour towards anyone is also sheer violence. Every man is inclined towards both truth and falsehood, but any addition of falsehood to one's propensities is bound to make the latter violence-oriented.

Violence has a wide scope and includes malice, jealousy, the desire to obstruct the progress of others, and the efforts to come in the way of their growing reputation. Similarly, it also encompasses such tendencies as striking fear in others, engineering adverse situations against them and creating difficulties in their way. Non-violence aims at totally abstaining from these tendencies and this constitutes its negative aspect.

Equality, friendship, self-restraint and such other noble feelings make up its positive aspect. Here non-violence is not interpreted literally in the narrow sense of non-killing. Such limitation robs non-violence of its comprehensive meaning. As to the concept of equality, it admits of no limits. Friendship can flourish only in a climate of equality. It gives rise to a feeling of fraternity. Only when inspired by this fraternal awareness can a man truly comprehend and practice non-violence.

A non-violent man is he who does not in the least discriminate between rich and poor or between friend and foe. He is free from all dialectics and therefore of the love of self and of malice towards others. He shuns killing, doing harm to others, oppressing them and making them dependent on himself. He transforms his thoughts, speech and actions by keeping them immune from all falsehood.

Non-violence is the greatest ideal of life. It engenders many other ideals. Truth, non-thieving, chaste living and greedlessness are all related to it. In worshipping non-violence ideally one automatically worships all other virtues.

Non-violence acts like an invincible armour which is proof against hatred, ill-feeling, malice, revenge, fear and lust. One who is gifted with it leads a carefree life. He remains unruffled by the memories of the past and the apprehensions about the future. He cannot be a party to the taking of a wrong decision under the desire to preserve and perpetuate his self.

In fact observance of non-violence does good both to oneself and to others. It is only in a climate of non-violence that opposing ideologies can peacefully coexist. The truth is that humanistic values cannot gain any recognition in a society or country where non-violence is not valued. Non-violence is the best guarantee of humanity's survival and progress. A truly non-violent man is ever awake and is incapable of harbouring any ill will.

Non-violence is to violence what light is to darkness, what nectar is to poison and what life is to death. Comprehending and internalizing non-violence is the greatest achievement of life.

SOURCE: Acharya Tulsi, *Acharya Tulsi: Fifty Years of Selfless Dedication*. Ladnun (Rajasthan): Jain Vishva Bharati, 1985, pp. 7–8

GLOSSARY

Ahimsa Principle of non-violence, based on reverence for all life.

Anekantavada The principle of **manifold aspects**, or the relativity of knowledge.

Aparigraha (non-possessiveness), and Brahmacharya (chastity).

Digambara (atmosphere-clad) A nude Jain sect.

Five Jain Vows Ahimsa (non-violence), Satya (truthfulness), Asteya (non-stealing),

Jiva soul; every soul is potentially divine, and greatly influenced by karma.

Karma The cosmic law of consequences for moral action, leading to reincarnation.

Manifold aspects The multiplicity and relativity of all points of view, visible to perfected souls, promoting tolerance and non-violence.

Renunciation Reducing desires and minimizing consumption to free soul from karmic entanglements and lessen earthly pollution.

Stoicism Impassive indifference to pleasure or pain (Greek word).

Svetambara (white clad) A Jain sect that wears white clothing.

Syadvada The relativity of truth to different points of view.

Tirthankara (bridgebuilder) The 24 great enlightened Jain teachers.

HOLY DAYS

Most Jain festivals celebrate events in the lives of the Tirthankaras. Scriptures about their lives are read during the festivals.

Two of the most important are Paryushana and Diwali. **Diwali** is celebrated to commemorate Mahavira's attainment of *liberation*. **Paryushana** is the custom of the wandering monks staying in one place during the rainy season, when they meditate and teach local Jain householders the principles of the Dharma. **Pratikramana** is a meditation for reflecting on one's spiritual journey and renewing the faith. It may be daily, monthly or annually.

Samet Sikhar Yatra is a popular pilgrimage to Samet Sikhar in Bihar, India, where 20 Tirthankaras attained *nirvana*.

HISTORICAL OUTLINE

c. 900 BCE—life of 22nd Tirthankara, Arishtameni, who renounced the cruelty of society to become a wandering ascetic

c. 900–800 BCE—life of 23rd Tirthankara, "Beloved Parshva," a saintly teacher for 70 years

c. 599–527 BCE—life of Mahavira, greatest Jain saint and 24th Tirthankara

c. 100 CE—division of Jains into Svetambara (white-clad) and Digambara (atmosphere-clad, i.e. naked) sects

c. 300 BCE–*c.* 500 CE—lives of *Kevalins*

(omniscient beings) such as Siddhasena; emergence of new orders (e.g. Mula-Sangha) c. 1200—emergence of modern Jain communities

1526–1818—further orders and *Kevalins* emerge under Muslim Mughal rule (e.g. Tulsi Das, 1532–1623)

1818 onward—Jain teachers spread out from India

REVIEW QUESTIONS

1   From your study of Jain history and texts, what kind of society did they emerge from? How did that affect their beliefs?
2   Tell the story of Mahavir and his teachings.
3   Explain how Jains practice *ahimsa*, how it has influenced the wider world, and your opinion of its origin and effectiveness.
4   What are the five Jain vows? Do they seem severe? Why?
5   Contrast Western consumerism with Jain asceticism and evaluate each.
6   Does the Jain principle of manifold aspects of the relativity of truths have a place in religion, which usually stresses orthodoxy?

INFORMATION RESOURCES

Caillat, Colette, "Jainism," in *The Encyclopedia of Religion*, 1987, VII: 507–14.

De Bary, William T. ed. "Sources of Indian Tradition," vol. 1. New York: Columbia University Press, 1958.

Introduction to Jainism
<www.cs.colostate.edu/~malaiya/jainhlinks.html>

Jain Holy Days
<www.cs.colostate.edu/~malaiya/paryushan.html>

Jain Studies
<www.library.dmu.ac.uk/electinfo/subjainf.htm>

"**Jaina Sutras**," in Max Muller, ed. *Sacred Books of the East*. vols. XLV and XXII. Oxford: Oxford University Press, 1895.

Jain, Surender K. ed. *Glimpses of Jainism*. Delhi: Motilal Banarsidass Publishers, 1997.

Jain words glossary
<www.cs.colostate.edu/~malaiya/jaingloss.html>

Kund-Kund, Acharya, *Barasa Anuvekelada*, Kund Kund Bharati, 18-B, Special Institutional Area, New Delhi 110067, New Delhi, 1990.

Mahavira and Jainism
<www.san.beck.org/EC8-Mahavira.html>

Sangave, Dr. Vilas A. *Aspects of Jaina Religion*. Bharatiya Jnanpith, 18, Institutional Area, Lodi Road, New Delhi 11003, India, 1990.

Shah, Unmakant, and G. Ralph Strohl, "Jainism," in *Encyclopedia Britannica*, XXII: 247–53, 1997.

Tobias, Michael, *Life Force: The World of Jainism*. Berkeley, CA: Asian Humanities Press, 1991.

CHAPTER 5

BUDDHISM

Siddhartha Gautama, it is told, was born prince of the Sakya clan in northeastern India, and probably lived 563–483 BCE. He renounced his comfortable life to seek the solution to suffering. He first sat with famous gurus, and practiced severe austerities, almost starving himself to death. Unsatisfied, he meditated, awakened to his true nature, then taught a "middle way" between luxury and austerity.

The one who had become a Buddha, or Awakened One, taught a practical way of escaping from suffering and achieving liberation. Monks and then nuns whom he trained were organized into orders, and the teachings spread throughout Asia, south into Sri Lanka and southeast Asia, north into Tibet and China, and east into Korea and Japan. Three major historical traditions developed: the **Theravada**, the **Mahayana**, and the **Vajrayana**. Contemporary Buddhism, as it spreads across the globe, is strengthening an earlier theme: engaged Buddhism.

To become a Buddhist is to adopt the Three Refuges: "I take refuge in The Buddha, the Dharma, and the Sangha [community of practicing Buddhists]." It is not the Buddha who saves. It is by living by the Dharma which the Buddha taught that one achieves liberation from the continual painful round of births and deaths into the blissful state known as **nirvana**. The techniques for becoming conscious of the workings of the mind and for bringing it under control have become highly appealing to contemporary citizens of industrial societies who are seeking peace of mind.

Buddha taught the Four Noble Truths: **1.** Life inevitably involves suffering; **2.** Suffering originates in desires for transient things; **3.** Suffering can be ceased by the eradication of desires; **4.** The path to liberation from desires is the Eightfold Path: *a.* Right understanding, *b.* Right thoughts or motives, *c.* Right speech, *d.* Right action, *e.* Right livelihood, *f.* Right effort, *g.* Right mindfulness, and *h.* Right meditation. Buddhists undertake a further set of basic obligations or Precepts (*sila*): **1.** Not harming living beings; **2.** Not taking anything not given; **3.** Not misusing sensual pleasures; **4.** Not speaking falsely or abusively; **5.** Not taking intoxicating drinks or drugs; **6.** Not eating solid food after mid-day; **7.** Not engaging in frivolous amusements; **8.** Not adorning one's body; **9.** Not sleeping in a high or luxurious place; and **10.** Not being involved with money.

The Awakened One

Several elaborated traditional texts about the Buddha's life have been preserved and revered, notably the account told by Asvaghosha, who lived during the second century CE. In his Sanskrit epic *Buddhacarita*, or *Acts of the Buddha*, Asvaghosha shows a deep reverence for the Buddha.

Defeat of Mara and Enlightenment
by Asvaghosha

The enlightenment of the Buddha is described in detail in Asvaghosha's Acts of the Buddha. *Here Sakya Gautama, at age thirty-five, meditating at the foot of a Bodhi tree, is tempted by Mara, Hindu personification of evil. His temptations, such as sensual gratification and wantonness, are resisted by the Buddha, whose steadfast tranquillity defeats all of Mara's many beastly lures and transforms his thunderous wrath into harmless flowers. Similarly, Jesus defeats Satan's temptation during his desert retreat. Thus, enlightenment blossomed and Gautama became the Buddha.*

When the great sage, the scion of a line of royal seers, sat down there, after making his vow for liberation, the world rejoiced, but Mara, the enemy of the good Law, trembled. . . .

His three sons, Caprice, Gaiety and Wantonness, and his three daughters, Discontent, Delight and Thirst, asked him why he was depressed in mind, and he answered them thus:

"The sage, wearing the armour of his vow and drawing the bow of resolution with the arrow of wisdom, sits yonder, desiring to conquer my realm; hence this despondency of my mind." . . .

Then as soon as Māra thought of his army in his desire to obstruct the tranquillity of the Sākya sage, his followers stood round him, in various forms and carrying lances, trees, javelins, clubs and swords in their hands;

Having the faces of boars, fishes, horses, asses and camels, or the countenances of tigers, bears, lions and elephants, one-eyed, many-mouthed, three-headed, with pendulous bellies and speckled bellies; . . .

Then Māra gave orders to his raging army of demons for terrifying the sage. Thereon that army of his resolved to break down his steadfastness with their various powers.

Some stood trying to frighten him, their many tongues hanging out flickering, their teeth sharp-pointed, their eyes like the sun's orb, their mouths gaping, their ears sticking up stiff as spikes.

As they stood there in such guise, horrible in appearance and manner, he was no more alarmed by them or shrank before them than before over-excited infants at play. . . .

Some lifted up rocks and trees, but were unable to hurl them at the sage. Instead they fell down with the trees and rocks, like the spurs of the Vindhyas when shattered by the levin.[1] . . .

Thereon others spat out snakes from their mouths as from rotten treetrunks; as if bound by spells, they did not hiss or raise themselves or move in his presence.

Others transformed themselves into huge clouds, accompanied by lightning and the fearsome crash of thunder-stones, and let loose on the tree a shower of stones, which turned into a pleasant rain of flowers. . . .

The less the sage was afraid of the fearsome troops of that array, the more was Māra, the enemy of the upholders of the Law, cast down with grief and wrath.

Then a certain being of high station and invisible form, standing in the sky and seeing that Māra was menacing the seer . . . addressed him with imperious voice:

"Māra, you should not toil to no purpose, give up your murderous intent and go in peace. For this sage can no more be shaken by you than Meru, greatest of mountains, by the wind. . . .

For such is his vow, his energy, his psychic power, his compassion for creation, that he will not rise up till he has attained the truth, just as the thousand-rayed sun does not rise without dispelling the darkness. . . .

His purpose is to deliver creation which is bound fast in mind by the snares of delusion." . . .

And when Māra heard that speech of his and observed the great sage's unshakenness, then, his efforts frustrated, he went away dejectedly with the arrows by which the world is smitten in the heart. . . .

The heavens shone with the moon like a maiden with a smile, and there fell a rain of sweet-smelling flowers filled with water. . . .

Then, after conquering Māra's host by his steadfastness and tranquillity, he, the master of trance, put himself into trance in order to obtain exact knowledge of the ultimate reality. . . .

As though living them over again, he recalled thousands of births, that he had been so-and-so in such-and-such a place and that passing out of that life he had come hither.

Then the compassionate one was filled with compassion for all living beings. . . .

Then with that completely purified divine eyesight he beheld the entire world, as it were in a spotless mirror.

His compassionateness waxed greater, as he saw the passing away and rebirth of all creatures according as their acts were lower or higher.

Those living beings whose acts are sinful pass to the sphere of misery, those others whose deeds are good win a place in the triple heaven.

[1.] Levin—lightning.

The former are reborn in the very dreadful fearsome hell and, alas, are woefully tormented with sufferings of many kinds. . . .

Thus with the divine eyesight he examined the five spheres of life and found nothing substantial in existence, just as no heartwood is found in a plantain tree when it is cut open. . . .

"Alas! Living creatures obtain but toil; over and over again they are born, grow old, die, pass on and are reborn.

Further man's sight is veiled by passion and by the darkness of delusion, and from the excess of his blindness he does not know the way out of this great suffering." . . .

Penetrating the truth to its core, he understood that old age and death are produced, when there is birth. . . .

Then he saw rightly that birth is produced from existence due to the power of the act.

With his divine eyesight he saw that active being proceeds from the act, not from a Creator or from Nature or from a self or without a cause. . . .

Then this conclusion came firmly on him, that from the annihilation of birth old age and death are suppressed, that from the destruction of existence birth itself is destroyed. . . .

Further the latter is suppressed through the suppression of thirst; if sensation does not exist, thirst does not exist. . . .

Similarly if name-and-form is rightly suppressed, all the six organs of sense are destroyed too; and the former is suppressed through the suppression of consciousness. . . .

The best of men saw no self anywhere from the summit of existence downwards and came to tranquillity, like a fire whose fuel is burnt out, by the eightfold path of supreme insight, which starts forth and quickly reaches the desired point. . . .

Pleasant breezes blew softly, the heaven rained moisture from a cloudless sky, and from the trees there dropped flowers and fruit out of due season as if to do him honour. . . .

At that moment none gave way to anger, no one was ill or experienced any discomfort, none resorted to sinful ways or indulged in intoxication of mind; the world became tranquil, as though it had reached perfection.

The companies of deities, who are devoted to salvation, rejoiced; even the beings in the spheres below felt joy. Through the prosperity of the party who favoured virtue the *dharma* spread abroad and the world rose above passion and the darkness of ignorance. . . .

Then for seven days, free from discomfort of body, he sat, looking into his own mind, his eyes never winking. The sage fulfilled his heart's desire, reflecting that on that spot he had obtained liberation.

Then the sage, who had grasped the principle of causation and was firmly fixed in the system of impersonality, roused himself, and, filled with great compassion, he gazed on the world with his Buddha-eye for the sake of its tranquillity.

Seeing that the world was lost in false views and vain efforts and that its passions were gross, seeing too that the law of salvation was exceeding subtle, he set his mind on remaining immobile.

Then remembering his former promise, he formed a resolution for the preaching of tranquillity....

Then, wishing to preach tranquillity in order to dispel the darkness of ignorance, as the rising sun the darkness, Gautama proceeded to the blessed city.

SOURCE: Asvaghosha, *The Buddhacarita, or Acts of the Buddha*, trans. E. H. Johnson. Delhi: Motilal Banarsidass, new edn 1984, pp. 188–217

Speculations Undeclared
from the Culamalunkya Sutta

One of the Buddha's most notable teachings was his practical rejection of most metaphysical speculation. In this passage from the Culamalunkya Sutta, he teaches Māuenkyāputta, a disciple, that efforts to answer speculative questions such as whether the world is eternal are fruitless. They are like a man shot with an arrow who refuses to allow medical treatment until he is told the social caste of his attacker, his size, his skin color, his home town, and the details of his weapon. Before he learned all this, he would die. The Buddha left such speculative metaphysics undeclared because they do not lead to the direct meditative experience of enlightenment that overcomes suffering.

Thus have I heard. On one occasion the Blessed One was living at Sāvatthī in Jeta's Grove, Anāthapindika's Park.

Then, while the venerable Mālunkyaputta was alone in meditation, the following thought arose in his mind:

"These speculative views have been undeclared by the Blessed One, set aside and rejected by him, namely: 'the world is eternal' and 'the world is not eternal'; 'the world is finite' and 'the world is infinite'; 'the soul is the same as the body' and 'the soul is one thing and the body another'; and 'after death a Tathāgata[2] exists' and 'after death a Tathāgata does not exist' and 'after death a Tathāgata both exists and does not exist' and 'after death a Tathāgata neither exists nor does not exist.' The Blessed One does not declare these to me, and I do not approve of and accept the fact that he does not declare these to me, so I shall go to the Blessed One and ask him the meaning of this." ...

"Suppose, Mālunkyāputta, a man were wounded by an arrow thickly

---

[2] Tathāgata—("transcendent one") one who has realized the truth.

smeared with poison, and his friends and companions, his kinsmen and relatives, brought a surgeon to treat him. The man would say: 'I will not let the surgeon pull out this arrow until I know whether the man who wounded me was a noble or a brahmin or a merchant or a worker.' And he would say: 'I will not let the surgeon pull out this arrow until I know the name and clan of the man who wounded me; . . . until I know whether the man who wounded me was tall or short or of middle height; . . . until I know whether the man who wounded me was dark or brown or golden-skinned; . . . until I know whether the man who wounded me lives in such a village or town or city; . . . until I know whether the bow that wounded me was a long bow or a crossbow; . . . until I know whether the bowstring that wounded me was fibre or reed or sinew or hemp or bark; . . . until I know whether the shaft that wounded me was wild or cultivated; . . . until I know with what kind of feathers the shaft that wounded me was fitted—whether those of a vulture or a crow or a hawk or a peacock or a stork; . . .

"All this would still not be known to that man and meanwhile he would die. . . .

"Mālunkyāputta, if there is the view 'the world is eternal,' the holy life cannot be lived; and if there is the view 'the world is not eternal,' the holy life cannot be lived. Whether there is the view 'the world is eternal' or the view 'the world is not eternal,' there is birth, there is ageing, there is death, there are sorrow, lamentation, pain, grief, and despair, the destruction of which I prescribe here and now. . . .

"Therefore, Mālunkyāputta, remember what I have left undeclared as undeclared, and remember what I have declared as declared. And what have I left undeclared? 'The world is eternal'—I have left undeclared. 'The world is not eternal'—I have left undeclared. 'The world is finite'—I have left undeclared. 'The world is infinite'—I have left undeclared. 'The soul is the same as the body'—I have left undeclared. 'The soul is one thing and the body another'—I have left undeclared. 'After death a Tathāgata exists'—I have left undeclared. 'After death a Tathāgata does not exist'—I have left undeclared. 'After death a Tathāgata both exists and does not exist'—I have left undeclared. 'After death a Tathāgata neither exists nor does not exist'—I have left undeclared.

"Why have I left that undeclared? Because it is unbeneficial, it does not belong to the fundamentals of the holy life, it does not lead to disenchantment, to dispassion, to cessation, to peace, to direct knowledge, to enlightenment, to Nibbāna.[3] That is why I have left it undeclared.

"And what have I declared? 'This is suffering'—I have declared. 'This is the origin of suffering'—I have declared. 'This is the cessation of suffering'—I have declared. 'This is the way leading to the cessation of suffering'—I have declared.

---

[3] Nibbāna—nirvana.

"Why have I declared that? Because it is beneficial, it belongs to the fundamentals of the holy life, it leads to disenchantment, to dispassion, to cessation, to peace, to direct knowledge, to enlightenment, to Nibbāna. That is why I have declared it.

"Therefore, Mālunkyāputta, remember what I have left undeclared as undeclared, and remember what I have declared as declared."

That is what the Blessed One said. The venerable Mālunkyāputta was satisfied and delighted in the Blessed One's words.

SOURCE: *The Middle Length Discourses of the Buddha*, trans. Bhikkhu Nanamoli and Bikkhu Bodhi. Boston: Wisdom Publications, 1995.

Theravada

The Theravada ("Teaching of the Elders") traditions are the traditions of Buddhism as it spread south, to Sri Lanka (largely in the third century CE), then to southeast Asia, to regions now called Myanmar, Malaysia, Indonesia, and Cambodia (eleventh to fourteenth centuries). Theravada adheres to early scriptures (Suttas) and monastic renunciation. Its texts are drawn from the Pali Canon, recorded in Sri Lanka as early as the first century BCE. Theravadan mediation emphasizes stages of attainment and mindfulness or **Vipassana** (insight) meditation. The ideal Buddhist is the arhat, a monk taking refuge in the Buddha, an accomplished ascetic who attains nirvana (nibbana in Pali) through self-effort.

The Fully Enlightened
from the Dhammapada

The Dhammapada ("Teaching of the Verses") is a collection of 423 key Buddhist verses of wide influence and importance. Teachers are often expected to conclude a discourse with a key verse (gatha), and this text is a collection of such verses. It urges a life of peace and non-violence, and teaches that hatred can never be overcome by hatred, only by kindness. **Karmic** *consequences follow from all actions, and actions follow naturally from thoughts. This extract emphasizes the importance of restraint and awakening to transcendence, rather than resorting simply to a life of seclusion. The texts are recorded in Pali, Tibetan, Chinese, and other languages. One traditional commentary is attributed to Buddhaghosha.*

Whose victory is not turned into defeat,
Whose victory no one in this world reaches,
That Awakened One whose range is limitless,
Him, the trackless, by what track will you lead?

For whom craving there is not, the netlike, the clinging,
To lead him wheresoever,

That Awakened One whose range is limitless,
Him, the trackless, by what track will you lead?

Those who are intent on meditating, the wise ones,
Delighting in the calm of going out,
Even gods long for them,
The Fully Enlightened Ones, the mindful.

Difficult is the attainment of the human state.
Difficult the life of mortals.
Difficult is the hearing of dharma true.
Difficult the appearance of Awakened Ones.

Refraining from all that is detrimental,
The attainment of what is wholesome,
The purification of one's mind:
This is the instruction of Awakened Ones.

Forbearing patience is the highest austerity;
Nibbāna is supreme, the Awakened Ones say.
One who has gone forth is not one who hurts another,
No harasser of others is a recluse.

No faultfinding, no hurting, restraint in the [laws],
Knowing the measure regarding food, solitary bed and chair,
Application, too, of higher perception:
This is the instruction of the Awakened Ones.

Not even with a rain of golden coins
Is contentment found among sensual pleasures.
"Sensual pleasures are of little delight, are a misery."
Knowing so, the wise one
Takes no delight
Even for heavenly sensual pleasures.
One who delights in the ending of craving
Is a disciple of the Fully Enlightened One.

Many for refuge go
To mountains and to forests,
To shrines that are groves or trees—
Humans who are threatened by fear.

This is not a refuge secure,
This refuge is not the highest.

Having come to this refuge,
One is not released from all misery.

But who to the Buddha, Dhamma,
And Sangha as refuge has gone,
Sees with full insight
The four noble truths;

Misery, the arising of misery,
And the transcending of misery,
The noble Eightfold Path
Leading to the allaying of misery.

This, indeed, is a refuge secure.
This is the highest refuge.
Having come to this refuge,
One is released from all misery.

SOURCE: *The Dhammapada*, trans. John Ross Carter and Mahinda Palihawadana, New York and Oxford: Oxford University Press, 1987, pp. 44–5

Rejection of Birth Castes
from the Vasettha Sutta

When the Buddha was living, there were several religious movements in India that arose out of dissatisfaction with the external religious formalities and the rigid social implications of the Hindu brahmanic caste system. Some protested against this system by becoming wandering ascetics. The Hindu Upanishads literature grew out of this movement, emphasizing renunciation and transcendental knowledge, rather than ritual and caste. In northeastern India, less influenced by the brahmanic traditions, arose several non-orthodox sects, including Buddhism. This extract, from the Vasettha Sutta, *is a Buddhist statement rejecting the belief that one is born into one's social caste, and affirming that one's merit is determined by one's actions.*

One is not a brahmin by birth,
Nor by birth a non-brahmin.
By action is one a brahmin,
By action is one a non-brahmin.

For men are farmers by their acts,
And by their acts are craftsmen too;
And men are merchants by their acts,
And by their acts are servants too.

And men are robbers by their acts,
And by their acts are soldiers too
And men are chaplains by their acts,
And by their acts are rulers too.

SOURCE: Bhikkhu Nanamoli and Bhikkhu Bodhi. Boston: Wisdom Publications, 1995, p. 806

Mahayana

Mahayana ("Large Vehicle") Buddhism is most prominent in Tibet, Mongolia, China, Korea, Vietnam, and Japan. The Mahayana **dharma** (teaching) emphasizes one's inherent wisdom and compassion for all sentient beings. The ideal practitioner (**bodhisattva**) honors the Pali Canon, yet delays his/her own nirvana in the effort to liberate other beings. Mahayana texts (sutras) emphasize the Buddha-nature (Buddhata) in all things and the importance of direct experience. The Buddha is not seen as primarily a historical person, as in Theravada, but is now seen rather as a universal principle, a cosmic presence. Images of this Buddha-nature are common, although they are not to be conceived of as divinities. Two widespread bodhisattvas expressing compassion and mercy are Avalokiteshvara (masculine) and Kwan-Yin (feminine). Mahayana dharma also teaches the emptiness of all things, in paradoxical language meant to take the mind beyond ordinary thought.

Emptiness
by Nagarjuna

Sunyata *(emptiness) is a basic element of Mahayana Buddhism. This is a very subtle and debatable term, full of paradox. Early Buddhism initially rejected the brahmanic notion of the Atman, or eternal soul, and opposed it with the Anatman. For Buddhists, the five aggregates (**skandhas**) composing a human are empty of a permanent soul. This concept was soon extended to deny any permanent self-existing essence or substance in all of the universe. Buddhists emphasize that when we envision the independent existence of things, we cling to them. Seeing their basic emptiness permits us to release the clinging. Nagarjuna was a major Buddhist philosopher who lived in India about 150–250 CE. His philosophy of emptiness has had enduring importance in subsequent Buddhist thought, and is central to Mahayana's Prajnaparamita (Perfection of Wisdom) literature. The source of existence, he argues, cannot be described, but only realized meditatively, due to its undifferentiated nature. In sunyata all oppositions between earth and heaven, nirvana and **samsara**, disappear. Worldly appearances, gods, and the self do have a conventional nature, but no independent substance, or self-existent thing-ness. Nagarjuna's "emptiness" is not the Western void of a hellish meaninglessness, or a denial of the world, but the very reason that the world exists.*

An Analysis of a Self-existent Thing

1   The production of a self-existent thing by a conditioning cause is not possible, [for,] being produced through dependence on a cause, a self-existent thing would be "something which is produced."

2   How, indeed, will a self-existent thing *become* "something which is produced"?
Certainly, a self-existent thing [by definition] is "not-produced" and is independent of anything else.

3   If there is an absence of a self-existent thing, how will an other-existent thing come into being?

SOURCE: Streng, Frederick, *Emptiness: A Study in Religious Meaning.* Nashville: Abingdon Press, p. 199

The Heart Sutra

The Heart Sutra comes from the Indian Prajnaparamita literature, about 350 CE. It distills the teachings on emptiness. The goal is to become a bodhisattva, seeking complete understanding, and dedicated to serving others by skillful means. Simultaneously, the realization is that there is no such thing as a bodhisattva, understanding, dedication, or attainment. To realize this emptiness is to approach perfection of wisdom.

Homage to the Perfection of Wisdom, the lovely, the holy!

Avalokita,[4] the holy Lord and Bodhisattva, was moving in the deep course of the wisdom which has gone beyond. He looked down from on high, he beheld but five heaps,[5] and he saw that in their own-being they were empty.

Here, O Sariputra,[6] form is emptiness, and the very emptiness is form; emptiness does not differ from form, form does not differ from emptiness; whatever is form, that is emptiness, whatever is emptiness, that is form. The same is true of feelings, perceptions, impulses and consciousness.

Here, O Sariputra, all dharmas are marked with emptiness; they are not produced or stopped, not defiled or immaculate, not deficient or complete.

Therefore, O Sariputra, in emptiness there is no form, nor feeling, nor perception, nor impulse, nor consciousness; no eye, ear, nose, tongue, body, mind; no forms, sounds, smells, tastes, touchables or objects of mind; no sight-organ-element, and so forth until we come to: no mind-consciousness-element; there is no ignorance, no extinction of ignorance, and so forth until we come to: there is no decay and death, no extinction of decay and

[4] Avalokita—a form of the Buddha emphasizing compassion.
[5] Heaps—the skandhas or five aggregates.
[6] Sariputra—one of the Buddha's two principal followers.

death; there is no suffering, no origination, no stopping, no path; there is no cognition, no attainment, and no non-attainment.

Therefore, O Sariputra, it is because of his indifference to any kind of personal attainment that a Bodhisattva, through having relied on the perfection of wisdom, dwells without thought-coverings. In the absence of thought coverings he has not been made to tremble, he has overcome what can upset, and in the end he attains to Nirvana. All those who appear as Buddhas in the three periods of time fully awake to the utmost, right and perfect enlightenment because they have relied on the perfection of wisdom.

Therefore one should know the Prajnaparamita as the great spell, the spell of great knowledge, the utmost spell, the unequalled spell, allayer of all suffering, in truth—for what could go wrong? By the Prajnaparamita has this spell been delivered. It runs like this: *Gate! Gate! Paragate! Parasamgate! Bodhi Svaha!* (Gone, Gone, Gone beyond, Gone altogether beyond, O what an awakening) All Hail! This completes the Heart of Perfect Wisdom.

SOURCE: Edward Conze, ed., *Buddhist Scriptures*. Harmondsworth, Middx: Penguin, 1986, pp. 162–4

Discovering Universal Emptiness
by Dogen

Dogen was a leading Japanese Buddhist philosopher who lived 1200–1253 in Kyoto and had a major influence on Zen. Orphaned at age seven, he joined a monastery at age thirteen, then traveled to China, returned to Japan, founded the Soto Zen sect, and the still-active Eiheiji temple. He struggled with questions such as whether enlightenment is gradual or instantaneous, and concluded that in all zazen *(sitting meditation) one is in the midst of realizing Buddha-nature. Some said all things* have *the Buddha-nature, but he said that all things* are *the Buddha-nature, although this realization remains dormant until awakened in Buddhist practice. Zazen is the practice of non-thinking, which goes beyond ideas of good or bad, enlightenment or illusion, because universal emptiness is as close as your nose.*

When we reflect upon our experience and practice of zazen we actualize the life of the Buddhas and Patriarchs and receive their right transmission which has been handed down from generation to generation. Our subject today is universal emptiness—the universal emptiness that is in our entire body, skin, flesh, bones and marrow. Universal emptiness has numerous meanings and interpretations—the twenty kinds, the 84,000 kinds and so on—[and if you can define it properly you can be said to be a Buddha or Patriarch].

Zen Master Shakyō Ezō once asked Zen Master Seidō Chizō, who was Shakyō's senior, "Do you know how to comprehend universal emptiness?" "Of course," Seidō answered. "How?" Shakyō wanted to know. Seidō grasped a handful of air. "Aha! You don't know how to grasp it then!" Shakyō exclaimed. Seidō challenged Shakyō to show him universal emptiness. Shakyō grabbed Seidō's nose and yanked it until he cried out in pain. "Now I've got it!" Seidō said. "Yes, now you know what it is," Shakyō agreed.

The purpose of Shakyō's initial question was to find whether or not our entire body is hands and eyes [i.e., universal emptiness]. Seidō's "Of course" was a defilement of Buddhism. To say you understand universal emptiness is to defile the truth—universal emptiness falls to the earth. When Shakyō asked Seidō how he understood universal emptiness he was asking him to show the "suchness" of universal emptiness; that is, show the true state of reality. However, we must be careful about this since circumstances are constantly changing the form of "suchness." When Seidō grabbed a handful of air it revealed that he understood only the head, but not the tail, of universal emptiness. Shakyō then saw that Seidō's understanding was limited and he could not even dream about universal emptiness. It was too profound and absolute for him. Therefore, Seidō asked Shakyō to show him universal emptiness. Half of the answer was already contained in Seidō's request but he had to discover the rest by himself. Shakyō grabbed his nose; he hid in Seidō's nostril so to speak. At that time universal emptiness in the form of Seidō and universal emptiness in the form of Shakyō were united and only universal emptiness remained. Prior to having his nose yanked Seidō thought that universal emptiness existed outside himself, but now he has cast off body and mind. Yet you must be careful not to cling to such a discovery of universal emptiness—do not defile yourself but practice within your own universal emptiness. Shakyō confirmed Seidō's understanding but did not try to grasp universal emptiness with his hands—universal emptiness cannot be grasped with our hands. After all, the entire world is universal emptiness; there is absolutely no room for doubt. We can now see why this koan[7] is so famous.

SOURCE: Dogen Zenji, *Shobogenzo (The Eye and Treasury of the True Law)*, vol. 1, trans. Kosen Nishiyama and John Stevens. Sendai, Japan: Daihokkaikaku, 1975, pp. 130–31

Zen and Koans
by Daisetz T. Suzuki

D. T. Suzuki (1870–1966), a major early popularizer of Zen in the United States, taught Buddhist philosophy in Kyoto, Japan. He began Zen training at age twenty-two, then spent thirteen years in the U.S., translating and writing about Zen. He spoke to Westerners in the language of ego ("We are too ego-centered"), love (which gives us "a glimpse into the infinity of things"), and tragedy ("God gives tragedies to perfect man"), as we can see in the first part of the extract below. In the second part,

---

[7] Koan—a paradoxical riddle in Zen training, challenging the student to break through conventional thought.

Suzuki discusses the classic method of learning by the Zen koan, *a riddle given to a student by a Zen master. Classic koans are "What is the sound of one hand clapping?" or "Show me your face before you were born." It may create a frustrating crisis for the student, but the Master strives to guide one past the merely intellectual answer into the Buddha-mind.*

We are too ego-centred. The ego-shell in which we live is the hardest thing to outgrow. We seem to carry it all the time from childhood up to the time we finally pass away. We are, however, given many chances to break through this shell, and the first and greatest of them is when we reach adolescence. This is the first time the ego really comes to recognize the "other". I mean the awakening of sexual love. An ego, entire and undivided, now begins to feel a sort of split in itself. Love hitherto dormant deep in his heart lifts its head and causes a great commotion in it. For the love now stirred demands at once the assertion of the ego and its annihilation. Love makes the ego lose itself in the object it loves, and yet at the same time it wants to have the object as its own. This is a contradiction, and a great tragedy of life. This elemental feeling must be one of the divine agencies whereby man is urged to advance in his upward walk. God gives tragedies to perfect man. The greatest bulk of literature ever produced in this world is but the harping on the same string of love, and we never seem to grow weary of it. But this is not the topic we are concerned with here. What I want to emphasize in this connection is this: that through the awakening of love we get a glimpse into the infinity of things, and that this glimpse urges youth to Romanticism or to Rationalism according to his temperament and environment and education.

When the ego-shell is broken and the "other" is taken into its own body, we can say that the ego has denied itself or that the ego has taken its first steps towards the infinite. Religiously, here ensues an intense struggle between the finite and the infinite, between the intellect and a higher power, or, more plainly, between the flesh and the spirit. . . .

What is a koan?

A koan, according to one authority, means "a public document setting up a standard of judgment," whereby one's Zen understanding is tested as to its correctness. A koan is generally some statement made by an old Zen master, or some answer of his given to a questioner. The following are some that are commonly given to the uninitiated:

1. A monk asked Tung-shan, "Who is the Buddha?" "Three *chin* of flax."

2. Yun-men was once asked, "When not a thought is stirring in one's mind, is there any error here?" "As much as Mount Sumeru."

3. Chao-chou answered, "*Wu!*" (*mu* in Japanese) to a monk's question, "Is there Buddha-nature in a dog?" *Wu* literally means "not" or "none", but when this is ordinarily given as a koan, it has no reference to its literal signification; it is "*Wu*" pure and simple.

4. When Ming the monk overtook the fugitive Hui-neng, he wanted Hui-neng to give up the secret of Zen. Hui-neng replied, "What are your original features which you have even prior to your birth?"

5. A monk asked Chao-chou, "What is the meaning of the First Patriarch's visit to China?" "The cypress tree in the front courtyard."

6. When Chao-chou came to study Zen under Nan-ch'uan, he asked, "What is the Tao (or the Way)?" Nan-ch'uan replied, "Your everyday mind, that is the Tao."

7. A monk asked, "All things are said to be reducible to the One, but where is the One to be reduced?" Chao-chou answered, "When I was in the district of Ch'ing I had a robe made that weighed seven *chin*."

8. When P'ang the old Zen adept first came to Ma-tsu in order to master Zen, he asked, "Who is he who has no companion among the ten thousand things of the world?" Ma-tsu replied, "When you swallow up in one draught all the water in the Hsi Ch'iang, I will tell you."

When such problems are given to the uninitiated for solution, what is the object of the master? The idea is to unfold the Zen psychology in the mind of the uninitiated, and to reproduce the state of consciousness, of which these statements are the expression. That is to say, when the koans are understood the master's state of mind is understood, which is satori[8] and without which Zen is a sealed book.

In the beginning of Zen history a question was brought up by the pupil to the notice of the master, who thereby gauged the mental state of the questioner and knew what necessary help to give him. The help thus given was sometimes enough to awaken him to realization, but more frequently than not puzzled and perplexed him beyond description, and the result was an ever-increasing mental strain or "searching and contriving" on the part of the pupil, of which we have already spoken in the foregoing pages. In actual cases, however, the master would have to wait for a long while for the pupil's first question, if it were coming at all. To ask the first question means more than half the way to its own solution, for it is the outcome of a most intense mental effort for the questioner to bring his mind to a crisis. The question indicates that the crisis is reached and the mind is ready to leave it behind. An experienced master often knows how to lead the pupil to a crisis and to make him successfully pass it. . . .

The worst enemy of Zen experience, at least in the beginning, is the intellect, which consists and insists in discriminating subject from object. The discriminating intellect, therefore, must be cut short if Zen consciousness is to unfold itself, and the koan is constructed eminently to serve this end.

SOURCE: D. T. Suzuki, *Zen Buddhism*, ed. William Barrett. New York: Doubleday, 1956, pp. 6–7, 134–7

---

[8] Satori—awakening, or enlightenment.

Nothing to Do with Rules
by Bankei

In a radical form Buddhism challenges one to live so fully from the Buddha mind that rules and precepts would not be necessary to guide behavior. A sense of rightness would so naturally flow that externally imposed rules would be superfluous. This is the view articulated here by the seventeenth-century Zen master Bankei (1622–1693). Zen was becoming overly formalized in Japan in his time, so he insisted on spontaneity and such a clear everyday awareness of the Unborn Buddha Mind that precepts (the basic obligations undertaken by Buddhists) would be dispensable. In the West this view is echoed by Augustine's saying "Love and do what you will."

A certain master of the Precepts School asked: "Doesn't your Reverence observe the precepts?"

The Master said: "Originally, what people call the precepts were all for wicked monks who broke the rules; for the man who abides in the Unborn Buddha Mind, there's no need for precepts. The precepts were taught to help sentient beings—they weren't taught to help buddhas! What everyone has from his parents innately is the Unborn Buddha Mind alone, so abide in the Unborn Buddha Mind. When you abide in the Unborn Buddha Mind, you're a living buddha here today, and that living buddha certainly isn't going to concoct anything like taking the precepts, so there aren't any precepts for him to take. To concoct anything like taking the precepts is not what's meant by the Unborn Buddha Mind. When you abide in the Unborn Buddha Mind, there's no way you can violate the precepts. From the standpoint of the Unborn, the precepts too are secondary, peripheral concerns; in the place of the Unborn, there's really no such thing as precepts."

SOURCE: *Bankei Zen: Translations from the Record of Bankei*, trans. Peter Haskel. New York: Grove Press, 1984, p. 7

Vajrayana

Vajrayana ("Diamond Vehicle") Buddhim began in India, perhaps in Nagarjuna's time, and spread to Tibet. It encourages students to learn from both Theravada and Mahayana principles, then study Vajrayana. This school teaches that emptiness (*sunyata*) is complemented by the compassion of the bodhisattva (*karuna*), and also that the wisdom (*prajna*) of emptiness has an indestructible, diamond (*vajra*) quality that cuts through dualistic illusions. Compassion is the dynamic means (*upaya*) of acting in the world. Enlightenment emerges when wisdom and compassion are experientially discovered to be one. Further, physical-mental processes can also become vehicles for enlightenment. This approach is related to Hindu Tantric ritual practices, and requires guidance from a compassionate teacher (*lama*). Rich in artistry, Vajrayana uses images of divinities, *mudras* (meditative gestures and postures), *mantras* (sacred syllables and phrases), and *mandalas* (sacred circular designs) as aids to meditation.

Love, Kindness, and Universal Responsibility
by the Dalai Lama

Today, since Tibetan Buddhism was forced into exile in India and Nepal beginning with the Chinese takeover of Tibet in 1950, the current Dalai Lama, Tenzin Gyatso, Tibet's religious and temporal leader, has become a global spokesman for Vajrayana Buddhism. He has spoken with such peaceful integrity and wisdom that he was awarded a Nobel Peace Prize in 1989, for his adherence to Buddhist non-violence in the struggle with China. This is an extract from his Nobel Prize acceptance speech. He speaks of the dangers of the population and environmental crises, consumerism, religious intolerance, and the need for non-violence and compassion. In exile, he has attempted to shift his culture from a theocratic to a democratic government. A leader forcefully exiled from his country, still he inspires many by translating Buddhist principles of compassion and patience into contemporary application.

I believe that every individual has a responsibility to help guide our global family in the right direction. Good wishes alone are not enough; we have to assume responsibility. . . .

As the twentieth century draws to a close, we find that the world has grown smaller and the world's people have become almost one community. Political and military alliances have created large multinational groups, industry and international trade have produced a global economy, and worldwide communications are eliminating ancient barriers of distance, language and race. We are also being drawn together by the grave problems we face: over-population, dwindling natural resources, and an environmental crisis that threatens our air, water, and trees, along with the vast number of beautiful life forms that are the very foundation of existence on this small planet we share.

I believe that to meet the challenge of our times, human beings will have to develop a greater sense of universal responsibility. Each of us must learn to work not just for his or her own self, family or nation, but for the benefit of all mankind. Universal responsibility is the real key to human survival. It is the best foundation for world peace, the equitable use of natural resources, and through concern for future generations, the proper care of the environment. . . .

Whether we like it or not, we have all been born on this earth as part of one great human family. Rich or poor, educated or uneducated, belonging to one nation or another, to one religion or another, adhering to this ideology or that, ultimately each of us is just a human being like everyone else: we all desire happiness and do not want suffering. Furthermore, each of us has an equal right to pursue these goals.

Today's world requires that we accept the oneness of humanity. In the past, isolated communities could afford to think of one another as fundamentally separate and even existed in total isolation. Nowadays, however, events in one part of the world eventually affect the entire planet. Therefore we have to treat each major local problem as a global concern from the moment it begins. We can no longer invoke the national, racial or ideological barriers that separate us without destructive repercussion. In the context of our new interdependence, considering the interests of others is clearly the best form of self-interest.

I view this fact as a source of hope. The necessity for cooperation can only strengthen mankind, because it helps us recognize that the most secure foundation for the new world order is not simply broader political and economic alliances, but rather each individual's genuine practice of love and compassion. For a better, happier, more stable and civilized future, each of us must develop a sincere, warm-hearted feeling of brother- and sisterhood. . . .

I believe that despite the rapid advances made by civilization in this century, the most immediate cause of our present dilemma is our undue emphasis on material development alone. We have become so engrossed in its pursuit that, without even knowing it, we have neglected to foster the most basic human needs of love, kindness, cooperation and caring. If we do not know someone or find another reason for not feeling connected with a particular individual or group, we simply ignore them. But the development of human society is based entirely on people helping each other. Once we have lost the essential humanity that is our foundation, what is the point of pursuing only material improvement?. . . .

In particular, a tremendous effort will be required to bring compassion into the realm of international business. Economic inequality, especially that between developed and developing nations, remains the greatest source of suffering on this planet. Even though they will lose money in the short term, large multinational corporations must curtail their exploitation of poor nations. Tapping the few precious resources such countries possess simply to fuel consumerism in the developed world is disastrous; if it continues unchecked, eventually we shall all suffer. Strengthening weak, un-diversified economies is a far wiser policy for promoting both political and economic stability. As idealistic as it may sound, altruism, not just competition and the desire for wealth, should be a driving force in business. . . .

One religion, like a single type of food, cannot satisfy everybody. According to their varying mental dispositions, some people benefit from one kind of teaching, others from another. Each faith has the ability to produce fine, warmhearted people and all religions have succeeded in doing so, despite their espousal of often contradictory philosophies. Thus there is no reason to engage in divisive religious bigotry and intolerance and every reason to cherish and respect all forms of spiritual practice. . . .

Throughout history, mankind has pursued peace one way or another. Is it too optimistic to imagine that world peace may finally be within our grasp? I do not believe that there has been an increase in the amount of people's hatred, only in their ability to manifest it in vastly destructive weapons. On the other hand, bearing witness to the tragic evidence of the mass slaughter caused by such weapons in our century has given us the opportunity to control war. To do so, it is clear we must disarm.

Disarmament can occur only within the context of new political and economic relationships. Before we consider this issue in detail, it is worth imagining the kind of peace process from which we would benefit most. This is fairly self-evident. First we should work on eliminating nuclear weapons, next, biological and chemical ones, then offensive arms, and, finally, defensive ones. At the same time, to safeguard the peace, we should start developing in one or more global regions an international police force made up of an equal number of members from each nation under a collective command. Eventually this force would cover the whole world. . . .

Our planet is blessed with vast, natural treasures. If we use them properly, beginning with the elimination of militarism and war, truly, every human being will be able to live a wealthy, well-cared-for life. . . .

I believe that the very process of dialogue, moderation and compromise involved in building a community of Asian states would itself give real hope of peaceful evolution to a new order in China. From the very start, the member states of such a community might agree to decide its defense and international relations policies together. There would be many opportunities for cooperation. The critical point is that we find a peaceful, nonviolent way for the forces of freedom, democracy and moderation to emerge successfully from the current atmosphere of unjust repression. . . .

I see Tibet's role in such an Asian Community as what I have previously called a "Zone of Peace": a neutral, demilitarized sanctuary where weapons are forbidden and the people live in harmony with nature. This is not merely a dream—it is precisely the way Tibetans tried to live for over a thousand years before our country was invaded. . . .

Another hopeful development is the growing compatibility between science and religion. Throughout the nineteenth century and for much of our own, people have been profoundly confused by the conflict between these apparently contradictory world views. Today, physics, biology and psychology have reached such sophisticated levels that many researchers are starting to ask the most profound questions about the ultimate nature of the universe and life, the same questions that are of prime interest to religions. Thus there is real potential for a more unified view. In particular, it seems that a new concept of mind and matter is emerging. The East has been more concerned with understanding the mind, the West with understanding matter. Now that the two have met, these spiritual and material views of life may become more harmonized.

The rapid changes in our attitude towards the earth are also a source of hope. As recently as ten or fifteen years ago, we thoughtlessly consumed its resources, as if there was no end to them. Now, not only individuals but governments as well are seeking a new ecological order. . . .

I think we can say that, because of the lessons we have begun to learn, the next century will be friendlier, more harmonious, and less harmful. Compassion, the seed of peace, will be able to flourish. I am very hopeful. At the same time, I believe that every individual has a responsibility to help guide our global family in the right direction. Good wishes alone are not enough; we have to assume responsibility. Large human movements spring from individual human initiatives.

Source: Tenzin Gyatso, *Love, Kindness and Universal Responsibility*. New Delhi: Paljor Publications, n.d., pp. 50–71

Living engaged Buddhism

How strong is the evidence that the Buddha fought for the common person against the establishment of his time, attempting to change society? He did oppose the birth caste system and the privileges of the brahmanic priestly caste. But his focus on individual consciousness does not seem like a direct critique of institutionalized social injustices. With the advent of modern technologies and increased resources far beyond those available during the Buddha's time, a renewed movement called "engaged Buddhism" is emerging with a critique of social problems. The Dalai Lama is one leader critical of violence and consumerism, and others are applying Buddhist principles to rectify injustices in such areas as the environmental crisis and gender inequalities. Some of the traditional practices of Buddhism, such as monastic celibacy, are being called into question and modified in the global context of contemporary Buddhism.

Engaged Buddhism in Asia
by Christopher Queen and Sallie King

Christopher Queen and Sallie King, in their book Engaged Buddhism: Buddhist Liberation Movements in Asia, *show the growing influence of social activism among Asian Buddhists. There is a debate about whether Buddhism is essentially a withdrawn, reflective spiritual practice, focusing on overcoming one's own desires and attachments, or whether it also authentically includes a valid movement into social and political arenas to improve the situation of poor, oppressed peoples and victims of war. Queen, King, and others argue that traditional Buddhist teachings and the modern situation do justify a Buddhist movement toward changing not only individual consciousness, but also oppressive social structures.*

To most people in the West, the term "Buddhism" means a religion of introspective withdrawal. Yet the reality of contemporary Asian Buddhism is often something very different. "Buddhism" in contemporary Asia means energetic engagement with social and political issues and crises at least as much as it means monastic or meditative withdrawal. . . .

In the socially engaged Buddhism of modern Asia, the liberation sought has been called a "mundane awakening" (*laukodaya*), which includes individuals, villages, nations, and ultimately all people (*sarvodaya*), and which focuses on objectives that may be achieved and recognized in this lifetime, in this world. George Bond has summarized the comprehensive nature of the liberative vision that inspires volunteers in the Sarvodaya Shramadana movement, including moral, cultural, spiritual, social, political, and economic dimensions. Thus, in addition to being a society based on the Buddhist precepts and offering opportunities for obtaining wisdom, happiness, and peace, Ariyaratna[9] and his colleagues have focused on the "ten basic human needs" that must be met for liberation to be possible: a clean and beautiful environment, an adequate and safe water supply, clothing, balanced diet, simple housing, basic health care, communication facilities, energy, education related to life and living, and free access to cultural and spiritual resources. The list is offered as a modern version of the Buddhist "middle way"—a balancing of the material and spiritual aspects of social change.

We may conclude that a profound change in Buddhist soteriology[10]—from a highly personal and other-worldly notion of liberation to a social, economic, this-worldly liberation —distinguishes the Buddhist movements in our study. The traditional conceptions of karma and rebirth, the veneration of the bhikkhu sangha,[11] and the focus on ignorance and psychological attachment to account for suffering in the world (the second Noble Truth) have taken second place to the application of highly rationalized reflections on the institutional and political manifestations of greed, hatred, and delusion, and on new organizational strategies for addressing war and injustice, poverty and intolerance, and the prospects for "outer" as well as "inner" peace in the world. . . .

Contemporary Buddhist liberation movements are as likely to apply their interpretive and organizational efforts to the critique and reform of social and political conditions as they are to propose and practice new spiritual exercises. The evils of war and genocide, of ethnic hatred and caste violence, and of economic disparity and degradation figure prominently in engaged Buddhist writings. On the other hand, the democratization, if not

---

[9] Ariyaratna—Ariyaratna, E. T., *Buddhism and Sarvodaya: The Sri Lankan Experience*, Delhi: Sri Satguru Publications, 1996.

[10] Soteriology—doctrine of salvation through suffering.

[11] Bhikkhu sangha—members of the Buddhist monastic communities.

the transformation, of spiritual practices—for example, meditation and ritual
initiations as now appropriated by lay practitioners—has been seen as an
integral concomitant to the shift to mundane awakening.

To advance their vision of a new world, Buddhist liberation movements
have harnessed modern methods of education, mass communication,
political influence and activism, jurisprudence and litigation, and yes, even
fund-raising and marketing. Many examples of these new "skillful means"
may be cited.

If practical education is a basic human need, according to villagers in Sri
Lanka, then the Buddhist liberation movements have concentrated major
resources to this end. Among the first activities of the Buddhist women
reformers in Sri Lanka at the turn of the century was the founding of
primary schools for girls. . . .

"Buddhism is based on service to others," wrote Walpola Rhula, the
eminent Sinhalese scholar-monk and activist, in 1946. . . .

Rahula's summary of the history of monastic engagement in the social
and political life of Ceylon begins with a picture of the primitive sangha at
the time of the Buddha. Here the founder and his followers are seen giving
practical advice to villagers who were "poor, illiterate, not very clean, and
not healthy . . . [who] needed simple moral ideas conducive to their material
well-being and happiness rather than deep and sublime discourses on
philosophy, metaphysics, or psychology as taught in the *Abhidhamma*. Such
ideas, taken from early Pali scriptures (*suttas*) Rahula was well-qualified to
interpret, included the view that crime and immorality in society are rooted
in poverty (*Cakkavatti-sihanada-sutta*), that employment opportunities must
be provided to ensure the common weal (*Kutadanta-sutta*), that merchants
should be diligent, savvy, and scrupulous in their dealings and that
laypersons should seek economic security, freedom from debt, good health,
and wholesome associations (*Sigala-sutta; Anguttara-nikaya*), and that political
leaders should observe the Ten Duties of the King, including liberality,
morality, self-sacrifice, integrity, nonviolence, and so on
(*Dhammapadatthakatha*). In short, "the Buddha and the bhikkhus taught
such important ideas pertaining to health, sanitation, earning wealth,
mutual relationships, well-being of society, and righteous government—all
for the good of the people." . . .

In his introduction to the writings of contemporary engaged Buddhists,
Kenneth Kraft has noted their agreement that "the principles and even some
of the techniques of an engaged Buddhism have been latent in the tradition
since the time of its founder. Qualities that were inhibited in pre-modern
Asian settings . . . can now be actualized through Buddhism's exposure to
the West, where ethical sensitivity, social activism, and egalitarianism are
emphasized." When these principles and techniques, regardless of their
provenance, are proclaimed and practiced in the name of the Awakened
One, in accord with the teachings of wisdom and compassion, and in the

spirit of the unbroken community of those seeking human liberation—that is, in harmony with the ancient refuges of Buddha, Dharma, and Sangha—then we may regard the catechism as authentically Buddhist. . . .

Simply put, in keeping with the Middle Path, Buddhist principles mandate that the poor need more attention given to the material dimension of life than do those who have enough; those who have more than enough need their attention turned to that fact. . . .

Buddhist liberation movements, collectively, constitute a major turning point in the development of Buddhism and will continue to play a role of substantial importance in the evolution of Buddhism into the foreseeable future.

SOURCE: Christopher S. Queen and Sallie B. King, eds., *Engaged Buddhism: Buddhist Liberation Movements in Asia*. Albany, NY: State University of New York Press, 1996, pp. ix, 9–33, 411–35

Buddhism Comes Home
by Jean Latz Griffin

Jean Griffin, a freelance writer, reports on the effects that Buddhism is having on the United States, and the changes that Western culture is bringing to Buddhism. A new kind of ecumenical, gender-neutral, and socially active Buddhism is emerging in several Western cultures. Not all cultural traditions of Asia will blend comfortably with modern culture, she says, yet the essential heart of Buddhism must not be lost in the translation. Traditional monastic centers of Buddhism (sanghas) were usually masculine. Now periodic practice retreats, rather than a monastic life of renunciation, serve a generation of women and men practitioners who find that "Caring for a baby is incredibly similar to monastic practice."

Growth in the numbers of Americans practicing some form of Buddhism has been phenomenal. Enrollment in the Naropa Institute in Boulder, Colorado, the country's only accredited, contemplative based institution of higher learning, has doubled in the past two years, and more than a thousand meditation centers have sprung up in North America since the 1960s, half of them in the last decade. A parallel but much smaller growth has taken place among Asian immigrants who have brought their traditions with them and built temples that use their native languages and are centered in mostly devotional Buddhist practices.

But American Buddhism has developed differently from Asian Buddhism. For example, most Buddhist practitioners here are lay men and women with families and jobs rather than monks and nuns living in monasteries and convents. In the West, women are more likely to be leaders, not just of other women, but of mixed-gender *sanghas* and retreat centers. And the structure of the sanghas themselves is more democratic than hierarchical, with many people contributing their ideas and insights.

Engaged Buddhism, in which social action is considered essential to Buddhist practice, has become a strong thread in American Buddhism. One can trace its roots to the Vietnam War when Thich Nhat Hanh, a Vietnamese Zen monk, began doing peace work in the form of underground support for Vietnamese draft resisters, social relief programs, and lectures in the United States. . . .

Another segment of American Buddhism focuses inward. Robert Thurman, head of the American Institute of Buddhism at Columbia University and author of several books, including *Inner Revolution*, once described Buddhism as "a therapy the Buddha developed for demented human beings." Although Thurman has also called Buddhism a world religion, a contemplative discipline, a counter-force to militarism, and an "evolutionary sport," the mental and emotional benefits of Buddhist meditative practice make it a natural companion of psychotherapy.

Kenneth Porter, a New York psychiatrist who has been a Vipassana practitioner for 13 years, says Buddhism has become closely linked to psychotherapy because meditative approaches that help people let go of attachments are similar to techniques that Western psychotherapists use to help patients overcome certain problems. In addition, Porter said, the Buddhist teaching that the core of all human beings is a sane and healthy "Buddha nature" is a welcome, healing corrective to the feelings of self-hatred that plague so many people who enter therapy. . . .

Western Buddhism is also much more ecumenical than it is in Asia, both within its own house and in relationship to other world religions. The three major traditions—Zen, Tibetan, and the Vipassana branch of Theravada, which have been separated for thousands of years in different Asian countries—are learning from and influencing each other through shared practices and cross-fertilization here. In addition, many Americans are combining Buddhist meditation with their Christian or Jewish religious practices.

Yvone Rand, meditation teacher at the Redwood Creek Buddhist Temple in Muir Beach, California, says she knows many people "who are absolutely committed to their Christian or Jewish faith traditions, but are also dedicated Buddhist meditators." Rand says she has no problem with this eclectic approach, and quotes one of her teachers, Shunryu Suzuki, the author of *Zen Mind, Beginner's Mind*, as saying that "Buddhism coming to the West would help people be better Christians."

However, Rand warns that a superficial smorgasbord approach to spirituality does pose a particular danger. "We are likely to end up with not much taproot if we just take a little of this and a little of that," Rand said. "There is a point in one's spiritual practice where going deep is very important.". . .

In China, Tibet, and Japan, the development of new forms of Buddhism took hundreds of years. But the *Dharma* has come to America in a time of automobiles, telephones, airplanes, fax machines and Web sites. The result: The rapidity of change in our culture has produced a unique form of Buddhism within decades rather than centuries and is forcing the first generation of Western-born Buddhist leaders to ask some difficult questions. How do you keep the essence of the Buddha's teachings while letting go of the Asian cultural trappings that don't speak to Western sensibilities? How much interaction between the Zen, Tibetan, and Vipassana traditions can take place without losing their unique contributions? Will too much popularization of Buddhism—in movies, music and elsewhere—water down the *Dharma*? Could what has been called *"Dharma-Lite"* be dangerous if people try to meditate without a trained teacher? And how do you build relationships between teachers and students that are free of the abuses of power that have plagued not only Buddhism but other religions in America?

These questions are being asked gently but firmly, with great respect for the generations of teachers who have gone before them, but with a clear sense that what current Western teachers do now will have a lasting impact....

But while some Buddhist leaders worry that the *Dharma* will be diluted or overly commercialized, Thurman, one of the more controversial Buddhist writers, has predicted that "Buddhism will not be able to succeed in its mission in America unless it is able to perform that mission without being Buddhism." In other words, Thurman told the first "Buddhism in America" conference held in 1997, Buddhist teachings will have to enter American society somewhat surreptitiously, without creating tensions with existing religions or requiring Americans to adopt cultural baggage from Japan or China or Tibet.

"If we try to bring Buddhist teachings to America on a religious basis, it's a hopeless project," he said. "Americans can pray to Jesus or Mary or Moses, it doesn't matter. But the heart has to be open." An example of a successful strategy that inserts Buddhist principles into a crucial arena of American life without creating tensions between existing religions is Jon Kabat-Zinn's work in which Buddhist meditative principles are applied in a program aimed at easing chronic pain.

The core teaching that Buddhism can bring to America, according to Thurman, is that "individuals, one by one, person by person, begin to live beyond life and death. You have to feel connected to the future infinitely, so that what you do is infinitely significant."...

Integration of Buddhism into family life, even though it is stronger in America than in Asia, is still difficult. That is part of the challenge of bringing a monastically focused practice to a new land and trying to adapt it in a way that fits into a busy family life. In Asia, families practice Buddhism by performing devotions in temples and giving alms to the monks and nuns. But most do not engage in serious meditation practice. In contrast, the prevalent religions in the United States—Christianity and Judaism— emphasize family involvement.

"When I was starting out, the first obstacle was the idea that to be a serious practitioner you had to leave everything and go to a monastery," a Zen priest in Illinois, Susan Myoyu Andersen said. "On the one hand, the intensive practice is very important and I am glad I have that under my belt. I also see that most people simply can't leave their jobs and families for years or even three months." One solution that Buddhist sanghas and centers across the country are developing is to offer weekend or week-long silent retreats and encourage people to do as much as they can without pushing them or making them feel guilty that they can't devote their entire lives to meditation. Most meditate alone daily and with a group once or twice a week. Another solution to the dilemma is to recognize everyday life as a practice. Andersen said that realization hit her full-force when she had her first child.

"Caring for a baby is incredibly similar to monastic practice," she said. "Your time is not your own, you're tired all the time, you are there to serve another human being. And a lot of time, it doesn't seem like you are really accomplishing anything. You learn to appreciate just holding the baby for its own sake. Some day you will go back to gardening and redecorating your living room, but right now, you are just holding the baby.". . .

As Buddhism changes and is changed by its interaction with American society, growing into a more ecumenical, psychologically oriented, lay-based, and gender-equal system than it has ever been before, leaders point to two strengths that are likely to carry it through future generations—its relative lack of institutionalization and its adaptability.

"Buddhism is a religion, but a funny kind of religion," said Kenneth Porter. "It is as much of a spiritual technology, which is compatible with many different religions, as it is a path in itself. It doesn't require the same kind of total ideological loyalty that some other religions require."

In addition, Buddhism in America is part of a broader movement in which people want to develop the spiritual dimension of their lives. "It is part of the stage our society is in," Porter said. "Since the essential, transcendent core experience that makes up spirituality can lose its spark when it becomes institutionalized into religion, [many people] may find the Judaism and Christianity they grew up with somewhat ossified. Buddhism is new and fresh."

SOURCE: Jean Latz Griffin, "Buddhism Comes Home," *Common Boundary*, vol. 17, no. 1 (Jan/Feb 1999), pp. 16–22

Precepts for an Engaged Buddhism
by Thich Nhat Hanh

Thich Nhat Hanh, a Vietnamese Zen master, was chairman of the Vietnamese Buddhist Peace Delegation during the Vietnam war. Due to his active efforts to reconcile the two warring sides, he was exiled. He has settled in France, where he teaches, writes, gardens, and helps other refugees. His several books have introduced many readers to a new brand of Buddhist activism. In his book Being Peace *he outlines a number of new precepts for an engaged Buddhism, "The Precepts of the Order of Interbeing." They clearly reflect careful study of both modern and ancient problems, such as religious intolerance, fanatical political ideology, and forceful indoctrination of children.*

First: Do not be idolatrous about or bound to any doctrine, theory, or ideology, even Buddhist ones. All systems of thought are guiding means; they are not absolute truth....

Second: Do not think that the knowledge you presently possess is changeless, absolute truth. Avoid being narrow-minded and bound to present views. Learn and practice non-attachment from views in order to be open to receive others' viewpoints. Truth is found in life and not merely in conceptual knowledge. Be ready to learn throughout your entire life and to observe reality in yourself and in the world at times....

Third: Do not force others, including children, by any means whatsoever, to adopt your views, whether by authority, threat, money, propaganda, or even education. However, through compassionate dialogue, help others renounce fanaticism and narrowness....

Fourth: Do not avoid contact with suffering or close your eyes before suffering. Do not lose awareness of the existence of suffering in the life of the world. Find ways to be with those who are suffering by all means, including personal contact and visits, images, sound. By such means, awaken yourself and others to the reality of suffering in the world....

Fifth: Do not accumulate wealth while millions are hungry. Do not take as the aim of your life fame, profit, wealth, or sensual pleasure. Live simply and share time, energy, and material resources with those who are in need....

Sixth: Do not maintain anger or hatred. As soon as anger and hatred arise, practice the meditation on compassion in order to deeply understand the persons who have caused anger and hatred. Learn to look at other beings with the eyes of compassion....

Seventh: Do not lose yourself in dispersion and in your surroundings. Learn to practice breathing in order to regain composure of body and mind, to practice mindfulness, and to develop concentration and understanding....

Eighth: Do not utter words that can create discord and cause the community to break. Make every effort to reconcile and resolve all conflicts, however small....

Ninth: Do not say untruthful things for the sake of personal interest or to impress people. Do not utter words that cause division and hatred. Do not spread news that you do not know to be certain. Do not criticize or condemn things that you are not sure of. Always speak truthfully and constructively. Have the courage to speak out about situations of injustice, even when doing so may threaten your own safety. . . .

Tenth: Do not use the Buddhist community for personal gain or profit, or transform your community into a political party. A religious community should, however, take a clear stand against oppression and injustice, and should strive to change the situation without engaging in partisan conflicts. . . .

Eleventh: Do not live with a vocation that is harmful to humans and nature. Do not invest in companies that deprive others of their chance to life. Select a vocation which helps realize your ideal of compassion. . . .

Twelfth: Do not kill. Do not let others kill. Find whatever means possible to protect life and to prevent war. . . .

Thirteenth: Possess nothing that should belong to others. Respect the property of others but prevent others from enriching themselves from human suffering or the suffering of other beings. . . .

Fourteenth: Do not mistreat your body. Learn to handle it with respect. Do not look on your body as only an instrument. Preserve vital energies (sexual, breath, spirit) for the realization of the Way. Sexual expression should not happen without love and commitment. In sexual relationships be aware of future suffering that may be caused. To preserve the happiness of others, respect the rights and commitment of others. Be fully aware of the responsibility of bringing new lives into the world. Meditate on the world into which you are bringing new beings.

SOURCE: Thich Nhat Hanh, *Being Peace*. Berkeley, CA: Parallax Press, 1987, pp. 89–100

GLOSSARY

Bodhisattva ("enlightenment being," Sanskrit; **bodhisatta**, Pali) In Theravada, an historical Buddha before Buddhahood was attained; in Mahayana, a compassionate being who vows to become a Buddha for all sentient beings.

Buddha In Theravada, the historical persons who awaken to truth, such as Gautama; in Mahayana, an enlightened person and a universal principle of all beings.

Dharma (**dhamma**, Sanskrit/Pali) Cosmic law, the teachings of Buddha, and the realization and practice of truth; the second of the Three Jewels (Buddha, dharma, sangha).

Karma Our actions and their effects on this life and lives to come.

Mahayana ("Large Vehicle," Sanskrit). The form of Buddhism from northern Asia which teaches the effort to liberate other beings and emphasizes the Buddha-nature in all things and the importance of direct experience.

Nirvana (**nibbana**, Sanskrit/Pali) Not only a heavenly realm discovered after death: Mahayana teachings affirm that nirvana is a state of awakening during life. It is the discovery of the path beyond ego's desires and passions, the realization of the union of opposites, the transcendence of mind's limits. It is peace and tranquility on earth, coming from beyond the duality of ordinary life.

Samsara In some Asian religions, cycles of birth and death through reincarnation involving the consequences of karma; the world of illusion to be escaped.

Skandhas The five aggregates which constitute a human appearance, such as sensation and consciousness; they are not fixed or substantial, but impermanent and co-dependently arising.

Sunyata ("emptiness," or "no-self"; "Anatman," Sanskrit) The lack of a permanent, self-existing soul in the skandhas and all reality.

Theravada ("Teaching of the Elders," Pali) Form of Buddhism from southern Asia which adheres to early scriptures and monastic renunciation; its texts are the Pali Canon.

Vajrayana ("Diamond Vehicle," Sanskrit) Form of Buddhism which teaches that emptiness is complemented by compassion and action. The Dalai Lama is its leader in the Tibetan tradition.

Vipassana ("See clearly," Pali) The central focus of meditation in Theravada practice, which stresses mindfulness and tranquility, leading to liberation.

Zen A Chinese and Japanese form of Buddhism emphasizing immediate experience. Of the two main schools, Rinzai, influenced by Hakuin, uses the koan to promote satori ("awakening"), while Soto, influenced by Dogen, uses more "silent illumination."

HOLY DAYS

Celebrating the Buddha Buddhist cultures celebrate the events and the meaning of the life of the Buddha in several ways.

1 Buddha's Day, or Visaka Puja in Theravada, is often the most holy day of the year, commemorating the birth, life, and death of the Buddha. It is usually celebrated on the full moon. Devotees gather at monasteries, have processions, chant, listen to sermons, water local Bodhi trees, serve the poor and sick, honor relics such as the Buddha's eyetooth, and bathe Buddha images.

2 Relics, such as teeth or bones supposedly preserved from his body, are commemorated as ways of participating in the magical power of his divine presence with rituals such as a procession and sprinkling holy water. Sometimes kings attempt to legitimate their rule by using such relics to empower and bless their state.

3 Honoring the Dharma is celebrated by chanting sacred texts. In Tibet the Feast of the First Discourse is held on a full moon. Thais celebrate the Buddha's teaching this to his mother, and his establishing the core of the monastic discipline.

4 The founding of the sangha/samgha, or "gathering community" of Buddhists, is celebrated annually. The miraculous, unannounced gathering of 1,250 wandering arhats before the Buddha in Rajagrha is recalled as the founding time of the first sangha. In Sri Lanka, thousands of people come to celebrate the arrival of Buddhism on the Island, brought by Mahind, son of King Ashoka, and his sister Sanghamitta, who brought a branch of Buddha's sacred Bodhi tree.

5 The saints of Buddhism are celebrated in annual festivals, honoring popular mythic events such as the Chinese Kuan-yin's birthday, enlightenment and entry into nirvana. Holidays celebrate historical leaders such as Bodhidharma, the first Chinese Patriarch who brought Cha'n/Zen to China, Hakuin, leader of the Rinzai Zen sect in Japan, and Padmasambhava, the leading missionary from India to Tibet.

Seasonal celebrations The Buddhist calendar also incorporates festivals of seasonal changes, agricultural events, and human life and death rituals. New Year's day is commonly celebrated, as are the origin of spring, the equinoxes, harvest thanksgiving, and festivals for the dead ancestors. These holidays are highly syncretic, blending Buddhist and ancient folk religion together. In Tibet, the New Year festival (Lo-gsar) combines the Buddhist miracle of Sravasti with the exorcism of the old year's evil, and calling up good fortune for the new year. In Thailand the onset of the monsoon rains is the occasion of intensified monastic retreat activities, alongside New Year's sympathetic magic intended to ensure the new rains necessary to planting rice.

HISTORICAL OUTLINE

c. 563–483 BCE—Life of Gautama Buddha

c. 258 BCE—King Asoka spreads Buddhism outside India

2nd century BCE—Asvaghosha writes *Acts of the Buddha*

200 BCE–200 CE—Theravada Buddhism develops

100 BCE—Theravada Pali Canon written down

c. 50 CE—Buddhism taken to China and East Asia

c. 100 CE—Mahayana Buddhism develops

c. 200 CE—Nagarjuna teaches Emptiness

c. 500 CE—Buddhism taken to Japan

589–845 CE—Peak of Chinese Buddhism

606 CE—Seng-tsan, Third Buddhist Patriarch in China, dies

775 CE—Padmasambhava establishes first Buddhist monastery in Tibet

c. 1079–1153—Milarepa influences Tibetan Buddhism

1222–82—Nichiren teaches in Japan

13th century—Buddhism begins to lose influence in India

c. 13th century—Ch'an Buddhism taken from China to Japan, becomes Zen

c. 1250—Nichiren Dogen develops Soto Zen Buddhism

c. 1750—Hakuin revitalizes Rinzai Zen Buddhism

1950—China annexes Tibet, Dalai Lama flees, Buddhism spreads to West

1966—Thich Nhat Hanh leaves Vietnam for the West

from 1970s—Dalai Lama teaches widely in the West

REVIEW QUESTIONS

1   What did Mara have to gain by thwarting the great Sage's attempt at enlightenment?
2   What needs to be suppressed and what realized in order to achieve enlightenment.
3   What are the "middle path," the four noble truths, the eightfold path? What does it mean to be free from delusions? Why is this important to Buddhists?
4   What questions did the Buddha leave undeclared? Why? What is more important?
5   Describe the similarities and contrast the differences of the Theravada, Mahayana, and Vajrayana traditions, naming and quoting classic texts in each tradition.
6   What refuge does the Dhammapada recommend? Why?
7   Why did the Buddha reject the Hindu caste system?

8   What are the different meanings of "emptiness" for Buddhists? Name three major writers/texts on the theme.
9   What is a koan? What is its purpose? Give an example.
10   How could Bankei's challenge to rules coexist in the same religion with the precepts?
11   What principles of Buddhism is the Dalai Lama applying to the modern world?
12   Do you think today's engaged Buddhism in Asia is a valid application of traditionally introspective Buddhism?
13   Do you think that the new Western support for home practice is a valid form of Buddhism? Why?
14   Do you think that Thich Nhat Hanh's new "Precepts of the Order of Interbeing" are perfectionist and unrealistic?

INFORMATION RESOURCES

Buddhaghosha, *Buddhaghosha's Parables*, trans. T. Rogers. London, 1870.

Carter, Robert E. *The Nothingness Beyond God*. St. Paul, MN: Paragon House, 1997.

Chodron, Pema, *When Things Fall Apart*. Boston and London: Shambhala, 1997.

Conze, Edward, ed. *Buddhist Scriptures*. Harmondsworth, Middx: Penguin, 1986.

Cousins, L. S. "Buddhism," in *A New Handbook of Living Religions*, ed. John R. Hinnels. Oxford: Blackwell, 1997.

DharmaNet Interlinks: Buddhist Studies www.dharmanet.org>

Goddard, Dwight, ed. *A Buddhist Bible*. Boston: Beacon Press, 1966.

Gross, Rita M. *Buddhism After Patriarchy*. Albany: State University of New York Press, 1993.

Kapleau, Philip, *The Three Pillars of Zen*. Boston: Beacon Press, 1965.

Loori, John Daido, "The Precepts and the Environment," *Mountain Record*, vol. 14, no. 3 (Spring 1996), pp. 12–17.

Macy, Joanna, *World as Lover, World as Self*. Berkeley: Parallax Press, 1991, p. 4–13.

McGreal, Ian P. *Great Thinkers of the Eastern World*. New York: HarperCollins, 1995.

Nishitani, Keiji, *Religion and Nothingness*. Berkeley: University of California Press, 1982.

Pilgrim, Richard, *Buddhism and the Arts of Japan*. Chambersburg, PA: Anima Press, 1993.

Powell, Andrew, *Living Buddhism*. Berkeley and Los Angeles: University of California Press, 1989.

Ramanan, K. Venkata, *Nagarjuna's Philosophy*. Delhi: Motilal Banarsidass, 1966

Reynolds, Frank, and Charles Hallisey, "Buddhism: An Overview," in *The Encyclopedia of Religion*, ed. M. Eliade, vol. 2, pp. 334–51. New York: Macmillan, 1986.

Reynolds, Frank, *et. al.* "The Buddha and Buddhism," in *The New Encyclopedia Britannica*, vol. 15, pp. 263–305. London, 1997.

Thurman, Robert, *The Tibetan Book of the Dead*. New York: Bantam, 1994.

Tricycle: the Buddhist Review, 92 Vandam St., New York, NY 10013 <www.tricycle.com>

CHAPTER 6

CONFUCIANISM

The ancient religious ways of China have developed into two distinct streams, known as Confucianism and Taoism. Confucianism is more humanistic and pragmatic; Taoism is more mystically inclined.

The stream known as Confucianism has developed from the ancient emphasis on veneration of ancestors and maintenance of proper rituals, or **li**, in order to stay in harmony with Heaven. Master K'ung, commonly known in the West by the latinized version of his name, Confucius, was an ardent proponent of the ancient rites as a practical base for an orderly and moral society. Born in approximately 551 BCE during a period of social chaos, he earnestly sought to advise rulers how to restore harmony. Failing to win their ear, he became a teacher of *li* and the arts of governance, so that his students might revive the ways of an idealized earlier period. The school of thought which he developed became the mainstream of Chinese philosophy for over two thousand years.

Confucius focuses much of his attention on the development of human virtues within relationships with others. A man or woman whom he calls "noble" or "superior" is not one of high birth but one who manifests such virtues as humanity (**jen**), filial regard for one's parents, reverence toward ancestors, and observance of proprieties in human relationships. A stable society, he maintained, depends upon compassion in the father and filial piety in the son; gentility on the part of the older brother and respect from the younger brother; righteousness in the husband and obedience in the wife; humanity in the older friend and deference in the younger friend; benevolence in rulers and loyalty in their subjects. Confucius himself was from a prominent family which had been reduced to poverty, but he always maintained and encouraged gentlemanly behavior even in humble surroundings.

Whereas Confucius's ideas were not embraced by the rulers of his time, by the Han dynasty (206 BCE–220 CE) they were adopted as a way of uniting the people behind the ruler, who was portrayed as the link between Heaven and the populace. Study of the Confucian Classics became mandatory for public service. This requirement lasted until the twentieth century, when all religious practice was disrupted by communism, but it has recently been revived, along with renewed interest in Confucian virtues as a guide to self-improvement.

The Confucian classics

As promoted by the Neo-Confucian scholars during the Sung dynasty (960–1279), the heart of Confucian teachings is found in the "Four Books"— The **Analects** of Confucius, Mencius, and two extracts from the ritual collections: "The Doctrine of the Mean" and "The Great Learning."

The Analects of Confucius

The Analects are terse sayings of Master K'ung, as collected by his students, some of whom are named.

Confucius said, "Is it not a pleasure to learn and to repeat or practice from time to time what has been learned? Is it not delightful to have friends coming from afar? Is one not a superior man if he does not feel hurt even though he is not recognized?"

Yu Tzu said, "Few of those who are filial sons and respectful brothers will show disrespect to superiors, and there has never been a man who is not disrespectful to superiors and yet creates disorder. A superior man is devoted to the fundamentals [the root]. When the root is firmly established, the moral law [Tao] will grow. Filial piety and brotherly respect are the root of humanity."

Tseng-Tzu said, "Every day I examine myself on three points: whether in counseling others I have not been loyal; whether in intercourse with my friends I have not been faithful; and whether I have not repeated again and again and practiced the instructions of my teacher."

Young men should be filial when at home and respectful to their elders when away from home. They should be earnest and faithful. They should love all extensively and be intimate with men of humanity. When they have any energy to spare after the performance of moral duties, they should use it to study literature and the arts.

Confucius said, "When a man's father is alive, look at the bent of his will. When his father is dead, look as his conduct. If for three years he does not change from the way of his father, he may be called filial."

Yu Tzu said, "Among the functions of propriety [*li*] the most valuable is that it establishes harmony. The excellence of the ways of ancient kings consists of this. It is the guiding principle of all things great and small. If things go amiss, and you, understanding harmony, try to achieve it without regulating it by the rules of propriety, they will still go amiss."

Confucius said, "The superior man does not seek fulfillment of his appetite nor comfort in his lodging. He is diligent in his duties and careful in his speech. He associates with men of moral principles and thereby realizes himself. Such a person may be said to love learning."

Confucius said, "A ruler who governs his state by virtue is like the north polar star, which remains in its place while all the other stars revolve around it."

Confucius said, "Lead the people with governmental measures and regulate them by law and punishment, and they will avoid wrongdoing but will have no sense of honor and shame. Lead them with virtue and regulate them by the rules of propriety, and they will have a sense of shame and, moreover, set themselves right."

Tzu-yu asked about filial piety. Confucius said, "Filial piety nowadays means to be able to support one's parents. But we support even dogs and horses. If there is no feeling of reverence, wherein lies the difference?"

When Confucius offered sacrifice to his ancestors, he felt as if his ancestral spirits were actually present. When he offered sacrifice to other spiritual beings, he felt as if they were actually present. He said, "If I do not participate in the sacrifice, it is as if I did not sacrifice at all."

Confucius said, "If you set your mind on humanity, you will be free from evil."

Confucius said, "Wealth and honor are what every man desires. But if they have been obtained in violation of moral principles, they must not be kept. Poverty and humble station are what every man dislikes. But if they can be avoided only in violation of moral principles, they must not be avoided. If a superior man departs from humanity, how can he fulfill that name? A superior man never abandons humanity even for the lapse of a single meal. In moments of haste, he acts according to it. In times of difficulty or confusion, he acts according to it."

Confucius said, "A superior man in dealing with the world is not for anything or against anything. He follows righteousness as the standard."

Confucius said, "If one's acts are motivated by profit, he will have many enemies."

Confucius said, "The superior man understands righteousness; the inferior man understands profit."

Confucius said, "I transmit but do not create. I believe in and love the ancients . . ."

Confucius said, "Set your will on the Way. Have a firm grasp on virtue. Rely on humanity. Find recreation in the arts."

Confucius said, "With coarse rice to eat, with water to drink, and with a bent arm for a pillow, there is still joy. Wealth and honor obtained through unrighteousness are but floating clouds to me."

Confucius never discussed strange phenomena, physical exploits, disorder, or spiritual beings.

Confucius said, "Heaven produced the virtue that is in me; what can Huan Tui[1] do to me?"

---

[1] Huan Tui—a minister of war who attempted to kill Confucius when he was 59 by felling a tree on him.

Confucius said, "The common people may be made to follow [the Way] but may not be made to understand it."

Confucius said, "Have sincere faith and love learning. Be not afraid to die for pursuing the good Way. Do not enter a tottering state nor stay in a chaotic one. When the Way prevails in the empire, then show yourself; when it does not prevail, then hide. When the Way prevails in your own state and you are poor and in a humble position, be ashamed of yourself. When the Way does not prevail in your state and you are wealthy and in an honorable position, be ashamed of yourself."

Confucius wanted to live among the nine barbarous tribes of the East. Someone said, "They are rude. How can you do it?" Confucius said, "If a superior man lives there, what rudeness would there be?"

Chi-lu [Tzu-lu] asked about serving the spiritual beings. Confucius said, "If we are not yet able to serve man, how can we serve spiritual beings?" "I venture to ask about death." Confucius said, "If we do not yet know about life, how can we know about death?"

Ssu-ma Niu, worrying, said, "All people have brothers but I have none." Tzu-hsia said, "I have heard [from Confucius] this saying: 'Life and death are the decree of Heaven; wealth and honor depend on Heaven. If a superior man is reverential [or serious] without fail, and is respectful in dealing with others and follows the rules of propriety, then all within the four seas are brothers.' What does the superior man have to worry about having no brothers?"

Tzu-kung asked about government. Confucius said, "Sufficient food, sufficient armament, and sufficient confidence of the people." Tzu-kung said, "Forced to give up one of these, which would you abandon first?" Confucius said, "I would abandon the armament." Tzu-kung said, "Forced to give up one of the remaining two, which would you abandon first?" Confucius said, "I would abandon food. There have been deaths from time immemorial, but no state can exist without the confidence of the people."

Chi K'ang Tzu asked Confucius about government. Confucius replied, "To govern [cheng] is to rectify [cheng]. If you lead the people by being rectified yourself, who will dare not be rectified?"

Chi K'ang Tzu asked Confucius about government, saying, "What do you think of killing the wicked and associating with the good?" Confucius replied, "In your government what is the need of killing? If you desire what is good, the people will be good. The character of a ruler is like wind and that of the people is like grass. In whatever direction the wind blows, the grass always bends."

Confucius said, "If a ruler sets himself right, he will be followed without his command. If he does not set himself right, even his commands will not be obeyed."

Confucius said, "A man who is strong, resolute, simple, and slow to speak is near to humanity."

Confucius said, "The superior man understands the higher things [moral principles]; the inferior man understands the lower things [profit]."

Confucius said, "There are three kinds of friendship which are beneficial and three kinds which are harmful. Friendship with the upright, with the truthful, and with the well-informed is beneficial. Friendship with those who flatter, with those who are meek and who compromise with principles, and with those who talk cleverly is harmful."

Tzu-chang asked Confucius about humanity. Confucius said, "One who can practice five things wherever he may be is a man of humanity." Tzu-chang asked what the five are. Confucius said, "Earnestness, liberality, truthfulness, diligence, and generosity. If one is earnest, one will not be treated with disrespect. If one is liberal, one will win the hearts of all. If one is truthful, one will be trusted. If one is diligent, one will be successful. And if one is generous, one will be able to enjoy the service of others."

Confucius said, "I do not wish to say anything." Tzu-kung said, "If you do not say anything, what will we little disciples ever learn to pass on to others?" Confucius said, "Does Heaven [*T'ien*, Nature] say anything? The four seasons run their course and all things are produced. Does Heaven say anything?"

SOURCE: Wing-tsit Chan, trans. and compiled. *A Sourcebook in Chinese Philosophy.* Princeton, New Jersey: Princeton University Press, 1963, pp. 18–47

The Book of Mencius

Mencius (c. 390–305 BCE), a major commentator on the teachings of Confucius, lived during a period of extreme chaos in China. Nonetheless, he maintained that rulers should govern not by force but by good will and humaneness, in cooperation with Heaven.

Mencius said, "For a man to give full realization to his heart is for him to understand his own nature, and a man who knows his own nature will know Heaven. By retaining his heart and nurturing his nature he is serving Heaven. Whether he is going to die young or to live to a ripe old age makes no difference to his steadfastness of purpose. It is through awaiting whatever is to befall him with a perfected character that he stands firm on his proper destiny."

Mencius said, "Though nothing happens that is not due to destiny, one accepts willingly only what is one's proper destiny. That is why he who understands destiny does not stand under a wall on the verge of collapse. He who dies after having done his best in following the Way dies according to his proper destiny. It is never anyone's proper destiny to die in fetters.". . .

Mencius said, "All the **Ten Thousand Things** are there in me. There is no greater joy for me than to find, on self-examination, that I am true to myself. Try your best to treat others as you would wish to be treated yourself, and you will find that this is the shortest way to benevolence."

Mencius said, "The multitude can be said never to understand what they practise, to notice what they repeatedly do, or to be aware of the path they follow all their lives. . . ."

Mencius said to Sung Kou-chien, "You are fond of travelling from state to state, offering advice. I shall tell you how this should be done. You should be content whether your worth is recognized by others or not."

"What must a man be before he can be content?"

"If he reveres virtue and delights in rightness, he can be content. Hence a Gentleman never abandons rightness in adversity, nor does he depart from the Way in success. By not abandoning rightness in adversity, he finds delight in himself; by not departing from the Way in success, he does not disappoint the people. Men of antiquity made the people feel the effect of their bounty when they realized their ambition, and, when they failed to realize their ambition, were at least able to show the world an exemplary character. In obscurity a man makes perfect his own person, but in prominence he makes perfect the whole Empire as well.". . .

Mencius said, "The people under a leader of the feudal lords are happy; those under a true King are expansive and content. They bear no ill-will when put to death, neither do they feel any gratitude when profited. They move daily towards goodness without realizing who it is that brings this about. A gentleman transforms where he passes, and works wonders where he abides. He is in the same stream as Heaven above and Earth below. Can he be said to bring but small benefit?"

Mencius said, "Benevolent words do not have as profound an effect on the people as benevolent music. Good government does not win the people as does good education. He who practises good government is feared by the people; he who gives the people good education is loved by them. Good government wins the wealth of the people; good education wins their hearts."

Mencius said, "What a man is able to do without having to learn it is what he can truly do; what he knows without having to reflect on it is what he truly knows. There are no young children who do not know loving their parents, and none of them when they grow up will not know respecting their elder brothers. Loving one's parents is benevolence; respecting one's elders is rightness. What is left to be done is simply the extension of these to the whole Empire.". . .

Mencius said, "Do not do what others do not choose to do; do not desire what others do not desire. That is all."

Mencius said, "It is often through adversity that men acquire virtue, wisdom, skill and cleverness. The estranged subject or the son of a concubine, because he conducts himself with the greatest of caution and is constantly on the watch out for possible disasters, succeeds where others would have failed."

Mencius said, "There are men whose purpose is to serve a prince. They will try to please whatever prince they are serving. There are men whose aim is to bring peace to the state. They achieve satisfaction through bringing this about. There are the subjects of Heaven. They practise only what could be extended to the whole Empire. They are the great men. They can rectify others by rectifying themselves."

Mencius said, "A gentleman delights in three things, and being ruler over the Empire is not amongst them. His parents are alive and his brothers are well. This is the first delight. Above, he is not ashamed to face Heaven; below, he is not ashamed to face man. This is the second delight. He has the good fortune of having the most talented pupils in the Empire. This is the third delight. A gentleman delights in three things and being ruler over the Empire is not amongst them."

Mencius said, "An extensive territory and a vast population are things a gentleman desires, but what he delights in lies elsewhere. To stand in the centre of the Empire and bring peace to the people within the Four Seas is what a gentleman delights in, but that which he follows as his nature lies elsewhere. That which a gentleman follows as his nature is not added to when he holds sway over the Empire, nor is it detracted from when he is reduced to straitened circumstances. This is because he knows his allotted station. That which a gentleman follows as his nature, that is to say, benevolence, rightness, the rites and wisdom, is rooted in his heart, and manifests itself in his face, giving it a sleek appearance. It also shows in his back and extends to his limbs, rendering their message intelligible without words."

SOURCE: D. C. Lau, trans. *Mencius*. London: Penguin, 1970, pp. 182–93.

The Doctrine of the Mean

The Doctrine of the Mean (the middle way) emphasizes conformity with the Tao, or way. This word is central to both Confucianism and Taoism, but is given different emphasis in the two traditions. In Confucianism, the Tao is the way of natural human sincerity, which reflects the Way of Heaven.

What Heaven (*T'ien*, Nature) imparts to man is called human nature. To follow our nature is called the Way. Cultivating the Way is called education. The Way cannot be separated from us for a moment. What can be separated from us is not the Way. Therefore the superior man is cautious over what he does not see and apprehensive over what he does not hear. There is nothing more visible than what is hidden and nothing more manifest than what is subtle. Therefore the superior man is watchful over himself when he is alone.

Before the feelings of pleasure, anger, sorrow, and joy are aroused it is called equilibrium (*chung*, centrality, mean). When these feelings are aroused and each and all attain due measure and degree, it is called harmony. Equilibrium is the great foundation of the world, and harmony its universal path. When equilibrium and harmony are realized to the highest degree, heaven and earth will attain their proper order and all things will flourish. . . .

Confucius said, "I know why the Way is not pursued. The intelligent go beyond it and the stupid do not come up to it. I know why the Way is not understood. The worthy go beyond it and the unworthy do not come up to it. There is no one who does not eat and drink, but there are few who can really know flavor.". . .

"The Way of the superior man functions everywhere and yet is hidden. Men and women of simple intelligence can share its knowledge; and yet in its utmost reaches, there is something which even the sage does not know. Men and women of simple intelligence can put it into practice; and yet in its utmost reaches there is something which even the sage is not able to put into practice. Great as heaven and earth are, men still find something in them with which to be dissatisfied. Thus with [the Way of] the superior man, if one speaks of its greatness, nothing in the world can contain it, and if one speaks of its smallness, nothing in the world can split it. The *Book of Odes*[2] says, 'the hawk flies up to heaven; the fishes leap in the deep.' This means that [the Way] is clearly seen above and below. The Way of the superior man has its simple beginnings in the relation between man and woman, but in its utmost reaches, it is clearly seen in heaven and on earth."

Confucius said, "The Way is not far from man. When a man pursues the Way and yet remains away from man, his course cannot be considered the Way. The *Book of Odes* says, 'In hewing an axe handle, in hewing an axe handle, the pattern is not far off.' If we take an axe handle to hew another axe handle and look askance from the one to the other, we may still think the pattern is far away. Therefore the superior man governs men as men, in accordance with human nature, and as soon as they change [what is wrong], he stops. Conscientiousness (*chung*) and altruism (*shu*) are not far from the Way. What you do not wish others to do to you, do not do to them.

"There are four things in the Way of the superior man, none of which I have been able to do. To serve my father as I would expect my son to serve me: that I have not been able to do. To serve my ruler as I would expect my ministers to serve me: that I have not been able to do. To serve my elder brothers as I would expect my younger brothers to serve me: that I have not been able to do. To be the first to treat friends as I would expect them to treat me: that I have not been able to do. In practicing the ordinary virtues

---

[2] *Book of Odes*—a basic Confucian text of poems and songs for official functions, largely compiled from older traditions.

and in the exercise of care in ordinary conversation, when there is deficiency, the superior man never fails to make further effort, and when there is excess, never dares to go to the limit. His words correspond to his actions and his actions correspond to his words. Isn't the superior man earnest and genuine?"...

Only those who are absolutely sincere can fully develop their nature. If they can fully develop their nature, they can then fully develop the nature of others. If they can fully develop the nature of others, they can then fully develop the nature of things. If they can fully develop the nature of things, they can then assist in the transforming and nourishing process of Heaven and Earth. If they can assist in the transforming and nourishing process of Heaven and Earth, they can thus form a trinity with Heaven and Earth....

The next in order are those who cultivate to the utmost a particular goodness. Having done this, they can attain to the possession of sincerity. As there is sincerity, there will be its expression. As it is expressed, it will become conspicuous. As it becomes conspicuous, it will become clear. As it becomes clear, it will move others. As it moves others, it changes them. As it changes them, it transforms them. Only those who are absolutely sincere can transform others.

It is characteristic of absolute sincerity to be able to foreknow. When a nation or family is about to flourish, there are sure to be lucky omens. When a nation or family is about to perish, there are sure to be unlucky omens. These omens are revealed in divination and in the movements of the four limbs. When calamity or blessing is about to come, it can surely know beforehand if it is good, and it can also surely know beforehand if it is evil. Therefore he who has absolute sincerity is like a spirit.

Sincerity means the completion of the self, and the Way is self-directing. Sincerity is the beginning and end of things. Without sincerity there would be nothing. Therefore the superior man values sincerity. Sincerity is not only the completion of one's own self, it is that by which all things are completed. The completion of the self means humanity. The completion of all things means wisdom. These are the character of the nature, and they are the Way in which the internal and the external are united. Therefore whenever it is employed, everything done is right....

Therefore absolute sincerity is ceaseless. Being ceaseless, it is lasting. Being lasting, it is evident. Being evident, it is infinite. Being infinite, it is extensive and deep. Being extensive and deep, it is high and brilliant. It is because it is extensive and deep that it contains all things. It is because it is high and brilliant that it overshadows all things. It is because it is infinite and lasting that it can complete all things. In being extensive and deep, it is a counterpart of Earth. In being high and brilliant, it is a counterpart of Heaven. In being infinite and lasting, it is unlimited. Such being its nature, it becomes prominent without any display, produces changes without motion, and accomplishes its ends without action.

The Way of Heaven and Earth may be completely described in one sentence: They are without any doubleness and so they produce things in an unfathomable way. The Way of Heaven and Earth is extensive, deep, high, brilliant, infinite, and lasting. The heaven now before us is only this bright, shining mass; but when viewed in its unlimited extent, the sun, moon, stars, and constellations are suspended in it and all things are covered by it. The earth before us is but a handful of soil; but in its breadth and depth, it sustains mountains like Hua and Yüeh without feeling their weight, contains the rivers and seas without letting them leak away, and sustains all things. The mountain before us is only a fistful of straw; but in all the vastness of its size, grass and trees grow upon it, birds and beasts dwell on it, and stores of precious things (minerals) are discovered in it. The water before us is but a spoonful of liquid, but in all its unfathomable depth, the monsters, dragons, fishes, and turtles are produced in them, and wealth becomes abundant because of it (as a result of transportation). The *Book of Odes* says, "The **Mandate of Heaven**, how beautiful and unceasing." This is to say, "This is what makes Heaven to be Heaven."

SOURCE: "The Doctrine of the Mean," in Wing-tsit Chan, *A Source Book in Chinese Philosophy*. Princeton, NJ: Princeton University Press, 1963, pp. 98–110

Scholars' Commentaries

Scholars were highly honored figures in traditional Confucianism. They assembled the teachings of Confucius, including his commentaries on ancient texts, and further developed his system of practical ethics.

The Great Commentary on *The Book of Changes*

The Book of Changes *(I Ching) is an ancient compilation of Chinese wisdom which serves as foundational material for both Confucianism and Taoism. Its basic text gives terse, cryptic images referring to a system of divination by throwing stalks of yarrow or coins and observing and interpreting the patterns they form. The system is seemingly dualistic: the stalks are long or short, or the coins fall on one side or the other. This interplay of two basic states of being is often referred to as yin ("the cloudy") versus yang ("brightness"), or "the yielding" versus "the firm," or "the receptive" versus "the creative." But in Chinese tradition, the two states are not seen as being opposed; rather, their dynamic coordination is at work in the continual flux of the cosmos. Wisdom therefore lies in understanding and harmonizing oneself with this flux. The Great Commentary is thought to be based at least in part on Confucius's interpretation of* The Book of Changes, *as later compiled by Confucian scholars.*

The Changes in the Universe and in *The Book of Changes*

1. Heaven is high, the earth is low; thus the Creative and the Receptive are

determined. In correspondence with this difference between low and high, inferior and superior places are established.

Movement and rest have their definite laws; according to these, firm and yielding lines are differentiated.

Events follow definite trends, each according to its nature. Things are distinguished from one another in definite classes. In this way good fortune and misfortune come about. In the heavens phenomena take form; on earth shapes take form. In this way change and transformation become manifest.

2.   Therefore the eight trigrams[3] succeed one another by turns, as the firm and the yielding displace each other.

3.   Things are aroused by thunder and lightning; they are fertilized by wind and rain. Sun and moon follow their courses and it is now hot, now cold.

4.   The way of the Creative brings about the male.
The way of the Receptive brings about the female.

5.   The Creative knows the great beginnings.
The Receptive completes the finished things.

6.   The Creative knows through the easy.
The Receptive can do things through the simple.

7.   What is easy, is easy to know; what is simple, is easy to follow. He who is easy to know attains fealty. He who is easy to follow attains works. He who possesses attachment can endure for long; he who possesses works can become great. To endure is the disposition of the sage; greatness is the field of action of the sage.

8.   By means of the easy and the simple we grasp the laws of the whole world. When the laws of the whole world are grasped, therein lies perfection.

On the Composition and the Use of *The Book of Changes*

1.   The holy sages instituted the hexagrams,[4] so that phenomena might be perceived therein. They appended the judgments, in order to indicate good fortune and misfortune.

2.   As the firm and the yielding lines displace one another, change and transformation arise.

3.   Therefore good fortune and misfortune are the images of gain and loss; remorse and humiliation are the images of sorrow and forethought.

4.   Change and transformation are images of progress and retrogression. The firm and the yielding are images of day and night. The movements of the six lines contain the ways of the three primal powers [heaven, earth, and humans].

5.   Therefore it is the order of the Changes that the superior man devotes himself to and that he attains tranquillity by. It is the judgments on the

---

[3] Trigrams—diagrams of some of the 64 possible throws of the yarrow stalks.
[4] Hexagrams—diagrams of some of the 64 possible throws of the yarrow stalks.

individual lines that the superior man takes pleasure in and that he ponders on.

6.   Therefore the superior man contemplates these images in times of rest and meditates on the judgments. When he undertakes something, he contemplates the changes and ponders on the oracles. Therefore he is blessed by heaven. . . .

The Deeper Implications of *The Book of Changes*

1.   The Book of Changes contains the measure of heaven and earth; therefore it enables us to comprehend the *tao* of heaven and earth and its order.

2.   Looking upward, we contemplate with its help the signs in the heavens; looking down, we examine the lines of the earth. Thus we come to know the circumstances of the dark and the light. Going back to the beginnings of things and pursuing them to the end, we come to know the lessons of birth and of death. The union of seed and power produces all things; the escape of the soul brings about change. Through this we come to know the conditions of outgoing and returning spirits [expanding and contracting phases].

3.   Since in this way man comes to resemble heaven and earth, he is not in conflict with them. His wisdom embraces all things, and his *tao* brings order into the whole world; therefore he does not err. He is active everywhere but does not let himself be carried away. He rejoices in heaven and has knowledge of fate, therefore he is free of care. He is content with his circumstances and genuine in his kindness, therefore he can practice love. . . .

Tao in its Relation to the Light Power and to the Dark Power

1.   That which lets now the dark, now the light appear is *tao*.

2.   As continuer, it is good. As completer, it is the essence.

3.   The kind man discovers it and calls it kind. The wise man discovers it and calls it wise. The people use it day by day and are not aware of it, for the way of the superior man is rare.

4.   It manifests itself as kindness but conceals its workings. It gives life to all things, but it does not share the anxieties of the holy sage. Its glorious power, its great field of action, are of all things the most sublime.

5.   It possesses everything in complete abundance; this is its great field of action. It renews everything daily: this is its glorious power.

6.   As begetter of all begetting, it is called change.

7.   As that which completes the primal images, it is called the Creative; as that which imitates them, it is called the Receptive.

8.   In that it serves for exploring the laws of number and thus for knowing the future, it is called revelation. In that it serves to infuse an organic coherence into the changes, it is called the work.

9.   That aspect of it which cannot be fathomed in terms of the light and the dark is called spirit.

SOURCE: "Ta Chuan: The Great Commentary," in *The Book of Changes*, trans. Richard Wilhelm, ed. Cary F. Baynes. Princeton: Princeton University Press, Bollingen Foundation, 1950, 1967, pp. 280–301

Principles for Women
by Pan Chao

Although the majority of Confucian scholars were men, there were also some female scholars. The most famous woman scholar was Pan Chao, who was historian for the Imperial Court of China in the first century CE. What follows is part of her advice to her daughters, and thus to women in general, on fulfilling their proper social roles.

Respect and Caution As *Yin* and *Yang* are not of the same nature, so man and woman have different characteristics. The distinctive quality of the *Yang* is rigidity; the function of the *Yin* is yielding. Man is honored for strength; a woman is beautiful on account of her gentleness. Hence there arose the common saying: "A man though born like a wolf may, it is feared, become a weak monstrosity: a woman though born like a mouse may, it is feared, become a tiger."

Now for self-culture nothing equals respect for others. To counteract firmness nothing equals compliance. Consequently it can be said that the Way of respect and acquiescence is woman's most important principle of conduct. So respect may be defined as nothing other than holding on to that which is permanent; and acquiescence nothing other than being liberal and generous. Those who are steadfast in devotion know that they should stay in their proper places; those who are liberal and generous esteem others, and honor and serve [them].

If husband and wife have the habit of staying together, never leaving one another, and following each other around within the limited space of their own rooms, then they will lust after and take liberties with one another. From such action improper language will arise between the two. This kind of discussion may lead to licentiousness. Out of licentiousness will be born a heart of disrespect to the husband. Such a result comes from not knowing that one should stay in one's proper place.

Furthermore, affairs may be either crooked or straight; words may be either right or wrong. Straightforwardness cannot but lead to quarreling: crookedness cannot but lead to accusation. If there are really accusations and quarrels, then undoubtedly there will be angry affairs. Such a result comes from not esteeming others, and not honoring and serving [them].

[If wives] suppress not contempt for husbands, then it follows [that such wives] rebuke and scold [their husbands]. [If husbands] stop not short of anger, then they are certain to beat [their wives]. The correct relationship between husband and wife is based upon harmony and intimacy, and [conjugal] love is grounded in proper union. Should actual blows be dealt, how could matrimonial relationship be preserved? Should sharp words be spoken, how could [conjugal] love exist? If love and proper relationship both be destroyed, then husband and wife are divided.

Womanly qualifications A woman [ought to] have four qualifications: (1) womanly virtue; (2) womanly words; (3) womanly bearing; and (4) womanly work. Now what is called womanly virtue need not be brilliant ability, exceptionally different from others. Womanly words need be neither clever in debate nor keen in conversation. Womanly appearance requires neither a pretty nor a perfect face and form. Womanly work need not be work done more skillfully than that of others.

To guard carefully her chastity; to control circumspectly her behavior; in every motion to exhibit modesty; and to model each act on the best usage, this is womanly virtue.

To choose her words with care; to avoid vulgar language; to speak at appropriate times; and not to weary others [with much conversation], may be called the characteristics of womanly words.

To wash and scrub filth away; to keep clothes and ornaments fresh and clean; to wash the head and bathe the body regularly, and to keep the person free from disgraceful filth, may be called the characteristics of womanly bearing.

With whole-hearted devotion to sew and to weave; to love not gossip and silly laughter; in cleanliness and order [to prepare] the wine and food for serving guests, may be called the characteristics of womanly work.

These four qualifications characterize the greatest virtue of a woman. No woman can afford to be without them.

SOURCE: Pan Chao, "Lessons for Women," in Serinity Young, ed., *An Anthology of Sacred Texts by and about Women*. New York: Crossroad Publishing Co., 1995, p. 359

Neo-Confucianism

As Buddhism spread into China, Confucianism was also revived. This "Neo-Confucianism," which became dominant after the tenth century CE, was more metaphysical than classical Confucianism, and it made extensive references to *The Book of Changes*.

The Great Ultimate
by Chou Tun-i

The philosopher Chou Tun-i (1017–73 CE) is considered the pioneer of Neo-Confucianism. His "Explanation of the Diagram of the Great Ultimate," which follows, became the basic framework for Neo-Confucian metaphysics and cosmology.

The Great Ultimate through movement generates yang. When its activity reaches its limit, it becomes tranquil. Through tranquillity the Great Ultimate generates yin. When tranquillity reaches its limit, activity begins again. So movement and tranquillity alternate and become the root of each other, giving rise to the distinction of yin and yang, and the two modes are thus established.

By the transformation of yang and its union with yin, the Five Agents of Water, Fire, Wood, Metal, and Earth arise. When these five material forces (*ch'i*) are distributed in harmonious order, the four seasons run their course.

The Five Agents constitute one system of yin and yang, and yin and yang constitute one Great Ultimate. The Great Ultimate is fundamentally the Non-ultimate. The Five Agents arise, each with its specific nature.

When the reality of the Ultimate of Non-being and the essence of yin, yang, and the Five Agents come into mysterious union, integration arises. **Ch'ien** (Heaven) constitutes the male element, and **K'un** (Earth) constitutes the female element. The interaction of these two material forces engenders and transforms the myriad things. The myriad things reproduce and reproduce, resulting in an unending transformation.

It is man alone who receives (the Five Agents) in their highest excellence, and therefore he is most intelligent. His physical form appears, and his spirit develops consciousness. The five moral principles of his nature (humanity or *jen*, righteousness, propriety, wisdom, and truthfulness) are aroused by, and react to, the external world and engage in activity; good and evil are distinguished; and human affairs take place.

The sage settles these affairs by the principles of the Mean, correctness, humanity, and righteousness (for the way of the sage is none other than these four), regarding tranquillity as fundamental. (Having no desire, there will therefore be tranquillity.) Thus he establishes himself as the ultimate standard for man. Hence the character of the sage is identical with that of Heaven and Earth; his brilliancy is identical with that of the sun and moon; his order is identical with that of the four seasons; and his good and evil fortunes are identical with those of spiritual beings. The superior man cultivates these moral qualities and enjoys good fortune, whereas the inferior man violates them and suffers evil fortune.

Therefore it is said that "yin and yang are established as the way of Heaven, the weak and the strong as the way of Earth, and humanity and righteousness as the way of man." It is also said that "if we investigate the cycle of things, we shall understand the concepts of life and death." Great is the *Book of Changes*! Herein lies its excellence!

SOURCE: Chou Tun-i, "An Explanation of the Diagram of the Great Ultimate," in *A Source Book in Chinese Philosophy*, trans. and ed. Wing-tsit Chan. Princeton: Princeton University Press, 1963, pp. 463–5

The Western Inscription
by Chang Tsai

Chang Tsai (1020–1077 CE) was another of the leading developers of Neo-Confucian thought; his "Western Inscription" is one of its most famous treatises. It was inscribed on the west window of his lecture room.

Heaven is my father and Earth is my mother, and even such a small creature as I finds an intimate place in their midst.

Therefore that which fills the universe I regard as my body and that which directs the universe I consider as my nature.

All people are my brothers and sisters, and all things are my companions.

The greater ruler [the emperor] is the eldest son of my parents [Heaven and Earth], and the great ministers are his stewards. Respect the aged—this is the way to treat them as elders should be treated. Show deep love toward the orphaned and the weak—this is the way to treat them as the young should be treated. The sage identifies his character with that of Heaven and Earth, and the worthy is the most outstanding man. Even those who are tired, infirm, crippled, or sick; those who have no brothers or children, wives or husbands, are all my brothers who are in distress and have no one to turn to.

When the time comes, to keep himself from harm—this is the care of a son. To rejoice in Heaven and to have no anxiety—this is filial piety at its purest.

He who disobeys [the Principle of Nature] violates virtue. He who destroys humanity is a robber. He who promotes evil lacks [moral] capacity. But he who puts his moral nature into practice and brings his physical existence into complete fulfillment can match [Heaven and Earth].

One who knows the principles of transformation will skillfully carry forward the undertakings [of Heaven and Earth], and one who penetrates spirit to the highest degree will skillfully carry out their will.

Do nothing shameful in the recesses of your own house and thus bring no dishonor to them. Preserve your mind and nourish your nature and thus [serve them] with untiring effort. . . .

Wealth, honor, blessing, and benefits are meant for the enrichment of my life, while poverty, humble station, and sorrow are meant to help me to fulfillment.

In life I follow and serve [Heaven and Earth]. In death I will be at peace.

SOURCE: Chang Tsai, "The Western Inscription," in *A Source Book in Chinese Philosophy*, trans. and ed. Wing-tsit Chan. Princeton: Princeton University Press, 1963, pp. 497–8

Living Confucianism

During the twentieth century, communism undercut the political, economic, and social base of Confucianism. However, Confucianism is not just a matter of past history, according to Confucian scholar Dr. Xinzhong Yao, Chairman of the Department of Religion, Ethics and Society at the University of Wales in Lampeter. He finds that even though Confucianism no longer molds Chinese social structure, its values continue to be significant and essential in Chinese life.

Confucianism and the Twenty-First Century
by Xinzhong Yao

Will Confucianism go into the twenty-first century merely as a remnant of history? Or will it have much to offer and to contribute to a meaningful life in a rapidly changing society? What elements or parts of the Confucian tradition enable it not to be a dead culture, nor to be a tradition of the past, but continually to be a living organism comprehensively functioning in a multi-cultural society, emotionally and rationally motivating the people, and naturally making contributions to world peace and prosperity?

The Modern Relevance of Confucianism With the Confucian retreat from political, social and economic stages in East Asia since the end of last century, the Confucian influence has been limited to a small area of learning, seeming to be alive only among tradition-minded people and merely as a social and psychological background of their activities. The political and religious role of Confucianism in Mainland China[5] changed from being the orthodox ideology to a "doctrinal furnishing" of feudalism and aristocracy, and its values and ideals were severely undermined or demolished both by radical revolutionaries and by radical liberals. For most academics and non-academic people, Confucianism represented the shadow of the past, the symbol and the reason of a backward, disadvantaged and powerless China. As a result three irreversible changes took place in relation to Confucianism: Confucian organizations and institutions disappeared, Confucians lost their social identity, and Confucian rituals no longer had spiritual values. Confucianism seemed to have been reduced to being merely a theory or a doctrine without practical meaning, an old image without effect on modern life.

However, this is only one side of the story of Confucianism in the twentieth century. The umbilical cord between the Confucian tradition and modern China cannot be easily cut off. The elements in the Confucian

---

[5] Mainland China—the current Communist state of the People's Republic of China, as opposed to the Republic of China which is the capitalist Nationalist state in Taiwan.

heritage have travelled to the present, either hidden in both Nationalist and Communist doctrines, principles, ethics, public opinions and the system of a bureaucratic elite, etc., or implicitly underlying the whole structure of Chinese community (family, community, society and the state), whatever forms it may take, either capitalist or socialist, Nationalist or Communist. The link between the Three Principles of the People initiated by Sun Zhongshan and the Confucian vision of the Grand Commonwealth Society (*datong shehui*) is so strong that very few people would deny that there exists a succession from the latter to the former. And Communism inherited a great deal from the Confucian moral code, so much so that . . . Communist ethics and Confucianism were not very different in practice.

After many years in which Confucianism suffered a setback, Confucianism is on the rise again in many states and areas of East Asia since the beginning of the 1980s, although the reasons and motives behind the Confucian popularity are quite different from one state to another. In any case, the revival of Confucianism is not simply a return to the tradition nor a wholesale restoration of the old practice and learning, but a renewal of the culture and a transformation of the heritage in order to redefine cultural identity and to guide social and economic development. . . .

It is agreed among the scholars in Confucian Studies that while the social structure of old Confucianism has gone, its doctrinal and idealistic values are inherent in Chinese psychology and underlie East Asian peoples' attitudes and behavior.

Despite criticism and caution about the relevance of Confucianism to modernization, Confucianism is nevertheless gradually regaining some of its lost place in people's lives and in intellectuals' minds. As a traditional organization Confucianism may not yet have obtained any new identity and those that are attached to old systems and old social structures may never be appreciated again. However, Confucian values have become functional once more and become more and more appealing to the people. For example, self-cultivation (*xiu shen*) as the basis for governing the state and bringing peace to the world has been partly accepted and deliberately adopted by this generation of students. The combination of Confucian values and modern qualities creates a new title for business leaders, "Confucian businessmen/women," praising the Confucian virtues of the industrial and commercial leaders, such as humaneness, trustfulness, sincerity and altruism in business dealings. Some people enthusiastically talk about "Marxist Confucianism" or "Confucian Marxism," while others see an opportunity in the economic experience of East Asia to merge Confucianism and the market economy, Capitalist Confucianism or Confucian Capitalism. Along with these new understandings of the nature and functions of Confucianism, efforts have also been made to rejuvenate and rehabilitate Confucian institutions, and interests in Confucian education, examination and academies are on the increase. For example, after the interval of more than half a century on the Mainland, the traditional civil service examination, which bears the hallmark of Confucianism, has partly been adopted as a modern means to recruit civil servants. Confucian academies are no longer regarded as "feudal institutes" but praised as centers for learning and education. In some Chinese communities in Hong Kong, Taiwan and South East Asia, a variety of Confucian organizations have been established aiming at restoring the spiritual functions of Confucianism; for example, the Confucian Academies, Confucian churches centered on the worship of Confucius, and even Confucian Sunday schools that take Confucian classics as their textbook. These may not be enough for Confucianism to reclaim the glorious image of its past. However, nobody would deny that it has become gradually relevant again to today's social/personal and religious life. There are obvious signs indicating that some aspects of the Confucian ethics are still useful and valuable, that the uniqueness of the Confucian religiosity is being recognized as an important dimension of human spirituality, and that the Confucian speculation on metaphysical views is considered conducive to the healthy growth of the global village. . . .

A Responsible Ethic Free choice is the foundation of modern society, and the pre-condition of market economy. However, freedom without responsibility would result in the collapse of the social network and in the conflict between individuals, and between individuals and society, and would lead to the sacrifice of the future in order to satisfy short-term needs. This has become a serious challenge to human wisdom and to human integrity. In this respect, Confucianism can make a contribution to a new moral sense, a new ecological view and a new code for the global village. Confucian ethics insists that the self be the centre of relationships, not in order to claim one's rights but to claim to be responsible; and that a sense of the community of trust must be modelled on the family, not in a way that excludes others but in a way that extends one's family affection to a wider world. According to a Confucian understanding, daily behaviour must be guided by an established ritual, not merely for restricting individuals, but more for cultivating the sense of holiness and mission in their heart. Education is essential for building up a good character, not primarily for building up one's physical power to conquer what is unknown, but for the ability to cooperate with others and to be in harmony with nature and the universe. . . .

The early twentieth-century critics have drawn us a dim and depressing picture of Confucian education in which human nature is distorted and human knowledge is confined to memorizing a few outdated classics. Confucian education certainly has its flaws and is insufficient to cope with modern subjects, nor is it enough to equip the people with technological tools to deal with modern problems. It would therefore be naïve or even foolish to try to replace modern education with Confucian moral training, and unprofessional to credit too much to the traditional ways while rejecting modern methodology of education. Nonetheless, it is still legitimate to raise such a question as: "Are there any useful elements in Confucian education that may be drawn out to serve the goal of a comprehensive education?"...

The purpose of education is not only to transmit knowledge. It is also to transmit and apply values. In this sense, all traditional forms of education are relevant, and Confucian education can be a useful and valuable supplement to modern school education.... Confucian learning was never meant to be a merely scholarly exercise. It had practical extensions, one of which was to put into practice the doctrinal understanding of individual, family, community and society, the core of values fostering a spirit of self-discipline, family solidarity, public morality and social responsibility. Confucian education is fundamentally humanistic; its primary purpose is learning to be fully human and becoming a qualified member of the community of trust; and its primary tools are enhancing self-cultivation and developing one's inner strength of assuming responsibilities for oneself, for one's family and for society at large....

The Confucian faith is fundamentally humanistic, which lays the responsibility for a better world and for a secured future, not in the hands of a supremely detached God, but in the hands of ordinarily engaged humans. In this sense, Confucianism provides us with an alternative way of dealing with the meaning of life and the meaning of death.... For a Confucian, the meaning of life can be realized only in learning and practice, in bringing oneself to the standard of a gentleman and the society to the standard of Great Unity: the destiny of a human can be fulfilled only in establishing words, merits and virtues for generations to come....

SOURCE: Xinzhong Yao, *Confucianism and the 21st Century: Confucian Moral, Educational and Spiritual Heritages Revisited.* Paper presented at First International Conference on Traditional Culture and Moral Education. Beijing, 1998

GLOSSARY

Analects (Lun-yu) The most revered scripture in Confucian tradition, a collection of his sayings, probably compiled by the second generation of his disciples.

Ch'i The vital energy in the universe and in individuals.

I Ching The Classic of Righteousness, an ancient text of divination and guidance.

Jen (ren) Benevolence, human-heartedness, humanistic love toward others; the highest Confucian virtue.

K'un Earth, a Yin element of creation.

Li Ritual, propriety, etiquette, social norms.

Mandate of Heaven Confucian sense of transcendent rightness of the state; may or may not be present in a ruler or a policy; closer to religion than most Confucian ideas, drawn from Chou dynasty's Duke of Chou (d.1094 BCE).

T'ai Chi The Great Ultimate (reality), that gives rise to Yin and Yang, drawn in a circle and embodied as a dance/exercise/meditation.
Tao (the **Way**) Living on the path of self-directing righteousness and harmony.
Ten Thousand Things Chinese phrase indicating "everything."

T'ien or **Ch'ien** Heaven or Nature—a Yang element of creation.
Yang The dark, receptive, "feminine" cosmic energy of **Ch'i**, like a river.
Yin The bright, assertive "masculine" cosmic energy of **Ch'i**, like a mountain.

HOLY DAYS

Explicitly Confucian holidays are celebrated in countries with remaining Confucian influence, such as Taiwan and South Korea.

Confucius's Birthday, September 28, is a state holiday in Taiwan, called "Teacher's Day," since Confucius advocated education not limited to aristocracy.

In South Korea on **Sokchonje** (March and September), traditional court orchestras play and costumed rituals are performed at Confucian shrines. The best place to see this ceremony is at Sungkyunkwan University in Seoul.

The Dragon Boat Festival, also known as the Double Fifth Festival, occurs on the fifth day of the fifth moon of the lunar calendar. It commemorates the Chinese scholar-statesman Chu Yuan (3rd century BCE). One of the three most important annual mainland Chinese festivals; the other two are the Autumn Moon Festival and Chinese New Year.

Domestic rites: these are implicitly Confucian. In the People's Republic the ancient tradition of ancestor memorials is celebrated on Ching Ming (Tomb Sweeping Day) in spring. Families clean and repair their ancestors' graves, place flowers, offer food, burn paper money to send wealth to ancestors in the spirit world. In South Korea, Chusok is Thanksgiving Day, the most important national holiday. People visit family tombs and present food offerings to their ancestors.

HISTORICAL OUTLINE

551–479 BCE—Confucius (Kong Qiu or Kung Ch'iu)

c. 300 BCE—birth of Hsun Tzu or Xunzi, who stressed the need for education

c. 391–308 BCE—Mencius (Meng Tzu or Mengzi)

250 BCE–220 CE—Han dynasty, during which Confucius's teachings became the basis of the state educational system

1130–1200 CE—Chu Hsi, Neo-Confucian scholar

1911—last of the Imperial dynasties overthrown

1949—Mao Tse-tung (Mao Zedong) and his Communist party take control of China

REVIEW QUESTIONS

1 Is Confucianism only a social philosophy, or does it have religious elements?
2 Do you think good ethics can be cultivated without an explictly religious motive? Did the Confucians do it? Give quotes.
3 Is Confucianism optimistic or pessimistic about human nature? How? What are the social implications of this belief?
4 Do you think the Confucian guide for women's behavior was unfair for that time?
5 Draw and explain the T'ai Chi diagram, explaining Yin and Yang.
6 Some modern Communists criticized Confucianism for breeding authoritarianism, nepotism, conservatism and male chauvinism. Does your reading of Confucian texts support this?
7 What elements of Confucianism do you consider valuable enough to keep for any society today?

INFORMATION RESOURCES

China Books and Periodicals
<www.chinabooks.com/Catalog/religion.html#cf>

China Introduction
<www.warriortours.com/intro/index.htm#Confucianism>

Chinese Holidays <www.sandiego-online.com/forums/chinese/htmls/holidays.htm>

Ching, Julia, Laurence Thompson and Wing-tsit Chan, "Confucian Thought" and "Confucius," in *The Encyclopedia of Religion*, ed. Mircea Eliade. IV: 15–42. New York: Macmillan, 1987.

Confucian and Taoist Texts

<http://acc6.its.brooklyn.cuny.edu/~phalsall/texts.html>

Kong Fu Zi–-Confucius
<www.albany.net/~geenius/kongfuzi/links.html>

Lau, D.C. trans. *Confucius: The Analects*. London: Penguin, 1979.

South Korean Holidays
<cair.kaist.ac.kr/korea/do/event.html#H1.4>

Taylor, Rodney, *The Religious Dimensions of Confucianism*. Albany, NY: State University of New York Press, 1990.

Tu Wei-ming, "Confucius and Confucianism," in *The Encyclopedia Britannica* XVI: 653–62, 1997.

CHAPTER 7

TAOISM

In contrast to the pragmatic logic of traditional Confucianism, the Taoist tradition is distinctly mystical. This mysticism actually had no name until scholars labeled it Taoism, lumping together ancient philosophical traditions and later religious sects which concentrate on the achievement of immortality.

Taoism is based on ancient Chinese ways and the teachings of **sages** whose remembrance is shrouded in the mists of time and legend. Most famous of these is Lao-tzu, who is traditionally thought to have lived during the sixth century BCE, To him is attributed the central scripture of Taoism, the **Tao-te Ching**. Whatever its source, the Tao-te Ching proposes a philosophical detachment, allowing things to take their own natural course without interference. By remaining quiet and receptive, one lives in harmony with the natural flow of life, with the **Tao**, the unnamable eternal Reality. In the Tao, all things are one, no matter how separate they may appear on the surface. Everything is to be accepted with equanimity, without preferences. The sage is like flowing water, which naturally flows into a valley from higher regions, makes it way around obstacles, and gently wears them down. He or she "does nothing," for the Tao if left to its own ways will express the underlying harmony in the universe. Energy is not to be wasted in artificial action, but may be expressed spontaneously and creatively when the natural energy is flowing in that direction. Favoring a low social profile, Taoist sages have traditionally withdrawn into the mountains to live contemplatively in nature.

The Traditional Canon

The central Taoist scripture is the Tao-te Ching, traditionally attributed to Lao-tzu, a curator of the royal library during the Chou dynasty of the sixth century BCE. According to legend, he was leaving society to retire to the mountains, at the age of 160, when a border guard requested him to share his wisdom. The terse five thousand characters thus inscribed have been translated more times than any book other than the Bible.

The Tao-te Ching
by Lao-tzu

The way that can be spoken of

Is not the constant way;
The name that can be named
Is not the constant name.
The nameless was the beginning of heaven and earth;
The named was the mother of the myriad creatures.
Hence always rid yourself of desires in order to observe its secrets;
But always allow yourself to have desires in order to observe its manifestations.
These two are the same
But diverge in name as they issue forth.
Being the same they are called mysteries,
Mystery upon mystery—
The gateway of the manifold secrets . . .

The way is empty, yet use will not drain it.
Deep, it is like the ancestor of the myriad creatures.
Blunt the sharpness;
Untangle the knots;
Soften the glare;
Let your wheels move only along old ruts.
Darkly visible, it only seems as if it were there.
I know not whose son it is.
It images the forefather of God . . .

The spirit of the valley never dies.
This is called the mysterious female.
The gateway of the mysterious female
Is called the root of heaven and earth.
Dimly visible, it seems as if it were there,
Yet use will never drain it . . .
When carrying on your head your perplexed bodily soul can you embrace in
    your arms the One
And not let go?
In concentrating your breath can you become as supple
As a babe?
Can you polish your mysterious mirror
And leave no blemish?
Can you love the people and govern the state
Without resorting to action?
When the gates of heaven open and shut
Are you capable of keeping to the role of the female?
When your discernment penetrates the four quarters
Are you capable of not knowing anything?
It gives them life and rears them.
It gives them life yet claims no possession;

It benefits them yet extracts no gratitude;
It is the steward yet exercises no authority.
Such is called the mysterious virtue . . .

The best of all rulers is but a shadowy presence to his subjects.
Next comes the ruler they love and praise;
Next comes one they fear;
Next comes one with whom they take liberties.
When there is not enough faith, there is lack of good faith.
Hesitant, he does not utter words lightly.
When his task is accomplished and his work done
The people all say, "It happened to us naturally." . . .

When the great way falls into disuse
There are benevolence and rectitude;
When cleverness emerges
There is great hypocrisy;
When the six relations[1] are at variance
There are filial children;
When the state is benighted
There are loyal ministers.

Exterminate the sage, discard the wise,
And the people will benefit a hundredfold;
Exterminate benevolence, discard rectitude,
And the people will again be filial;
Exterminate ingenuity, discard profit,
And there will be no more thieves and bandits.
These three, being false adornments, are not enough
And the people must have something to which they can attach themselves:
Exhibit the unadorned and embrace the uncarved block,
Have little thought of self and as few desires as possible . . .

There is a thing confusedly formed,
Born before heaven and earth.
Silent and void
It stands alone and does not change,
Goes round and does not weary.
It is capable of being the mother of the world.
I know not its name
So I style it "the way."

---

[1] Six relations—according to Wang Pi, these are father and son, elder and younger brother, husband and wife.

I give it the makeshift name of "the great."
Being great, it is further described as receding,
Receding, it is described as far away,
Being far away, it is described as turning back.
Hence the way is great; heaven is great; earth is great; and the king is also
  great. Within the realm there are four things that are great, and the king
  counts as one.
Man models himself on earth,
Earth on heaven,
Heaven on the way,
And the way on that which is naturally so . . .

In the pursuit of learning one knows more every day; in the pursuit of the
  way one does less every day. One does less and less until one does nothing
  at all, and when one does nothing at all there is nothing that is undone.
It is always through not meddling that the empire is won. Should you
  meddle, then you are not equal to the task of winning the empire.

SOURCE: Lao-tzu, *Tao-te Ching*, trans. D. C. Lau. London: Penguin, 1963, chapters 1,
4, 6, 10, 16, 17, 18, 19, 25, 48

The Great and Venerable Teacher
by Chuang Tzu

*The second major book in the traditional Taoist canon is a compilation of the often
humorous and ironic writings of the sage Chuang Tzu (c. 365-290 BCE). In the following passage, he refers to the ideal sage as the "True Man."*

He who knows what it is that Heaven does, and knows what it is that man
does, has reached the peak. Knowing what it is that Heaven does, he lives
with Heaven. Knowing what it is that man does, he uses the knowledge of
what he knows to help out the knowledge of what he doesn't know, and
lives out the years that Heaven gave him without being cut off midway—
this is the perfection of knowledge.

However, there is a difficulty. Knowledge must wait for something to fix
on to, and that which it waits for is never certain. How, then, can I know that
what I call Heaven is not really man, and what I call man is not really
Heaven? There must first be a **True Man** before there can be true knowledge.

What do I mean by a True Man? The True Man of ancient times did not
rebel against want, did not grow proud in plenty, and did not plan his
affairs. Being like this, he could commit an error and not regret it, could
meet with success and not make a show. Being like this, he could climb the
high places and not be frightened, could enter the water and not get wet,
could enter the fire and not get burned. His knowledge was able to climb all
the way up to the Way like this.

The True Man of ancient times slept without dreaming and woke without care; he ate without savoring and his breath came from deep inside. The True Man breathes with his heels; the mass of men breathe with their throats. Crushed and bound down, they gasp out their words as though they were retching. Deep in their passions and desires, they are shallow in the workings of Heaven.

The True Man of ancient times knew nothing of loving life, knew nothing of hating death. He emerged without delight; he went back in without a fuss. He came briskly, he went briskly, and that was all. He didn't forget where he began; he didn't try to find out where he would end. He received something and took pleasure in it; he forgot about it and handed it back again. This is what I call not using the mind to repel the Way, not using man to help out Heaven. This is what I call the True Man....

You hide your boat in the ravine and your fish net in the swamp and tell yourself that they will be safe. But in the middle of the night a strong man shoulders them and carries them off, and in your stupidity you don't know why it happened. You think you do right to hide little things in big ones, and yet they get away from you. But if you were to hide the world in the world, so that nothing could get away, this would be the final reality of the constancy of things.

You have had the audacity to take on human form and you are delighted. But the human form has ten thousand changes that never come to an end. Your joys, then, must be uncountable. Therefore, the sage wanders in the realm where things cannot get away from him, and all are preserved. He delights in early death; he delights in old age; he delights in the beginning; he delights in the end. If he can serve as a model for men, how much more so that which the ten thousand things are tied to and all changes alike wait upon!

The Way has its reality and its signs but is without action or form. You can hand it down but you cannot receive it; you can get it but you cannot see it. It is its own source, its own root. Before Heaven and earth existed it was there, firm from ancient times. It gave spirituality to the spirits and to God; it gave birth to Heaven and to earth. It exists beyond the highest point, and yet you cannot call it lofty; it exists beneath the limit of the six directions, and yet you cannot call it deep. It was born before Heaven and earth, and yet you cannot say it has been there for long; it is earlier than the earliest time, and yet you cannot call it old.

SOURCE: Chuang-tzu, *The Book of Chuang Tzu*, trans. Burton Watson. New York: Columbia University Press, 1968, pp. 77–83

Heaven's Gifts
by Lieh-tzu

Traditionally attributed to the Taoist philosopher Lieh Yu-kau, who claimed, perhaps metaphorically, that he could ride on the wind, the Lieh-tzu, the Classic of Complete

Emptiness, *is the third old scripture in the Taoist canon. Using stories and parables, it describes the universe according to classical Chinese thinking as being essentially composed of* **ch'i**, *meaning air or breath. This* ch'i *is itself insubstantial, but continually becomes more compacted and solid and then dissolves into nothingness.*

The Book of the Yellow Emperor[2] says: "When a shape stirs, it begets not a shape but a shadow. When a sound stirs, it begets not a sound but an echo. When Nothing stirs, it begets not nothing but something."

That which has shape is that which must come to an end. Will heaven and earth end? They will end together with me. Will there ever be no more ending? I do not know. Will the Way end? At bottom it has had no beginning. Will there ever be no more of it? At bottom it does not exist.

Whatever is born reverts to being unborn, whatever has shape reverts to being shapeless. But unborn it is not the basically Unborn, shapeless it is not the basically Shapeless. That which is born is that which in principle must come to an end. Whatever ends cannot escape its end, just as whatever is born cannot escape birth; and to wish to live forever, and have no more of ending, is to be deluded about our lot....

The thing which is shrinking there is swelling here, the thing which is maturing here is decaying there. Shrinking and swelling, maturing and decaying, it is being born at the same time that it is dying. The interval between the coming and the going is imperceptible; who is aware of it? Whatever a thing may be, its energy is not suddenly spent, its form does not suddenly decay; we are aware neither of when it reaches maturity nor of when it begins to decay. It is the same with a man's progress from birth to old age; his looks, knowledge and bearing differ from one day to the next, his skin and nails and hair are growing at the same time as they are falling away. They do not stop as they were in childhood without changing. But we cannot be aware of the intervals; we must wait for the fruition before we know.

There was a man of Ch'i country who was so worried that heaven and earth might fall down, and his body would have nowhere to lodge, that he forgot to eat and sleep. There was another man who was worried that he should be so worried about it, and therefore went to enlighten him.

"Heaven is nothing but the accumulated air; there is no place where there is not air. You walk and stand all day inside heaven, stretching and bending, breathing in and breathing out; why should you worry about it falling down?"

"If heaven really is accumulated air, shouldn't the sun and moon and stars fall down?"

"The sun and moon and stars are air which shines inside the accumulated air. Even if they did fall down, they couldn't hit or harm anyone."

---

[2] Yellow Emperor—a legendary ruler who is said to have ascended into Heaven on a great dragon and become one of the Immortals.

"What about the earth giving way?"

"The earth is nothing but accumulated soil, filling the void in all four directions; there is no place where there is not soil. You walk and stand all day on the earth, stamping about with abrupt spurts and halts; why should you worry about it giving way?"

The man was satisfied and greatly cheered; and so was the man who enlightened him.

When Ch'ang-lu-tzu heard of it, he said smiling:

"The rainbow, clouds and mist, wind and rain, the four seasons; these are formations in the accumulated air of heaven. Mountains and hills, rivers and seas, metal and stone, fire and wood; these are formations in the accumulated matter of earth. Knowing that they are accumulations of air and soil, how can we say that they will not perish? Heaven and earth are one tiny thing within the void, the largest among things that exist. It is no doubt true that it will be long before they reach their term and come to an end, and that it is no easy matter to estimate and predict when this will happen. To worry about them perishing is indeed wide of the mark; but to say they will never perish is also open to objection. Since heaven and earth are bound to perish, a time will come when they will perish. If we happen to be here when they do, why shouldn't we worry?"

When Lieh-tzu heard of it, he too smiled and said:

"It is nonsense to say either that heaven and earth will perish or that they will not. Whether they perish or not we can never know. However, from that side there is one point of view, from this side there is another. Hence the living do not know what it is like to be dead, the dead do not know what it is like to be alive. Coming, we do not know those who went before, going we shall not know those who came after. Why should we care whether they perish or not?"

Shun asked a minister:

"Can one succeed in possessing the Way?"

"Your own body is not your possession. How can you possess the Way?"

"If my own body is not mine, whose is it?"

"It is the shape lent to you by heaven and earth. Your life is not your possession; it is harmony between your forces, granted for a time by heaven and earth. Your nature and destiny are not your possessions; they are the course laid down for you by heaven and earth. Your children and grandchildren are not your possessions; heaven and earth lend them to you to cast off from your body as an insect sheds it skin. Therefore you travel without knowing where you go, stay without knowing what you cling to, are fed without knowing how. You are the breath of heaven and earth which goes to and fro; how can you ever possess it?"

SOURCE: *The Book of Lieh-tzu,* trans. A. C. Graham. London: John Murray; New York: Grove Press, 1960, pp. 22–31

Later developments

In addition to the philosophical system known as Taoism, as expressed in the preceding texts, from the second century CE onward various religious sects developed which are often referred to as "**Immortals** Taoism" or "Religious Taoism." Their relationship to the philosophical tradition is a matter of debate. These sects tend to focus on gods, spirits, magic, ritual and **alchemical** efforts to achieve physical immortality.

A complex medical system developed in China regarding relationships between physical and spiritual aspects of the universe with reference to yin and yang, the receptive and active energies within the Tao. The *Huang Ti Nei Ching Su Wen* ("The Yellow Emperor's Classic of Internal Medicine"), compiled during the Han era (206 BCE–220 CE), illustrates the specificity of this system, in contrast to the more general philosophical nature of the Taoist canon.

Communication of the Force of Life with Heaven
from *Huang Ti Nei Ching Su Wen*

Those who rebel against the basic rules of the universe sever their own roots and ruin their true selves. Yin and Yang, the two principles in nature, and the four seasons are the beginning and the end of everything and they are also the cause of life and death. Those who disobey the laws of the universe will give rise to calamities and visitations, while those who follow the laws of the universe remain free from dangerous illness, for they are the ones who have obtained Tao, the Right Way.

Tao was practiced by the sages and admired by the ignorant people. Obedience to the laws of Yin and Yang means life; disobedience means death. The obedient ones will rule while the rebels will be in disorder and confusion. Anything contrary to harmony (with nature) is disobedience and means rebellion to nature.

The Yellow Emperor said: "From earliest times the communication with Heaven has been the very foundation of life; this foundation exists between Yin and Yang and between Heaven and Earth and within the six points.[3] The (heavenly) breath prevails in the nine divisions,[4] in the nine orifices,[5] in the five viscera, and in the twelve joints; they are all pervaded by the breath of Heaven.

"Life has (the number) five, breath has (the number) three.[6] If people

---

[3] The six points—the four points of the compass, the Zenith and the Nadir.
[4] The nine divisions of China established under Yu the Great.
[5] The nine orifices: the eyes, the ears, the nostrils and the mouth, corresponding to the male principle, and the two lower orifices, the anus and the urethra, corresponding to the female principle.
[6] According to Wang Ping, the three factors are: the heavenly climate, the subtle spirit of the earth, and good fortune.

act contrary to these factors, then noxious influences will injure mankind. This (good conduct) is the foundation of long life. Just as the breath of the blue sky (is calm), so the will and the heart of those who are pure will be in peace, and the breath of Yang will be stable in those who keep themselves in harmony with nature. Even if there are noxious spirits they cannot cause injury to those who follow the laws of the seasons. Therefore the sages preserved the natural spirit and were in harmony with the breath of Heaven, and were thus in direct communication with Heaven. . . .

"The essence of the force of Yang protects the spirit, its gentleness protects the muscles. (If the atmosphere of Yang) cannot open and close, the cold air will follow and the result will be a great deformity. The deep pulse brings about ulcers which are transmitted to the flesh, and the breath of the ducts will become weakened, causing a propensity towards being easily frightened and startled. If the atmosphere of the (main) ducts is not harmonious with the system of the flesh, it will cause ulcers and swellings. Then the perspiration of the animal spirit is unable to reach out, one's body will be weakened, one's force of life will be melted, the '(acupuncture[7]) spots' will be closed, and there arise winds and intermittent fevers.

"Thus wind is the cause of a hundred diseases. When people are quiet and clear, their skin and flesh is closed and protected. Even a heavy storm, afflictions, or poison, cannot injure those people who live in accord with the natural order.

"If a sickness lasts for a long time, there is danger that it might spread, then the upper and the lower (parts of the body) cannot communicate; and even skillful physicians are then not able to help.

"If Yang accumulates excessively one will die from the (resulting) disease. If the force of Yang is blocked, the blockage should be dispelled. If one does not drain it thoroughly and guide away the rough matter, there will be destruction. The force of Yang should move outwards every day."

SOURCE: *Huang Ti Nei Ching Su Wen* ("The Yellow Emperor's Classic of Internal Medicine"), trans. Ilza Veith. Berkeley, CA: University of California Press, 1972, pp. 105–9

Awakening to Perfection
by Zhang Boduan (c. 983–1082)

In Immortals Taoism, there are thought to be various means of ascending from earthly life to immortal heavenly glory. The Yellow Emperor is said to have ascended on a celestial dragon with heavenly escort; some adepts simply vanish, while others leave their bodies while sitting in meditation and quaffing a highly poisonous elixir devel-

---

[7] Acupuncture—Chinese system of treating illness by means of needles inserted at specific points on the body.

oped from transmutation of base metals. Some Taoist adepts use spiritual practices to develop within themselves an immortal "embryo" which can traverse the heavenly realms, while still others undertake spiritual practices designed to develop their subtler energies until they ultimately dissolve into the Tao. One of the most important texts about the processes of inner alchemy is the Wuzhen pian *("Awakening to Perfection"). It was written by Zhang Boduan in 1075 to 1078. The text is highly metaphorical and has been interpreted on many different levels.*

First take the power of heaven and earth and make them into your crucible;[8]
Then isolate the essences of the sun and the moon:
Urge the two things to return to the Tao of the center:
Then work hard to attain the golden elixir[9]—how would it not come forth?

Secure your furnace, set up your crucible; always follow the power of
    heaven and earth.
Forge their essence and refine their innermost power, always keeping well
    in control of your yin and yang souls.
Congealing and dissolving, the incubating temperature produces
    transmutation.
Never discuss its mystery and wonder in idle conversation! . . .

Swallowing saliva and breathing exercises are what many people do,
Yet only with the method of this medicine can you truly transform life.
If there is no true seed in the crucible,
It is like taking water and fire and boiling an empty pot. . . .

"Empty the mind and fill the belly"—such profundity of meaning!
Just, to empty your mind, you must know it first.
Similarly, to refine your lead, you must first fill the belly:
Understand this to protect the mass of gold[10] that fills your halls within.

SOURCE: Zhang Boduan, "Awakening to Perfection," in *The Taoist Experience: An Anthology*, ed. Livia Kohn. New York: State University of New York Press, 1993, pp. 314–19

The Way of Perfect Truth
by Wang Che (1112–1170)

The new Taoist religious sects often freely mixed elements of Buddhism and Confucianism with Taoism, as these strands coexisted in Chinese culture without sharp

---

[8] Crucible—a vessel for melting at high temperatures, used in alchemy; a symbolic region of spirituality in inner alchemy.
[9] Elixir—alchemical medical potion believed to bestow longevity.
[10] Gold—an alchemical symbol for the spiritual treasure transformed from lead.

demarcations. For example, the twelfth-century teacher Wang Che (also known as Wang Ch'ung-yang, "Master Wang of Developed Yang") had studied and practiced both Confucian and Buddhist ways before becoming a master of the Tao, living as a recluse in the mountains and attracting many followers to his "Perfect Truth" sect. He gave the sect these basic precepts for the spiritual life.

On Residence and Covering Sleeping in the open air would violate the sun and the moon, therefore some simple thatched covering is necessary. However, it is not the habit of the superior man to live in great halls and lavish palaces, because to cut down the trees that would be necessary for the building of such grand residences would be like cutting the arteries of the earth or cutting the veins of a man. Such deeds would only add to one's superficial external merits while actually damaging one's inner credits. It would be like drawing a picture of a cake to ward off hunger or piling up snow for a meal—much ado and nothing gained. Thus the Perfect Truth Taoist will daily seek out the palace hall within his own body and avoid the mundane mind which seeks to build lavish external residences. The man of wisdom will scrutinize and comprehend this principle.

On Companionship A Taoist should find true friends who can help each other in times of illness and take care of each other's burials at death. However he must observe the character of a person before making friends with him. Do not commit oneself to friendship and then investigate the person's character. Love makes the heart cling to things and should therefore be avoided. On the other hand, if there is no love, human feelings will be strained. To love and yet not to become attached to love—this is the middle path one should follow.

There are three dimensions of compatibility and three of incompatibility. The three dimensions of compatibility are an understanding mind, the possession of wisdom, and an intensity of aspiration. Inability to understand the external world, lack of wisdom accompanied by foolish acts, and lack of high aspiration accompanied by a quarrelsome nature are the three dimensions of incompatibility. The principle of establishing oneself lies in the grand monastic community. The choice of a companion should be motivated by an appreciation of the loftiness of a person's mind and not by mere feelings or external appearance.

On Sitting in Meditation Sitting in meditation which consists only of the act of closing the eyes and seating oneself in an upright position is only a pretense. The true way of sitting in meditation is to have the mind as immovable as Mount T'ai[11] all the hours of the day, whether walking,

---

[11] Mount T'ai—a particularly Chinese sacred mountain.

resting, sitting, or reclining. The four doors of the eyes, ears, mouth, and nose should be so pacified that no external sight can be let in to intrude upon the inner self. If ever an impure or wandering thought arises, it will no longer be true quiet sitting. For the person who is an accomplished meditator, even though his body may still reside within this dusty world, his name will already be registered in the ranks of the immortals or free spirits and there will be no need for him to travel to far-off places to seek them out; within his body the nature of the sage and the virtuous man will already be present. Through years of practice, a person by his own efforts can liberate his spirit from the shell of his body and send it soaring to the heights. A single session of meditation, when completed, will allow a person to rove through all the corners of the universe.

On Pacification of the Mind There are two minds. One is quiet and unmoving, dark and silent, not reflecting on any of the myriad things. It is deep and subtle, makes no distinction between inner and outer, and contains not a single wandering thought. The other mind is that mind which, because it is in contact with external forms, will be dragged into all kinds of thoughts, pushed into seeking out beginnings and ends—a totally restless and confused mind. This confused mind must be eliminated. If one allows it to rule, then the Way and its power will be damaged, and one's Nature and Destiny will come to harm. Hearing, seeing, and conscious thoughts should be eliminated from all activities, from walking, resting, sitting, or reclining.

On Nurturing One's Nature The art of cultivating one's Nature is like that of playing on the strings of a musical instrument: too great a force can break the string, while too weak a pull will not produce any sound; one must find the perfect mean to produce the perfect note. The art of nurturing one's Nature is also like forging a sword: too much steel will make the sword too brittle while too much tin will make it too malleable. In training one's Nature, this principle must be recognized. When it is properly implemented, one can master one's Nature at will.

On Aligning the Five Primal Energies The Five Primal Energies are found in the Middle Hall. The Three Primal Energies are located at the top of the head. If the two are harmonized, then, beginning with the Green Dragon and the White Tiger [the supreme Yin-Yang pair], the ten thousand gods in the body will be arranged in perfect harmony. When this is accomplished, then the energy in the hundred veins will flow smoothly. Cinnabar[12] and mercury[13] will coalesce into a unity. The body of the adept

---

[12] Cinnabar—a heavy reddish ore of mercury, used in alchemical elixirs; a symbol for Nature.
[13] Mercury—a liquid metal element, symbol for Destiny.

may still be within the realm of men, but the spirit is already roving in the universe.

On the Union of Nature and Destiny Nature is spirit. Destiny is material energy. When Nature is supported by Destiny it is like a bird buoyed up and carried along by the wind—flying freely with little effort. Whatever one wills to be, one can be. This is the meaning in the line from the *Classic of the Shadowy Talismans*: "The bird is controlled by the air." The Perfect Truth Taoist must treasure this line and not reveal its message casually to the uninitiated. The gods themselves will chide the person who disobeys this instruction. The search for the hidden meaning of Nature and mind is the basic motif of the art of self-cultivation. This must be remembered at all times.

On the Path of the Sage In order to enter the path of the sage, one must accumulate patiently, over the course of many years, merit-actions and true practices. Men of high understanding, men of virtue, and men who have attained insight may all become sages. In attaining sagehood, the body of the person may still be in one room, but his Nature will already be encompassing the world. The various sages in the various Heavens will protect him, and the free spirits and immortals in the highest realm of the Non-Ultimate will be around him. His name will be registered in the Hall of the Immortals, and he will be ranked among the free spirits. Although his bodily form is in the world of dust, his mind will have transcended all corporal things.

On Transcending the Three Realms The Three Realms refer to the realms of desire, form, and formlessness. The mind that has freed itself from all impure or random thoughts will have transcended the first realm of desire. The mind that is no longer tied to the perception of objects in the object-realm will have transcended the realm of form. The mind that no longer is fixed upon emptiness will further transcend the realm of formlessness. The spirit of the man who transcends all three of these realms will be in the realm of the immortals. His Nature will abide forever in the realm of Jade-like Purity.

On Cultivating the Body of the Law The Body of the Law is formless form. It is neither empty nor full. It has neither front nor back and is neither high nor low, long nor short. When it is functioning, there is nothing it does not penetrate. When it is withdrawn into itself, it is obscure and leaves no trace: it must be cultivated in order to attain the true Way. If the cultivation is great, the merit will be great: if the cultivation is small, the merit will be small. One should not wish to return to it, nor should one be attached to this world of things. One must allow Nature to follow its own course.

On Leaving the Mundane World Leaving the mundane world is not leaving the body; it is leaving behind the mundane mind. Consider the analogy of the lotus: although rooted in the mud, it blossoms pure and white into the clean air. The man who attains the Way, although corporally abiding in the world, may flourish through his mind in the realm of sages. Those people who presently seek after non-death or escape from the world do not know this true principle and commit the greatest folly.

The words of these fifteen precepts are for our disciples of aspiration. Examine them carefully!

SOURCE: Wang Che, "The Way of the Taoist Tradition of Perfect Truth," in *Chinese Religion: An Anthology of Sources*, ed. Deborah Sommer. New York and Oxford: Oxford University Press, 1995, pp. 200–3

The Story of Ho Hsien Ku, a Female Immortal

In popular Taoism, many stories are told of the Eight Immortals, some of whom may have been based on historical figures. One of the Immortals is a female: Ho Hsien Ku. The following story illustrates how her selfless virtue, as well as her asceticism, won her a place among the Immortals.

An old woman owned a small farm at the foot of Mi-Lo Shan. She had never completed a full day's work and had no intention of doing so. As the years progressed she had become lazier and lazier, spending most of the day maliciously gossiping with her neighbours or giving abrupt orders to her servant.

Her latest servant was a young, beautiful and generous hearted girl called Ho Hsien Ku. However hard she worked the old woman was never satisfied. She continually harangued, scolded and punished the helpless girl. Ho Hsien Ku's day began at five o'clock in the morning and rarely finished before midnight.

Besides clearing the house and preparing the food she had to plant and reap the crops and feed and care for the animals. Ho Hsien Ku did this without complaint in return for food and lodgings, but at night, when she fell exhausted onto her straw mattress, she silently wept herself to sleep.

One day the old woman set off to visit her cousin, leaving the young girl to guard the house. Ho Hsien Ku placed a small wicker chair outside the front door and sat down with her sewing basket to repair the old woman's clothes.

Through the haze of the hot afternoon sun, she saw seven figures moving slowly towards her. As they drew closer, she saw their ragged clothes, gaunt faces and downcast eyes. The beggars eventually gathered around her. One stepped forward and in pleading tones addressed Ho Hsien Ku. "Could you please help us. We have not eaten a morsel of food in five days and now we are starving. Could you spare us a bowl of rice."

Ho Hsien Ku was moved by their distress. If she had had the choice, she would have given the beggars all the food in the house but she was hesitant. The old woman meticulously checked the amount of food in the house each day. If a handful of rice or a spoonful of oil was missing, she would beat the girl mercilessly. But Ho Hsien Ku could not turn the beggars away. She would rather be beaten black and blue than let these unfortunate ragged men starve by the roadside.

She beckoned the beggars to rest on the straw mats in front of the house then went into the kitchen to boil a pan of rice. Ten minutes later each beggar had a bowl of rice in his hands which he devoured eagerly and gratefully. The rice gave them renewed strength and after thanking Ho Hsien Ku profusely, the beggars wandered in the direction of the nearest town. No sooner had they disappeared from view, when the old woman returned home. Without acknowledging Ho Hsien Ku, she marched straight into the kitchen to check the rice, noodles, eggs, fish, oil and wood. Ho Hsien Ku sat trembling outside the door and within a few minutes a piercing scream of anger came from the kitchen. The old woman ran from the kitchen brandishing a wooden broom.

"You thief, you ungrateful wretch! What have you done with my rice? Have you eaten it or sold it?" she demanded as she held the girl's arm with a vise-like grip.

Holding back her tears, Ho Hsien Ku recounted the whole story but the old woman had a heart like iron. "I have no pity for these dirty beggars. You either find them and bring them back to me or I will beat your legs till you can no longer walk."

The old woman loosened her grip on Ho Hsien Ku's arm, just enough for Ho Hsien Ku to break free and dash after the beggars. She eventually caught up with them as they were resting by the dusty road-side. Standing breathlessly before them she pleaded desperately.

"I am sorry to ask you this, but could you return with me to prove to my mistress that you ate the rice. If you do not come she will beat me black and blue."

The beggars were only too willing to help the girl who had taken pity on them and they returned home with her. The old woman was still in a furious temper when they arrived.

"How dare you eat the food that belongs to a poor old woman," she screamed. "I demand that you vomit every morsel on the floor in front of me. If you don't, I will make sure that nobody in this district offers you food or water. You deserve to starve."

The beggars had no choice but to do as they were told. One by one they vomited the noodles on to the packed earth floor in front of the house. The old woman then turned to Ho Hsien Ku and demanded vehemently, "Eat every single noodle that has been vomited. This is the price you have to pay for feeding dirty beggars."

She pushed the tearful and frightened Ho Hsien Ku to the floor and the helpless girl was forced to put a handful of the vomited noodles into her mouth. As soon as the noodles touched her tongue she felt her body become lighter and lighter. She felt her legs rise from the ground and her body began to float away from the spiteful old woman, away from the home where she had suffered so miserably.

The old woman began to panic and turned round to demand an explanation from the beggars, but they too had risen high above the house. She caught a last glimpse of the beggars before they disappeared into the clouds and her servant, Ho Hsien Ku, was in their midst.

The Seven Immortals had come to earth to test the young girl's character and she had proved herself worthy of immortality. Because she had endured suffering without complaint and given to the poor without thought for herself, she could work alongside the Immortals for eternity.

SOURCE: "The Story of Ho Hsien Ku," from Kwok Man Ho and Joanne O'Brien, *The Eight Immortals of Taoism*, in Serinity Young, ed., *An Anthology of Sacred Texts by and about Women*, New York: Crossroad, 1995, pp. 394–5

The Essence of T'ai Chi
by Al Chung-liang Huang

Today there is considerable global interest in Taoism, with many translations of the ancient texts being undertaken and some of the spiritual practices being taught to people from other societies. Even under atheistic Communist rule, decades of Chinese have begun their days with T'ai-chi-ch'uan exercises for the sake of health and longevity. These slow, graceful movements were developed over two thousand years ago as a spiritual means of mental discipline and a physical aid to allowing the vital breath (ch'i) to flow freely through the body. In addition to the millions of people in East Asia who practice Tai-chi-ch'uan, Taoist masters such as Al Huang are teaching the practice to Westerners.

The yin/yang symbol is the interlocking, melting together of the flow of movement within a circle. The similar—and at the same time obviously contrasting—energies are moving *together*. Within the black area there is a white dot and within the white fish shape, there is a black dot. The whole idea of a circle divided in this way is to show that within a unity there is duality and polarity and contrast. The only way to find real balance without losing the centering feeling of the circle is to think of the contrasting energies moving together and in union, in harmony, interlocking. In a sense this is really like a white fish and a black fish mating. It's a union and flowing interaction. It's a kind of consummation between two forces, male and female, mind and body, good and bad. It's a very important way of living. People identify with this kind of concept in the Orient much more than in our Western culture, where the tendency is to identify with one force and to reject the contrasting element. If you identify with only one side of the duality, then you become unbalanced. **T'ai chi** can help you to realize how you are unbalanced and help you to become centered again as you re-establish a flow between the two sides. So don't get stuck in a corner, because a circle has no corners. If you think in this way, you open up more, and you don't feel like you have to catch up with anything.

Someone said that the difference between an Oriental man and a Western man is this: The Oriental man is very empty and light up here in the head and very heavy down here in the belly and he feels very secure. The Western man is light in the belly and very heavy up here in the head, so he topples over. In our Western society so much is in the head, so much is in talking and thinking about things, that we can analyze everything to pieces and it's still distant from us, still not really understood. We have so many mechanical gadgets to do our work for us that our bodies are underemphasized. In order to regain balance we have to emphasize the body and we must work with the mind-body together.

Some people realize that their bodies need more work, so they run, jog, ride bicycles, swim, and then say "O.K. I have done my share of exercise." But this is still a separation of "body time" and "mind time," like the separation of work and play that most people experience. You work very hard so that you can take a vacation and come to a beautiful place to enjoy yourself. This brings a separation in your life. Working shouldn't be such a chore. Playing shouldn't be such a straining for fun, fun, fun. Work and play can combine. Non-verbal activities are a very important way to regain balance and find unity in your life. When you stop talking you have a chance to open up and become receptive to what is happening in your body and to what is going on around you.

T'ai chi is one of the many ways to help you to discipline your body and find a way to release that tension within you. T'ai chi can be a way of letting your body really teach you and be with you and help you to get through the conflicts you encounter every day. . . .

We work on a continuous flow. This is another aspect of t'ai chi, which ties in exactly with the **I Ching**, the *Book of Changes*. Change is yin and constant is yang, or vice versa. So the constant thing is that we all can fit into the changing rise and fall. The change is constant; the constant is change. In movement, we learn to really understand this intellectual concept. Part of our everyday conflict is how to cope with the changes and how to be happy with the constant. We are usually bored with the constant, and we get frantic with the change. We have all kinds of gimmicks: "Meditate!" "Pull yourself together!" "Relax!" "Do therapy!" But these all boil down to one thing: Accept *both* the constant and the change. Learn how to be resilient and responsive to your surroundings, to time, and to yourself.

In t'ai chi practice, you move very slowly. By moving very slowly you have time to be aware of all the subtle details of your movement and your relationship to your surroundings. It's so slow that you really have no way of saying this is slower than that or faster than that. You reach a level of speed that is like slow motion, in which everything is just happening. You slow it to the point that you are fully involved in the process of each moment as it happens. . . .

Pay attention to the circular movement of your breathing. Allow the breathing pattern to really circulate inside of you, inside of your torso. Let it flow into your arms, up to your neck, to the top of your head, and down the backbone into your legs. Then energy can begin to expand to all directions at once. Feel all the energy from outside coming towards you, and your energy reaching out as your arms begin to lift. The rising of your arms is balanced by a sinking into your base, as the energy of the circle expands. Think of an expansion instead of a cut-and-dried hand-lift and knee-bend. . . . Think of that expansion into all directions from the center of your body and then the coming together, the collecting back to straight upright center support. Let that feeling of energy open you out into a curving yin/yang intertwining up/down flow as you expand in your arms and settle into your base. Then the outward energy curves and turns inward as your arms sink and your pelvis rises and you return to center. This energy must be a part of you; you must never move as an objective outsider observing. You must always be inside of it, with it. This is the only way you can do t'ai chi. . . .

Wherever you are, whatever you do, you can always come back to this marvelous sense of stillness, the feeling of yourself, very, very much *here*. This is your reference point; this is your stability. This is your life force that gives you balance. This is your home you carry around with you wherever you are. This is your powerhouse, your reservoir, your endless inexhaustible resource, that center you. . . . And the movement goes on and on and on.

SOURCE: Al Chung-liang Huang, *Embrace Tiger, Return to Mountain*. Moab, UT: Real People Press, 1973, pp. 12–19, 182–185.

GLOSSARY

Alchemy In Chinese tradition, an external search for a potion for immortality; an internal quest for immortal soul by meditation, bodily control and breathing.

Ch'i (breath) The universe's vital energy, found in the world and our bodies; harmony comes from balancing its Yin and Yang sides.

Emptiness The imperceptible, undifferentiated void giving birth to all existence.

I Ching (Classic Book of Changes) A manual of ancient divination.

Immortals (Pa-hsien) Eight Taoist perfected persons.

Sage A wise man, both scholar and teacher.

T'ai chi chuan (Power of the Great Ultimate) Stylized, graceful physical exercises practiced daily to enter into harmony with the universe, the Tao.

Tao (the Way) A term used by all Chinese schools of thought; in Taoism it means the ineffable, ultimate, universal reality, hidden behind existence.

Tao-te Ching (The Classic of the Way of Power) The primary text of Taoism attributed to Lao-tzu, addressed to a sage-king; condensed paradoxical poetry.

True Man (in Chuang Tzu) Mythical perfect person who lives in perfect freedom, untroubled by the world.

Yang The dark, receptive, "feminine" cosmic energy of Ch'i, like a river.

Yin The bright, assertive "masculine" cosmic energy of Ch'i, like a mountain.

HOLY DAYS

Taoist priests share ritual feasts for initiation into the hierarchy, advancement in rank, or the consecration of an oratory. They meditate, practice abstinences, perform temple ceremonies to consult, appease or drive off deities and ancestor spirits present in everyday events such as birth, marriage, burial, house construction, business affairs, and treatment of illness. In a trance, the priest may become the mouthpiece of a deity or deceased relative.

HISTORICAL OUTLINE

c. 1111–255 BCE—Chou dynasty rule

c. 500–400 BCE—Lao-tzu may have lived at this time

475–221 BCE—Chuang-tzu probably lived during this time

200–300 CE—Ko Hung's writings on alchemy

364–370 CE—the visionary Yang Hsi at the imperial court

c. 400–448 CE—Emperor T'ai Wu Ti of Northern Wei dynasty declares Taoism official imperial religion

618–907 CE—T'ang dynasty; Emperor Li Yuan, founder, claims descent from Lao-tzu

1949—Chang En-pu, 63rd Celestial Master, moves to Taiwan

REVIEW QUESTIONS

1   Why does the Tao-te Ching speak in paradoxical riddles? Explain some.
2   What is Emptiness for Lao-tzu? Illustrate.
3   Explain Chuang-tzu's "True Man."
4   What does Lieh-tzu mean by "it is being born at the same time that it is dying"?
5   How was the influence of Yin and Yang on illness explained to the Yellow Emperor?
6   What kind of alchemy does the "Awakening to Perfection" teach?
7   What are the goals of Taoist meditation?
8   Tell the story of Ho Hsien Ku.
9   Explain the meaning of the Yin/Yang circle.
10   Describe T'ai Chi-chuan.

INFORMATION RESOURCES

Al Chung-liang Huang, *Embrace Tiger, Return to Mountain: The Essence of T'ai Chi.* Moab, UT: Real People Press, 1973.

Baldrian, Farzeen, "Taoism: An Overview," in Mircea Eliade, ed., *The Encyclopedia of Religion*, IV: 288–306. New York: Macmillan, 1987.

Chuang-tzu, *Basic Writings*, trans. Burton Watson. New York: Columbia University Press, 1964.

Huai-Chin Nan, *Tao & Longevity*, trans. Wen Kuan Chu. Shaftesbury, UK: Element Books.

Kohn, Livia, *The Taoist Experience: An Anthology.* Albany, NY: State University of New York Press, 1993.

Seidel, Anna, and Michael Strickmann, "Taoism," in *The Encyclopedia Britannica*, XXVIII: 383–96, 1997.

Young, Serinity, ed. *An Anthology of Sacred Texts by and about Women.* New York: Crossroad, 1995.

CHAPTER 8

JUDAISM

In the West, the oldest of the major global religions is Judaism. It is in fact the seminal tradition for the two largest existing world religions: Christianity and Islam. They all share a central belief in **monotheism**; all also refer back to the first Hebrew patriarch: Abraham. It is thought that he lived perhaps somewhere between 1900 and 1700 BCE. God is said to have called him to Canaan and made a covenant with him that he would be the father of a great nation. In addition, his first son, Ishmael, is considered the progenitor of the Muslim lineage.

In addition to Abraham, Jewish tradition recognizes many later patriarchs and prophets. Moses is thought to have led the Israelites out of bondage in Egypt, to have spoken directly to God, and to have received God's commandments for the people. The revered King David united the kingdoms of Judah and Israel and established his capital in Jerusalem. His son Solomon ruled from approximately 967 to 928 BCE, increasing the extent, wealth, and power of the kingdom of Israel, and building the great Temple in Jerusalem for the priests to strengthen Hebrew piety. But the strength of the nation afterward declined until in 586 BCE, when Babylonia captured Jerusalem, destroyed the Temple, and took many Jews into exile. Fifty years later some were allowed to return and rebuild the Temple, but the Hebrew kingdom had by then become a dispersed people (the **Diaspora**).

After the Second Temple was destroyed by the Roman occupiers in 70 CE, Judaism was maintained and shaped primarily by **rabbis**, who were teachers, decision-makers, and interpreters of the written and oral traditions. Outside Israel, Babylon became a center of Jewish theological activity; Jewish intellectual life also flourished in Spain, France, and Germany, and under Muslim rule in Baghdad. Despite their growing cultural and financial power, Jewish people were eventually oppressed by certain Christians in Western Europe, which led to large-scale massacres, ultimately including the murder of over a third of the world's Jews by Nazi Germany during World War II. A special "homeland" for Jews was established in Palestine and given the ancient name of Israel, but it has never been free from tensions with the earlier and surrounding inhabitants of that area.

Today many people who are Jewish by birth do not practice the **Orthodox** tradition. Nevertheless, there is a renewal of interest in Judaism today, both among **conservatives** and among **Reform** Jews who are reinterpreting their traditions to find their relevance to contemporary life.

The Jewish Bible: Tanakh

The Jewish Bible, written in the Hebrew language, is called the **Tanakh**, an acronym for its three parts:

1. The **Torah**, which is the first five books: Genesis, Exodus, Leviticus, Numbers, Deuteronomy. These are traditionally believed to have been given by God and written by Moses; they are also known as the "**Pentateuch**," or "five scrolls." They contain the major founding traditions of the faith: creation, the first humans, the flood, the patriarchs from Abraham to Moses, the Exodus from slavery in Egypt led by Moses, and the founding of the Law, or Torah.

2. The "**Prophets**" (*Nevi'im*) are a group of books ascribed to leading reformers such as Isaiah. The prophets spoke boldly and critically of the flaws in their society, but also promised a messiah to free them and lead them to power.

3. The "Wisdom Literature", or "Writings" (*Kethuvim*) is a diverse collection of texts, ranging from poetic Psalms to the nearly tragic drama of Job.

With many parts originating as oral tradition, the Tanakh was slowly written down over hundreds of years, particularly during the Exile, 587–539 BCE. It was translated into Greek from about 200 BCE. Following the destruction of Jerusalem in 70 CE the **Canon** was gradually collected and finalized by the rabbis.

The Five Books of Moses—The Torah ("teaching" or "law")—includes the Books of Genesis, Exodus, Leviticus, Numbers, and Deuteronomy.

Genesis includes two stories of God's Creation, Adam and Eve's disobedience, Noah's flood, and the Patriarchal families: Abraham, Sarah, Hagar and Ishmael; Isaiah and Rebecca; Jacob and Esau among others.

Exodus tells of God's liberation of the Hebrews from Egyptian slavery, led by Moses, and his reception of the Torah's first Ten Commandments at the holy Mount Sinai.

Leviticus is a manual of rules for the ancient Hebrews.

Numbers records the movement of the tribes from Sinai to Canaan.

Deuteronomy includes a long farewell address from Moses and his death.

Traditionally Moses recorded God's revelations in the Torah. Since the nineteenth century, scholars with a more critical eye have made historical and literary analyses of the texts. They have found evidence that the Pentateuch is woven like a rope from strands of four different texts, from different historical periods: the **Yahwist**, the **Elohist**, the **Priestly**, and the **Deuteronomic**.

In the Beginning
The First Creation Account in Genesis

The first book of the Torah begins with creation, which scholars divide into two accounts. The first (a "Priestly" text) is the cosmic account of God's cosmic creation, from Genesis 1:1 to 2:4. In six days, God created the universe from a void, then the earth, vegetation, and humans, male and female in the divine image, then God gave humans responsibility for creation. On the seventh day he rested, which is why the Sabbath is kept as a holy day each week.

In the second creation account, from 2:4 to 3:2 (a "Yahwist" text), God first created one human, ha'adam *("earthling," from* ha'adamah, *"earth"). Later he created a second human being, as the first one was lonely, and thus created* ish *and* ishshah, *man and woman (Adam and Eve). This is why "a man leaves his parents and cleaves to the woman and the two become one flesh." God then created vegetation and animals in the Garden of Eden. Eve, tempted by the serpent, took the fruit of the Tree of Life. She gave some to Adam; then both ate. Their punishment was to labor—Eve in childbirth, Adam in the fields. Death was the ultimate punishment. This creation account can be contrasted with the neighboring Babylonian "Enuma Elish" in which many gods fight with each other until chaotic Tiamat is killed by heroic Marduk. On the contrary, the Genesis 6 flood story of Noah is very similar to the Babylonian "Epic of Gilgamesh" and with Noah's twin, Utanapishtim.*

When God began to create heaven and earth—the earth being unformed and void, with darkness over the surface of the deep and a wind from God sweeping over the water—God said, "Let there be light"; and there was light. God saw that the light was good, and God separated the light from the darkness. God called the light Day, and the darkness He called Night. And there was evening and there was morning, a first day.

God said, "Let there be an expanse in the midst of the water, that it may separate water from water." God made the expanse, and it separated the water which was below the expanse from the water which was above the expanse. And it was so. God called the expanse Sky. And there was evening and there was morning, a second day.

God said, "Let the water below the sky be gathered into one area, that the dry land may appear." And it was so. God called the dry land Earth, and the gathering of waters He called Seas. And God saw that this was good. And God said, "Let the earth sprout vegetation: seed-bearing plants, fruit trees of every kind on earth that bear fruit with the seed in it." And it was so. The earth brought forth vegetation: seed-bearing plants of every kind, and trees of every kind bearing fruit with the seed in it. And God saw that this was good. And there was evening and there was morning, a third day.

God said, "Let there be lights in the expanse of the sky to separate day from night; they shall serve as signs for the set times—the days and the years; and they shall serve as lights in the expanse of the sky to shine upon the earth." And it was so. God made two great lights, the greater light to dominate the day and the lesser light to dominate the night, and the stars. And God set them in the expanse of the sky to shine upon the earth, to dominate the day and the night, and to separate light from darkness. And God saw that this was good. And there was evening and there was morning, a fourth day.

God said, "Let the waters bring forth swarms of living creatures, and birds that fly above the earth across the expanse of the sky." God created the great sea monsters, and all the living creatures of every kind that creep, which the waters brought forth in swarms, and all the winged birds of every kind. And God saw that this was good. God blessed them, saying, "Be fertile and increase, fill the waters in the seas, and let the birds increase on the earth." And there was evening and there was morning, a fifth day.

God said, "Let the earth bring forth every kind of living creature: cattle, creeping things, and wild beasts of every kind." And it was so. God made wild beasts of every kind and cattle of every kind, and all kinds of creeping things of the earth. And God saw that this was good. And God said, "Let us make man in our image, after our likeness. They shall rule the fish of the sea, the birds of the sky, the cattle, the whole earth, and all the creeping things that creep on earth." And God created man in His image, in the image of God He created him; male and female He created them. God blessed them and God said to them, "Be fertile and increase, fill the earth and master it; and rule the fish of the sea, the birds of the sky, and all the living things that creep on earth."

God said, "See, I give you every seed-bearing plant that is upon all the earth, and every tree that has seed-bearing fruit; they shall be yours for food. And to all the animals on land, to all the birds of the sky, and to everything that creeps on earth, in which there is the breath of life, [I give] all the green plants for food." And it was so. And God saw all that He had made, and found it very good. And there was evening and there was morning, the sixth day.

The heaven and the earth were finished, and all their array. On the seventh day God finished what work that He had been doing, and He ceased on the seventh day from all the work that He had done. And God blessed the seventh day and declared it holy, because on it God ceased from all the work of creation that He had done. Such is the story of heaven and earth when they were created.

SOURCE: Genesis 1:1–2:4, in *Tanakh: A New Translation of the Holy Scriptures*. Philadelphia: Jewish Publication Society, 1985

The Second Creation Account in Genesis

When the Lord God made earth and heaven—when no shrub of the field was yet on earth and no grasses of the field had yet sprouted, because the Lord God had not sent rain upon the earth and there was no man to till the soil, but a flow would well up from the ground and water the whole surface of the earth—the Lord God formed man from the dust of the earth. He blew into his nostrils the breath of life, and man became a living being.

The Lord God planted a garden in Eden, in the east, and placed there the man whom He had formed. And from the ground the Lord God caused to grow every tree that was pleasing to the sight and good for food, with the tree of life in the middle of the garden, and the tree of knowledge of good and bad.

A river issues from Eden to water the garden, and it then divides and becomes four branches. The name of the first is Pishon, the one that winds through the whole land of Havilah, where the gold is. (The gold of that land is good; bdellium[1] is there, and lapis lazuli.[2]) The name of the second river is Gihon, the one that winds through the whole land of Cush. The name of the third river is Tigris, the one that flows east of Asshur. And the fourth river is the Euphrates.

The Lord God took the man and placed him in the garden of Eden, to till it and tend it. And the Lord God commanded the man, saying, "Of every tree of the garden you are free to eat; but as for the tree of knowledge of good and bad, you must not eat of it; for as soon as you eat of it, you shall die."

The Lord God said, "It is not good for man to be alone; I will make a fitting helper for him." And the Lord God formed out of the earth all the wild beasts and all the birds of the sky, and brought them to the man to see what he would call them; and whatever the man called each living creature, that would be its name. And the man gave names to all the cattle and to the birds of the sky and to all the wild beasts; but for Adam no fitting helper was found. So the Lord God cast a deep sleep upon the man; and, while he slept, He took one of his ribs and closed up the flesh at that spot. And the Lord God fashioned the rib that He had taken from the man into a woman; and He brought her to the man. Then the man said, "This one at last is bone of my bones and flesh of my flesh. This one shall be called Woman, for from man was she taken."

Hence a man leaves his father and mother and clings to his wife, so that they become one flesh. The two of them were naked, the man and his wife, yet they felt no shame.

Now the serpent was the shrewdest of all the wild beasts that the Lord God had made. He said to the woman, "Did God really say: You shall not eat of any tree of the garden?" The woman replied to the serpent, "We may eat of the fruit of the other trees of the garden. It is only about fruit of the tree in the middle of the garden that God said: 'You shall not eat of it or touch it, lest you die.'" And the serpent said to the woman, "You are not going to die, but God knows that as soon as you eat of it your eyes will be opened and you will be like divine beings who know good and bad." When the woman saw that the tree was good for eating and a delight to the eyes, and that the tree was desirable as a source of wisdom, she took of its fruit and ate. She also gave some to her husband, and he ate. Then the eyes of both of them

---

[1] Bdellium—a tree whose resin is the basis for perfume.
[2] Lapis lazuli—a deep blue semi-precious stone.

were opened and they perceived that they were naked; and they sewed together fig leaves and made themselves loincloths.

They heard the sound of the Lord God moving about in the garden at the breezy time of day; and the man and his wife hid from the Lord God among the trees of the garden. The Lord God called out to the man and said to him, "Where are you?" He replied, "I heard the sound of You in the garden, and I was afraid because I was naked, so I hid." Then He asked, "Who told you that you were naked? Did you eat of the tree from which I had forbidden you to eat?" The man said, "The woman You put at my side— she gave me of the tree, and I ate." And the Lord God said to the woman, "What is this you have done!" The woman replied, "The serpent duped me, and I ate." Then the Lord God said to the serpent, "Because you did this, more cursed shall you be than all cattle and all the wild beasts: on your belly shall you crawl and dirt shall you eat all the days of your life. I will put enmity between you and the woman, and between your offspring and hers; they shall strike at your head, and you shall strike at their heel." And to the woman, He said, "I will make most severe your pangs in childbearing; in pain shall you bear children, yet your urge shall be for your husband, and he shall rule over you."

To Adam He said, "Because you did as your wife said and ate of the tree about which I commanded you, 'You shall not eat of it,' cursed be the ground because of you; by toil shall you eat of it all the days of your life: thorns and thistles shall it sprout for you. But your food shall be the grasses of the field; by the sweat of your brow shall you get bread to eat, until you return to the ground—for from it you were taken. For dust you are, and to dust you shall return."

The man named his wife Eve, because she was the mother of all the living. And the Lord God made garments of skins for Adam and his wife, and clothed them.

And the Lord God said, "Now that the man has become like one of us, knowing good and bad, what if he should stretch out his hand and take also from the tree of life and eat, and live forever!" So the Lord God banished him from the garden of Eden, to till the soil from which he was taken. He drove the man out, and stationed east of the garden of Eden the cherubim and the fiery ever-turning sword, to guard the way to the tree of life.

SOURCE: Genesis 2:4–3:24, in *Tanakh: A New Translation of the Holy Scriptures*. Philadelphia: Jewish Publication Society, 1985

Abraham's Covenant
Genesis

Essential to Judaism is the **Covenant**. *Like contracts made between individuals, states, and kings with their subjects, God made numerous covenants with Israel ("I* *shall be your God and you shall be my people"; Leviticus 26:12). Most notable are: 1. the covenant with Noah, signified by the rainbow, that God would never again destroy humanity with a flood (Genesis 9:8); 2. the covenant with Abraham, signified by male circumcision, that God had chosen Israel as his people and that they would have the land that "you sojourn in" and be numerous (Genesis 17); 3. with Moses, signified by the laws of the Torah, that, if Israel obeyed God's Law, they would be God's treasured "kingdom of priests and a holy nation" (Exodus 19:5); and 4. with King David, that he should build a temple in Jerusalem, and that his "throne shall be established forever" (II Samuel 7:16).*

When Abram was ninety-nine years old, the Lord appeared to Abram and said to him, "I am El Shaddai. Walk in My ways and be blameless. I will establish My covenant between Me and you, and I will make you exceedingly numerous."

Abram threw himself on his face; and God spoke to him further, "As for Me, this is My covenant with you: You shall be the father of a multitude of nations. And you shall no longer be called Abram, but your name shall be Abraham, for I make you the father of a multitude of nations. I will make you exceedingly fertile, and make nations of you; and kings shall come forth from you. I will maintain My covenant between Me and you, and your offspring to come, as an everlasting covenant throughout the ages, to be God to you and to your offspring to come. I assign the land you sojourn in to you and your offspring to come, all the land of Canaan, as an everlasting holding. I will be their God."

SOURCE: Genesis 17:1–12, in *Tanakh: A New Translation of the Holy Scriptures.* Philadelphia: Jewish Publication Society, 1985

The Mosaic Covenant

Exodus records the heart of much of Jewish tradition, focusing on God's power to liberate the chosen people from unjust suffering. The Hebrews were slaves in Egypt, and the infant Moses was saved from Pharaoh's destruction to grow up a prince in Pharaoh's household. But he ran away, then returned to lead his people out of slavery after a great struggle with Pharaoh around 1250 BCE. At Sinai, the Hebrews were given the Ten Commandments, the first of the 613 Laws of the Torah, when Moses ascended the holy mountain.

Moses led the people out of the camp toward God, and they took their places at the foot of the mountain. Now Mount Sinai was all in smoke, for the Lord had come down upon it in fire; the smoke rose like the smoke of a kiln, and the whole mountain trembled violently. . . .

God spoke all these words, saying:

I the Lord am your God who brought you out of the land of Egypt, the house of bondage: You shall have no other gods besides Me.

You shall not make for yourself a sculptured image, or any likeness of what is in the heavens above, or on the earth below, or in the waters under the earth. You shall not bow down to them or serve them. For I the Lord your God am an impassioned God, visiting the guilt of the parents upon the children, upon the third and upon the fourth generations of those who reject Me, but showing kindness to the thousandth generation of those who love Me and keep My commandments.

You shall not swear falsely by the name of the Lord your God; for the Lord will not clear one who swears falsely by His name.

Remember the sabbath day and keep it holy. Six days you shall labor and do all your work, but the seventh day is a sabbath of the Lord your God: you shall not do any work—you, your son or daughter, your male or female slave, or your cattle, or the stranger who is within your settlements. For in six days the Lord made heaven and earth and sea, and all that is in them, and He rested on the seventh day; therefore the Lord blessed the sabbath day and hallowed it.

Honor your father and your mother, that you may long endure on the land that the Lord your God is assigning to you.

You shall not murder.

You shall not commit adultery.

You shall not steal.

You shall not bear false witness against your neighbor.

You shall not covet your neighbor's house: you shall not covet your neighbor's wife, or his male or female slave, or his ox or his ass, or anything that is your neighbor's

SOURCE: Exodus 19–20, in *Tanakh: A New Translation of the Holy Scriptures.* Philadelphia: Jewish Publication Society, 1985

An Eye for an Eye

For millennia the typical form of justice was clan vengeance. If someone killed a member of your clan, you were justified in killing a member of that clan. Neither was a sense of fair punishment for a crime common. So the Torah, along with other cultures' earlier legal documents, such as Hammurabi's Code in Babylon (1792–1750 BCE), attempted to set up fair punishment systems enacted by judges in court. Hammurabi's Code, inscribed on a stone pillar, listed among its laws "If a son has struck his father, his hands shall be cut off," and "If a man had destroyed the eye of another free man, his own eye shall be destroyed." This selection from Leviticus also shows the "eye for an eye" law. This was an effort to limit excessive retaliation and revenge, which at the time was a refinement of justice.

And to the Israelite people speak thus: Anyone who blasphemes his God shall bear his guilt; if he also pronounces the name Lord, he shall be put to death. The whole community shall stone him; stranger or citizen, if he has thus pronounced the Name, he shall be put to death.

If anyone kills any human being, he shall be put to death. One who kills a beast shall make restitution for it: life for life. If anyone maims his fellow, as he has done so shall it be done to him: fracture for fracture, eye for eye, tooth for tooth. The injury he inflicted on another shall be inflicted on him.

SOURCE: Leviticus 24, in *Tanakh: A New Translation of the Holy Scriptures.* Philadelphia: Jewish Publication Society, 1985

Choose Life

In Deuteronomy the Mosaic Covenant is restated, emphasizing Israel's obligation to "choose life" by living by the Torah, in order to fulfill the human side of the Covenants. This condition stands in contrast with the Davidic Covenant's unconditional promise of a secure kingship "forever."

I call heaven and earth to witness against you this day: I have put before you life and death, blessing and curse. Choose life—if you and your offspring would live—by loving the Lord your God, heeding His commands, and holding fast to Him. For thereby you shall have life and shall long endure upon the soil that the Lord your God swore to your ancestors, Abraham, Isaac, and Jacob, to give to them.

SOURCE: Deuteronomy 30, in *Tanakh: A New Translation of the Holy Scriptures.* Philadelphia: Jewish Publication Society, 1985

The Davidic Covenant

"Further, say thus to My servant David: Thus said the Lord of Hosts: I took you from the pasture, from following the flock, to be ruler of My people Israel, and I have been with you wherever you went, and have cut down all your enemies before you. Moreover, I will give you great renown like that of the greatest men on earth. I will establish a home for My people Israel and will plant them firm, so that they shall dwell secure and shall tremble no more. Evil men shall not oppress them any more as in the past, ever since I appointed chieftains over My people Israel. I will give you safety from all your enemies.

"The Lord declares to you that He, the Lord, will establish a house for you. When your days are done and you lie with your fathers, I will raise up your offspring after you, one of your own issue, and I will establish his kingship. He shall build a house for My name, and I will establish his royal throne forever. I will be a father to him, and he shall be a son to Me. When he does wrong, I will chastise him with the rod of men and the affliction of mortals; but I will never withdraw My favor from him as I withdrew it from Saul, whom I removed to make room for you. Your house and your kingship shall ever be secure before you; your throne shall be established forever."

SOURCE: II Samuel 7, in *Tanakh: A New Translation of the Holy Scriptures.* Philadelphia: Jewish Publication Society, 1985

Prophets

In the Ancient Near East, prophets (Nevi'im) were well-known cultic revealers of divine will. Known for their states of trance, and speaking ecstatically, they performed miracles and symbolic actions. The biblical pre-classical prophets, Samuel, Nathan, Elijah and Elisha, were known for foretelling future events and performing miracles, and were consulted by kings. The classical prophets, Isaiah, Jeremiah, Ezekiel, and the twelve minor prophets, also spoke in the name of God, beginning around 750 BCE, while Israel was being attacked by Assyria and Babylonia. They emphasized ethical **monotheism** rather than cult activities and foretelling the future. They criticized their society's hypocrisies and injustices and pleaded with Israel to repent. They also promised God's forgiveness and the coming of the **Messiah.**

The Prophecies of Isaiah

The prophecies of Isaiah son of Amoz, who prophesied concerning Judah and Jerusalem in the reigns of Uzziah, Jotham, Ahaz, and Hezekiah, kings of Judah.

"What need have I of all your sacrifices?" says the Lord. "I am sated with burnt offerings of rams, and suet of fatlings, and blood of bulls; and I have no delight in lambs and he-goats. That you come to appear before Me—Who asked that of you? Trample My courts no more; bringing oblations is futile, incense is offensive to Me. New moon and sabbath, proclaiming of solemnities, assemblies with iniquity, I cannot abide. . . .

Wash yourselves clean; put your evil doings away from My sight. Cease to do evil; learn to do good. Devote yourselves to justice; aid the wronged. Uphold the rights of the orphan; defend the cause of the widow.

"Come, let us reach an understanding," says the Lord. "Be your sins like crimson, they can turn snow-white; be they red as dyed wool, they can become like fleece. If, then, you agree and give heed, you will eat the good things of the earth; but if you refuse and disobey, you will be devoured [by] the sword." For it was the Lord who spoke.

SOURCE: Isaiah 1:11–20, in *Tanakh: A New Translation of the Holy Scriptures.* Philadelphia: Jewish Publication Society, 1985

The Earth Will Teach You

Wisdom literature is common in Ancient Near Eastern cultures. In the Tanakh it is called Kethuvim, and includes Proverbs, Job and Ecclesiastes; several Psalms are also in the Wisdom tradition. Proverbs is a collection of short oral sayings. Ecclesiastes is the book most skeptical of religion, raising many doubts. Psalms is a collection of songs. Job is a drama adapted from a Babylonian source in which Job's faith is tested by terrible suffering when he loses all his wealth and children and is stricken with illness. Here we select two quotes from Job: one showing a sense of ecological harmony with nature, and one showing God's grand cosmic answer to Job's suffering.

But ask the beasts, and they will teach you; the birds of the sky, they will tell you, or speak to the earth, it will teach you; the fish of the sea, they will inform you. Who among all these does not know that the hand of the Lord has done this? In His hand is every living soul and the breath of all mankind.

SOURCE: Job 12:7–10, in *Tanakh: A New Translation of the Holy Scriptures.* Philadelphia: Jewish Publication Society, 1985

Where Were You When I Laid the Earth's Foundations?

Then the Lord replied to Job out of the tempest and said: Who is this who darkens counsel, speaking without knowledge? Gird your loins like a man; I will ask and you will inform Me.

Where were you when I laid the earth's foundations? Speak if you have understanding. Do you know who fixed its dimensions or who measured it with a line? Onto what were its bases sunk?

Who set its cornerstone when the morning stars sang together and all the divine beings shouted for joy? ...

Have you ever commanded the day to break, assigned the dawn its place, so that it seizes the corners of the earth and shakes the wicked out of it? ...

Have the gates of death been disclosed to you? Have you seen the gates of deep darkness? Have you surveyed the expanses of the earth? If you know of these—tell Me.

SOURCE: Job 38:1–18, in *Tanakh: A New Translation of the Holy Scriptures.* Philadelphia: Jewish Publication Society, 1985

Commentaries on the Tanakh

Over many centuries rabbis collected numerous interpretations and extrapolations of Jewish Law, adapting them to the era in which they lived. The

Midrash are mainly concerned with interpreting Tanakh texts. The earliest Midrash may well be the Passover ritual **Haggadah**, now preserved in many elaborated versions. The **Mishnah** is a collection of laws originally handed down orally on festivals, marriage, damages, holy things, and purities. The **Talmud** is the body of teachings commenting on earlier Mishnah.

The Passover Seder Meal Ceremony

Uncover the Matzah *and lift the plate for all to see. The recital of the Passover Story begins with the following words*: This is the bread of affliction which our ancestors ate in the land of Egypt. All who are hungry—let them come and eat. All who are needy—let them come and celebrate the Passover with us. Now we are here; next year may we be in the Land of Israel. Now we are slaves; next year may we be free

The plate is put down, the Matzah *is covered, and the second cup of wine is filled. The youngest present asks the Four Questions.*

The Four Questions How different is this night from all other nights? On all other nights we may eat either leavened or unleavened bread; on this night, only unleavened bread. On all other nights we may eat any vegetable; on this night we are required to eat bitter herbs. On all other nights we are not bidden to dip our vegetables even once; on this night we dip them twice. On all other nights we eat our meals in any manner; on this night, why do we sit around the table together in a ceremonial fashion?

Uncover the Matzah *and begin the reply.*

The Answer "We were slaves of Pharaoh in Egypt," and the Lord our God brought us forth from there "with a strong hand and an outstretched arm." If the Holy One, blessed be He, had not brought forth our ancestors from Egypt, then we and our children, and our children's children, would still be enslaved to Pharaoh in Egypt. Therefore, even if we are all learned and wise, all elders and fully versed in the Torah, it is our duty nonetheless to retell the story of the Exodus from Egypt. And the more one dwells on the Exodus from Egypt, the more is one to be praised.

Point to the shank bone: The Passover offering which our ancestors ate in Temple days, what was the reason for it? It was because the Holy One, blessed be He, passed over the houses of our ancestors in Egypt, as it is written: "And you shall say, 'It is the Passover offering to the Lord, Who passed over the houses of the children of Israel in Egypt, when He smote the Egyptians, and spared our houses.' And the people bowed their heads and worshipped."

Point to the Matzah: This *Matzah* which we eat, what is the reason for it? It is because there was not enough time for the dough of our ancestors to rise when the King of all kings, the Holy One, blessed be He, revealed

Himself to them and redeemed them, as it is written: "And they baked the dough which they had brought out from Egypt into cakes of unleavened bread; for it had not leavened, because they were driven out of Egypt and they could not tarry; nor had they prepared any provisions for themselves."

Point to the bitter herbs: These bitter herbs which we eat—what is their meaning? It is because the Egyptians embittered the lives of our ancestors in Egypt, as it is written: "And they embittered their lives with hard labor, with mortar and bricks, and with every kind of work in the fields; all the work which they made them do was cruel."

In every generation one must see oneself as though having personally come forth from Egypt, as it is written: "And you shall tell your child on that day, 'This is done because of what the Lord did for me when I came forth, from Egypt.'" It was not our ancestors alone whom the Holy One, blessed be He, redeemed; He redeemed us too, with them, as it is written: "He brought us out from there that He might lead us to, and give us, the land which He had promised to our ancestors."

SOURCE: Rabbi Nathan Goldberg, trans. *Passover Haggadah*. Hoboken, NJ: Ktav Publishing, 1949/1993

Midrash

These two brief midrash show God telling Adam not to desolate God's world, and two approaches to teaching. In "The Rest is Commentary," an unbeliever approached the influential rabbi Shammai (c. 50 BCE–30 CE), who was a strict interpreter of Torah. Then he approached the sage Hillel, who lived about the same time, and was a prominent, less rigorous interpreter of Torah. He became president of the Sanhedrin, the supreme religious, political and judiciary body of Israel.

Your World
In the hour when the Holy One, blessed be he, created the first man,
he took him and let him pass before all the trees of the garden of Eden,
and said to him:
See my works, how fine and excellent they are!
Now all that I have created for you have I created.
Think upon this, and do not corrupt and desolate my world;
for if you corrupt it, there is no one to set it right after you.

The Rest is Commentary
Once a heathen came before Shammai. He said to him:
I will be converted, if you can teach me all the Torah while I stand on one leg.
Shammai pushed him away with the builder's measure he had in his hand.
The man came before Hillel. He converted him.
He said to him:

What is hateful to you, do not do to your fellow.
That is all the Torah. The rest is commentary—go and study.

SOURCE: Nahum N. Glatzer, ed. *Hammer on the Rock*. New York: Schocken, 1962, pp. 13, 80

Talmud

*The Talmud is the large body of commentary on the Mishnah's oral traditions. The Jerusalem Talmud dates from about 500 CE, and the Babylonian Talmud was completed about 600 CE. Its contents are notably historical, containing folklore, manners, customs, proverbs, prayers, ritual, and medical advice. The literary style is that of a discussion in an academy (yeshivah), led by scholars such as Ben Zoma. The visual format places a text in the middle of the page, and commentaries (gemara) are written around it. One-third of the Talmud's two and a half million words is commentary on **Halakhah** (written, oral and customary laws) and two-thirds on Haggadah (Passover Seder ritual).*

Ben Zoma says: Who is a wise man? He that learns from all men, as it is said, *From all my teachers have I got understanding* (Psalm 119:99).

Who is a mighty man? He that subdues his evil impulse, as it is said, *He that is slow to anger is better than the mighty, and he that ruleth his spirit than him that taketh a city* (Proverbs 16:32).

Who is a rich man? He that is content with his portion, as it is said, *When thou eatest the labor of thy hands happy shalt thou be and it shall be well with thee* (Psalm 128:2): *Happy shalt thou be* in this world, *and it shall be well with thee* in the world to come.

Who is an honorable man? He that honors mankind, as it is said, *For them that honor me I will honor and they that despise me shall be lightly esteemed* (I Samuel 2:30).

A Wise Man: It is he who is ready to learn even from his inferiors. With such readiness, if his inferior should present him with a wise view, he will not be ashamed to accept it and will not treat his words with contempt. This was characteristic of David, King of Israel, who said, "I would pay attention to any man who came to teach me something."

The Gentile philosophers say that even if a person were to know everything [as it were], if he does not want to increase his knowledge, he is not a wise man but a fool.... On the other hand, one who passionately loves to increase his wisdom, may be called a wise man even if he were to know nothing. Only this way can you attain true wisdom and discover the will of God.

SOURCE: Judah Goldin, ed. and trans. *The Living Talmud*. New Haven: Yale University Press, 1957

Evolving theology and spirituality

Jewish theology has continually elaborated and interpreted the principles of the faith in the light of contemporary life and thought. The Spanish and North African philosopher Maimonides (1135–1204) blended Jewish theology with Greek and Muslim philosophy. His "Thirteen Principles of Faith" affirms his interpretation of the Creator, the Law, and the Messiah.

The spiritual literature of Judaism expresses the experiences of the soul's mystical journey toward God. Mystical Kabbalism began during the Second Temple period and its esoteric teachings developed especially during the European Middle Ages. It developed complex images such as the *sefirot*, or aspects of God's being, drawn as a Tree of Life. The Baal-Shem Tov showed the way of a passionate spirituality and thus began the path of Hasidism, which persists today in various forms. The European philosopher Martin Buber lived from 1878 to 1965; his translation of religion into twentieth-century language likewise reflects his era's concern with I–It and I–Thou relations.

Thirteen Principles of Faith
by Maimonides

1   I believe with perfect faith that the Creator, blessed be his name, is the Author and Guide of everything that has been created, and that he alone has made, does make, and will make all things.

2   I believe with perfect faith that the Creator, blessed be his name, is a Unity, and that there is no unity in any manner like unto his, and that he alone is our God, who was, is, and will be.

3   I believe with perfect faith that the Creator, blessed be his name, is not a body, and that he is free from all the accidents of matter, and that he has not any form whatsoever.

4   I believe with perfect faith that the Creator, blessed be his name, is the first and the last.

5   I believe with perfect faith that to the Creator, blessed be his name, and to him alone, it is right to pray, and that it is not right to pray to any being besides him.

6   I believe with perfect faith that all the words of the prophets are true.

7   I believe with perfect faith that the prophecy of Moses our teacher, peace be unto him, was true, and that he was the chief of the prophets, both of those that preceded and of those that followed him.

8   I believe with perfect faith that the whole Law, now in our possession, is the same that was given to Moses our teacher, peace be unto him.

9   I believe with perfect faith that this Law will not be changed, and that there will never be any other law from the Creator, blessed be his name.

10 I believe with perfect faith that the Creator, blessed be his name, knows every deed of the children of men, and all their thoughts, as it is said, It is

he that fashioneth the hearts of them all, that giveth heed to all their deeds.

11 I believe with perfect faith that the Creator, blessed be his name, rewards those that keep his commandments and punishes those that transgress them.

12 I believe with perfect faith in the coming of the Messiah, and, though he tarry, I will wait daily for his coming.

13 I believe with perfect faith that there will be a resurrection of the dead at the time when it shall please the Creator, blessed be his name, and exalted be the remembrance of him for ever and ever.

SOURCE: Maimonides, "Thirteen Principles of Faith," trans. S. Singer, in *The Authorized Daily Prayer Book of the United Hebrew Congregations of the British Empire.* London: Eyre & Spottiswoode, 1912, pp. 89–90

From Strength to Strength
by Baal-Shem Tov

The founder of the mystical Jewish Hasidic sect in Eastern Europe in the eighteenth century was Rabbi Israel ben Eliezer, called the Baal-Shem Tov (Master of God's Name; c. 1700–60). The legends handed down about him tell of the longing of the Hasidim, who to this day strive to live the Torah with passionate mystical insight, guided by God's principles: Ecstasy (Hitlahavut), embracing God beyond time and space, Service (Avoda) to God in time and space, Intention (Kavana), the mystery of the soul directed to redeeming the world, and Humility (Shiflut). This legend tells how a bereaved youth is consoled by his lost friend who visits him from heaven in a dream.

In the days of the Baal-Shem there lived two friends. They stood in that most beautiful time of youth when the last dawn still glows in heaven, enchanting and undefined: auroral dreams still hover near by, but soon the sun will draw near, the stern master, and his kingdom of forms will become visible.

Often the friends sat together, leaning against the bare wall of their little room, and talked of the meaning of life. To one of them the world was revealed through the word of the Baal-Shem. From each thing he received a message, and with every action he gave a response. He threw himself down on the green field, greeted the wind and the water and the beautiful animals that glided swiftly by, and his greeting was a prayer. Thus for him the meaning of life was founded in the Creator. His companion flew into a passion against him and declared that all this was a sin against the spirit of truth. For each thing has many surfaces and each creature many forms, but he who submits himself to a faith now sees of the multiple reality only one surface and one form; his way becomes at once secure and impoverished, and the search for truth, for the meaning of life, dies away in him. To this the other replied that in the world of enlightenment there are no surfaces and forms, rather each thing and creature stands there in its purity. Thus the friends often argued with each other.

Then it happened that a serious illness overtook that youth who was devoted to the Baal-Shem. In the pitiless intensity of the pain he recognized the message of a power which must bring his earthly life to its end. So he did not resist it, but rather yielded himself to the mighty element. Nonetheless, horror lay encamped on the road to that which would take place in the abyss of eternity. He let the Baal-Shem know that he was preparing himself for death, and when the master stood by his bed, he said, "Rabbi, how and by what means shall I proceed? A horror lies before me and disturbs my peace."

The Baal-Shem took the hand of the sick boy in his hands and said to him, "Child, recall: have you not always gone from strength to strength and from goal to goal? So you shall also move onward in the gardens of eternity." He touched the forehead of the sick boy and said to him, "Because the hour of the last dawn is still over you, and because you have lived in it genuinely and have not been afraid of its happiness, I shall write my sign on your forehead so that no one can terrify your way and hinder your path. So go hence, child, when death summons you." He bent over him, laid forehead to forehead, and blessed him.

When the master had gone, the other youth slipped into the room and knelt by the bed. He kissed the hand of the sick boy and said, "My beloved, they wish to take you away, and I know that you do not resist. Recall how we used to talk with each other among the birches of a summer evening, and finally you said only, 'Yes, it is,' and I said, 'No, it is not.' Now I am terribly frightened, for you are going away from me, are willingly going away with these, your eyes. My beloved, the birches are in your eyes, and also the summer evening. And everything says, 'Yes, it is.' I feel that it is, I myself say it, indeed, and know it too, for otherwise there were no meaning in everything, and yet you are going away from me. Whither are you going?" He sobbed over the hand of his friend and kissed it again and again.

The dying boy spoke, "Dear one, I go farther on the way. When I am on the way, I shall think of you and of our love. I will come to you to tell you of my path. Give me your hand."

Then the other cried out, "You shall not go, I shall keep you, you shall not go!"

But the dying boy spoke out of his peace, "Not so, you cannot strive against the Lord. You shall hold my hand until my pulse ceases to beat, and this is my promise to you that I shall return to behold the beautiful earth and you."

The gates of the firmament opened before the sign on his forehead and he ascended. He moved from goal to goal and from holiness to holiness and received the meaning of life. Time grew still and there was no space, only the way of becoming without place and lapse of time.

Suddenly his step was checked, time roared in his ears, and space struck him with cruel fists. Then he stood there in the midst of silent watchmen. He showed them the sign on his forehead. But they stared at him and shook their heads, and he knew that his forehead no longer bore a sign. Human despair threatened to overcome him, but he withstood it. Then he saw an old man before him who asked, "Why do you halt here?"

"I can go no farther," he answered. "This thing is not good," said the old man. "For if you tarry here, then the life of the spirit will abandon you and you will remain here as an unfeeling stone. For all the life of the world to come is this: to move from strength to strength unto the abyss of eternity."

"What can I do?" the youth asked him.

"I shall go into the sanctuary," replied the old man, "and find out why this has happened to you." He went, came back, and said, "You promised your friend that you would come to him and tell him of your way. You have forgotten to do this and have broken your promise. Therefore, the sign has been removed from your forehead and you have been prevented from entering the sanctuary of truth."

Then the youth beheld his friend on earth and grieved at having forgotten him. "What shall I do in order to free myself from my guilt?" he asked.

The old man answered, "Descend into the nightly dream of your friend and tell him what he desires to know."

The youth descended to earth and entered into the dream of his friend. He stroked the forehead of the sleeping man and whispered in his ear, "Dear one, I have come to tell you of my way. But do not be angry at me for having delayed so long. For how can one think of a man, even though he be the most beloved, in the midst of the terror of God's vortex that overflows all limits?"

But the other rose up in his sleep, pressed his hand to his eyes and hissed forth the words of his chagrin from out of clenched teeth, "Depart from me, lying image, I will no longer let myself be made a fool of by you. I have waited and waited, and the promised one did not come. And now my spirit is rotted by waiting so that night after night your phantom visits me. But now I will no longer let myself be made a fool of. I command you, dissolve and appear to me no more!"

Then the youth threw himself trembling on his companion and clung to him. "Truly, I am no phantom, but your friend," he said, "and I have come to you out of the world of being. Think how we sat among the birches of a summer evening. Think how our right hands clasped each other in the hour of my death."

But the dreamer shouted, "You say the same night after night, and you catch me and I lift myself to you, then you vanish into the shadows. So let go of me now. See, I free myself of you!"

Once more the dead youth strove with his friend and cried, "Did not you say yourself, 'Yes, it is'?"

But the other only laughed in a hard voice, "Indeed I spoke thus, and I also waited. But the promised one did not come, and now I know that I was the plaything in the hand of a cruel hour. It was this hour that enslaved me and shamed me and brought the yes of betrayal to my lips. But I cry out against you, 'No, it is not!' "

Then the youth yielded and turned to disappear, but a last hope came to him and out of the faint distance he called to his comrade, "Then I will return in broad daylight and bring you a sign."

In the upper world he hurried to the temple of truth, sought out the old man and questioned him, "Help me and say what sign I can bring my friend to show that it is really I?"

"On this too I shall give thee counsel, my son," answered the old man, "and God be with thee. At noon of every Sabbath the Baal-Shem preaches on the mysteries of the teaching in the house of study that stands in the heaven of holy knowledge. And at the third Sabbath meal which unites heaven and earth he preaches on these mysteries before the ears of men, after his word has received the consecration of the upper world. Therefore, go at noon of the Sabbath and listen to the speech of your master in heaven; then descend to your friend and report to him the speech. This then will serve him as a sign; he will come to the holy meal in the house of the Baal-Shem and receive the word out of his mouth."

The youth did as he was advised, he absorbed the speech of the master, descended, entered into the day-dream of his friend and poured out the word over him like a balm. After that he bent over him and kissed him, mouth on mouth, with the kiss of heaven. Then he fled.

The other arose at once, and it seemed to him as if he had experienced the unexperienceable. He went outside; there stood the birches in the midday sun. He sat for a long time under the birches like one who knows.

When the sun began to sink, he went to the house of the Baal-Shem, not out of doubt but out of yearning. Now he stood in the door and heard the words out of the mouth of the Baal-Shem. He bowed himself at the feet of the speaker and said, "Rabbi, bless me for I want to die. For what is there left for me here?"

"Not so," replied the master. "Go outside to the birches that again stand in the summer evening and speak to them in your joy, 'Yes, it is.' And I do indeed bless you, but not for death, rather that now and here you may move from goal to goal, from strength to strength, and thus for ever and ever."

SOURCE: Martin Buber. *The Legend of the Baal-Shem*, trans. Maurice Friedman. New York: Harper and Row, 1955

I and Thou
by Martin Buber

Martin Buber (1878–1965) emphasized the reality of God as encountered by Jews, not as an interior subjective experience, a metaphysical or moral idea made up and projected into the heavens by humans, but as a real appearance of the divine. He translated traditional religious language into twentieth-century thought, pointing to the "I–Thou" relation as the experiential point of the encounter with eternal being. "I–it" relationships characterize industrial society's impersonal, utilitarian views of objects, but "I–Thou" relationships, mutual, direct, open human soul relationships, lead to the eternal Thou, traditionally known as God. Raised in Germany, Buber settled in Israel in 1938, and lectured internationally.

To man the world is twofold, in accordance with his twofold attitude.

The attitude of man is twofold, in accordance with the twofold nature of the primary words which he speaks.

The primary words are not isolated words, but combined words.

The one primary word is the combination *I–Thou*.

The other primary word is the combination *I–It*; wherein, without a change in the primary word, one of the words *He* and *She* can replace *It*.

Hence the *I* of man is also twofold.

For the *I* of the primary word *I–Thou* is a different *I* from that of the primary word *I–It*.

Primary words do not signify things, but they intimate relations.

Primary words do not describe something that might exist independently of them, but being spoken they bring about existence.

Primary words are spoken from the being.

If *Thou* is said, the *I* of the combination *I–Thou* is said along with it.

If *It* is said, the *I* of the combination *I–It* is said along with it.

The primary word *I–Thou* can only be spoken with the whole being.

The primary word *I–It* can never be spoken with the whole being.

When *Thou* is spoken, the speaker has no thing for his object. For where there is a thing there is another thing. Every *It* is bounded by others; *It* exists only through being bounded by others. But when *Thou* is spoken, there is no thing. *Thou* has no bounds.

When *Thou* is spoken, the speaker has no *thing*; he has indeed nothing. But he takes his stand in relation.

In every sphere in its own way, through each process of becoming that is present to us we look out toward the fringe of the eternal *Thou*; in each we are aware of a breath from the eternal *Thou*; in each *Thou* we address the eternal *Thou*.

The *Thou* meets me through grace—it is not found by speaking. But my speaking of the primary word to it is an act of my being, is indeed *the* act of my being.

The *Thou* meets me. But I step into direct relation with it. Hence the relation means being chosen and choosing, suffering and action in one; just as any action of the whole being, which means the suspension of all partial actions and consequently of all sensations of actions grounded only in their particular limitation, is bound to resemble suffering.

The primary word *I–Thou* can be spoken only with the whole being. Concentration and fusion into the whole being can never take place through my agency, nor can it ever take place without me. I become through my relation to the *Thou*; as I become *I*, I say *Thou*.

All real living is meeting.

The relation to the *Thou* is direct. No system of ideas, no foreknowledge, and no fancy intervene between *I* and *Thou*. The memory itself is transformed, as it plunges out of its isolation into the unity of the whole.

. . . in so far as man rests satisfied with the things that he experiences and uses, he lives in the past, and his moment has no present content. He has nothing but objects. But objects subsist in time that has been.

The present is not fugitive and transient, but continually present and enduring. The object is not duration, but cessation, suspension, a breaking off and cutting clear and hardening, absence of relation and of present being.

True beings are lived in the present, the life of objects is in the past.

. . . the thing, like the *I*, is produced late, arising after the original experiences have been split asunder and the connected partners separated. In the beginning is relation—as category of being, readiness, grasping form, mould for the soul; it is the *a priori* of relation, *the inborn Thou*.

The extended lines of relations meet in the eternal *Thou*.

Every particular *Thou*, is a glimpse through to the eternal *Thou*; by means of every particular *Thou* the primary word addresses the eternal *Thou*. Through this meditation of the *Thou* of all beings fulfilment, and non-fulfilment, of relations comes to them: the inborn *Thou* is realized in each relation and consummated in none. It is consummated only in the direct relation with the *Thou* that by its nature cannot become *It*.

The description of God as a Person is indispensable for everyone who like myself means by "God" not a principle (although mystics like Eckhart sometimes identify him as "Being") and like myself means by "God" not an idea (although philosophers like Plato at times could hold that he was this): but who rather means by "God," as I do, him who—whatever else he may be—enters into a direct relation with us men in creative, revealing and redeeming acts, and thus makes it possible for us to enter into a direct relation with him. This ground and meaning of our existence constitutes a mutuality, arising again and again, such as can subsist only between persons.

The concept of personal being is indeed completely incapable of declaring what God's essential being is, but it is both permitted and necessary to say that God is *also* a Person.

SOURCE: Martin Buber *I and Thou*, trans. Ronald George Smith. New York: Charles Scribner's Sons, 1958

Contemporary Judaism

Contemporary Jewish experience has been haunted by the question of how to respond to the Nazi Holocaust; it has been challenged by the rise of new women rabbis; and it has been enlivened by a renewal movement.

Surviving Auschwitz
by Viktor Frankl

The systematic destruction of Jews and others from 1933 to 1945 by the Nazis, the **Holocaust**, *killed six million Jews in concentration camps such as Auschwitz, Poland. Those lost are remembered annually on Holocaust Remembrance Day. A range of theological responses has followed from this immense tragedy. Some, like Richard Rubenstein, have declared God dead. Others have not lost their faith. One is the psychologist Viktor Frankl. While surviving Auschwitz, he observed that survivors of the death camps had to have a meaning, and he discovered four meanings that he found helped them make it: Love—even if his wife was dead, Frankl found solace in the love they shared; Art—the beauty of a sunset, flowers, music, prisoners' cabarets and jokes expressed their hope; Freedom—to choose one's response to suffering; and Faith in eternal life. He was moved by what one woman said about this just before she died.*

1. "Love goes very far beyond the physical person of the beloved. It finds its deepest meaning in his spiritual being, his inner self; whether or not he is actually present, whether or not he is still alive at all, ceases somehow to be of importance . . . love is as strong as death."
2. "As the inner life of the prisoner became more intense, he also experienced the beauty of art and nature as never before . . . we were carried away by nature's beauty, which we had missed for so long."
3. "Man can preserve a vestige of spiritual freedom, of independence of mind, even in such terrible conditions of psychic and physical stress. We who lived in concentration camps can remember the men who walked through the huts comforting others, giving away their last piece of bread."
4. "This young woman knew that she would die in the next few days. But when I talked to her she was cheerful in spite of this knowledge. 'I am

grateful that fate has hit me so hard,' she told me. 'In my former life I was spoiled and did not take spiritual accomplishments seriously.' Pointing through the window of the hut, she said, 'This tree here is the only friend I have in my loneliness.' Through that window she could see just one branch of a chestnut tree, and on the branch were two blossoms. 'I often talk to this tree,' she said to me. I was startled and didn't quite know how to take her words. Was she delirious? Did she have occasional hallucinations? Anxiously I asked her if the tree replied. 'Yes.' What did it say to her? She answered, 'It said to me, "I am here—I am life, eternal life."'"

SOURCE: Viktor Frankl. *Man's Search for Meaning*. New York: Washington Square Press, 1994, pp. 58–90. Reprint of 1st edn, Boston: Beacon, 1946

Jewish Feminism
by Susannah Heschel

In 1997 some educated Orthodox women in Queens, New York, were publicly reading Torah and having their daughters read Torah at their **bat mitzvahs** *(Onishi). One woman rabbi found congregants saying to her: "Rabbi, I can't tell you how different I felt about services because you are a woman. I found myself feeling that if you can be a rabbi, then maybe I could be a rabbi, too" (Geller). Other women have revised traditional prayers to say: "Blessed is She who spoke and the world became. Blessed is She. Blessed is She who in the beginning, gave birth," and modified Miriam's song in Exodus 15:1–18, "I will sing my praise to the Lord, To Her alone I will sing praise. The Lord is my Mother, my Strength, I will exalt her all my days ... Sing daughters of Israel, sing aloud ..." (Janowitz). These are examples of twentieth-century Jewish feminism, with a range of views, from the orthodox women who abide by Torah and accept traditional roles for women, to reformers who welcome women rabbis and new ritual language, to revolutionaries who strive to reawaken the ancient goddess tradition. Here Professor Heschel (daughter of Professor Abraham Heschel) outlines the varieties of contemporary Jewish feminism.*

Jewish feminism focuses on three issues: attaining complete religious involvement for Jewish women; giving Jewish expression to women's experiences and self-understanding; and highlighting the imagery, language, and rituals already present within Jewish tradition that center around the feminine and women. These efforts involve changing or eliminating aspects of Jewish law, customs, and teachings that prevent or discourage women from developing positions of equality to men within Judaism as well as bringing new interpretations to bear on the tradition. The implications of the proposed radical reevaluations go to the heart of Jewish beliefs concerning

God, revelation, and Torah. For example, if the Torah holds women in positions of subservience or contempt, contradicting women's self-understanding, then, feminism concludes, either the God who has revealed the Torah is a malevolent deity or the Torah is not God's revelation, but merely the projection of a patriarchal society intent on preserving its status quo.

Such conclusions lead some feminists away from Jewish theology to a secularized revision of Jewish beliefs and community completely outside the framework of Torah. Another conclusion contends that the Torah's claim to revelation must be understood to allow interpretations of its content in consonance with feminist values and principles. This option seeks to place feminism in the context of other major revisions in Judaism, such as the shift from sacrificial to liturgical worship after the destruction of the Temple.

Making feminist goals comparable in magnitude to those achieved after the destruction of the Temple raises broad implications that have only recently begun to be recognized. During the last two decades most Jewish feminist writings called for specific, concrete changes in Jewish observance and maintained a tone of optimism. Feminism and Judaism were not in the least contradictory, many argued, and equality of women and men was for the good of the entire community. Such optimism grew from a theological position that emphasized the intentionality of Jewish sources. According to this position, equality of women and men was honestly intended by Judaism's prophetic teachings of justice and by the devotion to God underlying talmudic law. The intention had not been realized during the course of Jewish history for sociological, not theological, reasons.

Cynthia Ozick has articulated this position by arguing that Torah itself, while lacking a commandment stating "Thou shalt not lessen the humanity of women," nonetheless contains the basis for eliminating its own diminution of women's humanity in its proclamation of justice as an absolute requirement. Yet her argument fails to address the problem of how a teaching that claims to be divinely revealed can legislate practices that are in opposition to its self-proclaimed goal of justice. If Torah is the revealed word of God, how can it be other than just and right in all its aspects? Moreover, how can we even claim knowledge of what is just and right without that divine source of knowledge? Finally, Ozick's argument shares with those of other Jewish theologians the seemingly insoluble quandary of determining what constitutes the revealed, immutable essence of Judaism and what should be viewed as merely a temporal, human invention.

In recent years, Jewish feminists have sought new approaches to Judaism by attempting to redefine both feminism and Judaism. The starting point for this newly emerging Jewish feminism is the application of the classic formulations of feminist thought to Jewish texts, beliefs, and practices. Feminist writers such as Mary Daly and Simone de Beauvoir define patriarchy as the situation in which men's experiences and expressions of those experiences are equated with normative human nature and behavior. Women stand as Other to those norms and are denied the opportunity to define themselves except in relation to men. De Beauvoir writes, "Thus humanity is male and man defines woman not in herself but as relative to him, she is not regarded as an autonomous being.... She is defined and differentiated with reference to man and not he with reference to her; she is the incidental, the inessential as opposed to the essential. He is the Subject, he is the Absolute, she is the Other."

Turning to Judaism, feminists discover a structure in which women are viewed as Other not only in the **synagogue** or within the Orthodox community but also within basic Jewish teachings, symbols, and language. Women stand as Other while men are the Subjects in the liturgy, in halakhah, and even in Judaism's theological formulations of God as father and king. Woman as Other is expressed, for example, by Judaism's "purity" laws, in which women convey impurity not to themselves or to other women but only to the men with whom they come into contact. Women enter into the discussions of Judaism's law codes only insofar as the codes affect men's lives and, with only rare exceptions, women have historically been banned from writing and studying Jewish texts. As Judith Plaskow writes, "Men are the actors in religious and communal life because they are the normative Jews. Women are 'other than' the norm; we are less than fully human."

The significance of the Otherness of women within Judaism has received different evaluations. Most Jewish feminists today agree with de Beauvoir's definition of woman as Other, but differ as to whether and how women's status can be shifted from Other to Subject. Increasing numbers of feminists insist that the incorporation of female language, particularly about God, is the most important and perhaps the only way this shift can be brought about. As long as God is described and addressed solely in male language and imagery, they argue, women will remain identified as Other. Only when God is addressed as She or as Goddess will women become subjects in the monotheistic religious framework. A key problem for feminists is what should be the source of this language and imagery. Naomi Goldenberg, Rita Gross, and others draw mainly from personal, inner symbols and experiences in their description of the Goddess and urge that these sources be brought into a Jewish context. Simply employing female imagery is not enough, they argue; it is the type of imagery that matters. They reject as patriarchal the imagery already present within the kabbalistic tradition, which views the feminine aspect of the godhead as passive and receptive. Instead, feminists suggest strong, dynamic, creative, and active images of the female.

Addressing God as She or as Goddess raises the question whether Jewish feminists are giving a new name to the traditional God of Jewish patriarchy or evoking a Goddess of the ancient world, worshiped, according to the Bible, by many ancient Israelites. Feminists such as Savina Teubal and Jane Litman argue that biblical and talmudic sources hint at a vibrant tradition of women's religiosity eventually excluded from the mainstream of Jewish religion. Those traditions of prior generations of Jewish women that can be reconstructed from the scanty sources are being urged as the basis for a new, feminist Judaism. Such reconstructions would include the celebration of the New Moon as a woman's holiday and the fifteenth day of the month of Av as a day for women to dance and rejoice.

Other feminists, such as Lynn Gottlieb and Arthur Waskow, argue that the ways women have traditionally been viewed—for example, as sensitive, accommodating, gentle, intuitive—have been denigrated by patriarchal society. Rather than such attributes being rejected in favor of traditionally masculine values, they require recognition as significant human values for men as well as women. Waskow argues that the status of women as Other within Judaism and the denigration of women's attributes are not accidental but are intrinsic to a masculine way of thinking characterized by dualism and projection. According to Waskow, by eliminating the dominance of masculine thinking and encouraging the adoption by men and women of traditionally feminine modes of thinking not only will women become equal with men, but Judaism will achieve its own goal of redeeming the world. A feminist Judaism, in this vision, will emphasize God's immanence rather than transcendence. Equality would not be achieved simply by women performing the Jewish rituals heretofore limited to men. Rather, this group of feminists urges a renewal of customs traditionally limited to women, such as immersion in the mikveh, hallah baking, and praying separately. Not only will the values that emerge from women's experiences be strengthened, but so will the sense of identity with the historical experience of Jewish women.

At issue in all the approaches are both the relationships of women to Jewish history and tradition and feminism as a mode of reinterpreting Judaism. In trying to maintain a link to the historical experiences of Jewish women, some feminists fear they may simply perpetuate the view of women created by patriarchal culture. Yet in breaking with traditional women's roles and identities feminists also risk the danger of making maleness the goal for women. The broader theological implications of feminism are shared by all interpreters of texts, history, and symbols. A central point is whether feminists are explicating the deeper meaning of Jewish tradition or grafting onto it their own, new concerns. The more radical feminists question whether aspects of Judaism that have functioned during history to keep women in a position of Other can today be made meaningful through reinterpretation. Most Jewish feminists try to remain within Judaism's framework, viewing their efforts as a new stage in a continually developing Judaism. But they are faced with the problem of trying to justify the continued relevance of traditions and beliefs they want to retain. Once the

laws and teachings regarding women are viewed as an outgrowth of a
particular historical period, we need a theological justification for the
relevance of all traditions and texts that we might wish to observe and
study, from the Sabbath to the Talmud. This last problem, which has only
recently come to be articulated by feminists, joins women with other Jewish
theologians and places feminism at the forefront of current theological
discussion.

SOURCE: Susannah Heschel. *On Being a Jewish Feminist*. New York: Schocken, 1983,
pp. 255–9

Making Judaism More Alive
by Michael Lerner

A liberal Jewish renewal movement in our times is described and encouraged by
Michael Lerner, a philosopher, psychologist and founder of Tikkun *magazine. A lead-*
ing Jewish "liberation theologian," Lerner advocates a sweeping renewal of Judaism,
rooted in Torah, that incorporates a deep understanding of repressed feelings, fear and
a new generation's yearning for spiritual authenticity, social conscience, and genuine
transcendence in a vital Jewish community. Out of a genuine love for Judaism, Lerner
urges a release of the silent pain inherited from the Holocaust, with a call to free all
Jews, whether Orthodox, Conservative, or Reform, from a sense of victimization. He
calls for liberation from sexism, homophobia, and ecological harm, along with a
renewal of spirituality and prayer.

Jewish renewal is not a denominational phenomenon. There are people
within every Jewish denomination who are seeking to build Jewish-renewal
consciousness, and there are people who are building Jewish renewal quite
apart from any of the official denominations.

Whenever you find a community of people who are actually witnessing
the existence of God and who are challenging the world of oppression in the
name of *this* God, there you find renewal energy. Whenever you have
people who understand themselves as part of the people whose task it is to
be partners with God in the transformation of the world, who
simultaneously approach that task with awe, wonder, and radical
amazement at the grandeur of the universe, and rejoice in God's presence
that fills the entire universe, there you have renewal energy. So renewal
energy is possible (and necessary) in every religious tradition in the modern
world.

Renewal becomes *Jewish* renewal when it is brought into the framework
of the historical experience of the Jewish people, commits itself to Jewish
rituals and traditions, seeks to rediscover God's voice through the medium of
the Torah tradition, and shares love for, compassion toward, and attachment
to the Jewish people. Within this Torah framework it seeks to figure out

how, in this moment of history, we can best be witnesses to God's presence
and the possibilities that that creates for us in transforming the world from
that which is to that which ought to be.

God Intoxication   If Jewish renewal can be found in any Jewish
denomination or in no denomination, how do you find it, recognize it, or
create it?

Look first for God intoxication. Not people who use the word God all
the time, or who yell out "Praise God!" or "*Baruch ha'Shem*!" but people who
are part of a community that seriously addresses itself to the obligation to be
God's witnesses today. Look for people who start each day by focusing on
the wonder of the world, allowing themselves to be astounded that anything
exists at all, overwhelmed with joy and excitement about the grandeur of
the universe, and who communicate to you and to others a real pleasure in
being able to serve God by working on healing and repairing the world.

Look for people who are constantly, almost unconsciously, engaged in
little acts of caring and compassion for others, and who radiate a warmth
and loving energy that is personal and specific (not the glazed eyes of "true
believers" who tell you that they love you, but don't seem to notice who
you are), the very focused love that comes from caring enough to get to
know you in all your particularity, respects you for who you are and not
just who they think you could or should be, and loves the God within you
not as a separate part of your soul which needs to be liberated from the rest,
but as a feature that flows through every part of your being.

Look for a community whose members do acts of charity and participate
in social action together, as a community, and who see their work as
testimony to God's presence in the world. Such a community would have
weekly meetings to discuss contemporary developments in the world and
how to respond to them. It would ensure that its members are actively
engaged as Jews in social-transformation movements.

Imagine such a community meeting. A group of Jews gather to pray and
celebrate God's presence in the world. Next, some joint study—a text is
presented and analysed. Then they check in with one another about their
own lives, about what has been happening in their families and work lives.
They share with one another their pains and their joys. Then they move on
to discuss the week's events. Reports are given by different members about
their involvement in social change activities. Group members help the
individuals figure out what might be the next moves or the strategic direction
for their activity in social change. Then the group discusses whatever *tzedakah*
or social-change activities it is doing together as a group. Finally, the group
celebrates its own solidarity, sings songs, moves together in dance.

Don't expect to find such communities at the moment, though there are
many communities where elements of this picture are being actualized.
Rather, the picture is drawn to indicate a direction. A Jewish-renewal

consciousness has existed in every major period of Jewish history. Its actual embodiment has always been imperfect and will be so in our historical epoch as well, though more of it will come into existence in the coming decades.

Getting Real, Psychologically and Spiritually   A history of pain has produced a population that lives its life in some degree of unconsciousness. The more pain, the more unconsciousness.

There are moments in history when the pain decreases, and people begin to experience themselves as "waking up." They talk about themselves and their lives as though they had noticed that they or previous generations seemed to be going through life in a sleeping state, zombielike.

Even when this doesn't happen for everyone, it can happen for some subset of people. When, for example, a group of people begin to "get" that the world is governed by God, they have this waking up experience. Various philosophers have described in similar terms the kind of enlightenment they experienced.

Over time, religious communities, as well as philosophical traditions and political, aesthetic, or psychological movements, may be lulled back into lower levels of consciousness, and what remains are the truths that were momentarily revealed and articulated, now embedded in these movements' words, symbols, rituals, communal practices, literature, and art. No longer able to fully experience life as it had been when people felt more alive, we still have these records of fuller awareness, beckoning us to return. The power in the symbols and the literature may still have the ability to transform us—if we awaken to what we are saying, but often we remain asleep.

There is no spiritual, political, or aesthetic tradition that is immune to being put back to sleep. One of the overwhelming consequences of contemporary culture is the increase of that level of collective amnesia. Over and over again we find ourselves surrounded by people who are in the process of forgetting what they once knew, increasingly unable to hold on to it. I believe that Alzheimer's is the paradigmatic sickness of the contemporary age, and that we live in the Alzheimer's society.

In such circumstances, those who have maintained the traditions are doing an important service. Rather than have to begin at the beginning, reinventing the history of human experience, people can reclaim from the tradition some of the elements that are most healthy and alive, while discarding those elements that represent the inevitable distortions of any particular age and experience. And as they reclaim, they can renew, by mixing that which has been with our own latest abilities to listen and hear what wisdom is being transmitted to us in the contemporary period (with all its inevitable distortions).

Jewish renewal is one of the many contemporary projects of people who are trying to reclaim and reawaken the frozen products of the past. There are people within psychoanalysis, feminism, Marxism, Christianity, Islam, art, music, philosophy, and many other areas who are trying to do the same thing in their own spheres.

How Real Does It Feel?   Another way to know if you are dealing with Jewish renewal or a counterfeit: Ask yourself how real the enterprise feels, how psychologically honest and alive, how spiritually centered and serious.

- Do people talk to one another in an honest fashion or are they on "good behavior"? Do they feign loving behavior and suppress all anger, or do they feel free to express a full range of emotions and feelings?
- Do people feel free to dispute the basic tenets of the community, to challenge its leadership, and to acknowledge the ways that they don't fit in?
- Do people feel free to express love and caring or excitement for one another without feeling that they are embarrassing other people or acting inappropriately?
- Can people acknowledge sexual attractions and pursue them, or is there a sexual straitjacket operating?
- Do people feel free to cry when they are sad, or to jump for joy when they are happy, or are these allowed only at specifically ritual moments?
- Can people really talk about the complexities of their experience with one another without fitting into some preestablished norm about what people are supposed to be feeling or thinking?
- Can people fully mourn when they are in mourning, or do they feel that they have to take care of others and assure them that they are really doing okay and going to survive the loss?
- Can people feel really joyous when something has happened in their personal lives that is good, or do they feel that they would be making others feel bad or jealous if they were to be "too" explicit about how good they feel?
- Does the community have some regular institutionalized way in which bad feelings among participants or between participants and the leadership of the community get put on the agenda, discussed, and worked through?
- Do people feel real in prayer? For example, when people pray with words like, "You shall rejoice in your holidays," are they actually rejoicing, or are they merely good-naturedly repeating an injunction, perhaps personally wishing they knew how to rejoice? When they say, "We are happy how good is our lot, how wonderful our portion, how pretty our inheritance," do you feel that people are actually happy? When people say, "Hear, O Israel, the Lord our God, the Lord is One," do you have the sense that they are actually trying to get their fellow

Jews to pay attention to this idea, or that they themselves are paying attention to it?

- When people greet you are they going through the motions with their "Shabbat Shalom," or do they actually seem to be hoping that you are going to have a peaceful Sabbath?

The list could go on.

My own experience is that most synagogue participation and most Jewish ritual are undergone in a semiconscious state. People sometimes know what they are saying, and if asked, they'd say they agree with much of it. But all too often they aren't fully there, fully into it. And, in fact, if you tried to become fully there or fully into it in most synagogues you'd probably look foolish.

To some extent, people feel embarrassed to let go of their sense of decorum, cynicism, self-restraint, and moderation—all of which might be compromised by letting themselves get into something that takes them beyond themselves. But this is not the whole story. I've watched people in Hasidic synagogues dance and sing excitedly, but then in my conversations with people afterward I've come to think that what people were getting excited *about* was the excitement itself, not the content of what they were supposedly praying for or to.

Getting real is different—it's actually meaning what you're saying, taking it seriously, staking your life on it.

This could be a demanding criterion for anyone to be expected to live in a world that is still dominated by pain and oppression. But it is a reasonable criterion of what counts as Jewish renewal.

If ever there was a category that seemed scary, it's this one: getting real. The more asleep people are, the more they feel threatened by the concept, dismiss it as New Agey or flakey or contentless.

The more awake you are, the more you've had experiences in which you've moved from being more unconscious to more conscious, and hence the more you understand what is being talked about.

SOURCE: Michael Lerner. *Jewish Renewal: A Path to healing and transformation.* New York: G. P. Puttman's Sons, 1994

GLOSSARY

Bar Mitzvah (son of the Commandment) An initiation for boys about 13 who have studied Judaism and ritually become responsible Jewish adult men.
Bat Mitzvah (daughter of the Commandment) An initiation for girls about 13 who have studied Judaism and ritually become responsible Jewish adult women, in some progressive congregations.
Canon Official list of authoritative books in a religion, inspired or revealed.
Conservatives A moderate branch of

modern Judaism, between Orthodoxy and Reform traditions.

Covenant Contracts between God and Israel, requiring circumcision and obedience to the Torah, and promising the land of Israel and prosperity.

Deuteronomic One of four strands of the Pentateuch, primarily Deuteronomy.

Diaspora (dispersion, exile) Jewish communities outside land of Israel.

Elohist One of four strands of the Pentateuch, using "Elohim" to name God.

Holocaust The destruction of Jews in Germany, Poland and other European countries by the Nazis before and during World War II.

Kabbalah The Jewish mystical tradition.

Messiah (the anointed one) Descendant of King David expected to restore the kingdom promised by the Prophets; blended with apocalyptic expectations.

Midrash Interpretations of scriptures, the basis of much of the Talmud. **Halakhah** are legal decisions, **Haggadah** are folklore, historical and spiritual teachings.

Mishnah A legal code based on the Torah, in oral traditions from around 200 CE.

Monotheism Belief in one supreme God.

Orthodox A Jewish group that strives to preserve the ancient practices, such as denial

of rabbinate to women; strong in Israel since 1948.

Priestly One of four strands of the Pentateuch, written late, with ritual concerns.

Prophets Oracular seers criticizing social injustices and promising the messiah.

Rabbi (teacher) The Jewish leader of a congregation; the local synagogue leaders who replaced the priests of the old central Temple in Jerusalem.

Reform Progressive movement from the 19th century in Europe and U.S.A.; accepts moral laws, rejects ritual laws inconsistent with modernity.

Synagogue A local center of worship, community and teaching; a focus that replaced the central Temple in Jerusalem during the Diaspora.

Talmud Body of commentary and discussion of interpretations of tradition.

Tanakh The complete Jewish Scriptures: Torah, Prophets and Writings.

Torah (teaching) Variously used to mean the first five scrolls of the Hebrew Scriptures (Pentateuch), all the Laws of Israel, or oral traditional law.

Yahwist (or Jahwist) One of four strands of the Pentateuch using "YaHWeH" to name God.

HOLY DAYS

Shabbat (Sabbath) The seventh day of the week, when Jews abstain from work. It begins after dark on Friday. Synagogue services are held Friday nights and Saturdays.

Rosh Hashanah (New Year) Around the Fall Equinox, the spiritual year begins with the blowing of a ram's horn and prayers.

Yom Kippur (Day of Atonement) To renew God's covenant, a time of inner spiritual cleansing, forgiveness and reconciliation.

Sukkot (Feast of Tabernacles) A fall harvest festival.

Hanukkah (Feast of Dedication) Around the Winter Solstice, eight candles are lit on a

candle-holder (menorah), one each night to commemorate God's increasing light.

Purim (Feast of Lots) A rowdy early spring remembrance of Esther and Mordecai's saving Jews from destruction by Persians.

Pesach (Passover) The spring celebration of the liberation of Jews from Egyptian slavery by Moses; opens with an instructional, symbolic Seder meal.

Yom Hashoah Holocaust memorial day, honoring the victims.

Yom Haatzuma-ut Israel Independence Day, celebrating May 14, 1948, when Israel again became a sovereign state, after centuries of the Diaspora.

HISTORICAL OUTLINE

c. 1900–1700 BCE?—Abraham, the first Patriarch

c. 1250 BCE—Exodus from Egypt led by Moses through Sinai to Promised Land

c. 1010–970 BCE—King David unites northern and southern Israel in Jerusalem

c. 961–931 BCE—First Temple built by David's son King Solomon

c. 750–250 BCE—Age of Classical Prophets: Isaiah, Jeremiah, Ezekiel and 12 Minor Prophets

722 BCE—Fall of Northern Kingdom (Israel) to Assyria

586 BCE—Fall of Southern Kingdom (Judah) to Babylon, Temple destroyed

c. 515 BCE—Exiles return from Babylon, rebuild Temple; Ezra and Nehemiah

168 BCE—Successful Maccabean Revolt against Hellenistic rulers

70 CE—Romans destroy Jerusalem and Temple; end of sacrifices and priests at Temple, beginning of Diaspora and Rabbinic leadership in synagogues

c. 90 CE—Canon of Tanakh agreed by consensus

c. 200 CE—Compilation of Mishnah

c. 500 CE—Jerusalem Talmud

c. 600 CE—Babylonian Talmud

c. 1135–1204—Maimonides adapts Jewish theology to philosophy

c. 1200–1300—Zohar appears in Spain, contributes to Kabbalah

1470—Spanish Inquisition begins to purge Muslims, Jews, other non-Christians

1492—Mass expulsion of Jews from Spain

c. 1555—Ghettos built in Italy and Germany

1700–60—Baal-Shem Tov in Eastern Europe begins Hasidism

1933–1945—Nazi Holocaust, reaching its climax during World War II

1948—State of Israel reestablished

REVIEW QUESTIONS

1   Describe the three major divisions of the Tanakh.
2   What is the Pentateuch?
3   What are the differences between the two Creation stories in Genesis?
4   What do these differences in Creation accounts tell us about how to interpret them? Discuss sequence of events, mastery of nature, and gender issues.
5   What is a Jewish Covenant? Describe three major Covenants.
6   What happened at Sinai in the Book of Exodus? Why is this important?
7   What were the two major messages of the classical Prophet Isaiah?
8   What was the essence of God's answer to Job when he was suffering?
9   What is the Talmud? Why do Jews need such commentaries?
10   What major themes did Maimonides see as central to Jewish faith?
11   What does the Baal-Shem Tov teach about life after death?
12   What does Martin Buber mean by "I–Thou" relations?
13   Describe three major theological responses to the Nazi Holocaust.
14   What view of Jewish feminism do you agree with? How would you defend it in discussion with Jewish men and women who see otherwise?
15   What is your opinion of Michael Lerner's *Jewish Renewal*?

INFORMATION RESOURCES

Bernstein, Ellen, ed. *Ecology and the Jewish Spirit*. Woodstock, VT: Jewish Lights Publishing, 1998.

Cohen, Arthur, and Paul Mendes-Flohr, eds. *Contemporary Jewish Religious Thought*. New York: Free Press/Macmillan, 1987

Commentary Magazine <www.Commentarymagazine.com>

Encyclopedia Judaica. Jerusalem: Keter Publishing, 1972

Fackenheim, Emil, *God's Presence in History*. New York: New York University Press, 1970

Gillman, Neil, *The Death of Death*. Woodstock, VT: Jewish Lights Publishing, 1997

Glatzer, Nahum, *Hammer on the Rock: A Short Midrash Reader*, trans. Jacob Sloan. New York: Schocken, 1948/62

Heschel, Abraham, *The Prophets*. New York: Harper and Row, 1962

Holz, Barry, *The Schocken Guide to Jewish Books*. New York: Schocken, 1992

Janowitz, Naomi, and Maggie Wenig, "Sabbath Prayers for Women," in Carol Christ and Judith Plaskow, *Womanspirit Rising*. San Francisco: Harper & Row, 1992

Jewish Film Archive Online <www.Jewishfilm.com>

Jewishnet

Judaism and Jewish Resources <www.shamash.org/trb/judaism.html>

Kaplan, Mordecai, *Judaism as a Civilization: Toward a Reconstruction of Jewish Life*. Philadelphia: Jewish Publication Society, 1934/1994

Neusner, Jacob, *An Introduction to Judaism*. Louisville, KY: Westminster/John Knox Press, 1991

Onishi, Norimitsu, "Reading Torah Women's Group Tests Tradition," in *The New York Times*, Metro Section, Feb. 16, 1997, pp. 43, 49.

Plaskow, Judith, *Standing Again at Sinai: Judaism from a Feminist Perspective*. San Francisco: Harper/San Francisco, 1990

Religion, Religions, Religious Studies: Judaism Page <www.clas.ufl.edu/users/gthursby/rel/judaism.htm>

Rubenstein, Richard L. *After Auschwitz*. Indianapolis: Bobbs-Merrill, 1966

Scholem, Gershom, *Major Trends in Jewish Mysticism*. New York: Schocken, 1946

Silverman, Lou. H. *et al*. "Judaism," in *Encyclopedia Britannica*, 1997, XXII: 379–456.

Virtual Religion Index: Jewish Studies <www.rci.rutgers.edu/~religion/links/judaic.html>

Zohar: The Book of Enlightenment, trans. Daniel Chanan Matt. New York: Paulist Press, 1983

CHAPTER 9

CHRISTIANITY

Christianity is such a widespread and influential religion that, around the world, dates are now commonly measured from the approximate birth date of Jesus, probably a few years before 1 CE. According to Christian tradition, he was born in Israel to a poor family under lowly circumstances, and his spiritual help was often offered to those who were neglected or rejected by society. When he began preaching openly at the age of about thirty, he was sharply critical of religious hypocrisy. Himself a Jew, he upheld the spirit of the teachings of the Torah while pointing out their abuses by religious authorities. To his followers, however, he was not just a reformer. He was known as a miracle worker; many who came to him were healed. Some became convinced that Jesus was the Messiah for whom they had long been waiting.

Jesus spoke often about the kingdom of God, but it seems that he was referring to a spiritual rather than a political realm. Nonetheless, the religious authorities and the Roman rulers of the region ultimately had him crucified in Jerusalem. Three days later, according to varied accounts in the Bible, he was miraculously resurrected and appeared again in the flesh to his closest disciples charging them to carry on his work. They, too, became great healers and preachers, despite persecution. One of the persecutors was reportedly transformed by a vision of Jesus, becoming the Apostle Paul. His extensive travels and writings were extremely influential in shaping Christianity as an organized religion and theology.

According to the biblical accounts, Jesus brought a message of love for all, especially the weak. He urged radical inner transformation and promised that God was forgiving to sinners who sincerely repented and turned toward Him. Paul's teachings brought the additional beliefs that Jesus was the incarnation of God and that Jesus's death offered atonement for the sins of a believer of any nationality. With this understanding, many Christians feel that, while other religions may have their saints and prophets, only Jesus offers the way to receiving God's grace.

Christian belief is not unitary; on the contrary, those professing belief in Jesus have over time separated into some 21,000 different denominations in three major divisions: Roman Catholic, Eastern Orthodox, and Protestant. Today there are lively conservative and liberal movements throughout Christianity.

Jesus the Christ

Stories of the life and teachings of Jesus and their theological interpretation appear in the New Testament of the Christian Bible, written in Greek and some Aramaic (spoken by Jesus). The Christian Bible also includes a version of the Hebrew Bible, or Tanakh, labeled as the "Old Testament." The New Testament begins with the four Gospels—Matthew, Mark, Luke, and John— and also includes material on the activities of Jesus's followers after his death, including letters from Paul to the newly developed Christian congregations.

The first three Gospels were written down between 70 and 90 CE. Mark is the oldest, and they all show evidence of earlier sources, oral and written. They are very similar, and are thus called the "**Synoptic**" Gospels. The fourth, the Gospel of John (*c.* 95), shows a more mystical and Greek influence (the Light, the Word). Paul's letters (Epistles) were written between 48 and 64 CE, before the Gospels took their present form. Other New Testament books were written down as late as 150. The following selections are taken from the **RSV**.

The Annunciation

In the sixth month the angel Gabriel was sent from God to a city of Galilee named Nazareth, to a virgin betrothed to a man whose name was Joseph, of the house of David; and the virgin's name was Mary. And he came to her and said, "Hail, O favored one, the Lord is with you!" But she was greatly troubled at the saying, and considered in her mind what sort of greeting this might be. And the angel said to her, "Do not be afraid, Mary, for you have found favor with God. And behold, you will conceive in your womb and bear a son, and you shall call his name Jesus. He will be great, and will be called the Son of the Most High; and the Lord God will give to him the throne of his father David, and he will reign over the house of Jacob for ever; and of his kingdom there will be no end." And Mary said to the angel, "How shall this be, since I have no husband?" And the angel said to her, "The Holy Spirit will come upon you, and the power of the Most High will overshadow you; therefore the child to be born will be called holy, the Son of God."

SOURCE: Luke 1:26–35

The Magnificat

And Mary said, "My soul magnifies the Lord, and my spirit rejoices in God my Savior, for he has regarded the low estate of his handmaiden. For behold, henceforth all generations will call me blessed; for he who is mighty has done great things for me, and holy is his name. And his mercy is on those who fear him from generation to generation. He has shown strength with his arm, he has scattered the proud in the imagination of their hearts, he has put down the mighty from their thrones, and exalted those of low degree; he has filled the hungry with good things, and the rich he has sent empty away. He has helped his servant Israel, in remembrance of his mercy, as he spoke to our fathers, to Abraham and to his posterity for ever."

SOURCE: Luke 1:46–55

Jesus's Birth

In those days a decree went out from Caesar Augustus that all the world should be enrolled. This was the first enrollment, when Quirinius was governor of Syria. And all went to be enrolled, each to his own city. And Joseph also went up from Galilee, from the city of Nazareth, to Judea, to the city of David, which is called Bethlehem, because he was of the house and lineage of David, to be enrolled with Mary, his betrothed, who was with child. And while they were there, the time came for her to be delivered. And she gave birth to her first-born son and wrapped him in swaddling cloths, and laid him in a manger, because there was no place for them in the inn. And in that region there were shepherds out in the field, keeping watch over their flock by night. And an angel of the Lord appeared to them, and the glory of the Lord shone around them, and they were filled with fear. And the angel said to them, "Be not afraid; for behold, I bring you good news of a great joy which will come to all the people; for to you is born this day in the city of David a Savior, who is Christ the Lord. And this will be a sign for you: you will find a babe wrapped in swaddling cloths and lying in a manger." And suddenly there was with the angel a multitude of the heavenly host praising God and saying, "Glory to God in the highest, and on earth peace among men with whom he is pleased!"

SOURCE: Luke 1:46–55

Jesus's Ministry Begins

And he went about all Galilee, teaching in their synagogues and preaching the gospel of the kingdom and healing every disease and every infirmity among the people. So his fame spread throughout all Syria, and they brought him all the sick, those afflicted with various diseases and pains, demoniacs,[1] epileptics, and paralytics, and he healed them. And great crowds followed him from Galilee and the Decapolis and Jerusalem and Judea and from beyond the Jordan.

SOURCE: Matthew 4:23–25

---

[1] Demoniac—person possessed by a demon.

The Beatitudes

Seeing the crowds, he went up on the mountain, and when he sat down his disciples came to him.

And he opened his mouth and taught them, saying:

"Blessed are the poor in spirit, for theirs is the kingdom of heaven.

"Blessed are those who mourn, for they shall be comforted.

"Blessed are the meek, for they shall inherit the earth.

"Blessed are those who hunger and thirst for righteousness, for they shall be satisfied.

"Blessed are the merciful, for they shall obtain mercy.

"Blessed are the pure in heart, for they shall see God.

"Blessed are the peacemakers, for they shall be called sons of God.

"Blessed are those who are persecuted for righteousness' sake, for theirs is the kingdom of heaven.

"Blessed are you when men revile you and persecute you and utter all kinds of evil against you falsely on my account. Rejoice and be glad, for your reward is great in heaven, for so men persecuted the prophets who were before you."

SOURCE: Matthew 5:1–12

Law

"Think not that I have come to abolish the law and the prophets; I have come not to abolish them but to fulfill them. For truly, I say to you, till heaven and earth pass away, not an iota, not a dot, will pass from the law until all is accomplished. Whoever then relaxes one of the least of these commandments and teaches men so, shall be called least in the kingdom of heaven; but he who does them and teaches them shall be called great in the kingdom of heaven. For I tell you, unless your righteousness exceeds that of the scribes and Pharisees, you will never enter the kingdom of heaven.

SOURCE: Matthew 5:17–20

Sincerely Motivated Faith and Works

"You have heard that it was said to the men of old, 'You shall not kill; and whoever kills shall be liable to judgment.' But I say to you that every one who is angry with his brother shall be liable to judgment; whoever insults his brother shall be liable to the council, and whoever says, 'You fool!' shall be liable to the hell of fire. So if you are offering your gift at the altar, and there remember that your brother has something against you, leave your gift there before the altar and go; first be reconciled to your brother, and then come and offer your gift."

SOURCE: Matthew 5:21–24

The Good Samaritan

[A lawyer said to Jesus:] "And who is my neighbor?" Jesus replied, "A man was going down from Jerusalem to Jericho, and he fell among robbers, who stripped him and beat him, and departed, leaving him half dead. Now by chance a priest was going down that road; and when he saw him he passed by on the other side. So likewise a Levite, when he came to the place and saw him, passed by on the other side. But a Samaritan,[2] as he journeyed, came to where he was; and when he saw him, he had compassion, and went to him and bound up his wounds, pouring on oil and wine; then he set him on his own beast and brought him to an inn, and took care of him. And the next day he took out two denarii [about 40 cents] and gave them to the inn-keeper, saying 'take care of him; and whatever more you spend, I will repay you when I come back.' Which of these three, do you think, proved neighbor to the man who fell among the robbers?" He said, "The one who showed mercy on him." And Jesus said to him, "Go and do likewise."

SOURCE: Luke 10:29–37

True Treasures

"Do not lay up for yourselves treasures on earth, where moth and rust consume and where thieves break in and steal, but lay up for yourselves treasures in heaven, where neither moth nor rust consumes and where thieves do not break in and steal. For where your treasure is, there will your heart be also."

SOURCE: Matthew 6:19–21

Healing the Blind

And as Jesus passed on from there, two blind men followed him, crying aloud, "Have mercy on us, Son of David." When he entered the house, the blind men came to him; and Jesus said to them, "Do you believe that I am able to do this?" They said to him, "Yes, Lord." Then he touched their eyes, saying, "According to your faith be it done to you." And their eyes were opened. And Jesus sternly charged them, "See that no one knows it."

SOURCE: Matthew 9:27–30

The Light of the World

In the beginning was the Word, and the Word was with God, and the Word was God. He was in the beginning with God; all things were made through him, and without him was not anything made that was made. In him was

---

[2] Samaritans—inhabitants of Samaria; Jews not exiled to Babylon in the 6th century BCE, and therefore rejected by returning refugees because of intermarriage.

life, and the life was the light of men. The light shines in the darkness, and the darkness has not overcome it.

SOURCE: John 1:1–5

The Word (*Logos*)

And the Word became flesh and dwelt among us, full of grace and truth; we have beheld his glory, glory as of the only Son from the Father.

SOURCE: John 1:14

The Last Supper

Then Judas Iscariot, who was one of the twelve [**disciples**], went to the chief priests in order to betray him to them. And when they heard it they were glad, and promised to give him money. And he sought an opportunity to betray him. And on the first day of Unleavened Bread, when they sacrificed the passover lamb, his disciples said to him, "Where will you have us go and prepare for you to eat the passover?" . . . And the disciples set out and went to the city, and found it as he had told them; and they prepared the passover. And when it was evening he came with the twelve. And as they were at table eating, Jesus said, "Truly, I say to you, one of you will betray me, one who is eating with me." They began to be sorrowful, and to say to him one after another, "Is it I?" He said to them, "It is one of the twelve, one who is dipping bread into the dish with me. For the Son of man goes as it is written of him, but woe to that man by whom the Son of man is betrayed! It would have been better for that man if he had not been born." And as they were eating, he took bread, and blessed, and broke it, and gave it to them, and said, "Take; this is my body." And he took a cup, and when he had given thanks he gave it to them, and they all drank of it. And he said to them, "This is my blood of the covenant, which is poured out for many. Truly, I say to you, I shall not drink again of the fruit of the vine until that day when I drink it new in the kingdom of God."

SOURCE: Mark 14:10-25

The Crucifixion

And Pilate again said to them, "Then what shall I do with the man whom you call the King of the Jews?" And they cried out again, "Crucify him." And Pilate said to them, "Why, what evil has he done?" But they shouted all the more, "Crucify him." So Pilate, wishing to satisfy the crowd, released for them Barabbas; and having scourged Jesus, he delivered him to be crucified. And the soldiers led him away inside the palace (that is, the praetorium[3]); and they

---

[3] Praetorium—the official residence of the governor of the Roman province.

called together the whole battalion. And they clothed him in a purple cloak, and plaiting a crown of thorns they put it on him. And they began to salute him, "Hail, King of the Jews!" And they struck his head with a reed, and spat upon him, and they knelt down in homage to him. And when they had mocked him, they stripped him of the purple cloak, and put his own clothes on him. And they led him out to crucify him. And they compelled a passer-by, Simon of Cyrene, who was coming in from the country, the father of Alexander and Rufus, to carry his cross. And they brought him to the place called Golgotha (which means the place of a skull). And they offered him wine mingled with myrrh; but he did not take it. And they crucified him, and divided his garments among them, casting lots for them, to decide what each should take.... So also the chief priests mocked him to one another with the scribes, saying, "He saved others; he cannot save himself. Let the Christ, the King of Israel, come down now from the cross, that we may see and believe." Those who were crucified with him also reviled him. And when the sixth hour had come, there was darkness over the whole land until the ninth hour. And at the ninth hour Jesus cried with a loud voice, *"Elo-i, Elo-i, lama sabach thani?"* which means, "My God, my God, why hast thou forsaken me?" And some of the bystanders hearing it said, "Behold, he is calling Elijah." And one ran and, filling a sponge full of vinegar, put it on a reed and gave it to him to drink, saying, "Wait, let us see whether Elijah will come to take him down." And Jesus uttered a loud cry, and breathed his last. And the curtain of the temple was torn in two, from top to bottom.... Joseph of Arimathea, a respected member of the council, who was also himself looking for the kingdom of God, took courage and went to Pilate, and asked for the body of Jesus. And Pilate wondered if he were already dead; and summoning the centurion, he asked him whether he was already dead. And when he learned from the centurion that he was dead, he granted the body to Joseph. And he bought a linen shroud, and taking him down, wrapped him in the linen shroud, and laid him in a tomb which had been hewn out of the rock; and he rolled a stone against the door of the tomb.

SOURCE: Mark 15:12–46

The Resurrection

And when the sabbath was past, Mary Magdalene, and Mary the mother of James, and Salome, bought spices, so that they might go and anoint him. And very early on the first day of the week they went to the tomb when the sun had risen. And they were saying to one another, "Who will roll away the stone for us from the door of the tomb?" And looking up, they saw that the stone was rolled back;—it was very large. And entering the tomb, they saw a young man sitting on the right side, dressed in a white robe; and they were amazed. And he said to them, "Do not be amazed; you seek Jesus of Nazareth, who was crucified. He has risen, he is not here; see the place where they laid him. But go, tell his disciples and Peter that he is going before you to Galilee; there you will see him, as he told you." And they went out and fled from the tomb; for trembling and astonishment had come upon them; and they said nothing to any one, for they were afraid.

SOURCE: Mark 16:1–8

Paul's Conversion

But Saul, still breathing threats and murder against the disciples of the Lord, went to the high priest and asked him for letters to the synagogues at Damascus, so that if he found any belonging to the Way, men or women, he might bring them bound to Jerusalem. Now as he journeyed he approached Damascus, and suddenly a light from heaven flashed about him. And he fell to the ground and heard a voice saying to him, "Saul, Saul, why do you persecute me?" And he said, "Who are you, Lord?" And he said, "I am Jesus, whom you are persecuting; but rise and enter the city, and you will be told what you are to do." The men who were traveling with him stood speechless, hearing the voice but seeing no one. Saul arose from the ground; and when his eyes were opened, he could see nothing; so they led him by the hand and brought him into Damascus. And for three days he was without sight, and neither ate nor drank.... So Ananias departed and entered the house. And laying his hands on him he said, "Brother Saul, the Lord Jesus who appeared to you on the road by which you came, has sent me that you may regain your sight and be filled with the Holy Spirit." And immediately something like scales fell from his eyes and he regained his sight. Then he rose and was baptized, and took food and was strengthened. For several days he was with the disciples at Damascus. And in the synagogues immediately he proclaimed Jesus, saying, "He is the Son of God."

SOURCE: Acts 9:1–20

The letters of Paul to the new Christian churches

Paul traveled and wrote to the new Christian communities, helping interpret the meaning of Jesus for them. His writings show the universalizing of the new faith, by taking it outside the Jewish Law and opening it to any believers.

Paul on Faith and Works

For we hold that a man is justified by faith apart from works of law. Or is God the God of Jews only? Is he not the God of Gentiles also? Yes, of Gentiles also, since God is one; and he will justify the circumcised on the ground of their faith and the uncircumcised through their faith. Do we then overthrow the law by this faith? By no means! On the contrary, we uphold the law.

SOURCE: Romans 3:28–31

Paul on Gender

Paul's ideas on gender are varied and reflect both his society and the more universalizing contradictions to his society that the new faith presented to him.

There is neither Jew nor Greek, there is neither slave nor free, there is neither male nor female; for you are all one in Christ Jesus.

SOURCE: Galatians 3:28

If there is anything they desire to know, let them ask their husbands at home. For it is shameful for a woman to speak in church.

SOURCE: I Corinthians 14:35

Paul on Faith, Hope, and Love

If I speak in the tongues of men and of angels, but have not love, I am a noisy gong or a clanging cymbal. And if I have prophetic powers, and understand all mysteries and all knowledge, and if I have all faith, so as to remove mountains, but have not love, I am nothing. If I give away all I have, and if I deliver my body to be burned, but have not love, I gain nothing. Love is patient and kind; love is not jealous or boastful; it is not arrogant or rude. Love does not insist on its own way; it is not irritable or resentful; it does not rejoice at wrong, but rejoices in the right. Love bears all things, believes all things, hopes all things, endures all things. Love never ends; as for prophecies, they will pass away; as for tongues, they will cease; as for knowledge, it will pass away. For our knowledge is imperfect and our prophecy is imperfect; but when the perfect comes, the imperfect will pass away. When I was a child, I spoke like a child, I thought like a child, I reasoned like a child; when I became a man, I gave up childish ways. For now we see in a mirror dimly, but then face to face. Now I know in part; then I shall understand fully, even as I have been fully understood. So faith, hope, love abide, these three; but the greatest of these is love.

SOURCE: I Corinthians 13:1–13

All excerpts from the Bible are taken from the Revised Standard Version. New York: Thomas Nelson, 1952. Available on The Bible Browser Home Page <http://goon.stg.brown.edu/bible_browser/pbform.shtml>

History and literature

When Jesus was healing two blind men he asked, "Do you believe that I am able to do this?" The history of Christianity has echoed with this question. What does it mean to believe that Christ was the Son of God on earth who can transform history? Does it mean that we are to interpret scripture as literally, factually true? Or, at the other extreme, can we read many biblical passages symbolically, such as Jesus healing the blindness of despair or bigotry? Or both? Christians have discussed these issues for two millennia. The emphasis on the historical, factual side has been strengthened by ancient texts. But recent discoveries of other texts from biblical times have raised controversial and fascinating questions. The question of how to interpret scripture is renewed by these religious texts, because they raise the question of the **canon**: how did the Bible come into history?

How to Interpret Scripture
by Origen

Jesus was known for stilling storms, feeding the hungry, healing the sick and blind, and raising the dead. From the beginning of the faith, thinkers questioned the proper ways to interpret these reports. Here Origen, an Egyptian theologian (c. 185–254 CE) makes the important distinction between a literal, historical, factual ("bodily") reading and a symbolic, metaphoric, spiritual interpretation.

The right way, as it appears to us, of approaching the scriptures and gathering their meaning, is the following, which is extracted from the writings themselves. We find some such rule as this laid down by Solomon in the Proverbs concerning the divine doctrines written therein: "Do thou portray them threefold in counsel and knowledge, that thou mayest answer words of truth to those who question thee" (Prov. 22:20, 21).

One must therefore portray the meaning of the sacred writings in a threefold way upon one's own soul, so that the simple man may be edified by what we may call the flesh of the scripture, this name being given to the obvious interpretation; while the man who has made some progress may be edified by its soul, as it were; and the man who is perfect and like those mentioned by the apostle: "We speak wisdom among the perfect; yet a wisdom not of this world, nor of the rulers of this world, which are coming to naught; but we speak God's wisdom in a mystery, even the wisdom that hath been hidden, which God foreordained before the worlds unto our glory" (I Cor. 2:6, 7)—this man may be edified by the spiritual law (Rom. 7:14), which has "a shadow of the good things to come" (Heb. 10:1). For just as man consists of body, soul, and spirit, so in the same way does the scripture, which has been prepared by God to be given for man's salvation.

But since there are certain passages of scripture which, as we shall show in what follows, have no bodily [literal] sense at all, there are occasions when we must seek only for the soul and the spirit, as it were, of the passage.

That it is possible to derive benefit from the first, and to this extent helpful meaning, is witnessed by the multitudes of sincere and simple believers.

But if the usefulness of the law and the sequence and ease of the narrative were at first sight clearly discernible throughout, we should be unaware that there was anything beyond the obvious meaning for us to understand in the scriptures.

Now what man of intelligence will believe that the first and the second and the third day, and the evening and the morning existed without the sun and the moon and stars? And that the first day, if we may so call it, was even without a heaven (Gen. 1:5–13)? And who is so silly as to believe that God, after the manner of a farmer, "planted a paradise eastward in Eden," and set in it a visible and palpable "tree of life," of such a sort that anyone who tasted its fruit with his bodily teeth would gain life; and again that one could partake of "good and evil" by masticating the fruit taken from the tree of that name (Gen. 2:8, 9)? And when God is said to "walk in the paradise in the cool of the day" and Adam to hide himself behind a tree, I do not think anyone will doubt that these are figurative expressions which indicate certain mysteries through a semblance of history and not through actual events (Gen. 3:8).

The aim of the divine power which bestowed on us the holy scriptures is not that we should accept only what is found in the letter; for occasionally the records taken in a literal sense are not true, but actually absurd and impossible, and even with the history that actually happened and the legislation that is in its literal sense useful there are other matters interwoven.

But someone may suppose that the former statement refers to all the scriptures, and may suspect us of saying that because some of the history did not happen, therefore none of it happened; and because a certain law is irrational or impossible when taken literally, therefore no laws ought to be kept to the letter; or that the records of the Savior's life are not true in a physical sense; or that no law or commandment of his ought to be obeyed. We must assert, therefore, that in regard to some things we are clearly aware that the historical fact is true ... [e.g.] that Jerusalem is the chief city of Judea, in which a temple of God was built by Solomon; and thousands of other facts.

For our contention with regard to the whole of divine scripture is, that it all has a spiritual meaning, but not all a bodily [literal] meaning; for the bodily meaning is often proved to be an impossibility. Consequently the man who reads the divine books reverently, believing them to be divine writings, must exercise great care.

SOURCE: "Origen on First Principles," in Hugh T. Kerr, ed., *Readings in Christian Thought*. Nashville, TN: Abingdon Press, 1966, pp. 45–7

Early non-canonical texts

Recent discoveries of ancient texts show that a number of non-canonical spiritual writings were circulating among Jews and Christians in Biblical times, notably the Dead Sea Scrolls and the Nag Hammadhi Library. This has highlighted the questions of how the Bible's content, the "canon," excluded certain texts and included others, and why. An example is the following "The Thunder, Perfect Mind."

The Thunder, Perfect Mind
from the Nag Hammadi Library

In 1945 Egyptian peasants discovered the first of many jars with scrolls, buried about 400 CE, written in the Coptic language, translated from Greek. These scrolls reveal new understandings of what is called "Gnosticism," a religious complex with roots in several religions that blended with Christianity from the first century. Some Gnostics postulated a remote supreme divinity and an inferior, imperfect creator god. They stressed mystical, experiential gnosis ("knowledge") as opposed to faith, and saw Jesus as more human than orthodox Christians did. Gnostics were rejected by the church as heretics in the second and third centuries for their theology, alleged elitism, opposition to church authority, and egalitarian view of women. However, the new discovery of the Nag Hammadi Library has given us a much better understanding of the Gnostics. As the following selection shows, they were capable of highly poetic, paradoxical and mystical insights.

I was sent forth from the power, and I have come to those who reflect upon me, and I have been found among those who seek after me.
Look upon me, you who reflect upon me, and you hearers, hear me.
You who are waiting for me, take me to yourselves.
And do not banish me from your sight. . . .

I am the wife and the virgin. I am [the mother] and the daughter.
I am the members of my mother.
I am the barren one and many are her sons.
I am she whose wedding is great, and I have not taken a husband. . . .

I am the silence that is incomprehensible
   and the idea whose remembrance is frequent.
I am the voice whose sound is manifold
   and the word whose appearance is multiple.
I am the utterance of my name.
Why, you who hate me, do you love me, and hate those who love me?
You who deny me, confess me, and you who confess me, deny me. . . .

But I am she who exists in all fears and strength in trembling.
I am she who is weak, and I am well in a pleasant place.
I am senseless and I am wise.
Why have you hated me in your counsels?
For I shall be silent among those who are silent,
   and I shall appear and speak. . . .

I am the one whose image is great in Egypt
   and the one who has no image among the barbarians.

I am the one who has been hated everywhere
  and who has been loved everywhere.
I am the one whom they call Life, and you have called Death.
I am the one whom they call Law, and you have called Lawlessness. . . .

I am she who does not keep festival,
  and I am she whose festivals are many.
I, I am godless, and I am the one whose God is great. . . .
Come forward to childhood,
  and do not despise it because it is small and it is little. . . .

For what is inside of you is what is outside of you,
  and the one who fashions you on the outside
  is the one who shaped the inside of you.
And what you see outside of you, you see inside of you;
  it is visible and it is your garment. . . .

SOURCE: "The Thunder, Perfect Mind," trans. George W. MacRae, in James M. Robinson, ed., *The Nag Hammadi Library*, revised edition. San Francisco: HarperCollins, 1990, pp. 272–7

The Formation of the Canon
by Athanasius

The process of selecting which of the numerous spiritual texts circulating about Jesus to include in the official Bible, the "canon," took over 300 years. Church leaders had varying lists of their favorite books. The list compiled in 367 by Athanasius (c. 296–373 CE), Bishop of Alexandria, is the oldest surviving one that approximates the current Christian Bible. A fairly official canon was approximately determined when in 405 Pope Innocent I proclaimed to be canonical a list very similar to Athanasius's. At the Council of Trent in 1546 **Roman Catholics** *reaffirmed their canon, which differs from* **Protestant** *and* **Orthodox** *versions. Generally the year 400 is accepted as the point when the Christian canon became consensus as Jerome's Latin translation (the Vulgate) was circulating. After listing a version of the Tanakh as the Old Testament, Athanasius proposed this New Testament canon:*

There are, then, of the Old Testament, twenty-two books in number; for, as I have heard, it is handed down that this is the number of the letters among the Hebrews; their respective order and names being as follows. The first is Genesis, then Exodus, next Leviticus, after that Numbers, and then Deuteronomy. Following these there is Joshua, the son of Nun, then Judges, then Ruth. And again, after these four books of Kings, the first and second being reckoned as one book, and so likewise the third and fourth as one book. And again, the first and second of the Chronicles are reckoned as one book. Again Ezra, the first and second are similarly one book. After these there is the book of Psalms, then the Proverbs, next Ecclesiastes, and the Song of Songs. Job follows, then the Prophets, the twelve being reckoned as one book. Then Isaiah, one book, then Jeremiah with Baruch, Lamentations, and the Epistle, one book; afterwards, Ezekiel and Daniel, each one book. Thus far constitutes the Old Testament.

Again it is not tedious to speak of the [books] of the New Testament. These are, the four Gospels, according to Matthew, Mark, Luke, and John. Afterwards, the Acts of the Apostles and Epistles (called Catholic), seven, viz. of James, one; of Peter, two; of John, three; after these, one of Jude. In addition, there are fourteen Epistles of Paul, written in this order. The first, to the Romans; then two to the Corinthians; after these, to the Galatians; next, to the Ephesians; then to the Philippians; then to the Colossians; after these, two to the Thessalonians, and that to the Hebrews; and again, two to Timothy; one to Titus; and lastly, that to Philemon. And besides, the Revelation of John.

SOURCE: from the *Nicene and Post-Nicene Fathers* series. <http://ccel.wheaton.edu/ fathers/NPNF2-04/Athanasius/Festal/t278.htm#t278.htm.2>

Theology and spirituality

Christians have struggled with many of the age-old questions that life poses and religions strive to answer. Are heroic spiritual reformers like Jesus merely humans, or was Jesus actually God appearing in history? Early creeds, such as the Athanasian Creed, affirmed that Jesus was divine, even simultaneously fully divine and fully human. What is the nature of the evil apparently behind life's atrocities? What rational investigations can convince thinkers of religious truths? What is the meaning of mystical experiences of divine presence? How much authority is the social convention of the day, such as the role of women, to be given in religion? What is the significance of mysterious, poetic religious language, such as "the incandescence of stillness"? Does the ascetic life of a priest, monk, or nun take one closer to God? Can religion really replace painful grief with transcendent joy? Is the Church a necessary mediator of God through sacraments, or does everyone have direct access to God? How are belief and ethics related?

The Confessions of St. Augustine
by Augustine of Hippo

*Augustine, Bishop of Hippo in North Africa (354–430), wrote the first surviving auto-biography showing an intense self-awareness. It also shows a detailed transformation from a pleasure-enjoying youth who fathered a child outside marriage, to a man awakened to deep spiritual realities. He struggled with the question of the nature of evil: is it a second cosmic force like God, as the **Manichaeans** believed (he was once a Manichaean), or is it a lack of God's goodness (*privatio boni*)? Augustine was per-*

suaded by the Neo-Platonists of a cosmic hierarchy, descending from an immaterial, eternal and intelligible God down to earth. He wrote several influential books: The City of God *criticizes "pagan" civic religions as bankrupt. He also wrote on the divine illumination of the intellect, the importance of introspection, and the need for God's grace to motivate morality.*

My sins were being multiplied, and my concubine being torn from my side as a hindrance to my marriage, my heart which clave unto her was torn and wounded and bleeding. And she returned to Afric,[4] vowing unto Thee never to know any other man, leaving with me my son by her. But unhappy I, who could not imitate a very woman, impatient of delay, inasmuch as not till after two years was I to obtain her I sought, not being so much a lover of marriage as a slave to lust, procured another, though no wife, that so by the servitude of an enduring custom, the disease of my soul might be kept up and carried on in its vigour, or even augmented, into the dominion of marriage. Nor was that my wound cured, which had been made by the cutting away of the former, but after inflammation and most acute pain, it mortified, and my pains became less acute, but more desperate. . . .

And to Thee is nothing whatsoever evil: yea, not only to Thee, but also to Thy creation as a whole, because there is nothing without, which may break in, and corrupt that order which Thou hast appointed it. But in the parts thereof some things, because unharmonizing with other some, are accounted evil: whereas those very things harmonize with others, and are good; and in themselves are good. And all these things which harmonize not together, do yet with the inferior part, which we call Earth, having its own cloudy and windy sky harmonizing with it. . . .

But after Thou hadst soothed my head, unknown to me, and closed mine eyes that they should not behold vanity, I ceased somewhat of my former self, and my frenzy was lulled to sleep; and I awoke in Thee, and saw Thee infinite, but in another way, and this sight was not derived from the flesh.

And I looked back on other things; and I saw that they owed their being to Thee; and were all bounded in Thee: but in a different way; not as being in space; but because Thou containest all things in Thine hand in Thy Truth; and all things are true so far as they be; nor is there any falsehood, unless when that is thought to be, which is not. And I saw that all things did harmonize, not with their places only, but with their seasons. . . . And I enquired what iniquity was, and found it to be no substance, but the perversion of the will, turned aside from Thee, O God, the Supreme, towards these lower things, and casting out its bowels, and puffed up outwardly. . . .

I had found the unchangeable and true Eternity of Truth above my changeable mind. And thus by degrees I passed from bodies to the soul,

---

[4] Afric—Africa, then referring only to the area of present-day Egypt, Libya, Algeria, and Morocco, as the rest of the continent was unknown to the Romans.

which through the bodily senses perceives; and thence to its inward faculty, to which the bodily senses represent things external, whitherto reach the faculties of beasts; and thence again to the reasoning faculty, to which what is received from the senses of the body is referred to be judged. . . .

Then I sought a way of obtaining strength sufficient to enjoy Thee; and found it not, until I embraced that Mediator betwixt God and men, the Man Christ Jesus, who is over all, God blessed for evermore, calling unto me, and saying, I am the way, the truth, and the life, and mingling that food which I was unable to receive, with our flesh. For, the Word was made flesh, that Thy wisdom, whereby Thou createdst all things, might provide milk for our infant state. For I did not hold to my Lord Jesus Christ, I, humbled, to the Humble; nor knew I yet whereto His infirmity would guide us. For Thy Word, the Eternal Truth, far above the higher parts of Thy Creation, raises up the subdued unto Itself.

SOURCE: Augustine of Hippo. *The Confessions of St. Augustine*, trans. Edward B. Pusey. New York: Washington Square Press, 1960, pp. 101, 119–22

A Medieval Argument for the Existence of God
by Anselm of Canterbury

Theologians explore questions such as what religious truths can be known by reason and which ones humans can know only by divine revelation. Thomas Aquinas (1225–74), for example, proposed five famous arguments that he thought could prove the existence of God by reason alone. But he concluded that some doctrines, such as the **Trinity** *and* **Incarnation**, *can be known only by revelation.*

Aquinas was preceded by Anselm of Canterbury (1033–1109) with his **ontological** *argument of metaphysical proof that God exists. Anselm was a Benedictine monk and an Archbishop of Canterbury. His argument for the existence of God is the earliest ontological argument. He contends that the greatest or most perfect thing that can be thought is God and, because of its perfection, it must exist. Later Emmanuel Kant (1724–1804) argued that existence is no more proven by the concept of perfection than the existence of money is proven by the concept of money. Later versions became the ontological question asking, "What makes existence itself possible?"*

That God Really Exists   Therefore, Lord, you who give knowledge of the faith, give me as much knowledge as you know to be fitting for me, because you are as we believe and that which we believe. And indeed we believe you are something greater than which cannot be thought. Or is there no such kind of thing, for "the fool said in his heart, 'there is no God' "? But certainly that same fool having heard what I just said, "something greater than which cannot be thought," understands what he heard, and what he understands is in his thought, even if he does not think it exists. For it is one thing for something to exist in a person's thought and quite another for the person to think that thing exists. For when a painter thinks ahead to what he will paint, he has that picture in his thought, but he does not yet think it exists, because he has not done it yet. Once he has painted it he has it in his thought and thinks it exists because he has done it. Thus even the fool is compelled to grant that something greater than which cannot be thought exists in thought, because he understands what he hears, and whatever is understood exists in thought. And certainly that greater than which cannot be understood cannot exist only in thought, for if it exists only in thought it could also be thought of as existing in reality as well, which is greater. If, therefore, that than which greater cannot be thought exists in thought alone, then that than which greater cannot be thought turns out to be that than which something greater actually can be thought, but that is obviously impossible. Therefore something than which greater cannot be thought undoubtedly exists both in thought and in reality.

That God Cannot be Thought Not to Exist In fact, it so undoubtedly exists that it cannot be thought of as not existing. For one can think there exists something that cannot be thought of as not existing, and that would be greater than something which can be thought of as not existing. For if that greater than which cannot be thought can be thought of as not existing, then that greater than which cannot be thought is not that greater than which cannot be thought, which does not make sense. Thus that than which nothing can be thought so undoubtedly exists that it cannot even be thought of as not existing.

And you, Lord God, are this being. You exist so undoubtedly, my Lord God, that you cannot even be thought of as not existing. And deservedly, for if some mind could think of something greater than you, that creature would rise above the creator and could pass judgment on the creator, which is absurd. And indeed whatever exists except you alone can be thought of as not existing. You alone of all things most truly exist and thus enjoy existence to the fullest degree of all things, because nothing else exists so undoubtedly, and thus everything else enjoys being in a lesser degree. Why therefore did the fool say in his heart "there is no God," since it is so evident to any rational mind that you above all things exist? Why indeed, except precisely because he is stupid and foolish?

SOURCE: Anselm of Canterbury, trans. David Burr, in Paul Halsall, ed. *The Medieval Sourcebook*, Virtual Religion Index, <www.rci.rutgers.edu/~religion>

Everything Lives in God
by Hildegard of Bingen

Hildegard (1098–1179) was a German nun of rare intelligence and originality. Beginning in childhood she had visions of God's light and angels and developed a spiritual wisdom based on her view that the Word of God is present in every living thing, expressed in its beauty. She also pressed forward her conviction of the spiritual equality of men and women, and was able to establish an independent Benedictine convent. She was a popular public speaker, and in an age when women seldom preached, she gave sermons to crowds at cathedrals. Her wisdom was sought by many for personal counsel and healing.

Your eyes are not strong enough to look at God. Your mind is not strong enough to comprehend his mysteries. You can only see and know what God allows. Yet in your desire to see and know more, you engage in all manner of foolish speculations, which cause your soul to stagger. Just as water is absorbed by the heat of a burning forge, so your soul is absorbed by the restlessness of your thoughts, as you try to grasp what is beyond your grasp.

The Word of God regulates the movements of the sun, the moon and the stars. The Word of God gives the light which shines from the heavenly bodies. He makes the wind blow, the rivers run and the rain fall. He makes trees burst into blossom, and the crops bring forth the harvest.

The sky above us imitates God. Just as the sky has no beginning and no end, so God has no beginning and end. Just as the stars sparkle, so spiritual stars emanate from the throne of God, to sparkle within people's souls.

The Word of God spoke, and brought all creatures into being. God and his Word are one. As the Word spoke, so God's eternal will was fulfilled. The echo of the Word awakened life from inanimate dust.

When the Word of God spoke at the moment of creation, his sound was implanted in every creature, and gave life to every creature.

The love of God is symbolized by a leaping fountain. All who come near to it are showered by its sparkling waters. And they can see their own image in the pool below.

Everything lives in God, and hence nothing can truly die, since God is life itself. God is the wisdom that brought all things into being. He breathes life into all things.

In all creation—in trees, plants, animals and stones—there are hidden secret powers which no one can discern unless they are revealed by God.

SOURCE: Robert Van de Weyer, ed. *Hildegard*. London: Hodder & Stoughton, 1997, pp. 32–4

Grief and Joy
by St. Gregory of Sinai

The Philokalia *(love of what is beautiful) is an ancient and growing collection of Orthodox writings, ascetic and mystical, reflecting the monastic life of the Eastern Church. It has a wide influence on the modern Orthodox world. This selection is from St. Gregory of Sinai, one of the bright lights of the fourteenth-century Church. Born c. 1265, he entered the monastic life at Sinai, then spent years at the famous Mount*

Athos monastery complex, perched precariously atop a remote mountain in Greece. Like other Orthodox, he practiced repetition of the "Jesus Prayer": "Jesus Christ, Son of God, have mercy on me," to bring God into his heart. Here he discusses the depths of grief and the heights of joy in meditation.

Unless your life and actions are accompanied by a sense of inner grief you cannot endure the incandescence of stillness. If with this sense of grief you meditate—before they come to pass—on the many terrors that await us prior to and after death you will achieve both patience and humility, the twin foundations of stillness. Without them your efforts to attain stillness will always be accompanied by apathy and self-conceit. From these will arise a host of distractions and day-dreams, all inducing sluggishness. In their wake comes dissipation, daughter of indolence, making the body sluggish and slack and the intellect benighted and callous. Then Jesus is hidden, concealed by the throng of thoughts and images that crowd the mind. . . .

For beginners prayer is like a joyous fire kindled in the heart; for the perfect is like a vigorous sweet-scented light. Or again, prayer is the preaching of the Apostles, an action of faith or, rather, faith itself, "that makes real for us the things for which we hope," active love, angelic impulse, the power of the bodiless spirits, their work and delight, the Gospel of God, the heart's assurance, hope of salvation, a sign of purity, a token of holiness, knowledge of God, baptism made manifest, purification in the water of regeneration, a pledge of the Holy Spirit, the exultation of Jesus, the soul's delight, God's mercy, a sign of reconciliation, the seal of Christ, a ray of the noetic[5] sun, the heart's dawn star.

SOURCE: Gregory of Sinai, ed. G. E. H. Palmer, *et al. The Philokalia*, vol. 4. London: Faber and Faber, 1995, pp. 236–7

The Reformation

Like any institution, the Church can require reforms. Jesus himself was a reformer, in the tradition of the Hebrew Prophets. The Eastern Orthodox Church split with the Roman Catholic Church in 1054 over theological disagreements after Constantinople was sacked by unrestrained Crusaders. Later the Protestant Reformation argued for certain theological principles, most importantly **justification** by faith, not only works and the priesthood of all believers. These code phrases unraveled a number of the Church's structures, and it was Martin Luther who boldly started the Reformation that splintered the Church. The Roman Catholic Reformation (also called the Counter-Reformation) was formalized at the Council of Trent (1545–63), which made other reforms. Rising European nationalism, global exploration, the expand-

---

[5] Noetic—intellectual or abstract.

ing capitalism, the growth of the middle class, the printing press, literacy, and democracy were all part of this great historical movement.

Faith Can Rule Only in the Inward Man
by Martin Luther

Luther (1483–1546) was a German priest and Doctor of Theology at Wittenberg University. He proclaimed many of the principles of the Protestant Reformation, beginning with his "95 Theses," his 1517 denunciation of the sale of indulgences (releases from spiritual punishment for sins). His inflammatory tracts resulted in his excommunication in 1521. In the following "Treatise" he argued for justification by faith rather than by works (human actions) alone. Luther said that God's grace and faith should lead to ethical action, but "religious" behavior alone is not sufficient to determine righteousness. He also argued for the priesthood of all believers—that everyone has direct access to God, with no need for ecclesiastical control. He proclaimed the Bible to be the authority in faith, and translated it into German (1534/45). He also opposed priestly celibacy, so in 1525 he married Catharine von Bora, a former nun.

One thing and one only is necessary for Christian life, righteousness and liberty. That one thing is the most holy Word of God, the Gospel of Christ. . . . The Word of God cannot be received and cherished by any works whatever, but only by faith. Hence it is clear that, as the soul needs only the Word for its life and righteousness, so it is justified by faith alone and not by any works; for if it could be justified by anything else, it would not need the Word, and therefore it would not need faith. But this faith cannot at all exist in connection with works, that is to say, if you at the same time claim to be justified by works, whatever their character; for that would be to halt between two sides, to worship Baal and to kiss the hand, which, as Job says, is a very great iniquity. . . . When you have learned this, you will know that you need Christ, Who suffered and rose again for you, that, believing in Him, you may through this faith become a new man, in that all your sins are forgiven, and you are justified by the merits of another, namely, of Christ alone.

Since, therefore, this faith can rule only in the inward man, as Romans 10 says, "With the heart we believe unto righteousness"; and since faith alone justifies, it is clear that the inward man cannot be justified, made free and be saved by any outward work or dealing whatsoever, and that works, whatever their character, have nothing to do with this inward man. . . .

Although, as I have said, a man is abundantly justified by faith inwardly, in his spirit, and so has all that he ought to have, except in so far as this faith and riches must grow from day to day even unto the future life: yet he remains in this mortal life on earth, and in this life he must needs govern his own body and have dealings with men. Here the works begin; here a man cannot take his ease; here he must, indeed, take care to discipline his body by fastings, watchings, labors and other reasonable discipline, and to make it subject to the spirit so that it will obey and conform to the inward man and to faith, and not revolt against faith and hinder the inward man, as it is the body's nature to do if it be not held in check. For the inward man, who by faith is created in the likeness of God, is both joyful and happy because of Christ in Whom so many benefits are conferred upon him, and therefore it is his one occupation to serve God joyfully and for naught, in love that is not constrained.

SOURCE: Martin Luther, "Treatise on Christian Liberty," Letter to Pope Leo X, in Clyde L. Manschreck, ed. *A History of Christianity*. Englewood Cliffs, NJ: Prentice Hall, 1964. Reprinted from *Works of Martin Luther II*, trans. W. A. Lambert. Philadelphia, PA: Muhlenburg Press, 1943, pp. 25–7

Living Christianity

Christian tradition encompasses dynamic movements that take many forms in our times. In the following excerpts, we offer a conservative evangelistic document as well as writings from some revered twentieth-century Christian figures, the argument of liberation theology, feminist voices, new ideas about how to imagine God, and a Christian engagement with the environmental cause.

An Evangelical Manifesto

The document excerpted below was drawn up in 1989 in Manila, Philippines, by 3,000 representatives from 170 countries who consider themselves "progressive evangelicals." It was headed "Calling the whole church to take the whole gospel to the whole world." It set out twenty-one affirmations, many of which are reprinted here.

We affirm our continuing commitment to the Lausanne Covenant[6] as the basis of our cooperation in the Lausanne movement.

We affirm that in the Scriptures of the Old and New Testaments God has given us an authoritative disclosure of his character and will, his redemptive acts and their meaning, and his mandate for mission.

We affirm that the biblical gospel is God's enduring message to our world, and we determine to defend, proclaim and embody it.

We affirm that human beings, though created in the image of God, are sinful and guilty, and lost without Christ, and that this truth is a necessary preliminary to the gospel.

---

[6] Lausanne Covenant—proceedings of the International Congress on World Evangelization, Lausanne, Switzerland, 1971.

We affirm that the Jesus of history and the Christ of glory are the same person, and that this Jesus Christ is absolutely unique, for he alone is God incarnate, our sin-bearer, the conqueror of death and the coming judge.

We affirm that on the cross Jesus Christ took our place, bore our sins and died our death; and that for this reason alone God freely forgives those who are brought to repentance and faith.

We affirm that other religions and ideologies are not alternative paths to God, and that human spirituality, if unredeemed by Christ, leads not to God but to judgment, for Christ is the only way.

We affirm that we must demonstrate God's love visibly by caring for those who are deprived of justice, dignity, food and shelter.

We affirm that the proclamation of God's kingdom of justice and peace demands the denunciation of all injustice and oppression, both personal and structural; we will not shrink from this prophetic witness.

We affirm that we who claim to be members of the Body of Christ must transcend within our fellowship the barriers of race, gender and class.

We affirm that the gifts of the Spirit are distributed to all God's people, women and men, and that their partnership in evangelization must be welcomed for the common good.

We affirm that we who proclaim the gospel must exemplify it in a life of holiness and love; otherwise our testimony loses its credibility.

We affirm that God is calling the whole church to take the whole gospel to the whole world. So we determine to proclaim it faithfully, urgently and sacrificially, until he comes.

SOURCE: "The Manila Manifesto," 1989. Reprinted in Rowland Croucher, *Recent Trends among Evangelicals,* 2nd edn. Victoria, Australia: John Mark Ministries, 1991, pp. 103–4

I Don't Want to Eat Any Sugar
by Mother Teresa

Mother Teresa's life (1910–97) and work are well known. This Albanian Catholic nun in Calcutta picked up off the street and cared for thousands of dying people; she wore a sari worth about a dollar. She crawled past piles of manure into caves to help frightened people with leprosy. What gave her strength was faith and love. This is an extract from her 1979 Nobel Prize acceptance speech.

Jesus too suffered in order to love us. He still suffers. To be sure that we might remember his great love he became our bread of life to satisfy our hunger for his love, our hunger for God, because it was for this love that we were created. We were created to love and to be loved, and he became man to enable us to love him as he loves us. He has become one with the hungry, the naked, the homeless, the sick, the persecuted, the lonely, the abandoned ones. . . .

I was amazed when I learned that in the West so many young people are on drugs. I tried to understand the reason for this. Why? The answer is, "because in the family there is nobody who cares for them." Fathers and mothers are so busy they have no time. Young parents work, and the child lives in the street, and goes his own way. . . .

The poor are good people. They can teach us much. One day a man came to thank us: "You who practice chastity have taught us very well how to plan our family, because self-control is nothing but love of one for the other." I think he was right. And many times these are people who have nothing to eat, nor a house to live in, yet they know how to be great.

The poor are wonderful people. One evening we picked up four in the street; one was in pitiful condition. I told the other Sisters: "You take care of the other three; I will see about this weakest one." I did all that my love enabled me to do: I put her in a bed, and on her face there appeared a marvelous smile. She took my hand, and after saying just one word: "Thanks!" she died. . . .

That is why we believe what Jesus said: "I was hungry, naked, homeless, unwanted, hated, nobody cared about me . . . And you did this for me!" . . .

There was a time in Calcutta when it was very difficult for us to get any sugar. I don't know how this came to the ears of the children, but a little four-year-old went home and said to his parents: "I don't want to eat any sugar for three days; I want to give it to Mother Teresa." Three days later his father and mother came to our house with the little fellow. I had never seen them before, and the child could hardly pronounce my name. But he knew very well why he had come: to share his love with others.

SOURCE: Lush Gjergji. *Mother Teresa: Her Life, Her Works*. New Rochelle, NY: New City Press, 1991, pp. 137–41

I've Seen the Promised Land
by Martin Luther King Jr.

Martin Luther King Jr. (1929–68) was the leader of the non-violent direct-action wing of the U.S. civil rights movement. Born in Atlanta, he became a Baptist minister in Montgomery, Alabama, and soon earned his doctorate in theology. King traveled widely and spoke often against racial prejudice. He organized many protests, using carefully planned non-violent resistant tactics inspired by Mahatma Gandhi. Only after research, then negotiations, failed would he permit protests against unjust, racially prejudiced customs or laws. He prohibited protesters from fighting back while protesting, in order to demonstrate the moral motives for their cause. His "Letter from a Birmingham Jail" and "I Have a Dream" speech (1963) articulated his principles and passions and won him the Nobel Peace Prize in 1964. He was assassinated in Memphis in 1968, shortly after he delivered the speech excerpted below.

Let us develop a kind of dangerous unselfishness. One day a man came to Jesus; and he wanted to raise some questions about some vital matters in life. At points, he wanted to trick Jesus, and show him that he knew a little more than Jesus knew, and through this, throw him off base. Now that question could have easily ended up in a philosophical and theological debate. But Jesus immediately pulled that question from mid-air, and placed it on a dangerous curve between Jerusalem and Jericho. And he talked about a certain man, who fell among thieves. You remember that a Levite and a priest passed by on the other side. They didn't stop to help him. And finally a man of another race came by. He got down from his beast, decided not to be compassionate by proxy. But with him, administered first aid, and helped the man in need. Jesus ended up saying, this was the good man, this was the great man, because he had the capacity to project the "I" into the "thou," and to be concerned about his brother. Now you know, we use our imagination a great deal to try to determine why the priest and the Levite didn't stop. At times we say they were busy going to church meetings—an ecclesiastical gathering—and they had to get on down to Jerusalem so they wouldn't be late for their meeting. At other times we would speculate that there was a religious law that "One who was engaged in religious ceremonials was not to touch a human body twenty-four hours before the ceremony." And every now and then we begin to wonder whether maybe they were not going down to Jerusalem, or down to Jericho, rather to organize a "Jericho Road Improvement Association." That's a possibility. Maybe they felt that it was better to deal with the problem from the causal root, rather than to get bogged down with an individual effort.

But I'm going to tell you what my imagination tells me. It's possible that these men were afraid. You see, the Jericho road is a dangerous road. I remember when Mrs. King and I were first in Jerusalem. We rented a car and drove from Jerusalem down to Jericho. And as soon as we got on that road, I said to my wife, "I can see why Jesus used this as a setting for his parable." It's a winding, meandering road. It's really conducive for ambushing. You start out in Jerusalem, which is about 1200 . . . feet above sea level. And by the time you get down to Jericho, fifteen or twenty minutes later, you're about 2200 feet below sea level. That's a dangerous road. In the days of Jesus it came to be known as the "Bloody Pass." And you know, it's possible that the priest and the Levite looked over that man on the ground and wondered if the robbers were still around. Or it's possible that they felt that the man on the ground was merely faking. And he was acting like he had been robbed and hurt, in order to seize them over there, lure them there for quick and easy seizure. And so the first question that the

Levite asked was, "If I stop to help this man, what will happen to me?" But then the Good Samaritan came by. And he reversed the question: "If I do not stop to help this man, what will happen to him?"

That's the question before you tonight. Not, "If I stop to help the sanitation workers, what will happen to all of the hours that I usually spend in my office every day and every week as a pastor?" The question is not, "If I stop to help this man in need, what will happen to me?" "If I do not stop to help the sanitation workers, what will happen to them?" That's the question.

Let us rise up tonight with a greater readiness. Let us stand with a greater determination. And let us move on in these powerful days, these days of challenge to make America what it ought to be. We have an opportunity to make America a better nation. And I want to thank God, once more, for allowing me to be here with you. . . .

And then I got into Memphis. And some began to say the threats, or talk about the threats that were out. What would happen to me from some of our sick white brothers?

Well, I don't know what will happen now. We've got some difficult days ahead. But it doesn't matter with me now. Because I've been to the mountaintop. And I don't mind. Like anybody, I would like to live a long life. Longevity has its place. But I'm not concerned about that now. I just want to do God's will. And He's allowed me to go up to the mountain. And I've looked over. And I've seen the promised land. I may not get there with you. But I want you to know tonight, that we, as a people will get to the promised land. And I'm happy, tonight. I'm not worried about anything. I'm not fearing any man. Mine eyes have seen the glory of the coming of the Lord.

SOURCE: Flip Schulke, ed. *Martin Luther King, Jr: A Documentary . . . Montgomery to Memphis*. New York and London: Norton, 1976, pp. 222–3. Reprinted in James Melvin Washington, ed. *A Testament of Hope*. San Francisco: Harper & Row, 1986, pp. 284–6

Not Development, but Liberation
by Gustavo Gutiérrez

In the late 1960s "Liberation theology" arose from indignation at the poverty of the masses in South America, led by Roman Catholic village priests and theologians such as Gustavo Gutiérrez. He opposed the destructive industrial world's surging "development" with a call to "liberation." He argued that the poor need ethical and economic preference, because God raises up those who suffer. Liberation theologies have expanded into feminist theologies, black theologies, and indigenous world theologies in general. Gutiérrez points out that Jesus's saying "the poor you will always have with you" assumes knowledge of its Deuteronomy 15:11 context: "For the poor will never cease out of the land; therefore I command you, You shall open wide your hand to your brother, to the needy, and to the poor in the land."

We can distinguish three reciprocally interpenetrating levels of meaning of the term *liberation*, or in other words, three approaches to the process of liberation.

In the first place, "liberation" expresses the aspirations of oppressed peoples and social classes, emphasizing the conflictual aspect of the economic, social, and political process which puts them at odds with wealthy nations and oppressive classes. In contrast, the word "development", and above all the policies characterized as developmentalist,[7] appear somewhat aseptic, giving a false picture of a tragic and conflictual reality. The issue of development does in fact find its true place in the more universal, profound, and radical perspective of liberation. It is only within this framework that "development" finds its true meaning and possibilities of accomplishing something worthwhile.

At a deeper level, "liberation" can be applied to an understanding of history. Man is seen as assuming conscious responsibility for his own destiny. This understanding provides a dynamic context and broadens the horizons of the desired social changes. In this perspective the unfolding of all of man's dimensions is demanded—a man who makes himself throughout his life and throughout history. The gradual conquest of true freedom leads to the creation of a new man and a qualitatively different society. This vision provides, therefore, a better understanding of what in fact is at stake in our times.

Finally, the word "development" to a certain extent limits and obscures the theological problems implied in the process designated by this term. On the contrary the word "liberation" allows for another approach leading to the Biblical sources which inspire the presence and action of man in history. In the Bible, Christ is presented as the one who brings us liberation. Christ the Savior liberates man from sin, which is the ultimate root of all disruption of friendship and of all injustice and oppression. Christ makes man truly free, that is to say, he enables man to live in communion with him; and this is the basis for all human brotherhood.

SOURCE: David Batstone *et al.*, eds. *A Theology of Liberation: History, Politics and Salvation*. Maryknoll, NY: Orbis Books, 1973, pp. 34–5

The Godhead as a Woman Giving Birth
by Virginia Mollenkott

Virginia Mollenkott is Professor Emerita of the William Paterson University in New Jersey. She publishes in the area of Christian feminist reform, the feminist effort to change the Church from within. This selection from her 1984 book The Divine Feminine: The Biblical Imagery of God as Female *uncovers the neglected femi-*

---

[7] Developmentalist— Gutiérrez uses the word *desarrollista*, "making worse."

nine images of God as, for example, mother, midwife, Shekinah, female beloved, and Dame Wisdom. Since then she has written Sensuous Spirituality: Out from Fundamentalism, *and (with Letha Scanzoni)* Is the Homosexual My Neighbor: A Positive Christian Response. *She is active in the Evangelical and Ecumenical Women's Caucus.*

More pervasive than any other biblical image of God as female is the image of a maternal deity. Not only is the Creator depicted as carrying in the womb or birthing the creation, but also Christ and the Holy Spirit are depicted in similar roles.

Isaiah 42:14 uses a simile of Yahweh's experiencing labor pains. Advancing like a hero against unjust idolators, Yahweh speaks: "From the beginning I have been silent,/ I have kept quiet, held myself in check./ *I groan like a woman in labor,*/ I suffocate, I stifle" (JB,[8] emphasis mine). Powerfully, God's anguish at the human failure to embody justice is captured in the image of a woman writhing, unable to catch her breath in the pain of her travail. This image makes God seem very much present alongside all those who are oppressed by the turmoil and suffering of our world. Out of God's travail comes a new world in which the blind are safely led, their darkness turning to light (Isaiah 42:16). . . .

Perhaps Jesus had all this in mind when he implied that his suffering on the cross initiated the birth-pangs or travail of bringing forth the New Humanity. He did that by using a birth image in John 16:21 (KJV[9]) to comfort the disciples concerning the difficulties they would confront in this world. A woman, he said, has sorrow when her *hour is come* and her birth contractions begin, but later her sorrow is turned to joy by the actual arrival of the baby. According to John's account it was only minutes later that Jesus began to pray with the words, "Father, the *hour is come*" (17:1). What hour? The hour of Christ-the-Mother's pain and sorrow: the hour of the birth pangs.

Paul utilized similar images in Romans 8:22: "From the beginning till now the entire creation, as we know, has been groaning in one great act of giving birth; and not only creation, but all of us who possess the first fruits of the Spirit, we too groan inwardly as we wait for our bodies to be set free" (JB). Salvation is here depicted as a birth process occurring not only within each individual (microcosm), but also within the natural creation as a whole (macrocosm). . . .

Because Paul understood that we Christians are intended to reflect God's motherhood in the nurturance of our own spirits and of each other, he did not hesitate to use female images concerning himself. He wrote to the Christians at Galatia, "I must go through the pain of giving birth to you all

---

[8] JB—Jerusalem Bible (1961 in French, 1966 in English).
[9] KJV—King James Version of the Bible.

over again, until Christ is formed in you" (4:19)—a double birth-image, since Paul says he would have to suffer renewed birth pangs until Christ's image had been fully conceived and gestated (formed) within the Galatians. When that had happened, of course, they could then proceed to give birth on their own.

Since Paul utilized mother-imagery in imitation of God-as-Mother, it should be no surprise to us that Cistercian abbots of the twelfth century also had no qualms about depicting their work in terms of motherhood. For instance, Bernard of Clairvaux urges prelates to "Learn that you must be mothers to those in your care, not masters."

Jesus spoke of the Holy Spirit as mother in John 3:6: "What is born of the flesh is flesh; what is born of the Spirit is spirit." To be born of the flesh is to emerge from a human mother; to be born of the spirit is to emerge from the divine Mother. Similarly John's Gospel asserts that those who believe in the Word "who was not born out of human stock" will themselves "become children of God," or in other words be "born of God" (1:12). And John's First Epistle asserts that everyone who loves is "born of God" (4:7). Such passages encourage us to see all "new-birth" or "born-again" images as affirmations of the female component in the divine nature. To proclaim that people "must be born again" is to urge them to experience the womb and the birth canal of God the Mother.

SOURCE: Virginia Ramey Mollenkott. *The Divine Feminine: The Biblical Imagery of God as Female*. New York: Crossroad, 1984, pp. 15–18

The Goddess and Women's Spirituality
by Charlene Spretnak

Charlene Spretnak teaches at the California Institute for Integral Studies in San Francisco. In this selection from her first book The Politics of Women's Spirituality, *she criticizes patriarchal religions as beyond reform and calls for a reawakening of the Goddess tradition as the best path to the divine for women. Her subsequent books have been* The Spiritual Dimension of Green Politics *(1986), and* States of Grace: The Recovery of Meaning in the Postmodern Age *(1991).*

The underlying rationale for patriarchal societies is patriarchal religion. Christianity, Judaism, Islam, and Hinduism all combine male godheads with proscriptions against woman as temptress, as unclean, as evil. We were all made to understand that Eve's act of heeding the word of the serpent caused the expulsion of the human race from the Garden of Eden. We were made to understand that, as a result of her act, it was decreed by God that woman must submit to the dominance of man. We were all raised in cultures that reflect this decree: men enjoy the secular and spiritual positions of power; women cook and clean for them and supply them with heirs.

Most of the four billion people currently living in accordance with the patriarchal order do not question it: things have been this way for a long time; it must be the natural order. But what if the patriarchy is only a few thousand years old? What if, for tens of thousands of years before that, societies were built around the concept of the Great Goddess? If this is the case, our entire overview of history is altered: We once passed through a very long phase of matrifocal[10] culture; we are now passing through a phase of patriarchal culture (which appears to be self-destructing after a relatively brief run); and the future phase is ours to design.

Manifestations of our reclaimed spirituality   *Anat, Aphrodite, Artemis, Asherah, Astarte, Athena, Attor, Au Set, Blodeuwedd, Britannia, Britomaris, Changing Woman, Demeter, Dictynna, Gaia, Hathor, Hecate, Hera, Ananna, Ishtar, Isis, Ix Chel, Kali, Kuan Yin, Magna Mater, Nut, Pandora, Persephone, Rhea, Rhiannon, Saraswati, Selene, Tara, Themis, White Goddess.*

Ours is the oldest spiritual tradition on Earth. Now we understand the symbolism in patriarchal myths wherein Apollo slays the python at Delphi, wherein evil comes to weak-willed Eve in the form of a snake, wherein Saint George fiercely slays the giant snake-like dragon, wherein Saint Patrick rids Ireland of the snakes—for in matrifocal spirituality snakes were a widespread symbol of cyclical renewal and regeneration, continually growing and shedding their skins. We understand why the animal declared unclean by the Judaic fathers was the pig, which had long been held sacred to Demeter[11] and other Mediterranean forms of the Goddess for its prolificacy.

The great silence has been broken at last. Women are coming together to cultivate the powers that can result from exploring matrifocal heritage, personal and collective mythology, natural healing, meditation, dreamwork, celebrating the cycles of nature (i.e., our surroundings and our own bodies), and ritual. As we all bear scars from having been raised under patriarchy, the ability to heal ourselves and each other psychically and physically is essential to the growth of women's culture. Ritual can generate and transform tremendous fields of force. That energy is always there for us to tap and manifest. Rituals created within a framework of women's spirituality differ in form and content from the empty, hierarchically imposed, patriarchal observances with which most of us grew up. They involve healing, strengthening, creative energy that expands with spontaneity from a meaningful core of values. . . .

SOURCE: Charlene Spretnak. *The Politics of Women's Spirituality*, 1982, pp. 394–5. Reprinted by permission of the author from *Chrysalis: A Magazine of Women's Culture*, no. 6, November 1978. © Charlene Spretnak 1978

---

[10] Matrifocal—focused on women as the leaders of society.
[11] Demeter—Greek goddess of fecundity and plenty.

Models of God
by Sallie McFague

Sallie McFague is Professor of Theology at Vanderbilt Divinity School. She explores the role of metaphor in theology and applies it to the problem of the masculine image of the biblical God, and to the ecological and nuclear crises. As a Christian she affirms the divine, personal power of God. But she also argues that, inevitably, imaginative metaphors involved in human expressions of faith become socially influenced models that are wrongly taken literally, such as the model of God the King, which reflects the monarchical, aristocratic society of the past. She calls for a constructive Christian, post-modern re-mythologizing of our models of God as mother, lover and friend.

In the closing stages of my last book, *Metaphorical Theology*, I experimented with the model of God as friend in an attempt to address the issues of idolatry and irrelevance leveled against the patriarchal imagery of the Christian tradition. The dominance of the patriarchal model, I felt, excluded the emergence of other models to express the relationship between God and the world, and so the model had become idolatrous and had rendered the tradition's imagery anachronistic. Since writing that book I have come to see patriarchal as well as imperialistic, triumphalist metaphors for God in an increasingly grim light: this language is not only idolatrous and irrelevant— besides being oppressive to many who do not identify with it—but it may also work against the continuation of life on our planet. Our nuclear capability places human beings of the late twentieth century on the verge of eliminating not only themselves but also most if not all other forms of life on earth. In this unprecedented danger, we must ask whether the Judeo-Christian tradition's triumphalist imagery for the relationship between God and the world is helpful or harmful. Does it support human responsibility for the fate of the earth, or does it, by looking to either divine power or providence, shift the burden to God? If a case can be made, as I believe it can, that traditional imperialistic imagery for God is opposed to life, its continuation and fulfillment, then we must give serious attention to alternatives. . . .

The nuclear issue is, however, part of a larger picture. I see the threat of a nuclear holocaust as epitomizing the genuinely novel context in which all constructive work in our time, including theology, must take place. To be sure, other eras undoubtedly considered their times as unprecedented as we find ours. But the crux for those of us who find our time exceptional is that the "old ways," the old solutions, will not do for us. The nuclear threat is but the most extreme example of what some call the post-modern sensibility. If the Enlightenment was the first watershed, thrusting us into the modern world, then the contemporary era must be called the second watershed, for its assumptions differ from those of the Enlightenment that created the modern world. Any listing of these assumptions will vary but will probably include some of the following: a greater appreciation of nature, linked with a chastened admiration for technology; the recognition of the importance of language (and hence interpretation and construction) in human existence; the acceptance of the challenge that other religious options present to the Judeo-Christian tradition; a sense of the displacement of the white, Western male and the rise of those dispossessed because of gender, race, or class; an apocalyptic sensibility, fueled in part by the awareness that we exist between two holocausts, the Jewish and the nuclear; and perhaps most significant, a growing appreciation of the thoroughgoing, radical interdependence of life at all levels and in every imaginable way. These assumptions, I believe, form the context for theology *if it is to be theology for our time*. The sorts of theological tasks that can be undertaken within this context are, of course, many, and the kind of reflection I will attempt in the present book is a modest, but I believe essential, one. It takes place at the level of the religious and theological imagination.

Let me try a sketch of what I am doing and then I will say a few words about the way I will do it. I begin with the assumption that what we can say with any assurance about the character of Christian faith is very little and that even that will be highly contested. Christian faith is, it seems to me, most basically a claim that the universe is neither indifferent nor malevolent but that there is a power (and a personal power at that) which is on the side of life and its fulfillment. Moreover, the Christian believes that we have some clues for fleshing out this claim in the life, death, and appearances of Jesus of Nazareth. Nevertheless, each generation must venture, through an analysis of what fulfillment could and must mean for its own time, the best way to express that claim. A critical dimension of this expression is the imaginative picture, the metaphors and models, that underlie the conceptual systems of theology. One cannot hope to interpret Christian faith for one's own time if one remains indifferent to the basic images that are the lifeblood of interpretation and that greatly influence people's perceptions and behavior. One of the serious deficiencies in contemporary theology is that though theologians have attempted to interpret the faith in new concepts appropriate to our time, the basic metaphors and models have remained relatively constant: they are triumphalist, monarchical, patriarchal. Much *deconstruction* of the traditional imagery has taken place, but little *construction*. If, however, metaphor and concept are, as I believe, inextricably and symbiotically related in theology, there is no way to do theology for our time with outmoded or oppressive metaphors and models. The refusal to deal with the constructive task results in either a return to anachronistic models—a conservative retreat—or a move away from all images toward abstract language. The first ghettoizes Christianity; the other renders it sterile. In this situation, one thing that is needed—and which I attempt in these pages—is a *remythologizing* of the relationship between God and the world. I will experiment with the models of God as mother, lover, and friend of the world, and with the image of the world as God's body. I will try to show that these metaphors are credible candidates for theology today from both a Christian and a postmodern perspective.

SOURCE: Sallie McFague. *Models of God: Theology for an Ecological, Nuclear Age.* Philadelphia, PA: Fortress Press, 1987, pp. ix–xi

The Green Patriarch: Environmental Orthodoxy
by Melba Newsome

His Holiness Bartholomew I is the Ecumenical Patriarch, the leader of the world's Orthodox Christians. His office in the Cathedral of St. George in Istanbul overlooks the Bosporus, the seaway that links the Black Sea to the Mediterranean Sea, both suffering from overfishing and pollution. Like some leaders in the Roman Catholic Church and the Protestant churches, he is speaking up for the need for restraint and stewardship toward nature by Christians. Orthodox Christians have always loved nature, he says, and so he has organized several environmental forums, speeches, and trips. He sharply defines Christian moral responsibility for the environment, saying: "For humans to cause species to become extinct and to destroy the biological diversity of God's creation ... these are sins."

Throughout his tenure as Patriarch, Bartholomew I has made environmental protection his crusade. His considerable work to promote the sanctity of our world's natural resources has earned him the sobriquet the Green Patriarch. In November 1997 Bartholomew advanced his agenda significantly. During a tour of the United States—when he became only the fifth religious leader awarded the Congressional Gold Medal—he made a historic speech at a symposium on religion, science, and the environment in Santa Barbara, California. "To commit a crime against the natural world is a sin," the Patriarch told an audience of eight hundred. "For humans to cause species to become extinct and to destroy the biological diversity of God's creation; for humans to degrade the integrity of the earth by causing changes in its climate, by stripping the earth of its natural forests, or destroying its wetlands; for humans to contaminate the earth's waters, its land, its air, and its life with poisonous substances—these are sins."

This wasn't the first time a religious leader had spoken about our responsibility to safeguard the environment. In 1971 the Anglican church declared environmental abuse blasphemous (that is, irreverent or impious). In 1989 Pope John Paul II called the environmental crisis a symptom of a deeper moral crisis. But the Patriarch's pronouncement is believed to be the first time a leader of a major international religion has explicitly linked environmental problems with sinful behavior.

"The Orthodox believe that bread and wine acquire personal characteristics by being made the body and the blood of Christ, and so creation is sanctified and affirmed as being 'very good.' The central concern of Orthodoxy is to enact through the Eucharist this new mode of being in which death ceases to exist. Precisely because creation is 'very good' it is worth preserving. The development of a special ethos of the sanctity of creation springing up from the Eucharist is valuable in the formation of a new environmental consciousness." ... Each of us has an obligation to God, who "placed the newly created human 'in the Garden of Eden to cultivate it and to guard it' " (Genesis 2:15). He imposed on humanity a stewardship role in relationship to the earth.

There is another aspect of personal responsibility that is close to the heart of Orthodoxy: *encratia*, or self-control, which is fundamental to Orthodox Christians. "Consuming the fruits of the earth unrestrained, we become consumed ourselves by avarice and greed. Asceticism is a corrective practice, a vision of repentance."

Voluntary restraint—and by implication, sustainable living—therefore is essential for practicing Orthodox Christians. "The Christian who harms the environment must start treating it for what it really is, namely, the extension of his or her own body, just as the church is the extension of Christ's physical body."

He has also made the Black Sea a priority. "The picture of the region is quite worrying," the Patriarch says, speaking about the long-term over-fishing and waste-dumping that have wrought havoc in the Black Sea; the last three monk seals spotted in 1996 now believed dead; the Black Sea's nutrient load, which has far exceeded the critical level; and the fishing fleets now idle. ... "We call upon the world's leaders to take action to halt the destructive changes to the global climate that are being caused by human activity. We must be spokespeople for an ecological ethic that reminds the world that it is not ours to use for our convenience. It is God's gift of love to us, and we must return that love by protecting it and all that is in it. Let us renew the harmony between heaven and earth, and transfigure every detail, every particle of life."

SOURCE: Melba Newsome, "The Green Patriarch: Environmental Orthodoxy," an interview with the Patriarch of Eastern Orthodoxy. *The Amicus Journal*, Winter 1999, vol. 20, No. 4, pp. 15–17 (<amicus@nrdc.org>)

GLOSSARY

Annunciation The biblical announcement to Mary of forthcoming motherhood by the angel Gabriel.

Apocrypha ("Hidden things") Non-canonical books associated with the Bible.

Canon ("Rule") A list of books that have authority in religion or culture.

Disciples The twelve companions of Christ, the first followers of his teachings.

Ecumenism The Christian quest for renewed unity among all Christian Churches; some seek a "wider ecumenism" incorporating all religions.

Grace God's freely given, unmerited love and forgiveness.

Heresy, heretic Belief contrary to the orthodox doctrine of Christianity; a follower of such beliefs.

Incarnation God (the Word) made flesh in the person of Jesus Christ.

Justification God's saving of humans from sin by **grace** through sacraments (Catholic) or faith (Protestant).

Manichaeism Third-century Iranian religion founded by Mani; a dualistic faith opposing God and matter; apostles of light fight powers of darkness.

Ontology Reflection on ultimate reality behind appearances.

Orthodox Branch of Christianity, once Church of the Byzantine Empire; broke with Roman Church in 1054; especially strong in Russia and Greece.

Protestant Branch of Christianity that began with Martin Luther in 1500s; stresses authority of Bible, priesthood of all believers, justification by faith, many denominations.

Roman Catholic Oldest branch of Christianity, centered in Rome, led by Pope; priests male and celibate, Mary honored, opposed to abortion.

RSV Revised Standard Version of the Bible: American English translation, twentieth century language (1946/52); the New RSV is more gender-inclusive (1989/95).

Synoptic The similar gospels of Matthew, Mark, and Luke, whose contents can be compared side-by-side in synopsis fashion.

Trinity Doctrine of One God in three persons: Father, Son, Holy Ghost or Holy Spirit.

HOLY DAYS

Epiphany 6 January, celebration of the three Kings' visit to the Child Jesus.

Ash Wednesday The beginning of Lent; ashes on the forehead initiate a 40-day period of self-restraint and reflection before Easter.

Palm Sunday Sunday before Easter, begins Holy Week, commemorating Christ's ride into Jerusalem.

Maundy Thursday The Thursday before Easter. Last Supper and betrayal of Christ by Judas.

Good Friday Christ's crucifixion.

Easter Sunday Christ's resurrection; Catholic and Protestant date is the Sunday after the full moon after the Spring Equinox; Orthodox later.

The Ascension Christ's withdrawal into Heaven 40 days after his resurrection.

Pentecost or **Whitsun** The Holy Spirit descends on Apostles.

The Assumption August 15, Roman Catholic feast, Virgin Mary taken body and soul into Heaven when she died, declared dogma by Pope Pius XII in 1950.

All Saints' Day 1 November, memorials for all saints and deceased, with requiem masses.

Immaculate Conception 8 December, Roman Catholic celebration of dogma of Mary's freedom from original sin.

Christmas 25 December, celebration of Christ's birth; absorbed festive atmosphere of Roman Saturnalia; Orthodox date is 6 January.

HISTORICAL OUTLINE

c. 4 BCE to 0 CE—Jesus born

c. 27–33 CE—Jesus crucified

c. 48–64 CE—Letters of Paul

c. 70–95 CE—Gospels written down

c. 150 CE—Last of New Testament writings

1st century CE—Josephus

c. 185–254—Origen

296–373—Athanasius

325—Nicene Creed

c. 400—Canon of Bible set

354–430—Augustine

800–1300—Consolidation of Papal Power

950–1350—Crusades

1033–1109—Anselm of Canterbury

1054—Division between Western and Eastern Orthodox Churches

1098–1179—Hildegard of Bingen

1182–1226—St. Francis of Assisi

1225–74—Thomas Aquinas

1200s—Building of European cathedrals

1521—Martin Luther excommunicated; Protestant Reformation begins

1545–63—Council of Trent: Roman Catholic Reformation, rejected indulgences

1945—Nag Hammadi scrolls discovered

1947—First of Dead Sea Scrolls discovered

1962—Vatican II

1915–1968—Thomas Merton

1929–1968—Martin Luther King

1910–97—Mother Teresa

REVIEW QUESTIONS

1   Why do you think it is told that Jesus was born in a stable, not in a palace?
2   How would you summarize the significance of the Beatitudes?
3   What was Jesus's view of the Jewish Law?
4   Did Jesus's teachings on reward in an afterlife help solve unjust suffering?
5   How would you interpret Jesus's healing of the blind to a scientist?
6   Why do you think Jesus suffered the Crucifixion?
7   What is the significance of the Resurrection?
8   How was Saul converted to Paul?
9   How did Paul interpret Jesus's teachings for non-Jews (Gentiles)?
10   How did Origen interpret scripture? Give an example.
11   Why do you think that *The Thunder, Perfect Mind* was not accepted in the Biblical canon?
12   What is the earliest text giving an approximation of the current biblical canon?
13   What change did Augustine go through? Quote from his concluding view.
14   Summarize Anselm's ontological argument? Does it convince you?
15   What did Hildegard of Bingen mean by "Everything lives in God"?
16   By what principles did Martin Luther change the Christian Church?
17   What are the main principles of the Manila Manifesto?
18   How do you think Mother Teresa endured the grief of seeing so many people she cared for die?
19   How did Martin Luther King relate the Good Samaritan to death?
20   How did Gustavo Gutiérrez compare "development" and "liberation"?
21   Compare the views of Virginia Mollenkott and Charlene Spretnak.
22   How does Sallie McFague think understanding metaphor helps religion?

INFORMATION RESOURCES

Cone, James, and Gayraud Wilmore, eds. *Black Theology: A Documentary History*. 2 vols. Maryknoll, NY Orbis, 1993

"Christian Tradition," Virtual Religion Index <www.rci.rutgers.edu/~religion/links/xnity.html>

Cross, F. L. ed. *The Oxford Dictionary of the Christian Church*. Oxford: Oxford University Press, 1997

Dillenberger, John, ed. *Martin Luther*. Garden City, NY: Anchor Doubleday, 1961

Ferme, Deane W. ed. *Third World Liberation Theologies: A Primer*. Maryknoll, NY: Orbis, 1986

Fox, Matthew, *The Coming of the Cosmic Christ*. San Francisco: Harper & Row, 1988

Freedman, David N. ed. *The Anchor Bible Dictionary*. 6 vols. New York: Doubleday, 1992

Furlong, Monica, *Visions and Longings: Medieval Women Mystics*. Boston: Shambhala, 1996

Harrington, Daniel, S.J. "Introduction to the Canon," in *The New Interpreter's Bible*, I: 7–21. Nashville: Abingdon Press, 1994

Kavanaugh, Kieran, ed. *John of the Cross. Selected Writings*. New York: Paulist Press, 1987

Keck, Leander, ed. *The New Interpreter's Bible*. 12 vols. Nashville: Abingdon Press, 1994

Küng, Hans, *et al.*, *Christianity and the World Religions*. Garden City, NY: Doubleday, 1986

Leith, John, *Creeds of the Churches*. Louisville, KY: John Knox Press, 1963

Lossy, Vladimir, *The Mystical Theology of the Eastern Church*. Crestwood, NY: St. Vladimir's Seminary Press, 1976

Marty, Martin, *et al.*, "Christianity," in *The Encyclopedia Britannica*, XVI: 251–366.

McGrath, Alister, ed. *The Blackwell Encyclopedia of Modern Christian Thought*. Oxford: Blackwell, 1993

Merton, Thomas, *Thomas Merton: Spiritual Master*, ed. Lawrence Cunningham. New York: Paulist Press, 1992

Pagels, Elaine, *The Gnostic Gospels*. New York: Random House, 1979

Pelikan, Jaroslav, "Christianity: An Overview," in *The Encyclopedia of Religion*. ed. Mircea Eliade. III: 348–62. New York: Macmillan.

Plaskow, Judith, and Carol Christ, *Weaving the Visions*. San Francisco: Harper & Row, 1989

Ruether, Rosemary, and Rosemary Keller, eds. *Women and Religion in America*. 3 vols. San Francisco: Harper & Row, 1981

Tillich, Paul, *A History of Christian Thought*. New York: Harper & Row, 1968

Walker, Williston, Richard Norris, Robert Handy, and David Lotz, *A History of the Christian Church*. New York: Scribner, 1985

Wilson, Ian, *Jesus: the Evidence*. New York: Harper & Row, 1984

Zefferelli, Franco, *Jesus of Nazareth*. Videorecording. RAI/ITC Entertainment, Ltd. 1977

CHAPTER 10

ISLAM

الله

In the sixth century CE, another great spiritual messenger appeared: the Prophet Muhammad. Although illiterate, he said he received revelations from an angel of God, and recited them in language so beautiful that to this day people weep when they hear it. Many of the revelations concern the absolute oneness of the Deity, Who has many names according to His attributes (such as the Merciful, the All-Knowing) but who is generally referred to with love and awe by the name of Allah. The most important virtue is submission to the will of Allah. This is one derivation of the word "Islam," which also means "peace."

The Prophet Muhammad is not considered divine, for in Islam worship is to be directed only toward Allah. Nevertheless, his life is considered a beautiful model for humanity, and his alleged sayings and doings have been lovingly recorded. Muslims consider him the last in a series of great prophets of monotheism, beginning with Abraham and the other Jewish patriarchs, and including Jesus. They thus tend to regard Judaism, Christianity, and Islam as a single evolving tradition which was renewed, corrected of historical distortions, and sealed by the Prophet Muhammad.

After early opposition in Mecca and subsequent withdrawal to Medina, the Prophet Muhammad became a strong political leader, returned triumphantly to Mecca, and made it a great center of monotheistic worship, which it remains to this day. Pilgrimage to Mecca's holy sites at least once in one's life is incumbent upon all Muslims, even though today they are spread around the world, forming the second largest and fastest-growing of all world religions. They are expected to regard all humanity as a single family, without racial distinctions, and to share the Prophet's message in a non-coercive way with non-Muslims so that they, too, may embark upon the straight path that leads to heavenly bliss, rather than the path of non-believers, which leads to hellish torments.

Non-Muslims commonly think of Islam as an attempt to create Muslim-dominated societies ruled by Muslim law, a desire which has spawned passionate revolutionary movements in many parts of the world. However, Islam has also given birth to great mystics and great intellectuals over the centuries, and its rich spirituality continues to coexist today with more politicized versions of the faith.

The Prophet Muhammad

The Prophet Muhammad was born in 570 CE* into an Arabic culture of clans who lived by farming, herding, and camel caravan trade between Asia and the Mediterranean, carrying valuables such as silks, cinnamon, and pepper. Their religions were polytheistic and nature-oriented; their ethics were tribally centered, the societies largely patriarchal. Prophecy was often practiced, involving trance visions and behavioral guidelines. Contact with nearby Jews and Christians was commonplace, and their religions were known to Muhammad's society. Many traditions of the actions and words of the Prophet, outside the Qur'an, were collected in **hadith,** accounts of the Prophet's actions. Two of the most important hadith concerning the faith tell of the Prophet's first revelations around 610 CE, and his **night journey** to the seventh heaven. They are told by Sahih Muslim in Chapters 74 and 75.

The Beginning of Muhammad's Revelation

'A'isha, the wife of the Apostle of Allah (may peace be upon him), reported: The first (form) with which was started the revelation to the Messenger of Allah was the true vision in sleep. And he did not see any vision but it came like the bright gleam of dawn. Thenceforth solitude became dear to him and he used to seclude himself in the cave of Hira', where he would engage in *tahannuth* (and that is a worship for a number of nights) before returning to his family and getting provisions again for this purpose. He would then return to **Khadija** and take provisions for a like period, till Truth came upon him while he was in the cave of Hira' There came to him the angel and said: Recite, to which he replied: I am not lettered. He took hold of me [the Apostle said] and pressed me, till I was hard pressed; thereafter he let me off and said: Recite. I said: I am not lettered. He then again took hold of me and pressed me for the second time till I was hard pressed and then let me off and said: Recite, to which I replied: I am not lettered. He took hold of me and pressed me for the third time, till I was hard pressed and then let me go and said: Recite in the name of your Lord Who created, created man from a clot of blood. Recite. And your most bountiful Lord is He Who taught the use of pen, taught man what he knew not (Qur'an xcvi: 1–4). Then the Prophet returned therewith, his heart was trembling, and he went to Khadija and said: Wrap me up, wrap me up! So they wrapped him till the fear had left him. He then said to Khadija: O Khadija! what has happened to me?—and he informed her of the happening, saying: I fear for myself. She replied: It can't be. Be happy. I swear by Allah that He shall never humiliate you. By Allah, you join ties of relationship, you speak the truth, you bear people's burden, you help the

---

* Some dates are given as After Hijrah (AH)/Common Era (CE).

destitute, you entertain guests, and you help against the vicissitudes which affect people. Khadija then took him to Waraqa b. Naufal b. Asad b. 'Abd al-'Uzza, and he was the son of Khadija's uncle, i.e. the brother of her father. And he was the man who had embraced Christianity in the Days of Ignorance (i.e. before Islam) and he used to write books in Arabic and, therefore, wrote Injil in Arabic as God willed that he should write. He was very old and had become blind. Khadija said to him: O uncle! listen to the son of your brother. Waraqa b. Naufal said: O my nephew! what did you see? The Messenger of Allah (may peace be upon him), then, informed him what he had seen, and Waraqa said to him: It is *namus*[1] that God sent down to Musa. Would that I were then (during your prophetic career) a young man. Would that I might be alive when your people would expel you! The Messenger of Allah (may peace be upon him) said: Will they drive me out? Waraqa said: Yes. Never came a man with a like of what you have brought but met hostilities. If I see your day I shall help you wholeheartedly.

This hadith has been narrated on the authority of 'A'isha with another chain of narrators like the one transmitted by Yunus, i.e. the first thing with which the revelation was initiated with the Messenger of Allah (may peace be upon him) except the words: By Allah, Allah would never humiliate you, and Khadija said: O son of my uncle! listen to the son of your brother.

This hadith has been reported from 'A'isha by another chain of transmitters and the words are: He (the Holy Prophet) came to Khadija and his heart was trembling. The rest of the hadith has been narrated like one transmitted by Yunus and Ma'mar, but the first part is not mentioned, i.e. the first thing with which was started the revelation to the Holy Prophet was the true vision. And these words like those transmitted by Yunus are mentioned thus: By Allah, Allah would never humiliate you. And there is also mention of the words of Khadija: O son of my uncle! listen to the son of your brother.

SOURCE: *Sahih Muslim*, trans. 'Abdul Hamid Siddiqi. Lahore, Pakistan: Sh. Muhammad Ashraf, Kashmiri Bazar, 1973 CE, vol. 1, pp. 96–8

The Night Journey

It is narrated on the authority of Anas b. Malik that the Messenger of Allah (may peace be upon him) said: I was brought al-Buraq who is an animal white and long, larger than a donkey but smaller than a mule, who would place his hoof at a distance equal to the range of vision. I mounted it and came to the Temple (Bait-ul-Maqdis[2] in Jerusalem), then tethered it to the ring used by the prophets. I entered the mosque and prayed two rak'ahs in it, and then came out and Gabriel brought me a vessel of wine and a vessel of

---

[1] *Namus*—the angel entrusted with divine secrets.
[2] Bait-ul-Maqdis—"The Much Frequented House;" The Dome of the Rock.

milk. I chose the milk, and Gabriel said: You have chosen the natural thing. Then he took me to heaven.

Gabriel then asked the (gate of the heaven) to be opened and he was asked who he was. He replied: Gabriel. He was again asked: Who is with you? He (Gabriel) said: Muhammad. It was said: Has he been sent for? Gabriel replied: He has indeed been sent for. And (the door of the heaven) was opened for us and lo! we saw Adam. He welcomed me and prayed for my good. Then we ascended to the second heaven. Gabriel (peace be upon him) asked the door of the heaven to be opened, and he was asked who he was. He answered: Gabriel; and he was again asked: Who is with you? He replied: Muhammad. It was said: Has he been sent for? He replied: He has indeed been sent for. The gate was opened. When I entered Isa b. Maryam and Yahya b. Zakariya (peace be upon both of them), cousins from the maternal side, welcomed me and prayed for my good. Then I was taken to the third heaven and Gabriel asked for the opening (of the door). He was asked: Who are you? He replied: Gabriel. He was (again) asked: Who is with you? He replied: Muhammad (may peace be upon him). It was said: Has he been sent for? He replied: He has indeed been sent for. (The gate) was opened for us and I saw Yusuf (peace of Allah be upon him) who had been given half of (world) beauty. He welcomed me and prayed for my well-being. Then he ascended with us to the fourth heaven. Gabriel (peace be upon him) asked for the (gate) to be opened, and it was said: Who is he? He replied: Gabriel. It was (again) said: Who is with you? He said: Muhammad. It was said: Has he been sent for? He replied: He has indeed been sent for. The (gate) was opened for us, and lo! Idris was there. He welcomed me and prayed for my well-being. (About him) Allah, the Exalted and the Glorious, has said: "We elevated him (Idris) to the exalted position" (Qur'an xix: 57).

Then he ascended with us to the fifth heaven and Gabriel asked for the (gate) to be opened. It was said: Who is he? He replied: Gabriel. It was (again) said: Who is with thee? He replied: Muhammad. It was said: Has he been sent for? He replied: He has indeed been sent for. (The gate) was opened for us and then I was with Harun (Aaron—peace of Allah be upon him). He welcomed me and prayed for my well-being. Then I was taken to the sixth heaven. Gabriel (peace to upon him) asked for the door to be opened. It was said: Who is he? He replied: Gabriel. It was said: Who is with thee? He replied: Muhammad. It was said: Has he been sent for? He replied: He has indeed been sent for. (The gate) was opened for us and there I was with Musa (Moses—peace be upon him). He welcomed me and prayed for my well-being. Then I was taken up to the seventh heaven. Gabriel asked the (gate) to be opened. It was said: Who is he? He said: Gabriel. It was said: Who is with thee? He replied: Muhammad (may peace be upon him). It was said: Has he been sent for? He replied: He has indeed been sent for. (The gate) was opened for us and there I found Ibrahim (Abraham—peace be upon him) reclining against the Bait-ul-Ma'mur and there enter into it seventy thousand angels every day, never to visit (this place) again.

Then I was taken to Sidrat-ul-Muntaha[3] whose leaves were like elephant ears and its fruit like big earthenware vessels. And when it was covered by the Command of Allah, it underwent such a change that none amongst the creation has the power to praise its beauty. Then Allah revealed to me a revelation and He made obligatory for me fifty prayers every day and night. Then I went down to Moses (peace be upon him) and he said: What has your Lord enjoined upon your **Ummah**? I said: Fifty prayers. He said: Return to thy Lord and beg for reduction (in the number of prayers), for your community shall not be able to bear this burden, as I have put to test the children of Isra'il and tried them (and found them too weak to bear such a heavy burden). He (the Holy Prophet) said: I went back to my Lord and said: My Lord, make things lighter for my Ummah. (The Lord) reduced five prayers for me. I went down to Moses and said: (The Lord) reduced five (prayers) for me. He said: Verily thy Ummah shall not be able to bear this burden, return to thy Lord and ask Him to make things lighter. I then kept going back and forth between my Lord Blessed and Exalted and Moses, till He said: There are five prayers every day and night, O Muhammad, each being credited as ten, so that makes fifty prayers. He who intends to do a good deed and does not do it will have a good deed recorded for him; and if he does it, it will be recorded for him as ten; whereas he who intends to do an evil deed and does not do, it will not be recorded for him; and if he does it, only one evil deed will be recorded. I then came down and when I came to Moses and informed him, he said: Go back to thy Lord and ask Him to make things lighter. Upon this the Messenger of Allah remarked: I returned to my Lord until I felt ashamed before Him.

It is narrated on the authority of Anas b. Malik that the Messenger of Allah (may peace be upon him) said: (The angels) came to me and took me to the Zamzam[4] and my heart was opened and washed with the water of Zamzam and then I was left (at my place).

Anas b. Malik reported that Gabriel came to the Messenger of Allah (may peace be upon him) while he was playing with his playmates. He took hold of him and lay him prostrate on the ground and tore open his breast and took out the heart from it and then extracted a blood-clot out of it and said: That was the part of Satan in thee. And then he washed it with the water of Zamzam in a golden basin and then it was joined together and restored to its place. The boys came running to his mother, i.e. his nurse, and said: Verily Muhammad has been murdered. They all rushed towards

---

[3] The Sidr is the Arabian Lote tree, known for its abundant shade.
[4] Zamzam or Zumzum—("abundant water") the legendary sacred spring at Mecca near the Kaaba stone, opened by Gabriel to save Hajira and Ismail from dying of thirst.

him (and found him all right). His colour was changed. Anas said: I myself saw the marks of needle on his breast.

SOURCE: *Sahih Muslim*, trans. Abdul Hamid Siddiqi. Lahore, Pakistan: Muhammad Ashraf, Kashmiri Bazar, 1973 CE, vol. 1, pp. 100–3

Islamic scripture: the Qur'an

The Holy Book of Islam, the Qur'an (Koran), was revealed to Muhammad, who was illiterate, and was written down by aides. Compared to the Jewish Tanakh, which was assembled over a thousand-year period, the Qur'an was recorded by the year 650, a scant eighteen years after Muhammad died. It has a stronger historical basis than many sacred texts of world religions, since it was written down more recently than most. Its original language—Arabic— has been carefully preserved, and it is felt that the Holy Qur'an cannot be translated properly from Arabic into any other language. Nonetheless, English translations have been attempted for the sake of those who do not understand Arabic. None of them is able to capture the musical, soulful quality of the Arabic, but they give some idea of the scripture's content. There follows a selection of passages, beginning with the **Fatiha** or opening chapter and covering topics such as right behavior, the family and **jihad**, as well as figures familiar from other religions—Adam, Abraham, Moses, Mary, and Jesus.

Fatiha

In the name of God, Most Gracious, Most Merciful.
Praise be to God, The Cherisher and Sustainer of the Worlds;
Most Gracious, Most merciful; Master of the Day of Judgment.
Thee do we worship, And Thine aid we seek,
Show us the straight way, The way of those on whom
Thou hast bestowed Thy Grace,
Those whose (portion) is not wrath, and who go not astray. (**Sura** 1)

Allah

There is no god but He; That is the witness of Allah, His angels, and those endued with knowledge, standing firm on justice. There is no god but He, the Exalted in Power, the Wise. (3:18)

He it is Who created the heavens and the earth in Six Days, and is moreover firmly established on the Throne (of Authority). He knows what enters within the earth and what comes forth out of it, what comes down from heaven and what mounts up to it. And He is with you wheresoever ye may be. And Allah sees well all that ye do.(57:4)

To Allah belongeth all that is in the heavens and on earth. Whether ye show what is in your minds or conceal it, Allah calleth you to account for it. He forgiveth whom He pleaseth, and punisheth whom he pleaseth, for Allah hath power over all things. (2:284)

To Allah belong the East and the West: Whithersoever ye turn, there is the presence of Allah. For Allah is all-Pervading, all-Knowing. (2:115)

He is the First and the Last, and the Outward and the Inward; and He is Knower of all things. (57:3)

He is the One Who sends to His Servant Manifest Signs, that He may lead you from the depths of Darkness into the Light and verily Allah is to you most kind and Merciful. (57:9)

Messengers

Muhammad is not more than an Apostle; many were the Apostles that passed away before him. (3:144)

We have sent thee inspiration, as We sent it to Noah and the Messengers after him: we sent inspiration to Abraham, Isma'il, Isaac, Jacob and the Tribes, to Jesus, Job, Jonah, Aaron, and Solomon, and to David We gave the Psalms. (4:163)

Say: "We believe in Allah, and in what has been revealed to us and what was revealed to Abraham, Isma'il, Isaac, Jacob, and the Tribes, and in (the Books) given to Moses, Jesus, and the prophets, from their Lord: We make no distinction between one and another among them, and to Allah do we bow our will (in Islam)." (3:84)

O mankind! The Apostle hath come to you in truth from God: believe in him; it is best for you. (4:170)

People of the Book

Mankind was one single nation, and Allah sent Messengers with glad tidings and warnings; and with them He sent the Book in truth, to judge between people in matters wherein they differed; but the People of the Book, after the clear Signs came to them, did not differ among themselves, except through selfish contumacy.[5] Allah by His Grace guided the believers to the

---

[5] Contumacy—stubborn rebellion.

Truth, concerning that wherein they differed. For Allah guides whom He will to a path that is straight. (2:213)

Say: "O People of the Book! come to common terms as between us and you: That we worship none but Allah; that we associate no partners with him; that we erect not, from among ourselves, Lords and patrons other than Allah." If then they turn back, say ye: "Bear witness that we (at least) are Muslims (bowing to Allah's Will)." (3:64)

Those who believe (in the Qur'an), and those who follow the Jewish (scriptures), and the Christians and the Sabians, any who believe in Allah and the Last Day, and work righteousness, shall have their reward with their Lord; on them shall be no fear, nor shall they grieve. (2:62)

Unity of Humanity

And hold fast, all together, by the Rope which God stretches out for you, and be not divided among yourselves; and remember with gratitude God's favor on you; for ye were enemies and He joined your hearts in love, so that by His Grace, ye became brethren. (3:103)

Righteousness

Those who believe, and do deeds of righteousness, and establish regular prayers and regular charity, will have their reward with their Lord; on them shall be no fear, nor shall they grieve. (2:277)

Allah hath promised to Believers, men and women, gardens under which rivers flow, to dwell therein, and beautiful mansions in gardens of everlasting bliss But the greatest bliss is the good pleasure of Allah: that is the supreme felicity. (9:72)

O ye who believe! Eat not up your property among yourselves in vanities: But let there be amongst you Traffic and trade by mutual good-will: Nor kill (or destroy) yourselves: for verily Allah hath been to you Most Merciful! (4:29)

They ask thee concerning wine and gambling. Say: "In them is great sin and some profit for men; but the sin is greater than the profit." (2:219)

Mecca

We see the turning of thy face (for guidance) to the heavens: now shall We turn thee to a Quibla[6] that shall please thee. Turn then thy face in the

---

[6] Quibla—the direction faced in prayer.

direction of the sacred Mosque: wherever ye are, turn your faces in that direction. (2:144)

For **Hajj** are the months well known. If any one undertakes that duty therein, Let there be no obscenity, nor wickedness, nor wrangling in the Hajj. And whatever good ye do, (be sure) Allah knoweth it. And take a provision (with you) for the journey, but the best of provisions is right conduct. So fear Me, o ye that are wise. (2:197)

Jihad

Not equal are those believers who sit (at home) and receive no hurt, and those who strive and fight in the cause of God with their goods and their persons. God hath granted a grade higher to those who strive and fight. (4:95)

Fight in the cause of God those who fight you, but do not transgress limits; for God loveth not transgressors. (2:190)

And fight them on until there is no more tumult or oppression, and there prevail justice and faith in God; but if they cease, let there be no hostility except to those who practice oppression. (2:193)

And if any strive (with might and main), they do so for their own souls: for Allah is free of all needs from all creation. (29:6)

Let there be no compulsion in religion: Truth stands out clear from Error: whoever rejects evil and believes in Allah hath grasped the most trustworthy hand-hold, that never breaks. And Allah heareth and knoweth all things. (2:256)

Gender, Family

O mankind! reverence your Guardian-Lord, who created you from a single person, created, of like nature, his mate, and from them twain scattered (like seeds) countless men and women; reverence Allah, through whom ye demand your mutual (rights), and (reverence) the wombs (that bore you); for Allah ever watches over you. (4:1)

Men are the protectors and maintainers of women, because God has given the one more (strength) than the other, and because they support them from their means. Therefore the righteous women are devoutly obedient, and guard in (the husband's) absence what God would have them guard. As to those women on whose part ye fear disloyalty and ill-conduct, admonish them (first), (next), refuse to share their beds, (and last) beat them (lightly); but if they return to obedience, seek not against them means (of annoyance): For God is Most High, Great (above you all). (4:34)

Do not marry unbelieving women (idolaters), until they believe: A slave woman who believes is better than an unbelieving woman, even though she allures you. Nor marry (your girls) to unbelievers until they believe: A man slave who believes is better than an unbeliever, even though he allures you. Unbelievers do (but) beckon you to the Fire. But Allah beckons by His Grace to the Garden (of bliss) and forgiveness, and makes His Signs clear to mankind: That they may celebrate His praise. (2:221)

If ye fear that ye shall not be able to deal justly with the orphans, marry women of your choice, two or three or four; but if ye fear that ye shall not be able to deal justly (with them), then only one, or (a captive) that your right hands possess, that will be more suitable, to prevent you from doing injustice. (4:3)

If a wife fears cruelty or desertion on her husband's part, there is no blame on them if they arrange an amicable settlement between themselves; and such settlement is best; even though men's souls are swayed by greed. But if ye do good and practice self-restraint, Allah is well-acquainted with all that ye do. (4:12)

So if a husband divorces his wife (irrevocably), he cannot, after that, remarry her until after she has married another husband and he has divorced her. In that case there is no blame on either of them if they re-unite, provided they feel that they can keep the limits ordained by Allah. (2.23)

If any do deeds of righteousness—be they male or female—and have faith, they will enter heaven, and not the least injustice will be done to them. (4:124)

Self-Restraint

O ye who believe! Fasting is prescribed to you as it was prescribed to those before you, that ye may (learn) self-restraint.... Ramadan is the (month) in which was sent down the Qur'an, as a guide to mankind, also clear (signs) for guidance and judgment (between right and wrong). So every one of you who is present (at his home) during that month should spend it in fasting, but if any one is ill, or on a journey, the prescribed period (should be made up) by days later. (2:183, 185)

Adam

He said: "O Adam! Tell them their names." When he had told them, Allah said: "Did I not tell you that I know the secrets of heaven and earth, and I know what ye reveal and what ye conceal? And behold, We said to the angels: "Bow down to Adam" and they bowed down. Not so Iblis: he refused and was haughty: He was of those who reject Faith.

We said: "O Adam! dwell thou and thy wife in the Garden; and eat of the bountiful things therein as (where and when) ye will; but approach not this tree, or ye run in harm and transgression."

Then did Satan make them slip from the (garden), and get them out of the state (of felicity) in which they had been. We said: "Get ye down, all (ye people), with enmity between yourselves. On earth will be your dwelling-place and your means of livelihood—for a time."

Then learnt Adam from his Lord words of inspiration and his Lord turned towards him; for He is Oft-Returning, Most Merciful. (2:33–37)

Abraham

And remember that Abraham was tried by his Lord with certain commands, which he fulfilled: He said: "I will make thee an **Imam** to the Nations." He pleaded: "And also (Imams) from my offspring!" He answered: "But My Promise is not within the reach of evil-doers." (2:124)

Moses

We sent an inspiration to Moses: "Travel by night with my servants, and strike a dry path for them through the sea, without fear of being overtaken (by Pharaoh) and without any other fear." Then Pharaoh pursued them with his forces, but the waters completely overwhelmed them and covered them up. Pharaoh led his people astray instead of leading them aright. O ye Children of Israel! We delivered you from your enemy, and We made a Covenant with you on the right side of Mount Sinai, and We sent down to you manna and quails (22:77–80)

Mary

Behold! the angels said: "O Mary! Allah hath chosen thee and purified thee—chosen thee above the women of all nations. . . . Behold! the angels said: "O Mary! Allah giveth thee glad tidings of a Word from Him: his name will be Christ Jesus, the son of Mary, held in honour in the world and the Hereafter and of (the company of) those nearest to Allah; He shall speak to the people in childhood and in maturity. And he shall be (of the company) of the righteous." She said: "O my Lord! How shall I have a son when no man hath touched me?" He said: "Even so: Allah createth what He willeth: When He hath decreed a plan, He but saith to it, 'Be,' and it is!" (3:42–47)

Jesus

Then will Allah say: "O Jesus the son of Mary! Recount My favour to thee and to thy mother. Behold! I strengthened thee with the holy spirit, so that thou didst speak to the people in childhood and in maturity. Behold! I taught thee the Book and Wisdom, the Law and the Gospel and behold! thou makest out of clay, as it were, the figure of a bird, by My leave, and thou breathest into it and it becometh a bird by My leave, and thou healest those born blind, and the lepers, by My leave. And behold! thou bringest forth the dead by My leave. And behold! I did restrain the Children of Israel from (violence to) thee when thou didst show them the clear Signs, and the unbelievers among them said: 'This is nothing but evident magic.'" (5:110)

Christ the son of Mary was no more than a messenger; many were the messengers that passed away before him. His mother was a woman of truth. They had both to eat their (daily) food. See how Allah does make His signs clear to them; yet see in what ways they are deluded away from the truth! (5:75)

That they said (in boast), "We killed Christ Jesus the son of Mary, the Messenger of Allah"; but they killed him not, nor crucified him, but so it was made to appear to them, and those who differ therein are full of doubts, with no (certain) knowledge, but only conjecture to follow, for of a surety they killed him not: Nay, Allah raised him up unto Himself; and Allah is exalted in Power, Wise. (4:157–158)

They say, "Allah hath begotten a son." Glory be to Him.—Nay, to Him belongs all that is in the heavens and on earth: everything renders worship to Him. (2:116)

If only they had stood fast by the Law, the Gospel, and all the revelation that was sent to them from their Lord, they would have enjoyed happiness from every side. There is from among them a party on the right course: but many of them follow a course that is evil. (5:66)

From those, too, who call themselves Christians, We did take a covenant, but they forgot a good part of the message that was sent them: so we estranged them, with enmity and hatred between the one and the other, to the day of judgment. And soon will Allah show them what it is they have done. (5:14)

The Day of Judgment

Then, on the Day of Judgment, He will cover them with shame, and say: "Where are My 'partners' concerning whom ye used to dispute (with the godly)?" Those endued with knowledge will say: "This Day, indeed, are the Unbelievers covered with shame and misery (namely) those whose lives the angels take in a state of wrong-doing to their own souls." Then would they offer submission (with the pretence), "We did no evil (knowingly)." (The angels will reply), "Nay, but verily Allah knoweth all that ye did; So enter the gates of Hell, to dwell therein. Thus evil indeed is the abode of the arrogant." To the righteous (when) it is said, "What is it that your Lord has revealed?" they say, "All that is good." To those who do good, there is good in this world, and the Home of the Hereafter is even better and excellent indeed is the Home of the righteous, Gardens of Eternity which they will enter: beneath them flow (pleasant) rivers: they will have therein all that they wish: thus doth Allah reward the righteous, (namely) those whose lives the angels take in a state of purity, saying (to them), "Peace be on you; enter ye the Garden, because of (the good) which ye did (in the world)." (16:27–32)

SOURCE: *The Holy Qur'an*, trans. with a commentary by Abdullah Yusuf Ali. Beirut, Lebanon: Dar Al Arabia, 1968 (© Khalil Al-Rawaf). Also on Internet <www.rci.rutgers.edu/~religion/links/islam.html#Quran>

Islamic theology and spirituality

Hadith, as we have seen, means "report" on the actions and words of the Prophet, outside the Qur'an, as told by his companions. Hadith range from grand revelations from Allah to descriptions of the Prophet's life, rules of war, marriage, **mosque** conduct, and personal behavior. Like all religious guidelines, they reflect their cultural environment. They are the second basis, after the Qur'an, for Islamic law, or **Shari'ah**. They contain references to their sources and seek to establish an authoritative "chain" (**isnah**) of transmission. For example, on Jihad, Abdullah Suhrawardy (1882–1935) wrote in *The Sayings of Muhammad*: "The most excellent Jihad is that for the conquest of self." Traditionally, the most authoritative and famous Hadith collections are the Sahih ("the Authentic") of Muhammad Ibn Ismail al-Bukhari (d.256/870, called "Bukhari") and the Sahih of Abu-l-Husayn Muslim ibn al-Hajjaj (d.261/875, called "Muslim"). The following are from Sahih Muslim (Volumes and pages given).

Seeking Consent for Marriage

Abu Huraira (Allah be pleased with him) reported Allah's Messenger (may peace be upon him) as having said: A woman without a husband (or divorced or a widow) must not be married until she is consulted, and a virgin must not be married until her permission is sought. They asked the Prophet of Allah (may peace be upon him): How her (virgin's) consent can be solicited? He (the Holy Prophet) said: That she keeps silent. (II: 714)

Fighting of Women Side by Side with Men

It has been narrated on the authority of Anas that, on the Day of Hunain, Umm Sulaim took out a dagger she had in her possession. Abu Talha saw her and said: Messenger of Allah, this is Umm Sulaim. She is holding a dagger. The Messenger of Allah (may peace be upon him) asked (her): What for are you holding this dagger? She said: I took it up so that I may tear open the belly of a polytheist who comes near me. The Messenger of Allah (may peace be upon him) began to smile (at these words). She said: Messenger of Allah, kill all those people—other than us—whom thou hast declared to be free (on the day of the Conquest of Mecca). (They embraced Islam because) they were defeated at your hands, (and as such their Islam is not dependable). The Messenger of Allah (may peace be upon him) said: Umm Sulaim, God is sufficient (against the mischief of the polytheists) and He will be kind to us (so you need not carry this dagger).

It has been narrated on the authority of Anas b. Malik who said that the Messenger of Allah (may peace be upon him) allowed Umm Sulaim and some other women of the Ansar to accompany him when he went to war; they would give water (to the soldiers) and would treat the wounded. (III: 1001)

Prohibition of Killing Women and Children in War

It is narrated on the authority of 'Abdullah that a woman was found killed in one of the battles fought by the Messenger of Allah (may peace be upon him). He disapproved of the killing of women and children.

It is narrated by Ibn 'Umar that a woman was found killed in one of these battles; so the Messenger of Allah (may peace be upon him) forbade the killing of women and children. (IV: 946)

Compel not Your Slave-Girls to Prostitution

Jabir reported that 'Abdullah b. Ubayy b. Salul used to say to his slave-girl: Go and fetch something for us by committing prostitution. It was in this connection that Allah, the Exalted and Glorious, revealed this verse: "And compel not your slave-girls to prostitution when they desire to keep chaste in order to seek the frail goods of their world's life, and whoever compels them, then surely after their compulsion Allah is Forgiving, Merciful" (xxiv. 33).

Jabir reported that 'Abdullah b. Ubayy b. Salul had two slave-girls; one was called Musaika and the other one was called Umaima and he compelled them to prostitution (for which 'Abdullah b. Ubayy b. Salul compelled them). They made a complaint about this to Allah's Messenger (may peace be upon him) and it was upon this that this verse was revealed: "And compel not your slave-girls to prostitute" up to the words: "Allah is Forgiving, Merciful." (IV: 1555)

Removal of the Idols from the Vicinity of the Ka'ba

It has been narrated by Ibn 'Abdullah who said: The Holy Prophet (may peace be upon him) entered Mecca. There were three hundred and sixty idols around the Ka'ba. He began to thrust them with the stick that was in his hand saying: "Truth has come and falsehood has vanished. Lo! falsehood was destined to vanish" (xvii. 8). Truth has arrived, and falsehood can neither create anything from the beginning nor can it restore to life. (III: 978)

The Merits of Jesus Christ (Peace Be Upon Him)

Abu Huraira reported Allah's Messenger (may peace be upon him) as saying: I am most akin to the son of Mary among the whole of mankind and the Prophets are of different mothers, but of one religion, and no Prophet was raised between me and him (Jesus Christ). (IV: 1260)

Merit of Love for the Sake of Allah

Abu Huraira reported Allah's Messenger (may peace be upon him) as saying: Verily, Allah would say on the Day of Resurrection: Where are those who have mutual love for My Glory's sake? Today I shall shelter them in My shadow when there is no other shadow but the shadow of Mine. (IV: 1362)

It is Forbidden to Commit Oppression

Abu Dharr reported Allah's Messenger (may peace be upon him) as saying that Allah, the Exalted and Glorious, said: My servants, I have made oppression unlawful for Me and unlawful for you, so do not commit oppression against one another. (IV: 1365)

The Merits of Forgiveness and Humility

Abu Huraira reported Allah's Messenger (may peace be upon him) as saying: Charity does not in any way decrease the wealth and the servant who forgives Allah adds to his respect, and the one who shows humility Allah elevates him in the estimation (of the people).

SOURCE: *Sahih Muslim*, trans. 'Abdul Hamid Siddiqi. Lahore, Pakistan: Sh. Muhammad Ashraf, Kashmiri Bazar, pp. 714–1369

Shari'ah

Muslim law is called Shari'ah ("the path leading to the watering place"), and is derived from the Qur'an, hadith, and practical reasoning, then applied by judges (*qadi*) as they interpret it for specific cases.

Iconoclasm, which prohibits images of divinity, is an example of Shari'ah and its various applications. Iconoclasm has been extended to all art in strict Muslim interpretation, but some cultures, such as the Iranian, are more lax.

Iconoclasm

In order to emphasize the ineffable transcendence of Allah, and in reaction against the numerous images of divinities in the polytheistic world, and in agreement with the iconoclastic Jewish prohibition of images of divinity, Muhammad banned all human and animal images. Consequently most Muslim art incorporates only calligraphy or plant life, as in the Taj Mahal in India. But not all Muslim cultures were strict about this rule. Persian (now Iranian) art illustrates Muhammad's Night Journey, for example. This Shi'ah hadith from Muwatta' Imam Malik records an account of the Prophet's rejection of imagery.

On Pictures and Images

Rafi' b. Ishaq, who was the freedman of Shifa', reported: I and 'Abd Allah b. Abi Talhah went together to Abu Sa'id Khudri to see him in his illness. Abu Sa'id said: The Apostle of Allah (may peace be upon him) told me that angels did not enter a house where there were pictures and images.

SOURCE: Malik, *Muwatta Imam Malik*, trans. with notes by Muhammad Rahimuddin. Lahore, Pakistan: Sh. Muhammad Ashraf, Kashmiri Bazar, 1980 CE, p. 409

Reason and revelation

The Qur'an serves as the basis of the Muslim's search for truth that guides the actions of believers. Thus the theological debates that developed are concerned with establishing with certainty the moral and ethical responsibility of the individual in relation to Allah. The early Mu'tazilah school were "occasionalists" and ([first cent. AH]/800 CE) emphasized the capacity, when aided by reason, to act in accordance with God's unity and justice.

Later, the Ash'arites ([second cent. AH]/900 CE), in asserting the omnipotence of Allah, attempted to shift the focus back to the Qur'an as the starting point of all ethical knowledge. Then, eventually, the incorporation and translation of Greek texts into Muslim ideals by subsequent philosophers refined the earlier systematic study of nature, from which values of right and wrong were deduced. Logic, reason's tool, became instrumental in developing the moral and ethical system of Islamic law.

Ibn Sina (Avicenna)

Ibn Sina ([370–429 AH]/980–1037 CE), the Persian philosopher, followed others such as al-Kindi (b. 800? CE) and al-Razi (d. 926 CE). But it was al-Farabi's (d. 950 CE) theories of logic, metaphysics and politics which set the foundations for Ibn Sina's causal system. In his Neoplatonist system, God's self-knowledge evokes a first intelligence, then successive intelligences. Of these, the Active intelligence produces all theoretical knowledge where logic, as well as the rational consideration of self-evident intuitive concepts, provides demonstrations of God's existence. Only prophets receive these principles directly, and they speak symbolically in their imaginative faculty so that believers can easily understand them. Here, like al-Farabi, Ibn Sina holds that religion is the imitation of philosophy. But his philosophical interpretations of his belief in the oneness of God, the prophethood of Mohammad, and so on, were considered unacceptable by al-Ghazali, his foremost critic.

That person upon whom the First Intelligence gazes, so that he or she becomes refined, cultivated, subtle, beautiful, brave, and perfect in intellect, becomes a prophet. The First Intelligence becomes for this person as our intellect (is for us). And intellect for him or her is on the level of our soul. Just as the soul that grasps a truth from the intellect is learned, the intellect that grasps from the First Intelligence is a prophet.

But this state varies. Either it occurs in sleep, since in wakefulness the preoccupations of the senses and the multitude of activities become a hindrance; or it occurs in wakefulness, since in sleep the imaginative faculty predominates; or in each it is full and true. The motion and repose of this person is pure in legislative function. It never admits abrogation or distortion. This person is free of worldly distractions and secular controls and is devoted to the affairs of the Necessary Existent. The First Intelligence nourishes his or her soul from itself. This nourishing is called sanctification. As the Qur'an states, "We have supported him with the Holy Spirit." (The First Intelligence) reveals itself to this person so that through (its) good auspices he or she comprehends. When he or she fully understands the universal[7], he or she attains knowledge of the included particulars,[8] since this person does not need time or delay (to understand matters). Thus (Muhammad) said "My Lord instructed me; and how well was my instruction; and I instructed 'Ali, and I instructed him well." Similarly (the Qur'an) said, "And We taught him knowledge from Us.". . . That which becomes clear from this summons is religion. And the law of that religion is religious creed. The acceptance of all this is faith. The name of that which prophets receive is revelation. When it is united with a human, and the Holy Spirit opens his or her way to itself and becomes governor of that disposition, it makes (that person) lofty in aspiration, and slight in greed, rancourless, without envy. Whatever this person does is through that Holy Power. Just as is (found) in the (prophetic) tradition, "I ask of you a faith that my heart touches."

---

[7] Universals—global principles, such as truth, justice, faith, or parenthood, e.g. Plato's ideas and Jung's archetypes.

[8] Particulars—specific, individual existing things or phenomena; instances of universals, such as an act of justice or a parent.

Thus the Holy Spirit is the noblest of all souls, for all (other) souls are subordinate to the Universal Intelligence. The Holy Spirit, however, is that which is the intermediary between the Necessary Existent and the First Intelligence. The faith of that Power is the prophet, who is the messenger and bearer of the Holy Emanation. That Power is the fruit of proximity to the First Intelligence....

Faith consists of two parts: real and metaphorical, the husk and the core. Prophets have real faith, the core, for they bear the core and the truth. Ordinary people bear the husk, the form. Their faith is sensible, not intelligible. With the aid of the (intellectual) faculty, (the prophet) draws down the Holy Spirit. As he said, "I feel the breath of the Merciful from the Yemen." This Holy Spirit is a divine faculty. It is not a body, nor a substance, nor an accident. It is the pure divine Command; "Indeed, His is the Command and the Creation." The intent of (the word Command) is not (physical) speech and expression. People who do not consider this appropriate and consider the Holy Spirit to be a result of the Command do so because they do not know the reality of Command. There is no nobility greater than a soul joined to the divine Command.... The Qur'an says, "A day in which the Spirit and the angels arise in a row."

When these preliminaries are known, it should (also) be known that reason comprehends truth through itself, while prophethood comprehends truths through Holy Support. Just as speech is not reason, reason is not summons, and summons is not prophethood. Recollection[9] stands between speech and reason, and apostleship between prophethood and summons. Hence, whatever rational concepts that the intellect wishes to convey to the senses, it does so by means of recollection. (The latter then) formulates it in sensible sounds and unites (it) with speech, so that hearing apprehends.

SOURCE: Peter Heath, *Allegory and Philosophy in Avicenna (Ibn Sina)*. Philadelphia, PA: University of Pennsylvania Press, 1992, pp. 118–19

Al-Ghazali

Al-Ghazali ([405–505 AH]/1058–1111 CE) was an Ash'ari theologian, jurist and mystic who criticized the rationalism of al-Farabi and Ibn Sina. Following a spiritual crisis, al-Ghazali concluded that systematic reasoning could not yield the insights of mysticism. In his treatise "The Incoherence of the Philosophers," he attacked philosophical theories which oppose religious principles. His metaphysics was "occasionalistic" and it was clearly irreconcilable with the uniformly rational, causal order of Ibn Sina, which took power away from God and did not permit miracles. However, al-Ghazali believed that logic was not tied to any metaphysical system, and was thus a neutral tool that could be used in expounding ethical rules of conduct. His criticism of

---

[9] Recollection—a Platonic concept: the eternal soul's recalling universals known in heaven before current reincarnation.

Ibn Sina had two effects: 1. in clarifying Ibn Sina's study of logic, he popularized it; 2. he thus made Greek modes of thinking more accessible.

When I had finished with these sciences, I next turned with set purpose to the method of mysticism (or Sufism). I knew that the complete mystic 'way' includes both intellectual belief and practical activity; the latter consists in getting rid of the obstacles in the self and in stripping off its base characteristics and vicious morals, so that the heart may attain to freedom from what is not God and to constant recollection of Him. . . .

I apprehended clearly that the mystics were men who had real experiences, not men of words, and that I had already progressed as far as was possible by way of intellectual apprehension. What remained for me was not to be attained by oral instruction and study but only by immediate experience and by walking in the mystic way. . . .

Next I considered the circumstances of my life, and realized that I was caught in a veritable thicket of attachments. I also considered my activities, of which the best was my teaching and lecturing, and realized that in them I was dealing with sciences that were unimportant and contributed nothing to the attainment of eternal life.

After that I examined my motive in my work of teaching, and realized that it was not a pure desire for the things of God, but that the impulse moving me was the desire for an influential position and public recognition. I saw for certain that I was on the brink of a crumbling bank of sand and in imminent danger of hell-fire unless I set about to mend my ways. . . .

For nearly six months beginning with Rajab[10] 488 AH [July 1095 CE], I was continuously tossed about between the attractions of worldly desires and the impulses towards eternal life. In that month the matter ceased to be one of choice and become one of compulsion. God caused my tongue to dry up so that I was prevented from lecturing. One particular day I would make an effort to lecture in order to gratify the hearts of my following, but my tongue would not utter a single word nor could I accomplish anything at all.

This impediment in my speech produced grief in my heart, and at the same time my power to digest and assimilate food and drink was impaired; I could hardly swallow or digest a single mouthful of food. My powers became so weakened that the doctors gave up all hope of successful treatment. "This trouble arises from the heart," they said, "and from there it has spread through the constitution; the only method of treatment is that the anxiety which has come over the heart should be allayed."

Thereupon, perceiving my impotence and having altogether lost my power of choice, I sought refuge with God most high as one who is driven to Him, because he is without further resources of his own. He answered me, He who "answers him who is driven (to Him by affliction) when he

---

[10] Rajab—the month during which Mohammad ascended to Heaven.

calls upon Him" (Qur'an 27, 63). He made it easy for my heart to turn away from position and wealth, from children and friends.

In due course I entered Damascus, and there I remained for nearly two years with no other occupation than the cultivation of retirement and solitude, together with religious and ascetic exercises, as I busied myself purifying my soul, improving my character and cleansing my heart for the constant recollection of God most high, as I had learnt from my study of mysticism. I used to go into retreat for a period in the mosque of Damascus, going up the minaret of the mosque for the whole day and shutting myself in so as to be alone.

At length I made my way from Damascus to the Holy House (that is, Jerusalem). There I used to enter into the precinct of the Rock every day and shut myself in.

Next there arose in me a prompting to fulfil the duty of the Pilgrimage, gain the blessings of Mecca and Medina, and perform the visitation of the Messenger of God most high (may peace be upon him).

I continued at this stage for the space of ten years, and during these periods of solitude there were revealed to me things innumerable and unfathomable. This much I shall say about that in order that others may be helped: I learnt with certainty that it is above all the mystics who walk on the road of God; their life is the best life, their method the soundest method, their character the purest character; indeed, were the intellect of the intellectuals and the learning of the learned and the scholarship of the scholars, who are versed in the profundities of revealed truth, brought together in the attempt to improve the life and character of the mystics, they would find no way of doing so; for to the mystics all movement and all rest, whether external or internal, brings illumination from the light of the lamp of prophetic revelation; and behind the light of prophetic revelation there is no other light on the face of the earth from which illumination may be received.

SOURCE: W. Montgomery Watt, *The Faith and Practice of the Al-Ghazali*. London: Allen & Unwin, 1953, pp. 54–61

Ibn Rushd (Averroes)

Ibn Rushd ([520–598 AH]/1126–1198 CE), physician, philosopher and judge, came from a stimulating philosophical movement in Spain, which also included Ibn Bajjah (Avempace, d. 1138 CE) and Ibn Tufayl (d. 1185 CE). His commentaries on Aristotle greatly influenced medieval Latin philosophy. His famous reply to al-Ghazali ("The Incoherence of the Incoherence") is a legal, theological, and philosophical defense of an Aristotelian causal view which contested al-Ghazali's Ash'ari conception of divine causality as well as Ibn Sina's Neoplatonism. The West hailed him as the originator of the theory of "two truths" where the higher truth was located in revelation. Rational truth was for philosophers, and religious truth for the masses. In Spain, Ibn Rushd was followed by Ibn al-'Arabi (d. 1240 CE).

Now since this religion is true and summons to the study which leads to knowledge of the Truth, we the Muslim community know definitely that demonstrative study does not lead to [conclusions] conflicting with what Scripture has given us; for truth does not oppose truth but accords with it and bears witness to it.

This being so, whenever demonstrative study leads to any manner of knowledge about any being, that being is inevitably either unmentioned or mentioned in Scripture. If it is unmentioned there is no contradiction, and it is in the same case as an act whose category is unmentioned, so that the lawyer has to infer it by reasoning from Scripture. If Scripture speaks about it, the apparent meaning of the words inevitably either accords or conflicts with the conclusions of demonstration about it. If this [apparent meaning] accords there is no argument. If it conflicts there is a call for allegorical interpretation of it. The meaning of "allegorical interpretation" is: extension of the significance of an expression from real to metaphorical significance, without forsaking therein the standard metaphorical practices of Arabic, such as calling a thing by the name of something resembling it or a cause or consequence or accompaniment of it, or other things such as are enumerated in accounts of the kinds of metaphorical speech.

SOURCE: *Averroes on the Harmony of Religion and Philosophy*, trans. George F. Hourani. London: Luzac & Co., 1967

Worship

How to Perform Salaat

Salaat *is Islamic ritual worship of the community at a mosque, especially on Friday noon, but also five times daily. Worshipers wash ritually first, then bow repeatedly facing the direction of* **Mecca** *(qibla), which is marked in a mosque by a niche (mihrab). A leader (imam) leads prayers. A prayer rug (sajjada) defines the sacred space for bowing. All prayers are spoken in Arabic. This is the first portion:*

Before Salaat:
Body, clothes and place of prayer must be clean.
Perform *wudu*[11] if needed.
Traditionally, women cover their hair.
Face the Qibla, the direction of Mecca.
Stand erect, head down, hands at sides, feet evenly spaced.
Recite Iqama (private call to prayer):
  Allaahu Akbar (4×)

---

[11] Wudu—ritual ablution.

Ashhadu an la ilaaha illa-Lah (2×)
Ash Hadu anna Muhamadar rasuulullah (2×)
Hayya' alas Salaah (2×)
Hayya' ala Falaah (2×)
[Fajr only: A-Salaatu Khayrun Mina-Naum (2×)]
Qad qaamitis Salaah (2×)
Allaahu Akbar (2×)
Laa ilaaha illa-Lah
God is the most great.
  I bear witness that there are not gods but God.
  I bear witness that Muhammad is the Messenger of God.
  Come to prayer.
  Come to felicity.
  [Prayer is better than sleep.]
  Our prayers are now ready. Our prayers are now ready.
  God is the most great.
  There is no deity save God.

Express intent to perform Salaat (niyyat):
I intend to offer the——rakats[12] of the——prayer, and face the Qibla for the
sake of Allah and Allah alone.
  (For example: "I intend to offer the 4 rakats of the Isha prayer and face
the Qibla for the sake of Allah and Allah alone.")

Salaat
Niyyat: Stand in respect and attention; put the world behind you.
Bring hands to ears, palms forward, thumbs behind earlobes.
  Allahu Akbar/God is the most great.
Qiyam: Place right hand over left, men below navel, women at chest level;
look at the ground in front of you.

Opening Supplication (optional):
  Subhaanaka alahumma wa bihamdik
  wa tabaaraka smuka wa ta'aalaa jadduka
  wa laa ilaaha ghairuk

  Glory to You, O Allah, and Yours is the praise.
  And blessed is Your Name, and exalted is Your Majesty.
  And there is no deity to be worshipped but You.

  A'uudhu billaahi minash shaitaan ar-Rajeem
  I seek refuge in Allah from Satan, the accursed. . . .

[Repetitions of bowing and more prayers . . . conclusion:]

---

[12] Rakat—one cycle of bowing and praying.

Look over right shoulder (toward the angel recording your good deeds), then the left (toward the angel recording your wrongful deeds); say each time:
   As Salaamu 'alaikum wa rahmatulaah
   Peace and blessings of God be upon you.

Say personal prayers with hands cupped and palms up at chest level.
Wipe face with palms.
If praying in a group, stand and greet each other individually, saying: "May God receive our prayers."

SOURCE: <www.sufism.org>

Sufi mysticism

Muslims who seek direct mystical experiences of Allah are known as **Sufis**. Initially Sufis stressed simplicity, a coarse woolen garment, even asceticism. Today many Muslims are associated with variations of Sufism, some stressing its uniquely Muslim quality, some its universalism. Techniques are practiced in order to induce trance states, such as *dhikr* (prayer), *sama* (music), or dance (the "Whirling Dervishes"), to refine spiritual awareness of Allah. Sufi spirituality is not contrary to Shari'ah law, but should lead to moral behavior. One notable Sufi, Ibn 'Arabi, perceived that in the world there is actually nothing but God, transcendent yet manifested on earth. The Sufi Order of the West, founded in London in 1910 by Hazrat Inyat Khan, furthered the universal theme of Sufism, seeking the unity of religions and relevance to the modern world. Three great Sufis were Rabi'a, Rumi and Ibn 'Arabi.

Rabi'a

Rabi'a al-Adawiyya ([c. 95–185 AH]/713–801 CE) was born into a poor family and sold into slavery, but later freed. She devoted herself to a life of prayer, poverty, and seclusion. Her asceticism and pure love of God banished hatred and inspired many Sufis thereafter. She believed that one should not love out of desire for paradise or fear of hell, but for love of God alone.

"Doorkeeper of the Heart"
Your hope in my heart is the rarest treasure
Your Name on my tongue is the sweetest word
My choicest hours
Are the hours I spend with You—

O God, I can't live in this world
Without remembering You—

How can I endure the next world
Without seeing Your face?

I am a stranger in Your country
And lonely among Your worshippers:
This is the substance of my complaint.

"Dream Fable"

I saw myself in a wide green garden, more beautiful than I could begin to understand. In this garden was a young girl. I said to her,

"How wonderful this place is!"

"Would you like to see a place even more wonderful than this?" she asked. "Oh yes," I answered. Then taking me by the hand, she led me on until we came to a magnificent palace, like nothing that was ever seen by human eyes. The young girl knocked on the door, and someone opened it. Immediately both of us were flooded with light. God alone knows the inner meaning of the maidens we saw living there. Each one carried in her hand a serving-tray filled with light. The young girl asked the maidens where they were going, and they answered her, "We are looking for someone who was drowned in the sea, and so became a martyr. She never slept at night, not one wink! We are going to rub funeral spices on her body."

"Then rub some on my friend here," the young girl said.

"Once upon a time," said the maidens, "part of this spice and the fragrance of it clung to her body—but then she shied away."

Quickly the young girl let go of my hand, turned and said to me:

"Your prayers are your light;
Your devotion is your strength;
Sleep is the enemy of both.
Your life is the only opportunity that life can give you.
If you ignore it, if you waste it,
You will only turn to dust."

Then the young girl disappeared.
In love, nothing exists between breast and Breast.
Speech is born out of longing,
True description from the real taste.
The one who tastes, knows;
The one who explains, lies.
How can you describe the true form of Something
In whose presence you are blotted out?
And in whose being you still exist?
And who lives as a sign for your journey?

SOURCE: *Rabi'a*, trans. Charles Upton. Brattleboro, VT: Threshold Books.

Rumi

Jalal ad-Din ar-Rumi ([605–672]/1207–1273) was one of the greatest of Muslim mystics. Living in Persia and Turkey, he founded the order of the Mevlevi, the "Whirling Dervishes," known for their spinning, ecstatic dances. His belief in reincarnation, his universalism, and his Platonic influence went beyond Islamic orthodoxy, but have been neglected in view of his strong influence otherwise.

With every breath the sound
of love surrounds us,
and we are bound for the depths
of space, without sightseeing.
We've been in orbit before
and know the angels there.
Let's go there again, Master,
for that is our land.
Yet we are beyond all that
and something more than angels.
Out beyond duality,
we have a home, and it is Glory.
That pure substance is
different from this dusty world.
What kind of place is this?
We once came down, soon we'll return.
A new happiness befriends us
as we work at offering our lives.
Muhammed, an ornament to the world,
is our caravan's chosen guide.
The sweetness we breathe on the wind
is from the scent of his hair,
and the radiance of this thought
is from the light of his day.
His face once split the moon in two—
she couldn't endure the sight of him.
Yet how lucky she was,
she who humbly received him.
Look into our hearts and see
the splitting moon in each breath.
Having seen that vision,
how can you still dream?
When the wave of *Am I not?* struck,
it wrecked the body's ship;
when the ship wrecks once more,
it will be the time of union.

SOURCE: William C. Chittick, *The Sufi Path of Love: The Spiritual Teachings of Rumi*. Albany, NY: State University of New York Press, 1983, pp. 36–7

Between the Yea and the Nay
by Ibn 'Arabi

Ibn 'Arabi Muhyi al-Din was born in Spain ([560 AH]/1165 CE). As a young man at a party in Seville, he heard a strange voice say: "O Muhammad, it was not for this that you were created." Disturbed, he retreated and had a vision in which he saw Jesus, Moses and Muhammad. He studied with several spiritual masters, then began traveling, and eventually wrote over 700 books, influencing many Sufis. He considered all prophets to be teachers of a primordial religion: "There is no knowledge except that taken from God." He taught a monism in which Being is essentially one: "There is nothing in Being but God." Ibn 'Arabi performed the pilgrimage to Mecca in 1202, then settled in Damascus in 1223 until his death ([638 AH]/1240 CE). In this passage he tells of his meeting with the great Ibn Rushd.

I spent the day in Cordoba at the house of Abu al-Walid Ibn Rushd. He had expressed a desire to meet me in person, since he had heard of certain revelations I had received while in retreat and had shown considerable astonishment concerning them. In consequence my father, who was one of his closest friends, took me with him on the pretext of business, in order to give Ibn Rushd the opportunity of making my acquaintance. I was at the time a beardless youth. As I entered the house, the philosopher rose to greet me with all the signs of friendliness and affection, and embraced me. Then he said to me "Yes," and showed pleasure on seeing that I had understood him. I, on the other hand, being aware of the motive for his pleasure, replied "No." Upon this Ibn Rushd drew back from me, his colour changed and he seemed to doubt what he had thought of me. He then put to me the following question, "What solution have you found as a result of mystical illumination and divine inspiration? Does it coincide with what is arrived at by speculative thought?" I replied, "Yes and no. Between the Yea and the Nay the spirits take their flight beyond matter, and the necks detach themselves from their bodies."

At this Ibn Rushd became pale, and I saw him tremble as he muttered the formula "there is no power save from God." This was because he understood my allusion ... After that he sought from my father to meet me in order to present what he himself had understood: he wanted to know if it conformed with or was different from what I had. He was one of the great masters of reflection and rational consideration. He thanked God that in his own time he had seen someone who had entered into the retreat ignorant and had come out like this—without study, discussion, investigation or reading.

SOURCE: *Sufis of Andalusia*, trans. R. W. J. Austin. 1971, repr. Beshara Publications, 1988, p. 23

Living Islam

Islam today is expanding and encountering the impact of technological cultures and their values. Two of the outstanding areas of debate are women and ecology.

Women and Islam
by Ruth Mas

Ruth Mas is a Ph.D. candidate at the Center for the Study of Religion at the University of Toronto. She is completing her dissertation on women and Islam.

The growing Muslim population in the culture of industrialized, secular North America and Europe is highlighting the role of Muslim women around the world. Media images have been fueled by the urgent political tensions in the Muslim world. As a consequence, Muslim women are, especially if veiled, often inaccurately portrayed as ignorant, oppressed and uneducated. The already existing notion that Islam is the cause of Muslim women's oppression is thus being repeatedly reinforced by the ongoing debates that surround the role of women in Islam.

The confrontation caused by Muslim ninth-century conquest of large parts of the Christian world and the later colonization of Muslim countries by Europe has provided the Western media with many stereotypical images. This, along with the confrontation of religions, nationalities, cultural origins and values, provides new challenges to those wishing to understand Muslim women.

Naturally, most of the discussions concerning the status of women in Islam are centred on the Qur'an. The plurality of textual interpretations throughout Islamic history is inevitable. However, women's views have been largely excluded from these interpretations. It is only recently that the social and historical frameworks supporting the Qur'an's position on women have been questioned by women. Many Muslim women believe in the relevance of the Qur'an to the present, but they insist on rethinking all their traditions: the Qur'an, the Hadith, and the Shari'ah. Women in the first idealized Muslim *ummah* (community) were liberated, freed from ancient tribal customs which, for example, promoted female infanticide, and were given equal status. The oppression of women today is interpreted by Muslim feminists as an inauthentic transformation of the values and ethics originally prescribed in the Qur'an. The challenges posed to the interpretation of the Qur'an are the same challenges made to other religions' scriptures by the Enlightenment and the industrial revolution. Increasingly, the Qur'an is being recognized as a socially and historically situated text which addressed the issues particular to its time. At some places in the Qur'an, women are clearly accorded the same status as men:

> O! Mankind, be conscious of your Sustainer who has created you out of
> one living entity, and out of it created its mate, and out of the two spread
> abroad a multitude of men and women (4:1).

Here the genderless origin of women and men is clear. Elsewhere, for
example, in reference to Judgment Day, the emphasis is placed on the
inauthenticity of hierarchy among individuals, regardless of race, culture, or
gender (49:13; 33:35).

One of the most problematic texts is the one which deals with the rights
of men to govern over women:

> Men are the protectors and maintainers of women, because Allah has
> given the one more (strength) than the other, and because they support
> them from their means. Therefore, the righteous women are devoutly
> obedient, and guard in the husband's absence what Allah would have
> them guard (4:34).

Also controversial is the text dealing with the value of women as legal
witnesses (2:282). Feminists are quick to point out that the attention paid to
the statement concerning the need of two female witnesses to replace one
male usually ignores the fact that this specific example refers to the role that
women played in financial contracts. Recognition of the social and economic
factors of the time would demonstrate that the earning potential and
therefore financial responsibility was limited to men long ago, and *not*
that it *should* be today. The same holds true for inheritance laws today
(4:11–12).

Texts that refer to witnessing in adultery, rape, unchastity, and the
witnessing of bequests, for example, do not make gender distinctions.
Therefore, they can be interpreted as a) giving equal value to both female
and male testimonies and b) stating that a woman's testimony can even
falsify that of a male (4:135; 24:6–9). Eliminating the patriarchal framework
upon which legal interpretations of the Qur'an have been codified is
contingent on historically and sociologically contextualizing Qur'anic
discourse.

Marriage contracts are another topic where the equality between
women and men as equal partners is another issue. Marriage, as defined in
the Qur'an, is contingent upon the consent of the woman and any
restrictions or requirements that she may put on the marriage (4:19). As a
contract, marriage can be lawfully discontinued through divorce, even
though it would be preferable that there be reconciliation:

> If a wife fears cruelty or desertion on her husband's part, there is no blame
> in them if they arrange an amicable settlement between themselves; and
> such settlement is best (4:128).

The congeniality of these statements immediately loses value when compared to the tabooed topic of polygamy:

> If ye fear that he shall not be able to deal justly with the orphans, marry women of your choice, two, or three, or four; but if ye fear that ye shall not be able to deal justly (with them), then only one, or (a captive) that your right hands possess. That will be more suitable, to prevent you from doing injustice (4:3).

How can an ethic so bound by issues regarding a tribal Arabia be used to justify polygamy today, in a post-industrial age? This very question has become the *bête noire* of inter-religious dialogue, feminist criticism, and condemnation from the West. After all, the practice of polygamy was, in this medieval context, already a widespread practice among Jews, Zoroastrians and Hindus. Islamic practice encouraged monogamy, but tolerated limited polygamy.

Obviously menstrual blood raises issue of taboo and impurity. The Islamic practice of isolating menstrual blood and restricting intercourse has now been interpreted to have actually terminated some previously held superstitions concerning sexual intercourse. All these advances in interpretation are the result of many modern Muslim women who are courageously speaking up.

Wearing the veil (*hijab*)[13] is another issue that has recently attracted enormous amounts of attention. The diverse cultural meanings given to wearing the veil are neglected by the West's identification of it as oppressive. These Western definitions given to the hijab have been adopted by modernizing regimes in the past. Turkey's abolition of the Shari'ah in 1926, and the adoption of the Swiss Civil Code, also abolished the right of women to wear the hijab. In addition, the hijab was forbidden under the Shah of Iran, but later readopted during the revolution. In the present, the increased use of the hijab in diasporic communities globally points to the fact that veiling is an issue of identity that opposes what Muslims see as the sexually lax morality of the West. Its adoption constitutes a symbol of the religious duty to keep Islam alive in a hostile environment.

Muslim women living in Muslim countries have always had to adjust their roles in society to the political situations that define them. Nothing short of an encyclopedia dedicated to the complex topic of the role of women in the different Muslim traditions would do justice to the nationalities, ethnicities, classes, political affiliations, functions, forms, and symbols of their lived and historical realities. An extensive list of phenomena important to women in Islam today can be specified. Here are but a few:

---

[13] Hijab—the veiling or segregation of women in Islamic societies for modesty.

A. 1) Marriage laws were rewritten in 1960 in Pakistan. Divorces and marriages were registered, the marriage age was raised, and polygamy was limited. 2) The introduction of Nizani Islam (the Islamic Order) in 1979 by General Zia ul-Haq who seized power in 1977. 3) The ability of women to vote under Benazir Bhutto.
B. The painful pre-Islamic custom of clitoridectomy and infibulation which still exists, for example, amongst the Nubians of West Aswan.
C. Mu'ta marriage (temporary marriage) in Iran.
D. The repudiation of law 44 in 1985 in Egypt, which stipulated that Muslim wives had the right to divorce their husbands if they chose a second wife, and had right to custody of their children and the acquisition of the marital domicile to raise children.
E. In Afghanistan, Taliban human rights violations and the violent imposing of the veil and forced exclusion of women from the public sphere and workforce.
F. The situation of Muslim women in all the states under the former Soviet Communist rule.
G. In Iraq, a throwback to "crimes of honour" under Saddam's regime, which carry the death penalty for women.
H. Algerian women's role in the continuing civil strife which has witnessed the slaughter of over 100,000 people.

Ultimately, as the situation of women in Algeria so urgently demonstrates, the issue of women in Muslim countries is inextricably bound with and informs our common humanity. The problem of the plight of these women is first and foremost an urgent intellectual, spiritual, and moral question for the industrialized modern world's secularist frameworks. It also challenges the judgments and categories that we make. To what extent can our use of "Muslim women" admit to the plurality of discourse, secularist and not, which exists in both traditionally Islamic and non-Islamic countries? To what extent does it include the lesbian, gay, cross-gendered and racially differing minorities which also form part of their communities and political struggles? To what extent should it take into account the lived realities of their male counterparts? The careful examination of all these changing phenomena should alert us to the urgency of together sharpening our critical intellectual tools so as to better the plight of others.

Ecology: A Sacred Science
by Seyyed H. Nasr

The ecology crisis will not be solved simply by social engineering, new technologies, or by creating an ethics expanded to include the non-human, argues Seyyed Nasr, Professor of Islamic Studies at Washington University. What is needed is a "scientia sacra," a sacred science that brings out our suppressed sense of the interconnectedness of all beings. We cannot bestow sacredness on nature, because it is already there. The major world religions have forgotten this, although the indigenous sacred ways of tribal peoples have long remembered it. Religions need also to respect the varied sacred ways of each other's traditions. Muslims in India, for example, need to respect the Hindu sense of the sacredness of the Ganges River. Awakening to the signature of God in everything will be the foundation of a new ecological ethic.

The Earth is bleeding and the natural environment suffering in an unprecedented manner from the onslaught of man. The problem is now too evident to deny, and the solutions proposed are many but for the most part insufficient. Earth will not be healed by some kind of social engineering or changes in a technology that cannot but treat the world of nature as pure quantity to be manipulated for human needs whether they be real or imaginary. All such actions are no more than cosmetics with an effect that is of necessity only skin deep.

What is needed is a rediscovery of nature as sacred reality and the rebirth of man as the guardian of the sacred, which implies the death of the image of man and nature that has given birth to modernism and its subsequent developments. It does not mean the "invention of a new man" as some have claimed, but rather the resurfacing of the true man, the pontifical man whose reality we still bear within ourselves. Nor does it mean the invention of a sacred view of nature, as if man could ever invent the sacred, but rather the reformulation of the traditional cosmologies and views of nature held by various religions throughout history. It means most of all taking seriously the religious understanding of the order of nature as knowledge corresponding to a vital aspect of cosmic reality and not only subjective conjectures or historical constructs. There must be a radical restructuring of the intellectual landscape to enable us to take this type of knowledge of nature seriously, which means to accept the findings of modern science only within the confines of the limitations that its philosophical suppositions, epistemologies,[14] and historical development have imposed upon it, while rejecting completely its totalitarian claims as *the* science of the natural order. It means to rediscover a science of nature that deals with the *existence* of natural objects in their relation to Being, with their subtle as well as gross aspects, with their interrelatedness to the rest of the cosmos and to us, with their symbolic significance and with their nexus to higher levels of existence leading to the Divine Origin of all things.

Furthermore, in speaking of the religious view of the order of nature we must now do so in a global context reflecting the global character of the problem at hand. It is necessary to delve into religions as different as the Shamanic and Hindu, Buddhist and Abrahamic, without a relativization that

---

[14] Epistemologies—theories of knowledge.

would destroy the sense of the sacred in each tradition. There are perspectives and schools within most religions that have not paid much attention to the domain of nature, as seen especially in Western Christianity, but within every integral tradition there *are* those schools that have dealt with the domain of nature both in its spiritual and cosmic reality. It is those schools that must be sought and studied across religious frontiers in a manner so as to preserve the authenticity of each tradition while bringing out the spiritual significance of nature in a universal fashion. . . .

On a more practical level, it is necessary to create respect on behalf of the followers of a particular religion for what is held to be sacred in another religion not only in the domain, say, of sacred art and architecture but also in the world of nature. A Muslim in Benares does not consider the Ganges to be sacred for himself but must accept its sacredness for the Hindus and respect it, as was done for Hindu holy places by traditional Muslims of Benares for centuries and vice versa as far as Muslim holy places were concerned; this mutual respect has continued for the most part and still survives to some extent despite recent communal tragedies. The respect accorded to manmade sites possessing religious significance must also be extended to natural ones despite difficulties that come about when two or three religions claim the same site or land as holy, as we find in Palestine and Israel, or when the economic considerations of a more powerful people confront the belief system of others who consider a particular forest, river, or mountain to be sacred. The despicable record of the modern world in overlooking the claims of others to the sacred not only in an abstract manner but also concretely, such as land, rivers, forests, etc.—as seen in the destruction of much of the habitat of the Native American peoples—has been itself a major cause of the present environmental crisis and cannot any longer act as a model for future dealings among peoples. In evoking the religious understanding of the order of nature, this sense of respect for the religious teachings concerning nature of religions other than our own must be strengthened in the same way that respect for other human beings or houses of worship of other faiths is encouraged, at least by the majority of those concerned with religion and spirituality on a global scale today.

Religions serve as the source of both an ethics involving the environment and a knowledge of the order of nature. They can abet and strengthen one another in both domains if authentic religious teachings are not compromised and diluted in the face of secularism. This is particularly true of Western Christianity, which for so long has tried to identify itself with a civilization that has grown more secular every day. Traditional Christian teachings even in the domain of nature are in fact much closer to those of other religions than to the modern secularist philosophies of the West, as witnessed by questions concerning the sanctity of life and abortion. . . .

Finally, every being in the world of nature not only issues from the

Divine Principle or the One, but also reflects Its Wisdom and, to use theistic language, sings the praises of the Lord. The religious understanding of the order of nature, which we can share only on the condition of conforming ourselves to the world of the Spirit, enables us to read the signatures of God upon the face of things and hear their prayers. It thereby re-creates a link between us and the world of nature that involves not only our bodies and psyches but also the Spirit within us and our final end. It enables us to see the sacred in nature and therefore to treat it not only with respect but also as part of our greater self. It reminds us how precious is each being created by God and how great a sin to destroy wantonly any creature that by virtue of its existence bears the imprint of the Divine and is witness to the One who is our Origin and End.

SOURCE: Seyyed H. Nasr, *Religion and the Order of Nature*. New York and Oxford: Oxford University Press, 1996, pp. 286–9

GLOSSARY

A'isha Muhammad's youngest wife, who was the source of many *hadith.*
Fatiha The first Sura of the Qur'an.
Hadith A traditional report about the Prophet's sayings or actions.
Hajj The holy pilgrimage to Mecca, taken at least once in the lifetime if affordable.
Hijrah (or Hegira) The journey of the Prophet from Mecca to Medina in 622 CE.
Imam A Muslim prayer leader, and a Shi'ite religious leader.
Iconoclasm Prohibition of images in art to prevent distortion of Allah's reality.
Isnah Authoritative chain of transmission of a Hadith.
Jihad The Muslim term for struggle, with two meanings: an inner struggle against evil, and an outer struggle for a Muslim social order.

Khadija Muhammad's first wife, who supported him when he received prophecies.
Mecca The holy city of Islam whose mosque is the goal of Hajj pilgrimages.
Mosque Sacred building for Muslim worship, usually an open-roofed rectangle with towers (minarets) for calling to prayer.
Night Journey Muhammad's visionary journey to Jerusalem and up through seven heavens to Allah to receive revelations.
Salaat The daily Islamic Ritual Prayer.
Shari'ah The divine law, as interpreted by judges, based on Qur'an and Hadith.
Sufi Muslim mystical tradition; some say Islamic only, some say universal.
Sunnah The actions of the Prophet and guides to legal interpretations.
Sura A chapter in the Qur'an.
Ummah The Muslim community as a whole.

HOLY DAYS

Friday Mosque Worship

Lunar Month	*Holy Day*
10th of Muharran	New Year
12th of Rabi'al-Awwai	The Prophet's Birthday

27th of Rajab	Muhammad's Ascension
Ramadan	Month of Fasting; Night of Power (27th)
1st of Shawwal	Breaking of the Fast; Pilgrimage Season
Dhu al-Qa'da	Pilgrimage Season
8th–13th of Dhu al-Hihha	Hajj: Pilgrimage to Mecca

HISTORICAL OUTLINE

c. 570 CE—Birth of Muhammad

c. 610 CE—Revelations of Qur'an begin

622 CE—Migration from Mecca to Medina (Hijrah)

c. 630 CE—Muhammad converts southern Arabian tribes

632 CE—Death of Muhammad

632 CE—Election of Abu Bakr as first caliph

633 CE—Spread of Islam begins, expanding to northern Egypt, Palestine, Iran

650 CE—Qur'an canon set

750 CE—Islam spreads to Spain, southern Russia, Afghanistan

750–1258—Islam reaches its peak under Abbasid caliphs

1500—Spread of Islam now includes

northern Africa, Eastern Europe into Hungary, Turkey, central Russia, India, and Indonesia

1171—Salah-al-Din recaptures Jerusalem from Crusaders

1300–1400s—Christians fight to retake Spain using Inquisition

1453—Turks conquer Constantinople, renaming it Istanbul

1556—Akbar becomes the Muslim Mughal emperor in India

1800–1900s—Many Muslim colonies come under European control

1947—Muslim Pakistan separates from Hindu India

1970s—Oil-wealthy Muslim nations start OPEC; Muslim resurgence begins

REVIEW QUESTIONS

1   Based on our readings, what kind of society did Muhammad encounter?
2   What is the Qur'an?
3   What are "Hadith"? Give examples.
4   Describe Muhammad's "Night Journey."
5   What is the "Fatiha"?
6   How does the Qur'an describe Allah?
7   What differing views of Jihad are in the Qur'an and Hadith?
8   What views of women, children and divorce does the Qur'an teach?
9   What is the spiritual purpose of Ramadan?
10   What is the Qur'an's view of Abraham, Moses, Mary, and Jesus?
11   What is the "Day of Judgment" in the Qur'an?
12   What is Shari'ah? Give an example.
13   Describe how three major Islamic philosophers saw the relation between reason and revelation.
14   What is Salaat? How is it performed?
15   What is Sufism? Describe the thoughts of three major Sufis.

16   Describe the contemporary situation of women in Islamic cultures.
17   What does S. H. Nasr say that Islam's role should be in environmental ethics?

INFORMATION RESOURCES

Ahmed, Leila, *Women and Gender in Islam.* New Haven, CT: Yale University Press, 1992.

Ask, Karen, and Marit Tjomsland, eds. *What is Islam?* New York: Oxford University Press, 1998.

Athar, Shahid, *What is Islam?* <www.islam-usa.com>

Bayat, Mojedh & Mohammad Ali Jamnia, *Tales from the Land of the Sufis.* Boston and London: Shambhala, 1994.

Beck, Lois, and Nikki Deddie, eds. *Women in the Muslim World.* Cambridge, MA: Harvard University Press, 1982.

Ernst, Carl W. *The Shambhala Guide to Sufism.* Boston and London: Shambhala, 1997.

Fakhry, Majid, *A History of Islamic Philosophy.* New York, 1983.

Glasse, Cyril, *The Concise Encyclopedia of Islam.* San Francisco: Harper & Row, 1989.

Hixon, Lex, *Heart of the Koran.* Wheaton, IL, and London: Theosophical Publishing House, 1988.

Islam video series, Insight Media, 2162 Broadway, New York, NY 10024, (212) 721–6316. An excellent source of videos on world religions www.insight-media.com/religion.html

Islamic Studies, Virtual Religion Index, Rutgers University Religion Dept. <www.rci.rutgers.edu/~religion/links/islam.html#Quran>

Jomier, Jacques, *How to Understand Islam.* New York: Crossroad, 1991.

Lawrence, Bruce B. *Defenders of God: The Fundamentalist Revolt Against the Modern Age.* San Francisco: Harper & Row, 1989.

Lester, Toby, "What is the Koran?" in *The Atlantic Monthly*, 43–56, Jan. 1999.

Martin, Richard C. *Islamic Studies: A History of Religions Approach.* Upper Saddle River, NJ: Prentice-Hall, 1982/96.

Medlevi Order, <www.sufism.org>

Mernissi, Fatima, *Beyond the Veil: Male-Female Dynamics in a Modern Muslim Society.* New York: Wiley, 1975.

Morewedge, Parvis, ed. *Islamic Philosophical Theology.* Albany, NY, 1979.

Nasr, Seyyed Hossein, *Ideals and Realities of Islam.* London: Allen & Unwin/Harper, 1966.

Smith, Huston, *Islamic Mysticism: The Sufi Way.* Videocassette. The Hartley Film Foundation: Cos Cob, CT.

Schimmel, Annemarie, *Islam: An Introduction.* Albany: State University of New York Press, 1992.

Shah, Idries, *The Way of the Sufi.* New York: Dutton, 1970.

Stern, S. M., Albert Hourani, and Vivian Brown, eds. *Islamic Philosophy and the Classical Tradition.* Columbia, SC, 1972.

Universal Islamic Declaration of Human Rights, Islamic Council of London, 1981.

Wadud-Muhsin, Amina, *Qur'an and Woman.* Kuala Lumpur: Penerbit Fajar Bakti Sdn. Bhd, 1992.

Watt, W. Montgomery, *et al.* "Muhammed and the Religion of Islam," in *The New Encyclopedia Britannica* XXII: 1–43.

CHAPTER 11

SIKHISM

From 1469 to 1708, not one but a continuous series of ten prophets appeared in north India, developing a tradition which has come to be known as Sikhism. In the Punjabi language of the founders, *sikh* means "student." And according to contemporary understanding of the religion, those who are known as Sikhs are students not only of the Ten Sikh **Gurus** but also of the founders and saints of other traditions. Even more so, Sikhs are those who love God, try to remember God in everyday life, and attempt to serve God in the world.

The first of the Sikh Gurus became known as Guru Nanak. He was born into a Hindu family but in his eleventh year, when the time came for him to be invested with the traditional sacred thread, he refused. He explained in inspired verse that the thread would wear out, in contrast to eternal spiritual virtues which should be inwardly cultivated. This preference for inward transformation and closeness to God rather than outward rituals is evident in many stories told about his life. Guru Nanak spent much of his adult life on long journeys, preaching to Hindus and Muslims alike about spiritual truth. During his last twenty years, he developed a unique village in which land was owned in common, people pooled their labor, and the food was offered to everyone freely in a **langar**, a communal kitchen. He praised women, cut through the caste system, and declared manual work holy, thereby challenging prejudices which had developed within Hindu society. He offered a straightforward path to God-realization: work hard to support yourself by honest means, share with others, and always recite the Name of God.

The mystical teachings, new social order, and practicality of Guru Nanak's path were continued and developed by his nine successors. Their spiritual power and the devotion of their followers were construed as threatening by the Mughal rulers, as well as the Hindu hill chiefs, and from time to time the Gurus and their Sikhs had to face armed attacks. The saintly Fifth and Ninth Gurus were martyred. Ultimately, the powerful Guru Gobind Singh, tenth of the Sikh masters, transformed his intimidated people into **Khalsa**, extraordinarily courageous warrior-saints pledged to protect people of all religions and castes from oppression. Sacrificing his entire family and ultimately himself, Guru Gobind Singh instructed his followers thenceforth to regard the sacred scriptures compiled by the Gurus as their master: the **Guru Granth Sahib**.

Guru Nanak at Mecca

Many stories are told about miracles occurring in the Gurus' lives. This one concerns Guru Nanak's journey to Mecca, the holy city to which only Muslims are allowed to travel.

The Guru after a fairly long sojourn at Kapurthala started for Mecca and joined a party of faqirs.[1] The Guru wore a long yellow robe on which were impressed some words and carried a staff such as a Haji[2] carried.

The faqirs watched him and one day asked, "What is your religion?"

"I belong to the religion of those who follow the path of God," replied the Guru.

The faqirs pressed him and to confess that he was a Muslim but the Guru refused to do so. The faqirs were greatly troubled. They were not sure whether they were right in having with them a man who was an infidel. The Guru read their hearts and disappeared from amongst them with his two attendants. They noticed that a cloud that used to protect them from the scorching rays of the sun also disappeared with him.

The faqirs thought that travelling by himself he would never reach Mecca. They were astonished when they found that the Guru had already arrived with his two attendants. They were even more puzzled when they were told that the Guru had been there for several days. They were convinced that he was some great soul and begged him to forgive them for their suspicions about him.

The keeper of the Kaaba[3] one night discovered that he was sleeping with his feet towards the Kaaba. It was time for prayers so he informed the priest that a pilgrim was committing a great sacrilege by turning his feet towards the house of God. The priest in high dudgeon rushed to where the Guru was sleeping.

"Wake up, you stupid fool," he explained, "and rub your face on the ground and beg to be forgiven for turning your feet towards the house of God."

The Guru did not move, but said, "Turn my feet towards the place where God does not dwell."

The priest could no more control himself and ordered the keeper to take him by the feet and turn him right about in the other direction. The door keeper obeyed but whichever direction they turned the Guru's feet they say that the Kaaba turned with them. The priest stood spell-bound. He saw that the house of God was in all directions.

---

[1] Faqir—Muslim ascetic.
[2] Haji—a pilgrim to Mecca.
[3] Kaaba—the Black Stone, the revered central cubic stone structure of the great mosque in Mecca.

The Guru rose and looked at the priest with eyes full of compassion, "Your eyes have been opened just for a moment," he said. "Don't forget what you have seen. The entire space is nothing but God's dwelling place."

The priest bowed before the Guru and then told his Chief of what had happened. The Chief was a seeker after truth. He hastened to the Guru in the hope of getting some glimpses of the eternal light.

He respectfully saluted, the Guru returned the salute, and then he sat down beside him.

"You are a godly man from all appearance," said Rukin-ud-Din, for this was his name, "but tell me to what religion you belong."

"I believe in the religion of Him, who is the master of all that is visible and invisible," answered the Guru.

"What do you mean by Him?" asked Rukin-ud-Din.

"He who is without a second," said the Guru, "to whom birth and death are not known. Who is beyond all change, and who pervades everywhere, lands, seas, air and skies."

"So you believe in one God; you must be a Muslim."

"I accept no creed," said the Guru. "I am His slave and slaves have not even their own will. How can they accept any creed who yield unwavering obedience to the Lord?"

"God as you have described Him, is the same God of which our Kalma[4] speaks," repeated Rukin-ud-Din. "Why not acknowledge yourself to be a Muslim?"

"The Vedas too speak of one God, the supreme God of all," said the Guru. "Then why should not I declare myself a Hindu? Truth remains Truth. It is the coloured lenses of the self that reflect it in various colours. A servant of God, aware of His presence, cannot accept creeds, which imprison truth and impose on it their own limitations."

"How do you make this out?" asked Rukin-ud-Din.

"You have an example before your eyes. You call this sacred temple a house of God. If you were a true believer, you would find there is no place where the house of God does not exist. Further, you say you believe in one God. Then why don't you recognize in men of diverse creeds a brother? If this truth dwelt in your heart, you would act in its light. You would not believe that kissing a black stone was the highest religious act."

Rukin-ud-Din was much impressed and said, "Come and join us tomorrow in the ceremony of sacrifice. I will provide a camel for you."

The Guru laughed and asked, "Why?"

"God is pleased with sacrifices," replied Rukin-ud-Din. "He bestows His mercy on those who offer a sacrifice."

---

[4] Kalma—profession of faith in one God and in Muhammad as Messenger.

"If a drop of blood pollutes your garments," said the Guru, "how can the spilling of blood be pleasing to God?"

"I do not know," said Rukin-ud-Din, "but sacrifice is prescribed by Shariat—the sacred law of the Muslims. To follow the law is the best of acts."

"The law of love ordains that one should be harmless in thought and act," said the Guru. "To treat others as you would that they should treat you. Righteousness is the unalterable law of living of all people."

"If you follow no written law, what about giving justice to others?"

"If we live justly, the need for administering justice does not arise. If we forgive those who harm us, we need invoke no man-made law. If we live as members of one human family, every individual living for the others, then we follow the divine law and if we follow the divine law we transform this world full of misery into a world of happiness. In such a kingdom there is no need of any law and for any administrators of law. It is because we fail to follow the divine law that we submit to man-made law to rectify the self-aggrandisement of men."

"How are sinners to be punished, if we do not follow the Shariat?" asked Rukin-ud-Din. "Tell me what is your conception of sin?"

"We sin," said the Guru, "when we fail to follow the divine law of love. We sin when we trespass on the rights of others for our own selfish ends, when we cause them injury. In short, to do harm is to sin."

"Such acts as do no harm to anyone and yet have their root in self, are they not sinful?"

"God reads hearts. He sees what passes in our minds; unselfish acts partake of the spirit of sacrifice and such acts are blessed, while selfish acts bring pain and suffering."

"What do you mean by sacrifice?" asked Rukin-ud-Din. "You refused to sacrifice when I invited you to do so."

"My good friend, we sacrifice when we deprive the self of what it holds dear, to serve others or to serve a good cause. To kill a sheep and feast on its flesh is no sacrifice," answered the Guru. "To give what one needs for one's self to another, whose need is greater, is an act of sacrifice. They who give and expect a return make no sacrifice. They are like a money-lender who makes advances at compound interest. They who give and want nothing in return are the real giver, but he who takes all he can without giving is below the human stage. The dead body of an animal and its bones are of some use, but the dead body of a man requires a plot of earth to be buried in or fuel for cremation. He who gives in the hope of a return is human, he who gives without any wish for a reward is divine."

Those who heard the Guru always wanted to hear more from him. The high priest was no exception. He asked, "Instruct me in the art of true living."

"Let your heart and mind put on the garb of a Qalandar.[5] Every hour of the night and day seek your Maker. Rub out from the tablet of the mind all that is written there and polish it into the brightness of a mirror. There will then appear on it a luminous spark. This spark will become the sun and a soundless sound will fill your heart with divine music and draw you near to God."

SOURCE: Sir Jogendra Singh and Raja Sir Daljit Singh, *The Great Humanist Guru Nanak*. Patiala, Punjab, India: Languages Department Punjab, 1970, pp. 52–5

Daily prayers

Traditional Sikhs spend several hours each day in reciting prayers composed under inspiration by the Gurus, in addition to trying always to recite the Name of God inwardly. The day begins early in the morning with prayer and recitation of five hymns. Another long prayer is recited at dusk, and another at bedtime. Repeated recitation of the prayers is a way of training the mind in thinking spiritually, and of increasing one's faith in and awareness of God. Excerpts from some of these prayers are offered below.

JapJi

Composed by Guru Nanak, JapJi sets forth the essence of Sikh philosophy. It is the first of the morning prayers.

There is one God
His Name is Truth
He is the Creator
He is without fear
He is without hate
Immortal is His form
He is not born to die or be born again
By the Guru's grace, He is obtained.

He was true before time began and He
   was the Truth when time began.
True He is even now and
   true He shall be hereafter.

By thinking alone one cannot know Him
   though one may think a hundred thousand times.
One cannot obtain peace of mind by
      keeping silent and remaining absorbed in Him.

[5] Qalandar—a Muslim saint.

The hunger (for knowing Him) can neither be
  appeased by remaining hungry, nor by
  accumulating all the good things of life.
No, by none of these, nor by a hundred thousand
  other devices can God be reached.
How then shall the truth be known and how the veil
  of false illusion torn?
Only by obeying, O Nanak! the will of the Lord.

By His will all forms are created
  but His will we do not know.
By His will are all beings infused with life and by His
  will some achieve greatness.
By His will some are made high, some low and by His
  will some get pleasure, some get pain.
By His will some are saved, others
  doomed to die, relive, and die again.
All are subject to His will, no one is exempt from it.
O Nanak! he who knows His will
  has no ego or pride....

True is the Master, True is His name and His
  speech is unbounded love.
His creatures ever cry, "Give O, give" and He,
  the bounteous never says "no."
What then should we offer at His feet so that
  we may see His court?
What should we speak, by hearing
  which He may give us his love?
In the sweet hours of the early morning,
  meditate on His greatness.
By good action this body is obtained,
  by His grace we get salvation.
Know then, that the True one is all by Himself.

SOURCE: *JapJi: The Morning Prayer*, trans. Bhagat Singh and G. P. Singh. New Delhi: Hemkunt Press, 1986, pp. 9–13

Jaap Sahib

Guru Gobind Singh's Jaap Sahib is the second morning prayer. In wave after wave of negative and positive epithets, it paints a vast picture of the Formless God.

Salutations to the Eternal, Salutations to the Merciful.
Salutations to the Formless, Salutations to the Peerless....

Salutations to the One beyond deeds,
Salutations to the One beyond creeds,
Salutations to the One beyond names,
Salutations to the One beyond any fixed locale.

Salutations to the Unconquerable,
Salutations to the Fearless.
Salutations to the Unshakeable,
Salutations to the Invincible.

Salutations to the One without colour or hue,
Salutations to the One who hath no beginning.
Salutations to the One who is impenetrable,
Salutations to the One who is unfathomable. . . .

Salutations to the Absolute One,
Who is yet manifest in myriad forms.
Salutations to the One beyond physical elements,
Salutations to the One beyond all bonds. . . .

Salutations to the One who is ever steady,
Salutations to the One beyond physical elements.
Salutations to the One who cannot be seen,
Salutations to the One beyond sorrow or grief. . . .

Salutations to the Divine Reveller,
Salutations to the Divine Ascetic.
Salutations to the Lord, without any hue,
Salutations to the Lord, ever Indestructible. . . .

Salutations to the One, who hath no caste,
Salutations to the One, who hath no lineage.
Salutations to the One, beyond confines of religions,
Salutations to the One, who is wonderful. . . .

Salutations to the Destroyer of all,
Salutations to the Creator of all.
Salutations to the Annihilator of all,
Salutations to the Preserver of all.

Salutations to the Lord of Light and Truth,
Salutations to the Lord, ever mysterious.
Salutations to the Lord, ever unborn,
Salutations to the Lord of beauty.

Salutations to the Lord, immanent everywhere,
Salutations to the Lord, who pervades everything.
Salutations to the Lord, manifest in all colours,
Salutations to the Lord, who destroys everything. . . .

Salutations to Thee,
Wielder of weapons and Pride of arms,
Perfect of knowledge and Mother of all.

O Lord,
Having Thy domain in all quarters,
Thou art the Reveller everywhere.
Self created, compassionate and auspicious,
Thou art ever united with everyone.
Destroyer of bad times,
Thou art the Embodiment of Compassion.
Ever so close to everyone,
Everlasting is the treasure of Thy glory and power.

SOURCE: Guru Gobind Singh, *Jaap Sahib*, trans. Shri Surendra Nath. New Delhi:
Gobind Sadan, 1991, rev. 1996, pp. 20–33, 174

Sukhmani Sahib

*"The Song of Greatest Spiritual Bliss" composed by the Fifth Guru, Sukhmani Sahib,
takes over an hour to recite, and thus it is not part of all Sikhs' daily practice.
Nevertheless, it contains many important concepts, including the passage given here,
a description of the* **Brahm-giānī**, *a God-realized being who lives in the world to
help society but is not entangled in worldliness. This is the Sikh spiritual ideal.*

The brahm-giānī is always uncontaminated,
Like the lotus, which is unaffected by muddy water.

The brahm-giānī is ever free from sins and remains pious;
(He burns others' sins), just as the sun burns and dries up things.

The brahm-giānī sees all men as equal;
Just as the wind blows on the rich and the poor without any distinction.

The brahm-giānī remains uniformly patient;
Like the earth, whether one digs it up or another smears it with precious
  sandal. . . .

Divine knowledge is the (spiritual) food of the brahm-giānī.
The brahm-giānī meditates on God alone, (says) (Gurū) Nānak.

The brahm-giānī has his hopes (only) on One.
The brahm-giānī shall never perish.

The brahm-giānī is steeped in humility.
The brahm-giānī takes joy in doing good to others.

The brahm-giānī is not entangled in worldly matters.
The brahm-giānī controls his wandering mind.

To the brahm-giānī, whatever is done (by God), is the best.
The brahm-giānī obtains the fruit of his human life.

In the company of the brahm-giānī, all are saved.
With the help of the brahm-giānī, the whole world worships and
    remembers God, (says) (Gurū) Nānak.

The brahm-giānī keeps love for One Supreme Being in his heart.
God lives with the brahm-giānī. . . .

The Lord of Supreme joy resides in the heart of the brahm-giānī.
The heart of the brahm-giānī is full of joy.

In the life of brahm-giānī every event is spontaneous.
The teachings of the brahm-giānī are pure.

He becomes brahm-giānī, whom God makes so.
The glory of brahm-giānī is great.

Who can estimate the greatness of the brahm-giānī?
Only a brahm-giānī knows the divine spiritual state of the brahm-giānī. . . .

The brahm-giānī is the helper of the helpless.
The brahm-giānī extends his hand over all.

The brahm-giānī owns the whole world.
The brahm-giānī is himself the Formless One. . . .

SOURCE: Guru Arjun Dev, *Sacred Sukhmani*, trans. Harbans Singh Doabia. Amritsar,
India: Singh Brothers, Mai Sewan, 1979, pp. 83–91

The Guru Granth Sahib

Sikhs treat their scripture with great reverence. It is a vast collection of mystical devotional poetry, some 5,867 hymns sung in classical musical forms.

They were composed by seven of the Sikh Gurus and also by numerous Hindu and Muslim saints of all castes. The overarching theme is devotion to God and inner detachment from worldly concerns. Living by the instructions of the Guru and remembering God's Holy Name are prescribed as antidotes to worldliness. A few selections from this unique inter-religious scripture are given below.

"Oh honey bee, thou art lost in worldly flowers"
by Guru Nanak

. . . . O my soul, thou honey-bee,
Buzzing around the blossoms to rifle their sweets,
Hear me, thy sorrow is great:
I asked the Guru in so many words
"What is the true path?"
And the Guru in so many words answered me:
O honey bee thou art lost in worldly flowers,
When the sun rises after death,
Thy soul will suffer as body scalded by oil.

Without the Word of the Guru
Man is stupid and cannot find his way,
He dieth and forever suffereth agony.
Forget not God, O heart of a fool, O honey bee:
On the other road lieth death,
On the other road lieth destruction, saith Nānak.

My soul thou art not a native of this world,
Wherefore then get caught in the net?
Entertain within thyself the Holy Name of God.
The fish like the human soul is ensnared in the net of death,
It weeps and gasps in agony,
And now she knows that life ever pleasant was a delusion.
Adore and cherish the Lord
And cast out baseless fears.
Pay heed, O my soul, to this admonition of Nānak:
My soul, thou art not native to this place,
In thine inner depths cherish the true Lord.

As streaming rivers that start from the same source
Are separated but meet in the Ocean,
So do souls meet in the Infinite,
One in a million knows
That age upon age

The world's illusions enchant and poison the soul.
Those that contemplate the Guru
Learn easily and realize God.

Those who do not cherish the Lord's Name
Wander, deceived and bewildered;
Without such cherishing of the Lord's Name,
Without the love of His Eternal Being,
Man can have no destiny except remorse and anguish.
Nānak utters a truth:
Through the Word of the Guru
The long estrangement of the soul and God end in meeting.

"Oh my mind, remember the Holy Name"
by Guru Amar Das (the Third Guru)

If the mind is unclean, all else is unclean;
And ceremonial washings cannot wash the mind.
This world is the realm of illusion:
There are few who grasp the Real.
O my mind, remember the Holy Name![6]
That is the precious gift of the Guru to men.
Were a man to learn all the postures of the most austere Yogis,
And mortify all his senses,
Not so would he cleanse the mind, or discard self-will.
There is no cure for the mind's sickness
But taking shelter at the Guru's feet.
To meet the Guru is to experience
A change of outlook that cannot be described
Saith Nānak: From the mind of him who dies to self
Through meeting the Guru, and is reborn through the Guru's Word,
All uncleanness is removed.

"My eyes are wet with the Lord's nectar"
by Guru Ram Das (the Fourth Guru)

My eyes are wet with the Lord's nectar; my soul is drenched
   in his Love.
He tested my heart with His touchstone: He found it pure
Through the Guru my soul and body are dyed as with deep
   crimson.

---

[6] Holy Name—*Nam,* remembrance of God by inner or outer recitation of one of God's
   names, a central Sikh practice.

Nānak, the slave, has made himself fragrant with musk:
My earthly life is blessed.

The hymn of the Lord's love is like a pointed arrow,
That hath pierced deep in my heart: who feels love's pain
  knows it
And he that dies to this life even while living
Has obtained his deliverance even in this life.
Saith Nānak: By meeting the True Guru
Life's dangerous ocean is crossed.

Ignorant and a fool though I am, I seek thy sanctuary.
May I attain to the love of my Beloved!
I reached God through the perfect Guru: may I seek nothing
  but His service.
My mind and body are soothed, O Lord, by Thy Word:
I repeat Thy Holy Name with thrilling delight.
Through meeting the saints and seeking Truth in their company
Nānak has attained to God.

Hear my prayer, O Thou who hast pity on the wretched!
I seek my shelter in the Name: I long for the Name to be on
  my lips.
O Lord, it is Thy Greatness to love Thy Saints and save the
  honour.
Humble Nānak has taken Thee as his stronghold:
Thy Name has helped him to cross the dangerous ocean.

"The true Guru is an ocean of pearls"
by Guru Arjun Dev (the Fifth Guru)

That man is blind within and blind without,
Though he pretendeth to sing of the Lord
And performeth ritual washings and puts on caste-marks,
If in his heart he runneth after Mammon.
He cannot remove his inner dirt of self sense.
In births he comes and goes,
Overwhelmed by sleep, played by lust,
And uttereth the name of God.
Though he call himself a Vaishnav,[7]
Since self-will is the goad of his actions

---

[7] Vaishnav—an ascetic devoted to some form of Lord Vishnu, such as Krishna.

What can he hope to gain?
Pretended holiness is like thrashing empty husks,
Or like the crane who sits among the swans,
Is still on the watch for fish. The swans find him an intruder.
They live upon pearls and precious stones, the crane on frogs,
And finally the poor crane flies away
In fear that the swans might spot his true nature.
Men do as God wills. Why should we blame anyone?
When anything happens, God wills that it should.
The True Guru is an ocean-wide lake of pearls:
The sincere seeker after his pearls shall find them.
The True Guru is the holy lake of Mansrover,[8]
And his Sikhs are there gathered like his swans.
The lake is full of pearls and precious stones;
However many the swans eat, they will not be exhausted.
The Sikhs are like swans who remain at the lake for ever
And banquet for ever on jewels. God has so willed it.
Nānak, blessed is the disciple who comes to the Guru:
The Guru will save him, save his family,
Nay, in the end he will save the whole world!

"The one who mingles with God"
by Guru Teg Bahadur (the Ninth Guru)

That man who in the midst of grief is free from grieving,
And free from fear, and free from the snare of delight,
Nor is covetous of gold that he knows to be dust,
Who is neither a backbiter nor a flatterer,
Nor has greed in his heart, nor vanity, nor any worldly
    attachment,
Who remains at his centre unmoved by good and ill fortune,
Who is indifferent to the world's praise and blame
And discards every wishful fantasy
Accepting his lot in a disinterested fashion,
Not worked upon by lust or by wrath,
In such a man God dwelleth.
The man on whom the Grace of the Guru alights
Understands the way of conduct:
His soul, O Nānak, is mingled with the Lord
As water mingles with water!

---

[8] Lake Mansrover—a holy lake high in the Himalayas.

Hymns of the Hindu and Muslim Saints
by Nam Dev

In addition to hymns of the Sikh Gurus, the Guru Granth Sahib includes compositions by numerous Hindu and Muslim saints and musicians. Many were of a very low caste, illustrating the Sikh conviction that the heights of spiritual realization transcend caste distinctions. Nam Dev (1270–1350) was a low-caste Hindu tailor. This first hymn by Nam Dev is called "God is the object of the yearning of my soul."

As water is precious
To the traveller in Marwar,
As the hungry camel
Yearns for the creeper,
As the wild deer at night
Hearken enrapt
To the hunter's bell,
So God is the object
Of the yearning of my soul!
Thy Name is beauty,
Thy Form is beauty,
Thy Hues are beauty,
O my living Lord!

As the dry earth yearneth
In thirst for the raindrops,
As the honey-bee yearneth
For the scent of the flowers,
As the kokil[9] loves the mango-tree,
So I long for the God.

As the sheldrake
Longs for sunrise,
As the swan yearneth
For Mansarowar Lake,
As the wife pines
For her husband,
So God is the object
Of the yearning of my soul!

As the babe yearneth
For his mother's breast-milk,

---

[9] Kokil—a type of bird.

As the chatrik[10] who drinketh
Only the raindrops
Yearneth for the rain,
As the stranded fish
Yearneth after water,
So God is the object
Of the yearning of my soul!

All seekers, sages, teachers
Yearn, O Lord, after Thee.
How few of them have seen Thee!
As Thy Name is yearned after
By Thy whole vast creation,
So for Nama God is the object
Of the yearning of his soul!

"How can there be any difference between me and Thee?"
by Ravidas

Ravidas was a fifteenth-century Hindu saint who was an extremely low-caste hide-tanner and shoemaker.

Between Thee and me, between me and Thee,
How can there be likeness or difference?
Likeness or difference as between gold
And a bracelet made of it, as between water
And the waves that move on its surface!
Were I not a sinner, O Eternal Lord,
How couldst Thou have the title of Redeemer of Sinners?
Thou, O Lord, art the Searcher of hearts.
Through God, the Master, we know the saints, His Servants:
Through the servants of God, we know God.
Grant me O Lord that my body may be Thy shrine.
Few, O Ravidas, see God in everything.

SOURCE: All above hymns from the *Guru Granth Sahib*: in *Selections from The Sacred Writings of the Sikhs*, trans. Trilochan Singh *et al*. New York: Samuel Weiser, Inc., 1973. According to the standard pagination of the Guru Granth Sahib, they are from page numbers 438, 558, 448, 633, 393, and 93, respectively.

[10] Chatrik—a type of bird, said to drink only raindrops.

"Pray crow, peck not these eyes, so that I may see the Beloved"
by Sheikh Farid, with commentary by Guru Nanak

The mystical poetry of several Muslim saints is also lovingly included in the Guru Granth Sahib. One is the great Sufi dervish, Sheikh Farid (1175–1265). His burning ardor for his Beloved is tempered by a commentary from Guru Nanak.

Mighty river, erode not thy banks; thou too to thy
   maker art answerable.
What power is in the river to flow this way or that?
God's Will guides its course.
Farid, thy days have been sorrow-filled, thy nights
   in suffering passed.
Now towards the close the Pilot shouts:
"Thy boat's in jaws of storm."
Life's long river flows on, bringing down the sandy banks;
Yet is the boat safe from the storm, if the Pilot be attentive.
Farid, scores profess to be my friends; but
   true friends see I nowhere.
For one true friend my heart yearns as in smouldering fire.
Farid, the body keeps ever a tumult, who will bear
   its suffering for ever?
Let me plug my ears,
Blow storm never so loud.
Farid, this life is like ripe dates and rivers of honey.
With each passing day comes closer the grip of death.
Farid, penance has left my body a skeleton;
Crows peck at my soles.
God still has not revealed Himself—
Such is my destiny.

Thou crow pecking at my emaciated body, eating away its flesh,
Pray touch not these two eyes, so I have sight of the Beloved.
Pray crow, peck not at my body; fly off from
   where thou art settled.
Swallow not the flesh of this body wherein is
   lodged the Beloved.
Farid, the lowly grave makes call to homeless
   man to come to his real abode—
Saying, come to me thou must; fear not death.
With these eyes have I beheld the vast world
   vanish into eternity.

Each in his own trials is caught;
Nor am I free from mine.

In separation from God my body burns like the oven;
My bones flame like firewood;
To find union with the Beloved
Could I walk till my feet be tired,
Would walk on my head.

Theme continued by Guru Nanak
Thou needst not burn thyself like the oven nor put in
    flames thy bones:
Why torture thy poor limbs? Behold the Beloved in
    thy own heart.

SOURCE: Sheikh Farid, with commentary from Guru Nanak, *Sri Guru Granth Sahib*, trans. Gurbachan Singh Talib. Patiala, Punjab: Punjabi University Publication Bureau, 1990, pp. 2761–4

Dasam Granth

When Guru Gobind Singh undertook the final compilation of the Guru Granth Sahib, including in it the poetry of his father, the martyred Guru Teg Bahadur, he included only one of his own compositions. However, the literature attributed to Guru Gobind Singh is vast and complex. It includes lengthy descriptions of "Hindu" deities, discipline for the Khalsa, the warrior-saints whom he pledged to defend, people of all castes and creeds, a powerful letter to the tyrannical Muslim ruler Aurangzeb, his spiritual autobiography (*Bacchitar Natak*), and *Akal Ustat*, assertions of the oneness of all religions and the unity of humankind. Portions from the latter two are given below.

"This is the purpose for which God sent me"
by Guru Gobind Singh

I now relate my own story,
How while doing "Tapasya"[11] I had to come to earth.
There is a mountain by the name of Hemkund,
Which is adorned by seven peaks.

There I remained in deep meditation

---

[11] Tapasya—austere meditation.

and performed "Tapasya" worshipping the
timeless and mighty God who transcends death.
In consequence of this "Tapasya,"
from the dual state, I became One with God.

Then under command of God,
I took birth in Kali Yug,[12]
My heart did not really wish to come down,
because I was totally immersed in
meditation at the feet of the Lord.
He then explained to me His purpose,
and sent me here with His command,

Lord (Akal Purukh) said:
"You are my chosen and cherished son
whom I have installed for strengthening faith and religion.
Go down to earth and propagate righteousness
and guide mankind away from wickedness."

This is the purpose for which Lord sent me
and in consequence I took birth on this earth.
I shall speak (and act) as directed by Lord
and shall not bear enmity to anyone.
But any people who address me as God,
will be consigned to the cauldron of hell.
Regard me only as the humble servant of God,
Let there be no doubt or mystery on this score.
I am the servant of the Supreme Lord,
come to earth to watch His play.
I shall utter on earth the word of Lord,
and shall not remain silent in this mortal world.

SOURCE: Guru Gobind Singh, *Bacchitar Natak*, in *Jap*. New Delhi: Gobind Sadan,
pp. xv–xvi

"Let all humanity be recognized as one"
by Guru Gobind Singh

There are monks with shaven heads; there are many kinds of yogis,
celibates, and ascetics, Hindus, Turks, Shi'ite Muslims, and Sunni Muslims.

---

[12] Kali Yug, or Kali Yuga—the last and darkest of the four ages which continually recur,
according to Indian thought.

But know that all of humanity is recognized as one race.
The Creator and the Beneficent One are the same; the Provider and the
    Merciful One are the same;
Let no one make the mistake of thinking there is a difference.
There is not one God for Hindus and another for Muslims.
Worship the one God who is the divine Preceptor for all, the One Form
    whose Light suffuses all.
Temples and mosques are the same,
Hindu worship and Muslim prayer are the same,
All people are the same.
It is only through erroneous thinking that they appear different.
Deities and demons, Muslims and Hindus wear their regional garb,
But all people have the same eyes, the same ears, the same body, the same
    composition of earth, air, fire, and water.
Allah and Abekh[13] are the same, the messages of the Puranas[14] and Qur'an
    are the same.
All are alike; one God created all.
As from one fire millions of sparks arise separately and then unite again in
    the fire,
As from one dustheap many dust particles fill the air and then resettle,
    blending with the dust,
As in one stream millions of waves are produced, but being made of water,
    become water again,
So from God's Form all non-sentient and sentient things are manifested,
    and springing from God, all shall be united in God again.

SOURCE: Guru Gobind Singh, *Manas ki jaat*, trans. Gobind Sadan, New Delhi

Living Sikhism

In 1999, Sikhs around the world jubilantly celebrated the 300th anniversary
of Guru Gobind Singh's creation of the Khalsa. In the process, many people
proclaimed the idealistic and universalist nature of the Gurus' mission.

The Sikh Gurus' Vision of an Ideal Society
by Dr. Dharam Singh

*Dr. Dharam Singh, a professor at Punjabi University in Patiala specializing in Guru
Gobind Singh's social philosophy, asserts that the Sikh Gurus' mission included
measures designed to develop an ideal classless society.*

---

[13] Abekh—a Name of God, meaning "without garb."
[14] Puranas—Sanskrit sacred writings.

Besides caste which is peculiar to Indian society, the economic factor is equally responsible for stratification of society into different classes all over the world. In such a set-up, the affluent and the haves generally adopt an oppressive and exploitative attitude towards the poor and the have-nots: this is equally true in the case of individuals as well as nations. This gulf between the two classes widens further as a result of the pace of social, material progress being different for these different classes. Since the economic factor comes to determine human social relations, man becomes unduly more unmindful of moral and ethical values in this struggle for economic betterment. Sikhism, however, believes in the universal brotherhood of mankind, and therefore holds everyone an equal claimant to the natural resources provided them by the universal Father. Any attempt to deny one's share in that heritage would amount to sacrilege against God. The ethics of the kingdom of God as taught in the Sikh scripture are the ethics of a classless society.

An important socio-religious directive for the Sikhs is to earmark a tithe[15] of their income for philanthropic purposes. Every Sikh, when he visits a *gurdwara*[16] to pay obeisance to the Guru Granth Sahib, offers some cash. There is no lower or higher limit on this offer and, in fact, it is not even obligatory if one is not in a position to offer any. This offer of cash, though made with religious faithfulness, is not to please the Guru or God: it is an individual's modest contribution towards general, communal purposes. . . .

Besides caste and class, religion is another very potent factor which divides mankind into diverse groups of different religious denomination. At the time Sikhism was born and during the period of its ascendancy, persecution of man in the name of religion was quite common. The Sikh Gurus felt it an insult to the divine essence in man, and declared that all human beings, irrespective of their religious denominations, are one. Guru Gobind Singh in his *Akal Ustati* refers to the diversity of religions followed by people of the world, and declares emphatically that followers of diverse religions are one. Religious labels are temporary and wither away with the bodily vesture whereas it is the worth of deeds done by man that is the criterion of judgment both in this world and the Divine Court. Guru Amar Das confers equal validity on all religions in helping man realize the ultimate end of life. The role of religion is not that of scissors that tears asunder but that of a needle that sews together the torn fabric of human society. . . .

The concept of the equality of mankind includes the womenfolk as well. Woman occupies a subordinate position in the patriarchal society, but her position becomes worse in the poor societies, especially in India where she suffers oppression as a woman and as a member of the oppressed caste or

---

[15] Tithe—a proportion, originally a tenth.
[16] Gurdwara—a Sikh temple.

class. The Indian woman of Guru Nanak's time was a victim of this sexist discrimination and oppression, and was completely denied an independent personality of her own. Infanticide, child marriage, malnutrition and *sati*[17] were some of the evils resulting from this *Weltanschauung*.[18] Sikhism makes no distinction between man and woman, and considers both as the equal manifestation of the Divine. Man and woman are equal but distinct because of the functional distinction they have in the historical order. Even if none of the Gurus was a woman, there is no inferiority for woman in the orthodox Sikh ecclesiology. Guru Nanak was perhaps the first personage in the religious history of mankind to raise his voice against her discrimination.

The Sikh Gurus not only provided ideational basis in their hymns for the socio-religious rehabilitation of women but also undertook and advised to undertake some widespread and practical steps in this direction. As a result of this, she came to occupy a place equal to man and play an active role in the socio-religious life. That the women were quite active as missionaries of Sikh faith during the Guru-period is confirmed by a *hukumnama*[19] issued by Guru Tegh Bahadur to the *sangat*[20] of Patna wherein he refers among others to one Bebe Peri Bai. The role played by Mai Bhago[21] during the pontificate of Guru Gobind Singh is common knowledge. Sikh tradition, supported by the *Rahitnama*[22] literature, lays injunctions against female infanticide, *purdah*[23] and *sati*. It also permits widow remarriage for her rehabilitation in social life. The Rahitnamas denounce any kind of marginalization of woman. Chastity and fidelity, two important constituents of the sanctity of the family life as well as of social relations, are no more the virtues expected of woman alone: they apply to women as much as they apply to men and even to the rulers. . . . The Sikhs in their daily supplication (*ardas*) seek the welfare of all—*sarbat da bhala*. . . .

There is no priestly class as such in Sikhism and anybody can lead the congregation. . . . In the appointment of leaders of congregation, caste, class and status are given no consideration, and the only criterion of merit is the incumbent's spiritual and moral state. . . .

In the *gurdwara*, everybody is welcome irrespective of his social or economic status, and none is favoured or discriminated against on any count. Here the prince and the pauper sit together and pray.

When membership of the *sangats* and the frequency of their visits to the *dharamsalas*[24] increased, it was considered imperative to arrange food for the

---

[17] *Sati, suttee*—the Hindu custom of a widow's self-immolation on her husband's funeral pyre.
[18] *Weltanschauung*—philosophy, literally "world view" (German).
[19] *Hukumnama*—spiritual instructions taken from opening the Guru Granth Sahib at random.
[20] *Sangat*—Sikh congregation.
[21] Mai Bhago—great female warrior and martyr in Sikh history.
[22] *Rahitnama*—disciplines prescribed for Sikhs.
[23] *Purdah*—veiling and separation of women.
[24] *Dharamsala*—holy place.

devotees. The institution of *langar* or *Guru-ka-Langar* (free community kitchen) started with a view to meeting this requirement. The institution became popular during the pontificate of Guru Angad Dev.... Guru Amar Das further consolidated the institution and made it mandatory for every visitor, high or low, to partake of food in the *langar* before seeing the Guru. Each successive Guru contributed to the consolidation of this institution, and today we find *langar* an integral part of almost every *gurdwara* or the Sikh place of worship the world over.

In the *langar*, the food is prepared communally, without anybody asking for the caste or class of the volunteer lending a helping hand. *Seva*[25] or service in the *langar* has been accepted as highly meritorious. All the visitors sit in *pangat* (row) without any distinction of caste, class or creed, and take their food. There is an injunction against providing a special seat or special food for anyone whosoever. The Sikh history stands witness that here princes have sat alongside peasants. This has been a very important step in translating the principle of equality into practice—more so, in a society where rigidity of casteism and sectarianism segregated people from one another. It has also served as a medium of social integration between the king and the commoner, the prince and the peasant....

The desire for *seva* is born of the feeling of love for others. Love is, as we have said earlier, the natural corollary of the Sikh precept of the universal brotherhood of mankind and universal fatherhood of God. All men, whatever their caste, clan or creed, are the children of God and all are spiritually united to each other and to the Creator-Lord. That is why, like *seva*, love has also been declared a very potent means of reaching God....

Love for all as equal members of the universal brotherhood of mankind and social service and other altruistic deeds done with humility and with absolutely no selfish motives naturally lead to the establishment of a social order which is marked by justice, communal harmony and peaceful co-existence. These social conditions are all the more needed in the modern social phenomena which are experiencing rapid socio-cultural transformations that do not, however, occur at a uniform pace. Consequently, the economically poor and the socially backward are in the world today at odds with the affluent and the socially and politically advanced. These inequalities cause personal and social insecurity, distrust and hatred in personal and social relations and gross violation of human rights and a widespread sense of fear and frustration.... It was to overcome these and such other negative tendencies that the Sikh Gurus preached a distinct metaphysical theory and then made it the *vis-a-tergo*[26] of their vision of an ideal social structure marked by humanitarian outlook.

According to the Sikh thought, *kirt karna* (to earn one's bread with the

---

[25] *Seva*—voluntary service in devotion to God.
[26] *Vis-a-tergo*—(Latin) literally "push from behind."

sweat of one's brow), *nam japna* (remember the Divine Name; ... feeling and realizing His presence in all beings and at all places), and *wand chhakna* (to share with others what one earns through honest means) are the three cardinal values in the Sikh vision of an ideal society.

SOURCE: Dharam Singh, *Sikhism: Norm and Form*. Patiala and New Delhi: Vision & Venture, 1997, pp. 120–9

GLOSSARY

Guru A teacher of religious knowledge and spiritual insight, a channel of divine understanding.
Guru Granth Sahib The collection of Sikh sacred scriptures.
Gurmukh A person who follows the commandments of the Guru rather than his or her own ideas.

Hukam Divine command.
Khalsa Sikh warrior-saints pledged to protect people of all religions and castes from oppression.
Langar Free community kitchen.

SIKH HOLY DAYS

Sikh celebrations usually include continuous reading of the entire Guru Granth Sahib over a period of 48 hours, followed by offering of a large communal meal. Dating of holy days has traditionally followed the lunar calendar.

January 14 Maghi, celebration of the martyrdom of 40 Immortals at Muktsar in Guru Gobind Singh's last battle against the Mughal forces.

April 13 or 14 Baisakhi, anniversary of the creation of the Khalsa, often including initiation of new members of the Khalsa with amrit (holy water stirred with a double-edged sword as the Sikh prayers are recited).

[June] 4th day of the lunar month of Jeth Martyrdom of Guru Arjun Dev by heat torture, commemorated by offering of a cooling drink to all passers-by.

[October–November] Full moon of the lunar month of Kartik Traditional celebration of Guru Nanak's birthday (although scholarship has placed the original date as April 15).

[November] 5th light part of the lunar month of Maghar Martyrdom of Guru Teg Bahadur.

[December–January] 7th light part of lunar month of Poh Birthday of Guru Gobind Singh.

HISTORICAL OUTLINE

1469–1539 CE—life of Guru Nanak, the first Sikh Prophet. After a vision of God, he began the Sikh faith by claiming God to be one, formless and omnipresent, not limited to one religion's beliefs. He traveled widely, including to Mecca, and finally settled in Kartarpur, now in Pakistan.

1563–1606—life of the Fifth Guru, Arjun Dev, tortured to death by the Mughal emperor Jahangir.

1621–75—life of the Ninth Guru, Teg Bahadur, who offered his life to protect Hindus' freedom of religion.

1666–1708—life of Guru Gobind Singh, the Tenth Guru, who took up arms against attacks by Hindus and Muslims and turned his followers into courageous saint-soldiers.

1699—Guru Gobind Singh initiated the order of Khalsa ("the pure"), creating a casteless community.

1708—At his death, Guru Gobind Singh installs the Guru Granth Sahib as the Guru of Sikhs.

1780–1839—Maharaja Ranjit Singh extends and rules a strong Sikh kingdom with regard for all religions.

1848—After Ranjit Singh's death, as the British move into the Punjab, Sikh rule falls.

1919—Bloody massacre by the British in the Sikh spiritual capital of Amritsar.

1947—Pakistan is established; its border divides the Sikh population, and some 2,500,000 Sikhs are compelled to leave Pakistan for India.

1984—The Indian army storms the Harimandir (Golden Temple) to dislodge Sikh militants. Prime minister Indira Gandhi assassinated by two Sikh bodyguards, starting widespread Hindu violence against Sikhs. Sikhs demand separate Sikh state.

April 1999—millions of Sikhs converge on Anandpur Sahib, home of the Guru Granth Sahib, to celebrate the 300th anniversary of the Khalsa.

REVIEW QUESTIONS

1   Based on your readings, to what kind of social structures is Sikh religion responding? How?
2   What are the three cardinal values in the Sikh vision of an ideal society?
3   Do Sikhs view the world to be ultimately an illusion or real?
4   How does Sikh theology reflect its environment? Discuss, for example, karma, reincarnation, caste, one formless God. How is Sikh theology and practice different from its environment?
5   Is Sikh faith focused on monastic retreats or active work? What view of society does this reflect?
6   Do Sikhs commune with God through mediators?

INFORMATION RESOURCES

Cole, W. Owen, and Piara Singh Sambhi, *The Sikhs: Their Religious Beliefs and Practices.* London: Routledge, 1985

Cole, W. Owen, and Piara Singh Sambhi, *A Popular Dictionary of Sikhism.* 1990

Duggal, K. S. *Sikh Gurus: Their Lives and Teachings.* New Delhi: UBS Publishers' Distributors Ltd., 1993

Gobind Sadan, <www.gobindsadan.org.>

Institute of Sikh Studies, <www.sikh-institute.org.>

Kohli, Surindar Singh, *The Life and Ideals of Guru Gobind Singh.* New Delhi: Munshiram Manoharlal Publishers Pvt. Ltd., 1986

Macauliffe, Max Arthur, *The Sikh Religion: Its Gurus, Sacred Writings, and Authors.* Oxford: Oxford University Press and Delhi: S. Chand and Company, 1963

Singh, Harbans, ed. *The Encyclopedia of Sikhism.* Patiala: Punjabi University. 1992–1999.

Singh, Nikky Gurinder Kaur, *The Feminine Principle in the Sikh Vision of the Transcendent.* Cambridge: Cambridge University Press, 1993

CHAPTER 12

NEW RELIGIOUS MOVEMENTS

From time immemorial, there have probably been visionaries and philosophers proclaiming spiritual truth. Some with particular abilities of leadership and spiritual qualities have attracted followers; those who have been especially successful in doing so are still honored today as the founders of the world's major living religions. Others are now forgotten. This process continues in the present, with thousands of new religious movements emerging since World War II and others withering away.

New religious movements have always been regarded skeptically by previously established religions. In general, most religions claim to be the best, perhaps the exclusive carriers of authentic spiritual truth. Whether institutionalization or human waywardness is the cause, people may drift away from the initial fervor of their religion. Spiritual renewal may then arise either within the religion as a reform movement or without, as a new religious movement which nonetheless is likely to have some links with past tradition.

New religious movements may be perceived not only as threats to earlier movements, but also as threats to their followers' mental health and personal safety. In our times, there have been group suicides by members of movements anticipating doomsday or even trying to be picked up by unidentified flying objects. Some groups have encouraged their followers to withdraw from their communities and families to develop a non-worldly lifestyle. Such behaviors have led to negative branding of new religious movements as **cults** or **sects**, and have led to vigorous anti-cult organizations in some parts of the world. However, the word "cult" is value-neutral and could be applied to some existing religions; it connotes a religion which is centered upon devotion to a single person or deity. Similarly, "sect" connotes a branch of a larger tradition. The term "new religious movements" is preferred today by scholars of religion. Below are examples of some types of new religious movements which are popular today.

Old religions in new skins

Some "new religions" are not new at all, but are rather imports from cultures other than one's own. Many Indian religious teachers, for instance, have brought versions of Hinduism to the West and adapted them to Western tastes.

Maharishi Mahesh Yogi has developed a world movement teaching "transcendental meditation" based on inner repetition of a **mantra**—a sacred word or phrase. Training in the method is quite expensive, and thus the movement has expanded into luxury services for the wealthy, cloaked in Indian mystique.

Transcendental Meditation Today
by Hemant Kumar

It's the biggest wooden house in the Netherlands. Not a single metal pin or nail has been driven into the seasoned cedar. Finnish artisans handcrafted wooden pins and rivets to take the place of metallic nails and screws. Famous German architect Ike Hartman pored over reams of original Vastu inscribed in *Sthapatya Ved*, to design the house. A generous coat of *neem* oil protects the wood from termite. When the cedar catches the late evening sun, its golden paint simply ignites. And the house glows—like a gigantic ladle overflowing with molten gold. And then, as the sun goes down, up goes the quartet of fountains on the sprawling lawns across the building. Transfixed, I watch the spectacle unfold like a giant slide show.

The place is Vlodrop, some 300 km south of Amsterdam. This is where the Maharishi Mahesh Yogi lives and from where he presides over his vast empire girdling the globe and growing ever larger. It's so quiet here you can hear yourself think. I enter the main building and a long, scented corridor lined with slippers. And yet, not a sound. I raise a questioning eyebrow at Atilla, the young Austrian driver who picked me up at Amsterdam's Schiphol airport. Fingers on his lips, he points out my room to me. I unlatch the door, and with a whispered "TM time. I must rush too," Atilla disappears down the hallway. My room would put any five-star hotel suite to shame. It's plush, elegant and beautifully decorated. It's part of a huge building, housing more than 500 people, each of them sitting absolutely still, deep in meditation—Transcendental Meditation (TM).

At this very moment the man responsible for this modern, mystical nirvana is meditating in his glass-encased veranda. At 85, the Maharishi still meditates six to seven hours daily and works longer than any of his ablest lieutenants can. It is said that no one knows how many hours the Maharishi actually sleeps. He turns in only after midnight and is up again before dawn.

In the swinging 60s, when he landed in Europe, the Maharishi encountered a dazed, confused generation. Rebellious youngsters freaking out on the decadent pop culture of the hippies. Marriages wrecking on the bedrock of alcoholism, mistrust and promiscuity. The Beatles and Flower Power. Anti-war demonstrations and the search for an elusive elixir. Inner peace? It was as rare as virginity on Pennsylvania Avenue. At first, they didn't understand what this short, dark man from the Far East was saying to them in his broken English and a deeply eastern accent. But soon enough, they began to trickle in. The trickle changed to a flood. And today, the Maharishi's organisation is a worldwide movement spanning 80 countries. For millions of people in these countries TM twice daily is as essential as brushing their teeth, probably more. . . .

It's morning. The Maharishi is listening to *Yajur Veda* chants on his music system. Outside, the whole place is abuzz with activity. The appetising sound of huge stainless-steel vessels clanging in the kitchen downstairs. The loud *"chhanngg"* of rai, hing and curry leaves crackling in pure ghee. Breakfast is being prepared for 500 people and for the Maharishi. A man is snipping white lilies in the sprawling lawn to make a bouquet for the Maharishi. Another pushes a wheelbarrow in the organic vegetable garden, whistling a tune. Indian, European or American, they all greet each other with hands folded and a "Jai Guru Dev." This heady cocktail of curry leaves, ghee, Jai Guru Dev, and kurta-pyjama in the heart of white man's Europe would seem ludicrous were it not so genuine and warm and natural in this setting. . . .

This is a modern rishi[1] who has harnessed technology to his advantage. A dish antenna links up straight from his room to a satellite for broadcasting on his 24-hour TV channel. Cellphones, laptops, Internet, video-conferencing. The works. "This is the Age of Information. How will you reach your message to the millions of people worldwide if you don't keep in step with technology." asserts Dr Bevan Morris, the man who heads the Maharishi's think-tank. . . .

Valkenberg showcases the Maharishi's finest and most exclusive Ayurvedic healing centre in the Netherlands. Housed in a castle-like mansion that used to be a monastery, it combines the best of Ayurveda— pulse diagnosed natural medicine, meditation and panchkarma.[2] Rich Europeans and Americans spend weeks here cleansing their minds and bodies of toxins. The mansion has scores of consultation rooms, treatment and massage facilities, meditation halls, dining halls and super-deluxe suites for guests.

The place is a mini-India minus, of course, the filth and stench. . . . Exquisitely designed treatment rooms for panchkarma are swathed in the sweet aroma of some of the choicest Indian flowers. . . . This is a huge, efficiently run corporation selling the ancient wisdom of India in a modern-day package. And its success is evident in the kind of resources it has, the

---

[1] Rishi—a sage or teacher.
[2] Panchkarma—an ancient Ayurvedic healing technique of body purification and massage.

talented people it attracts, the magnificent, peaceful beauty of its centres, and the mystic magnetism of its CEO.[3]

SOURCE: Hemant Kumar, "Maharishi's World," in *India Today: Plus*, fourth quarter 1998, pp. 50–58

Esoteric wisdom

There have long been people who claim to be privy to deeper secrets of religion which have been hidden from the general public. A famous nineteenth-century proponent of this idea was the Russian Madame Helena Blavatsky (1831–91). She said that she had received higher initiations by hidden Ascended Masters, some of them from Eastern religions, and proposed that the eternal truths which they revealed to her were the key to harmonizing all religions. The global Theosophical Society is an outgrowth of her teachings. The dialogue below is between an Enquirer and a Theosophist.

The Wisdom-Religion Esoteric in All Ages
by Madame Blavatsky

THEO. [Ammonius[4]] was born a Christian, but never accepted Church Christianity. As said of him by [Mosheim]:

"He had but to propound his instructions according to the ancient pillars of Hermes, which Plato and Pythagoras[5] knew before, and from them constituted their philosophy. Finding the same in the prologue of the Gospel according to St. John, he very properly supposed that the purpose of Jesus was to restore the great doctrine of wisdom in its primitive integrity. The narratives of the Bible and the stories of the gods he considered to be allegories illustrative of the truth, or else fables to be rejected." Moreover, as says the *Edinburgh Encyclopedia*, "he acknowledged that Jesus Christ was an excellent *man* and the 'friend of God,' but alleged that it was not his design entirely to abolish the worship of demons (gods), and that his only intention was to purify the ancient religion."

ENQ. Since Ammonius never committed anything to writing, how can one feel sure that such were his teachings?

THEO. Neither did Buddha, Pythagoras, Confucius, Orpheus, Socrates, or even Jesus, leave behind them any writings. Yet most of these are historical personages, and their teachings have all survived. The disciples of Ammonius (among whom Origen and Herennius) wrote treatises and explained his ethics. Certainly the latter are as historical, if not more so,

---

[3] CEO—chief executive officer.
[4] Ammonius Saccas (175–242 CE)—a philosopher of Alexandria, Egypt, whose most famous pupils were Origen and Plotinus.
[5] Plato, Pythagoras—ancient Greek philosophers.

than the Apostolic writings. Moreover, his pupils—Origen, Plotinus, and
Longinus (counsellor of the famous Queen Zenobia[6])—have all left
voluminous record of the Philaletheian System[7]—so far, at all events, as
their public profession of faith was known, for the school was divided into
exoteric and **esoteric** teachings.

ENQ. How have the latter tenets reached our day, since you hold that what
is properly called the Wisdom-Religion was esoteric?

THEO. The Wisdom-Religion was ever one, and being the last word of
possible human knowledge, was, therefore, carefully preserved. It preceded
by long ages the Alexandrian Theosophists, reached the modern, and will
survive every other religion and philosophy.

ENQ. Where and by whom was it so preserved?

THEO. Among Initiates of every country; among profound seekers after
truth—their disciples; and in those parts of the world where such topics
have always been most valued and pursued: in India, Central Asia, and
Persia

ENQ. Can you give me some proofs of its esotericism?

THEO. The best proof you can have of the fact is that every ancient
religious, or rather philosophical, cult consisted of an esoteric or secret
teaching, and an exoteric worship. Furthermore, it is a well-known fact
that the Mysteries of the ancients comprised with every nation the
"greater" (secret) and "Lesser" (public) Mysteries—e.g., in the celebrated
solemnities called the *Eleusinia*,[8] in Greece. From the Hierophants[9] of
Samothrace, Egypt, and the initiated Brahmins of the India of old, down to
the later Hebrew Rabbis, all preserved, for fear of profanation, their real
bona fide beliefs secretly. The Jewish Rabbis called their secular religious
series the *Mercavah* (the exterior body), "the vehicle," or, "the covering
which contains the hidden soul"—i.e., their highest secret knowledge. Not
one of the ancient nations ever imparted through its priests its real
philosophical secrets to the masses, but allotted to the latter only the husks.
Northern Buddhism has its "greater" and its "lesser" vehicle, known as the
Mahayana, the esoteric, and the *Hinayana*, the exoteric, Schools. Nor can
you blame them for such secrecy; for surely you would not think of feeding
your flock of sheep on learned dissertations on botany instead of on grass?
Pythagoras called his *Gnosis* "the knowledge of things that are," and
preserved that knowledge for his pledged disciples only: for those who
could digest such mental food and feel satisfied; and he pledged them to
silence and secrecy. Occult alphabets and secret ciphers are the

---

[6] Zenobia (d. *c.* 274 CE)—queen of Palmyra in Syria.

[7] Philaletheian System—an esoteric philosophical system of knowledge.

[8] Eleusinian Mysteries—in ancient Greece, rites sacred to Demeter, goddess of fruitfulness
    and the harvest.

[9] Hierophant—an interpreter of sacred mysteries.

development of the old Egyptian hieratic[10] writings, the secret of which was, in the days of old, in the possession only of the Hierogrammatists, or initiated Egyptian priests. Ammonius Saccas, as his biographers tell us, bound his pupils by oath not to divulge his higher doctrines except to those who had already been instructed in preliminary knowledge, and who were also bound by a pledge. Finally, do we not find the same even in early Christianity, among the Gnostics,[11] and even in the teachings of Christ? Did he not speak to the multitudes in parables which had a two-fold meaning, and explain his reasons only to his disciples? "To you," he says, "it is given to know the mysteries of the kingdom of heaven; but unto them that are without, all these things are done in parables" (Mark iv. 11). "The Essenes[12] of Judea and Carmel made similar distinctions, dividing their adherents into neophytes, brethren, and the perfect, or those initiated." Examples might be brought from every country to this effect.

ENQ. Can you attain the "Secret Wisdom" simply by study? Encyclopedias define Theosophy pretty much as Webster's Dictionary does, i.e., as "supposed intercourse with God and superior spirits, and consequent attainment of superhuman knowledge by physical means and chemical processes." Is this so?

THEO. I think not. Nor is there any lexicographer capable of explaining, whether to himself or others, how superhuman knowledge can be attained by physical or chemical processes. Had Webster said "by metaphysical and alchemical processes," the definition would be approximately correct: as it is, it is absurd. Ancient Theosophists claimed, and so do the modern, that the infinite cannot be known by the finite—i.e., sensed by the finite Self—but that the divine essence could be communicated to the higher Spiritual Self in a state of ecstasy. This condition can hardly be attained, like hypnotism, by "physical and chemical means."

ENQ. What is your explanation of it?

THEO. Real ecstasy was defined by Plotinus as "the liberation of the mind from its finite consciousness, becoming one and identified with the infinite." This is the highest condition, but not one of permanent duration, and it is reached only by the very very few. It is, indeed, identical with that state which is known in India as *Samadhi*. The latter is practised by the Yogis, who facilitate it physically by the greatest abstinence in food and drink, and mentally by an incessant endeavour to purify and elevate the mind. Meditation is silent and unuttered prayer, or, as Plato expressed it, "the ardent turning of the soul toward the divine; not to ask any particular good (as in the common meaning of prayer), but for good itself—for the universal

[10] Hieratic—priestly; relating to the Egyptian hierglyphic sacred texts.
[11] Gnostics—early Christian sect that embraced a mystical perception of spiritual knowledge.
[12] Essenes—a Jewish sect of *c.* 200 BCE–100 CE who lived in ascetic, monastic communities in the region of the Dead Sea in Palestine.

Supreme Good" of which we are a part on earth, and out of the essence of which we have all emerged. Therefore, adds Plato, "remain silent in the presence of the divine ones, till they remove the clouds from thy eyes and enable thee to see by the light which issues from themselves, not what appears as good to thee, but what is intrinsically good."

ENQ. Theosophy, then, is not, as held by some, a newly devised scheme?

THEO. Only ignorant people can thus refer to it. It is as old as the world, in its teachings and ethics, if not in name, as it is also the broadest and most catholic system among all.

SOURCE: H. P. Blavatsky, *The Key to Theosophy*. The United Lodge of Theosophists, Los Angeles, CA: 1920, pp. 5–9

Apocalyptic expectations

Throughout human history, there have been widespread expectations that life is about to come to a dramatic end. Expectations of an **apocalypse** have taken many forms, including the movement known as "Jehovah's Witnesses." It is based on a literal interpretation of Bible passages about the coming kingdom of God, as developed starting in the 1870s by Charles Taze Russell. By now it has a world headquarters in Brooklyn, New York, some three and a half million followers worldwide, and nearly half a million missionaries going door to door offering literature such as the following tract, which is also available on the Internet.

Life in a Peaceful New World
by Jehovah's Witnesses

God's Kingdom will bring earthly benefits beyond compare, accomplishing everything good that God originally purposed for his people to enjoy on earth. Hatreds and prejudices will cease to exist, and eventually everyone on earth will be a true friend of everyone else. In the Bible, God promises that he will "make wars to cease to the extremity of the earth." "Nation will not lift up sword against nation, neither will they learn war anymore"— Psalm 46:9; Isaiah 2:4.

The whole earth will eventually be brought to a gardenlike paradise state. The Bible says: "The wilderness and the waterless region will exult, and the desert plain will be joyful and blossom as the saffron. . . . For in the wilderness waters will have burst out, and torrents in the desert plain. And the heat-parched ground will have become as a reedy pool, and the thirsty ground as springs of water"—Isaiah 35:1, 6, 7.

There will be every reason to be happy in the Paradise earth. Never again will people hunger for lack of food. "The earth itself will certainly give its produce," the Bible says (Psalm 67:6; 72:16). All will enjoy the fruits of their own labor, as our Creator promises: "They will certainly plant vineyards and eat their fruitage.... they will not plant and someone else do the eating"—Isaiah 65:21, 22.

In God's new world, no longer will people be crammed into huge apartment buildings or run-down slums, for God has purposed: "They will certainly build houses and have occupancy.... They will not build and someone else have occupancy." The Bible also promises: "They will not toil for nothing" (Isaiah 65:21–23). Thus people will have productive, satisfying work. Life will not be boring.

In time, God's Kingdom will even restore the peaceful relations that existed in the garden of Eden between animals, and between animals and humans. The Bible says: "The wolf will actually reside for a while with the male lamb and with the kid the leopard itself will lie down, and the calf and the maned young lion and the well-fed animal all together; and a mere little boy will be leader over them"—Isaiah 11:6–9; Hosea 2:18.

Just imagine, in the Paradise earth all sicknesses and physical infirmities will also be healed! God's Word assures us: "No resident will say: 'I am sick'" (Isaiah 33:24). "[God] will wipe out every tear from their eyes, and death will be no more, neither will mourning nor outcry nor pain be anymore. The former things have passed away"—Revelation 21:4.

How It Is Possible for You Surely your heart must be moved by the promises of God regarding life in his new world of righteousness. And while some may consider the realizing of such blessings too good to be true, they are not too good to come from the hand of our loving Creator—Psalm 145:16; Micah 4:4.

Of course, there are requirements to be met if we are to live forever in the coming Paradise on earth. Jesus showed a principal one, saying in prayer to God: "This means everlasting life, their taking in knowledge of you, the only true God, and of the one whom you sent forth, Jesus Christ"—John 17:3.

So if we truly want to live in God's new world, we must first learn God's will and then do it. For it is a fact: This "world is passing away and so is its desire, but he that does the will of God remains forever," to enjoy eternally the blessings to be showered down by our loving Creator—1 John 2:17.

SOURCE: Jehovah's Witnesses, "Life in a Peaceful New World." *Watch Tower* <www.watchtower.org> April 1999. *Copyright* © 1999 *Watch Tower* Bible and Tract Society of Pennsylvania

Following a leader

Charismatic leadership often draws converts to new religious movements. During the twentieth century, many young people were drawn to give up their possessions and adopt a self-sacrificing lifestyle for the sake of others, while regarding a Korean former Christian Sunday school teacher, Reverend Sun Myung Moon, as the promised second coming of Christ. He teaches that Jesus's mission was incomplete, and that he and his wife have come to fulfill God's original plan as the "True Parents" of humankind.

The Lord of the Second Advent and the Ideal of True Parents
by Rev. Sun Myung Moon

Mary, when she was engaged to Joseph, received, from the Archangel Gabriel the surprising message that the Messiah would be born through her (Luke 1:31). In those days, if an unmarried woman became pregnant, she would be killed. But Mary accepted the will of God with absolute faith, saying, "Behold, I am the handmaid of the Lord; let it be to me according to your word" (Luke 1:38).

Mary consulted with the priest Zechariah, who was her relative and was highly respected. In this way, God let Mary, Zechariah, and Elizabeth know about the birth of the Messiah before anybody else. All of them had the absolutely crucial mission of following the will of God and serving Jesus. Zechariah's family let Mary stay in their house. Jesus was conceived in the house of Zechariah.

For the first time in history, there could be born on earth, free of satanic accusation and through a prepared womb, the seed of the Son of God—the seed of the True Father. In this way, the only begotten Son of God, the owner of the first love of God, was born for the first time in history.

Although the Son of God could be born on earth, he needed a wall of protection to grow up safely in the satanic world and fulfill the will of God. God had hoped that these three people in the family of Zechariah would establish that protective foundation.

Jesus was viewed as an illegitimate son, and lacking the protection of Zechariah's family and the love of Joseph, he grew up with an indescribable loneliness in his heart.

Jesus was aware of his path as the Messiah, and he lamented by himself these lonely circumstances and the serious obstacle they presented to fulfilling the will of God. The Messiah is the True Parent. And to fulfill that mission he needed to receive his substantial bride.

If Zechariah and Elizabeth, who had received the revelation and spiritual support from God, had maintained absolute faith, they would have served Jesus as the Son of God and as the Messiah and would have received God's will through Jesus and would have followed him absolutely. Also, John the Baptist was born to serve Jesus and should have brought his followers to believe in Jesus and receive salvation. But unfortunately, although

Zechariah, Elizabeth and John the Baptist testified at first to Jesus as the Son of God, there is no evidence that they served him as such. The respected priest Zechariah was simply a spectator. John the Baptist stood separate from Jesus. These circumstances blocked the people from following Jesus and made his path very difficult. And once this family lost faith in Jesus, looking at him through human eyes, there was no room for them to help him receive his bride.

Faced with the opposition of Mary, Zechariah, Elizabeth and finally John the Baptist, Jesus gave up hope for their protection as he sought to fulfill his mission. Therefore, Jesus left his home in search of a new spiritual foundation to restart the Providence of Salvation.

Now without a family and household, Jesus lamented, "Foxes have holes, and birds of the air have nests; but the Son of man has nowhere to lay his head" (Matt. 8:20). With his family-level foundation lost, Jesus sought to replace it. That was his three-year course.

In the end, as people disbelieved and the disciples lost faith, Jesus took Satan's attack. And as his foundation crumbled, he went the way of the cross.

Originally, Jesus came to the earth as the Messiah to give blessings to his disciples and all humankind. He was to build the sinless Kingdom of Heaven. But because of the lack of faith in him, he could not receive his bride, he could not become the True Parent and he could not accomplish his mission. This is why he promised to return.

The Lord of the Second Advent comes to perfect the foundation of God's Providence of Restoration left uncompleted by Jesus. That is to say, he comes as the seed of the original True Child to complete the ideal of creation. He comes to complete the idea of True Parents, who are the origin of the True Love, True Life and the True Lineage of God. He comes on the victorious foundation of the fundamental providence of God's side up to the time of Jesus. He also stands upon the victorious foundation of Jesus' life and finds the bride that Jesus could not find. Together they become the True Parents to save all humankind.

SOURCE: Rev. Sun Myung Moon, "The True Family Movement that will Save Mankind," *Founder's Address*. Washington, DC: Fourth Congress of the Inter-Religious Federation for World Peace, 1997 (© IRFWP 1997)

Spiritual psychotherapy

In today's individualistic milieu, many people are looking for help for their personal problems. A number of psychological self-help movements have sprung up to meet the demand. One is called the *Course in Miracles*. Its founders were professors of medical psychotherapy. One of them, Helen Schucman, discovered an inner Voice which dictated the *Course in Miracles* to her over a period of seven years. The Course has become the basis for study groups and retreat centers. The following explanation of the content of the *Course in Miracles* was itself received through inner dictation, according to Helen Schucman.

A Course in Miracles Summarized
by Helen Schucman

Nothing real can be threatened. Nothing unreal exists. Herein lies the peace of God.

This is how *A Course in Miracles* begins. It makes a fundamental distinction between the real and the unreal; between knowledge and perception. Knowledge is truth, under one law, the law of love or God. Truth is unalterable, eternal and unambiguous. It can be unrecognized, but it cannot be changed. It applies to everything that God created, and only what He created is real. It is beyond learning because it is beyond time and process. It has no opposite; no beginning and no end. It merely is.

The world of perception, on the other hand, is the world of time, of change, of beginnings and endings. It is based on interpretation, not on facts. It is the world of birth and death, founded on the belief in scarcity, loss, separation and death. It is learned rather than given, selective in its perceptual emphases, unstable in its functioning, and inaccurate in its interpretations. . . .

When you have been caught in the world of perception you are caught in a dream. You cannot escape without help, because everything your senses show merely witnesses to the reality of the dream. God has provided the Answer, the only Way out, the true Helper. It is the function of His Voice, His Holy Spirit, to mediate between the two worlds. He can do this because, while on the one hand He knows the truth, on the other He also recognizes our illusions, but without believing in them. It is the Holy Spirit's goal to help us escape from the dream world by teaching us how to reverse our thinking and unlearn our mistakes. Forgiveness is the Holy Spirit's great learning aid in bringing this thought reversal about. However, the Course has its own definition of what forgiveness really is just as it defines the world in its own way.

The world we see merely reflects our own internal frame of reference—the dominant ideas, wishes and emotions in our minds. "Projection makes perception." We look inside first, decide the kind of world we want to see and then project that world outside, making it the truth *as we see it*. We make it true by our interpretations of what it is we are seeing. If we are using the perception to justify our own mistakes—our anger, our impulses to attack, our lack of love in whatever form it may take—we will see a world of evil, destruction, malice, envy and despair. All this we must learn to forgive, not because we are being "good" and "charitable," but because what we are seeing is not true. We have distorted the world by our twisted defenses, and are therefore seeing what is not there. As we learn to recognize our perceptual errors, we also learn to look past them or "forgive." At the same time we are forgiving ourselves, looking past our distorted self-concepts to the Self that God created in us and as us.

Sin is defined as "lack of love." Since love is all there is, sin in the sight of the Holy Spirit is a mistake to be corrected, rather than an evil to be punished. Our sense of inadequacy, weakness and incompletion comes from the strong investment in the "scarcity principle" that governs the whole world of illusions. From that point of view, we seek in others what we feel is wanting in ourselves. We "love" another in order to get something ourselves. That, in fact, is what passes for love in the dream world. There can be no greater mistake than that, for love is incapable of asking for anything.

Only minds can really join, and whom God has joined no man can put asunder. It is, however, only at the level of Christ Mind that true union is possible, and has, in fact, never been lost. The "little I" seeks to enhance itself by external approval, external possessions and external "love." The Self that God created needs nothing. It is forever complete, safe, loved and loving. It seeks to share rather than to get; to extend rather than project. It has no needs and wants to join with others out of their mutual awareness of abundance. . . .

Perception is a function of the body, and therefore represents a limit on awareness. Perception sees through the body's eyes and hears through the body's ears. It evokes the limited responses which the body makes. The body appears to be largely self-motivated and independent, yet it actually responds only to the intentions of the mind. If the mind wants to use it for attack in any form, it becomes prey to sickness, age and decay. If the mind accepts the Holy Spirit's purpose for it instead, it becomes a useful way of communicating with others, invulnerable as long as it is needed, and to be gently laid by when its use is over. Of itself it is neutral, as is everything in the world of perception. Whether it is used for the goals of the ego or the Holy Spirit depends entirely on what the mind wants.

The opposite of seeing through the body's eyes is the vision of Christ, which reflects strength rather than weakness, unity rather than separation, and love rather than fear. The opposite of hearing through the body's ears is communication through the Voice for God, the Holy Spirit, which abides in each of us. His Voice seems distant and difficult to hear because the ego, which speaks for the little, separated self, seems to be much louder. This is actually reversed. The Holy Spirit speaks with unmistakable clarity and overwhelming appeal. No one who does not choose to identify with the body could possibly be deaf to His messages of release and hope, nor could he fail to accept joyously the vision of Christ in glad exchange for his miserable picture of himself.

Christ's vision is the Holy Spirit's gift, God's alternative to the illusion of separation and to the belief in the reality of sin, guilt and death. It is the one correction for all errors of perception; the reconciliation of the seeming opposites on which this world is based. Its kindly light shows all things from another point of view, reflecting the thought system that arises from knowledge and making return to God not only possible but inevitable. What was regarded as injustices done to one by someone else, now becomes a call for help and for union. Sin, sickness and attack are seen as misperceptions calling for remedy through gentleness and love. Defenses are laid down because where there is no attack there is no need for them. Our brothers' needs become our own, because they are taking the journey with us as we go to God. Without us they would lose their way. Without them we could never find our own. . . .

Through forgiveness the thinking of the world is reversed. The forgiven world becomes the gate of Heaven, because by its mercy we can at last forgive ourselves. Holding no one prisoner to guilt, we become free. Acknowledging Christ in all our brothers, we recognize His Presence in ourselves. Forgetting all our misperceptions, and with nothing from the past to hold us back, we can remember God. Beyond this, learning cannot go. When we are ready, God Himself will take the final step in our return to Him.

SOURCE: Helen Schucman, Preface to *A Course in Miracles*, April 1999 <www.acim.org> © 1995 Foundation for Inner Peace

Nature spirituality

In urbanized, industrialized cultures, many people now feel a longing to re-embrace nature-oriented spiritual ways, such as those practiced by indigenous societies. Not being directly connected with such cultures, some are now freely adapting spiritual practices which regard the cosmos as sentient and sacred, forming a movement often known as **Neo-paganism** Some Neo-pagans from the West draw particularly on ways that were thought to exist in pre-Christian Europe. Diane Mariechild, who leads rituals in the Boston area, offers the following explanation and guided meditation.

Witchcraft
by Diane Mariechild

Feminists, working to reclaim a positive image of female consciousness, are digging back to our roots. These excavations have led us into matriarchal time, a time when our foremothers had a very strong and valuable effect on each other, themselves and society. It was a time when women's values were the predominant values, a time when ancient women walked in harmony with their inner, cyclical natures, a time when women valued their intuitions and dreams.

One of humankind's oldest religions is Wicca, craft of the wise. Wise Ones—or witches, as they are more commonly known—worship the female creative force in the form of the Great Mother. The Great Mother, revered Creatress of Life, was the dominant figure for thousands of years. The worship of the Great Mother spanned the world and Her names were legion: Nut, Isis, Ishtar, Inanna, Diana, Hecate, Artemis, Selene, Demeter, Astarte, Hathor, Aphrodite, Kali, Bellona, Harmonia, Shin Moo, Rhea, Luna, Cybele, Trivia, Cerridwen.

The male force was secondary and was introduced much later as the son/lover. He was her consort; she the immortal mother of a mortal son. The horned god appeared as a later personification of nature, but the female principle, the Moon Goddess, was the Queen of Heaven. In all ancient Babylonian and Sumerian creation myths women and men were created together in pairs by the Goddess. Female and male values were not polarized then. The male was part of the female, and female and male doubled in power by manifesting side by side.

The witches' concept of a god is the life force of the universe. Feminist witches worship this life force as a triune Goddess—Artemis, Selene and Hecate—the maiden, the mother and the crone. The three-formed Goddess has also been identified with the three phases of the moon: Artemis, the waxing; Selene, the full; and Hecate, the waning. Each phase represents another manifestation of the life energy, so that the generating, the organizing and the destructive aspects are all included.

The female principle is an agent of transformation: she is both creator and destroyer. Hatred of the female principle stems from a fear of death. When we come to realize that death is only a transformation, not an end, it will no longer hold any fear. Witches do not accept death as a finality, nor do they conceive of any heaven or hell in the Christian sense. They accept, as do many other ancient religions, the reincarnational process.

Witches believe in magic. Magic is knowing that the world consists of more than a physical reality. Magic does not work against nature: rather it is a deep understanding of the highest workings of nature and a movement in accordance with it. The object of magic is not to tell the future, to communicate with the spirits or to make one's will work for various ends. These are only the means. A witch develops her powers of magic in order to develop herself. Magic requires that we begin to change the world by first changing ourselves.

Witches, acknowledging that the world is composed of more than physical reality, realize that humans also possess more than the five senses. The sixth sense, the psychic sense, which is latent in all of us enables us to connect with the world beyond the physical.

To learn the craft of the wise is to develop the powers of the deep mind. As these powers are developed, one has access to spiritual and psychic information and energy. Psychic sensitivity alone, however, will not develop the powers of the mind. Self-control and a strength of character must be combined with psychic awareness.

Witchcraft is more than a religion and the practice of magic. It is a philosophy, a way of life. Witchcraft offers us a beautiful synthesis of female and male energies. It integrates thought, feelings and intuition and provides a meaningful connection between the material and non-material worlds.

Witches celebrate each month when the moon is full, a time of great psychic energy. These celebrations are called "esbats." *Lady of Silver Magic* is a guided fantasy which enables you to create and experience a full moon ritual or esbat. . . .

Lady of Silver Magic. Relax, deepen and protect yourself. Float down now to a deserted beach. Here on this quiet beach lighted by the moon you sit and watch the moonbeams sparkling and shimmering across the water. The sparkling beams dancing on the waters carry you even deeper. And you begin a slow and steady walk. Winding your way along the shoreline, your path guided by the moon. And you feel once again that irresistible pull that draws you to her, Lady of Silver Magic.

And that magical force, shows you that you are in her presence. Whisper to her, lovely Lady of Silver Magic. And in so doing, you, her faithful daughter, find joy, serenity and peace in her presence.

Feeling that force rising within you, your pace quickens and you are pulled along, pulled as the tides are pulled, drawn back to the time of the great matriarchies, an age that is past, present and future all in one.

And ahead of you is a small grove of trees. Entering that grove now you remember a time when you were one of the wise ones and that time is now. The trees seem to part and there in the clearing is the space where your sisters gather once in the month "when the moonswell fills to brimming."

Together you silently gather the stones and begin to mark off the circle and build the small altar in the north corner.

And drawing the circle from east to north, the women, each in turn, enter the circle.

The fire is lit and facing the altar you speak: "My Lady of Silver Magic, I do build this circle, a space sacred and apart, in your honor."

Taking a torch and lighting the east you say, "Beautiful Lady of the Winds, the skies are yours. May I become as free as you."

Taking the torch and lighting the south you say, "Oh Goddess of warmth and fire, the seasons are yours. May each spring bring forth the richness of the natural world."

Taking the torch and lighting the west you say, "Oh, Lovely One, the sparking waters are yours. May the streams and rivers continue to flow clean and pure."

Taking the torch and lighting the north you say, "Oh, fertile lush Goddess of the earth, ancient mother who nourishes, who gives birth to all living things, the earth is yours. May it stay fertile and rich and free from spoil."

Facing the altar once again you speak, "Beautiful Ancient One, bless your daughters with your presence. Fill us with your light and love." All gathered now meditate on Her presence. *Pause about three minutes.*

Face the north and slowly extinguish the torch thanking the Goddess for Her presence.

Face the west and slowly extinguish the torch thanking the Goddess for Her presence.

Face the south and slowly extinguish the torch thanking the Goddess for Her presence.

Face the east and slowly extinguish the torch thanking the Goddess for her presence.

And facing the altar a final time you thank the Goddess for strengthening you with Her presence and slowly extinguish the fire.

Share farewells with your sisters and then quietly leave the grove, returning to the beach. And winding your way along the shoreline you move up and back to your usual waking reality. Return relaxed, refreshed and filled with energy. Take your time and then open your eyes and stretch your body.

SOURCE: Diane Mariechild. *Mother Wit. A Feminist Guide to Psychic Development.* Trumansburg, NY: The Crossing Press, 1981, pp. 125–9

Universalism

Certain other new religious movements have the stated goal of unifying humanity. One of these—Baha'i—has gained a worldwide membership of five million people from diverse cultural backgrounds. Its principal founder was Bahá'u'lláh (1817–92) from Iran, who claimed to be offering new revelations from God concerning human unity.

A New Revelation from the Unifier
by Bahá'u'lláh

This is the Day in which God's most excellent favors have been poured out upon men, the Day in which His most mighty grace hath been infused into all created things. It is incumbent upon all peoples of the world to reconcile their differences, and, with perfect unity and peace, abide beneath the shadow of the Tree of His care and loving-kindness. It behoveth them to cleave to whatsoever will, in this Day, be conducive to the exaltation of their stations, and to the promotion of their best interests. . . .

Beseech ye the one true God to grant that all men may be graciously assisted to fulfil that which is acceptable in Our sight. Soon will the present-day order be rolled up, and a new one spread out in its stead. Verily, thy Lord speaketh the truth, and is the Knower of things unseen.

This is the Day whereon the Ocean of God's mercy hath been manifested unto men, the Day in which the Day Star of His loving-kindness hath shed its radiance upon them, the Day in which the clouds of His bountiful favor have overshadowed the whole of mankind. Now is the time to cheer and refresh the down-cast through the invigorating breeze of love and fellowship, and the living waters of friendliness and charity.

They who are the beloved of God, in whatever place they gather and whomsoever they may meet, must evince, in their attitude towards God, and in the manner of their celebration of His praise and glory, such humility and submissiveness that every atom of the dust beneath their feet may attest the depth of their devotion. . . .

It is incumbent upon every man, in this Day, to hold fast unto whatsoever will promote the interests, and exalt the station, of all nations and just governments. Through each and every one of the verses which the Pen of the Most High hath revealed, the doors of love and unity have been unlocked and flung open to the face of men. We have erewhile declared— and Our Word is the truth—: "Consort with the followers of all religions in a spirit of friendliness and fellowship." Whatsoever hath led the children of men to shun one another, and hath caused dissensions and divisions amongst them, hath, through the revelation of these words, been nullified and abolished. From the heaven of God's Will, and for the purpose of ennobling the world of being and of elevating the minds and souls of men, hath been sent down that which is the most effective instrument for the education of the whole human race. The highest essence and most perfect expression of whatsoever the peoples of old have either said or written hath, through this most potent Revelation, been sent down from the heaven of the Will of the All-Possessing, the Ever Abiding God. Of old it hath been revealed: "Love of one's country is an element of the Faith of God." The Tongue of Grandeur hath, however, in the day of His manifestation proclaimed: "It is not his to boast who loveth his country, but it is his who loveth the world." Through the power released by these exalted words He hath lent a fresh impulse, and set a new direction, to the birds of men's hearts, and hath obliterated every trace of restriction and limitation from God's holy Book.

SOURCE: Bahá'u'lláh. *Gleanings from the Writings of Bahá'u'lláh*, trans. Shoghi Effendi. Wilmette, IL: Baha'i Publishing Trust, 1976, pp. 6–7, 94–6.

The fate of new religious movements

No matter how successfully a new prophet has gathered followers, the continuation of his or her mission depends upon what happens after he or she dies. Professor J. Gordon Melton discusses the organizational matters which come into play after the prophet's death.

After the Founder's Death
by J. Gordon Melton

In simple terms, the average founder of a new religion, especially one that shows some success during the first generation, is obviously an important factor in the growth and development of his/her movement. The movement is initially an extension of the founder's ideas, dreams, and emotional make-up. The leader may be valued as a teacher and/or venerated as a cosmic being or even divine entity. However, once the founder articulates the group's teachings and practices, they exist independently of him/her and can and do develop a life of their own. Once the follower experiences the truth of the religion, that experience also exists independently. Once a single spokesperson for the founder arises, the possibility of transmitting the truth of the religion independently of the founder has been posited. If a leader has developed a religious vision with the depth to gain a significant following during his/her lifetime, it will be a religion in which the role of the individual who created the religion, however important, will be but one element, not the overwhelming reality. Just as the disconfirmation of a prophecy rarely alters the direction of a group, so the death of the founder rarely proves fatal or leads to drastic alteration in the group's life. But what does happen when the founder dies? Generally the same thing that happens in other types or organizations, that is, very simply, power passes to new leadership with more or less smoothness depending upon the extent and thoroughness of the preparation that has been made ahead of time.

...When a new religion dies, it usually has nothing to do with the demise of the founder; it is from lack of response of the public to the founder's ideas or the incompetence of the founder in organizing the followers into a strong group. Most new religions will die in the first decade, if they are going to die.

In the overwhelming majority of cases, however, if a new religion finds some response and survives its initial phases of organization to attain a relative stability (the more so if it becomes fairly successful, with multiple centers and a mature leadership), the death of the founder will be experienced as a sad event but not a fatal or even traumatic one. In years past, the passing of a founder has often led to a power struggle, with the loser breaking away and taking some supporters to establish a rival organization. Such power struggles are a clear sign that leadership was allowed to develop in the group, though the final choice among several possible successors was postponed until after the founder's death.

Such power struggles, while momentarily important, are no more significant than any other issues that threaten schism. The more preparation is made for a smooth transition, the more likely an orderly succession is to occur. ...

One important factor that has served to further lessen the impact of succession problems on new religions is the control of property. In past years, the single leader of a group could have complete control of the group's assets. If no clear successor was named, the property was the bounty to be won by rivals. However, that concern has increasingly become a non-issue. . . . In the United States, almost all new religions are organized as corporations under the leadership of boards of directors who have formal legal control of the corporate assets. . . . Given the collective nature of the board leadership, it is not subject to the disturbances caused by the death of any single person, including a founder, in a leadership position. Imposed for tax purposes, the corporate structure has as a by-product given new religious groups an additional stability that no single leader could bequeath.

In Conclusion As we rid ourselves of the myths about new religions, we lose our naivete about their seriousness and the fullness of their religious life. We also can discard the inappropriate list of superlatives frequently used to describe new religions as totalistic societies under the absolute control of their charismatic leaders. Such talk is more rhetoric than reality and more polemic than analysis. While we observe the adulation of religious leaders in ritual setting, we also experience the ability of members to distance themselves emotionally when away from the presence of the guru. As the myths drop away, we become free to explore the rich storehouse of data available to us in the experience and operation of first-generation religion. Normal, creative people form new religious structures, and the continued generation of new religions is to be expected as a sign of health in any open society.

New religions as first generation religions, whether a new orthodox Christian movement such as eighteenth-century Methodism, or a new Hindu group built around a recently arrived guru, share many characteristics. During the first generation, the founder, whose new ideas led to the formation of the group, places a definitive stamp upon it. The first members are self-selected because of their initial confidence in the leader and/or their agreement with the leader's program. The first generation is also a time of experimentation and rapid change. The leader must discover the right elements to combine in a workable program, generate solutions to unexpected obstacles, choose and train capable leaders, and elaborate upon the initial ideas or vision that motivated the founding of the group in order to create a more complete theology. The group formally or informally gives feedback in the form of approval or disapproval of the leader's actions. The most successful leaders are continually adjusting and reacting to that feedback.

Over time, the choices open to the leader are narrowed. Structures (and expectations) develop. As the movement grows, and especially as branches are established, the leader has to work through intermediaries, and the lines of authority and communication become more impersonal. The leader's real ability to change structures, should s/he desire such adjustments, meets greater and greater resistance. Though the leader may retain some important pieces of control, the real task of managing the organization and administering the organization's affairs increasingly passes to the second and third echelon leadership. The analogy between religious and secular corporations, however much it offends religious sensibilities, is both appropriate to and informative of religious group dynamics.

Just as different religious groups will believe and act differently when their founders are alive, different groups will bring all of their unique experiences as new religions to bear in their responses to the leaders' deaths and to filling the vacuums created by those losses. . . . The problem of succession is not the determinative trauma it has often been considered to be and it in no way cuts off options limiting the group's determination of its own future course. Groups will tend to react to their leaders' deaths as they have previously reacted to other situations, and will make the necessary decisions in much the same way they have made decisions in the past.

SOURCE: J. Gordon Melton, Introduction to Timothy Miller, ed. *When Prophets Die: The Postcharismatic Fate of New Religious Movements*. New York: State University of New York Press, 1991, pp. 8–12

GLOSSARY

Apocalypse The coming of the dramatic end of the world, when evil will be eradicated and good saved by God.

Charisma Extraordinary personal magnetic appeal of a person.

Cult A religious group devoted to a single person or deity.

Esoteric Knowledge understood only by a restricted small group.

Exoteric Knowledge understood by a large group.

Mantra A syllable, phrase or verse whose repetition puts one in harmony with the divine, such as AUM (OM).

Neo-paganism A variety of ancient religions reawakening suppressed practices.

Second Advent The Second Coming of Jesus.

Sect A religious group somewhat different from an orthodox tradition.

REVIEW QUESTIONS

1   What are the current practices at the headquarters of the Transcendental Meditation movement?

2   What is Theosophy's teaching about the relationships of world religions and the esoteric/exoteric teachings?

3   What do you think would be required to bring about the utopian paradise described by the Jehovah's Witnesses?

4   Is Sun Myung Moon's appeal to the true parents and the bride of the returning

Jesus an extension of Jesus's biblical teaching? Does it matter whether it is an extension or not?

5   Can we distinguish between the psychological and the spiritual themes in "A Course in Miracles"? Discuss perception, projection, defenses, ego, truth, illusion, sin, forgiveness, God, Christ, Holy Spirit, divinity in each person.

6   How does the new Witchcraft movement differ from traditional stereotypes of Witches? Do you think conventional consciousness will accept this change?

7   Do you think that Baháu'lláh's universalism can erase people's identification with their countries? What in religion would it take to do that?

8   What effect does the death of the founder have on a new religion? Why?

9   Do you agree with J. Gordon Melton: "The continued generation of new religions is to be expected as a sign of health in any open society"? Or do you see new religions as unacceptable "cults"? Why?

10 Do you think that parents should have the legal right to hire "de-programmers" to kidnap their children under 18 who have joined what they consider a deceptive, manipulative, brainwashing "cult"? Why?

INFORMATION RESOURCES

Academic Info New Religious Movements & Alternative Spirituality, <www.academicinfo.net/nrms.html>

Beckford, James, *et al.* "New Religions," in *The Encyclopedia of Religion,* ed. Mircea Eliade, X: 390–413. New York: Macmillan, 1987

Cults, <www.rci.rutgers.edu/~religion/links/anthro.html#Cults>

Fisher, Mary Pat, *Religion in the Twenty-first Century.* New Jersey: Prentice Hall, 1999

"New Religious Movements," in *The Oxford Dictionary of World Religions,* ed. John Bowker. Oxford: Oxford University Press, 1997

New Religious Movements Links, <www.gtu.edu/library/LibraryNRMLinks.html>

The Religious Movements Page, <cti.itc.virginia.edu/~jkh8x/soc257/welcome/welcome.htm>

CHAPTER 13

THE INTERFAITH MOVEMENT

Reading the world's sacred scriptures and writings, one may be struck by the similarity of themes running through them. For example, whether in the Bible or the Bhagavad Gita or the Guru Granth Sahib, the reader is exhorted to be less attached to things of this world and more attentive to the eternal dimensions of existence, to purify the mind, and to love and serve others. Now that the world's scriptures are widely available, such similarities have become more readily apparent. Increasing pluralism within societies has also increased contact between religions. As a result, the twentieth century witnessed widespread attempts to bring people from different faith traditions closer in dialogue and spiritual relationship. The hope of those in this **interfaith movement** is that thereby the violence and hatreds which have sometimes characterized relationships between people of different religions may come to an end.

Differences definitely exist between religions. At the most basic level of religious practice, some pray with heads covered, some with heads bared; some sing jubilantly, some sit in silence. The doctrinal differences between atheistic beliefs, pluralistic approaches to divinity, and monotheism are not readily reconciled. Great divisions exist even within religions, sometimes to the point of violence. Theological distinctions are exacerbated by cultural differences, so a vegetarian Jain believing in non-violence to all life forms would find it very hard to appreciate the spiritual significance of a Santería animal sacrifice.

Many religions have developed exclusive claims to truth which make it difficult for followers of one religion to consider the possibility that other religions are also valid. Barriers between religions also exist at the managerial level. Religion has always offered its leaders the potential for amassing wealth and power. Thus people's religious sentiments have often been politicized and manipulated by those with vested interests in attracting and holding their flocks within their boundaries.

Nevertheless, the interfaith movement persists as sensitive people in each faith try to find ways to reconcile their deep beliefs in their own religion with their desire to find ways of cooperating with people of other faiths.

The oneness of religions

Mystics of all religions find underlying unity in their spirituality, which transcends the externals of religions. The following passage is from a great Sufi mystic from India who brought a universal spiritual message to the West early in the twentieth century.

Religion
by Hazrat Inayat Khan

Perhaps a person belongs to the best religion in the world. He does not live it, belongs to it. He says that he is a Muslim, or a Christian, or a Jew. He is sure it is the best religion, but at the same time he does not care to live it— he just belongs to it, and thinks that belonging to a certain religion, which is an accepted religion, is all that is needed. And people of all different religions have made it appear so, owing to their enthusiasm, and forced by their mission in life. For they have made facilities for those who belong to their particular religion, saying that by the very fact of their belonging to that particular religion they will be saved on the Day of Judgment, while others, with all their good actions, will not be saved, because they do not belong to that particular religion. This is a man-made idea, not God-made. God is not the Father of one sect; God is the Father of the whole world, and all are entitled to be called His children, whether worthy or unworthy. And in fact it is man's attitude toward God and Truth which can bring him closer to God, who is the idea of every soul. And if this attitude is not developed, then, whatever a man's religion be, he has failed to live it. Therefore, what is important in life is to try and live the religion to which one belongs, or that one esteems, or that one believes to be one's religion.

But one must always know that religion has a body and has a soul. Whatever body of religion you may touch, you touch the soul; but if you touch the soul, you touch all its bodies, which are like its organs. And all the organs constitute one body, which is the body of *the* religion, the religion which is the religion of Alpha and Omega, which was and which is and which will always be. Therefore the dispute, "I am right and you are wrong," in the path of religion is not necessary. We do not know what is the heart of man. If outwardly he seems to be a Jew, a Christian, a Muslim, or a Buddhist, we are not the judge of his religion, for every soul has a religion peculiar to itself, and no one else is entitled to judge its religion. There may be a person in a very humble garb, without any appearance of belief in God, or of piety or orthodoxy, and he may have a religion hidden in his heart which not everybody can understand. And there may be a person who is highly evolved, and his outward conduct, which alone manifests to people's views, may appear to be altogether contrary to their own way of looking at things, and they may accuse him of being a materialist or an unbeliever, or someone who is far from God and Truth. And yet we do not know; sometimes appearances are merely illusions; behind them there may be the deepest religious devotion or the highest ideal hidden, of which we know very little.

... Those who, with the excuse of their great faith in their own religion, hurt the feeling of another and divide humanity, whose Source and Goal is the same, abuse religion, whatever be their faith. The Message, whenever, at whatever period it came to the world, did not come to a certain section of humanity; it did not come to raise only some few people who perhaps accepted the faith, the Message, or a particular organized Church. No, all these things came afterwards. The rain does not fall in a certain land only; the sun does not shine upon a certain country only. All that is from God is for all souls. If they are worthy, they deserve it; it is their reward; if they are unworthy, they are the more entitled to it. Verily, blessing is for every soul; for every soul, whatever be his faith or belief, belongs to God. . . .

Every child is born in life a pupil, one who is willing to learn and willing to believe. As the Prophet Muhammad says: "Every soul is born on earth a believer; it is only afterwards that he turns into an unbeliever." It is certain that if one had not been born a believer one would never have learned the language of one's country, because if anyone had tried to teach the words and one had refused to accept the teachings as true, one would never have learned the names and character of things. For instance, if it were said, "This is water," and one had not believed it, and had thought, "It is fruit," then one would never really have known what was water and what fruit. A child is born with the tendency to believe and learn what it is taught.

The divine life has a certain capability to give life, and it gives this life as teaching to the children of earth, and this teaching is called *Dharma*, religion. Religions are many and different from one another, but only in form. Water is one and the same element, and formless, only it takes the shape of the channel which holds it and which it uses for its accommodation; and so the name water is changed into river, lake, sea, stream, pond, etc. So it is with religion; the essential truth is one, but the aspects are different. Those who fight about external forms will always fight, those who recognize the inner truth will not disagree, and thus will be able to harmonize the people of all religions.

Dharma has been given from time to time to the world, at times quietly, and sometimes with a loud voice; but it is a continual outpouring of the inner knowledge, of life, and of divine blessing.

SOURCE: Hazrat Inayat Khan, *The Unity of Religious Ideals*. New Lebanon, NY: Sufi Order Publications, 1979, pp. 5–8

Interfaith initiatives

One of the first global interfaith efforts was the groundbreaking 1893 Parliament of the World's Religions in Chicago, which for the first time gave many Westerners a sampling of the spiritual riches of Eastern religions. By the beginning of the twenty-first century, such conferences and organizations bringing together teachers and followers from many religions have become commonplace. At such gatherings, purple-robed Tibetan monks, feather-wearing leaders from indigenous religions, turban-clad Sikhs, and Christian priests wearing crosses may sit together and try to explore their common ground as well as their differences. There are also academic seminars examining points of religious similarity and difference, interfaith service projects in which people of different faiths try to live and work together, interfaith networking and conferences via Internet, and interfaith worship services. Many initiatives are also afoot to put together teams of respected religious leaders who would work together to address major social issues.

Global Imperatives for the Third Millennium
by Dr. Robert Muller

Dr. Robert Muller is a leading optimist about the possibility that humankind will develop a global consciousness. Dr. Muller was for decades the Assistant to the Secretary-General of the United Nations.

.... In my view, from all perspectives—scientific, political, social, economic, and ideological—humanity finds itself in the pregnancy of an entirely new and promising age: the global, interdependent, universal age; a truly quantum jump; a cosmic event of the first importance that is perhaps unique in the universe: the birth of a global brain, heart, senses and soul to humanity, of a holistic consciousness of our place in the universe and on this planet, and of our role and destiny in them.

Much of this new consciousness is enhanced by the prodigious advances in sciences and technology. Yet most people, governments and institutions—including religions—are bewildered by this phenomenon. They have difficulty adapting to it with understanding and creativity; they were not educated for it. They see the future with anxiety. Many of them turn and cling to the past or look inwards to the nation, ethnic group or religion which they know and where they feel secure. As a result, the world seems at a loss and is badly equipped and organized globally and politically.

But we will make it. We are learning. Once aware of our problems and errors, we are beginning to correct them. The *Encyclopedia of World Problems and Human Potential*, published by the International Union of International Associations in Brussels, lists more than 11,400 world problems but even more potentials to solve them. One progress is happening after another: the decolonization of the planet in less than forty years; no world war in half a century; the end of the cold war; the end of apartheid; a substantial decrease in child mortality; the eradication of major epidemics; the increase in human longevity, both in poor and in rich countries; a universal organization of nations; one world conference after the other, attended by more and more heads of states (the first world conference on the environment in 1972 in Stockholm was attended by only two heads of states; the second conference twenty years later in Rio de Janeiro was attended by 140); the creation of free trade areas and regional communities; and I could go on with this list. . . .

Nevertheless, one important dimension has been missing from this extraordinary journey of humanity in recent times, a dimension lamented by Secretaries-General Dag Hammarskjöld, U Thant and Javier Perez de Cuellar: the *spiritual* dimension, the highest, deepest, most common, universal and binding dimension of all. What science, politics, economics and sociology were trying to achieve, the religions knew long ago by virtue of transcendence, of elevated consciousness and union with the universe and time. This dimension is still missing, yet it is urgently needed in world affairs. . . .

The crucial task of the world's religious and spiritual traditions, and interfaith organizations is restoring a sense of spirituality to all that we do. The common heritages and institutional authority of the religions, combined with an emerging global spirituality, can make enormous contributions to the challenges and details of creating a better world. Though an atheist, André Malraux has said that "the third millennium will be spiritual or there will be no third millennium." Dag Hammarskjöld, a rational economist and world observer whom the UN transformed into a mystic, said, "I see no hope for permanent world peace, We have tried and failed miserably. Unless the world has a spiritual rebirth, civilization is doomed."

The religions are still accused of hindering peace, human progress and brotherhood. How often have I heard, after one of my speeches, "Mr. Muller, we agree with most of what you said, except one: forget about religions. They are one of the main troublemakers and dividing factors in the world." But I continue to preach about the spiritual and religious dimension. The new age we are entering will be an age of communities and of cooperation: it will be an age of family (celebrated by the UN in 1994), and of the family of nations. The family of religions cannot be absent; its absence could mean the retrocession and evanescence of religions, left behind by rapidly growing political, economic, scientific, ecological and sociological globalizations of the world. . . .

May I express my own overpowering conviction, born from five decades as a world servant? It is this:

At this crucial point of human history, on the eve of the third millennium, the main duty of the religions is not to propagate their dogmas and rituals or to try to increase their memberships. Their main *spiritual* duty is to give the world a desperately needed Renaissance from the extreme materialism and moral decay into which we have fallen. The issue is *not* whether we should pray standing or kneeling, our heads covered or uncovered; it is whether we will pray—period; whether we will be *good Samaritans* to those in need; whether we can give renewed hope to youth; whether we will revitalize the sacredness of life-giving, belief in the soul, marriage and fidelity. The main duty of religions must be to inspire love for all human brothers and sisters, especially the downtrodden, the poor, the handicapped, abandoned children, the homeless, the refugees, the innocent victims of violence. . . .

May we enter the 21st century consciously choosing to live in love, togetherness and fulfillment on this beautiful and miraculous celestial body—endowed with life and perhaps unique in the fathomless and mysterious universe.

SOURCE: Robert Muller, "Preparing for the Next Millennium," in Joel D. Beversluis, ed. *A SourceBook for Earth's Community of Religions*. Grand Rapids, MI, and New York: CoNexus Press and Global Education Associates, 1995, pp. 2–4

Declaration on the Elimination of All Forms of Intolerance and of Discrimination Based on Religion or Belief
by the United Nations

The following declaration was adopted by the General Assembly of the United Nations on November 25, 1981.

The General Assembly
Considering that one of the basic principles of the Charter of the United Nations is that of the dignity and equality inherent in all human beings, and that all Member States have pledged themselves to take joint and separate action in co-operation with the Organization to promote and encourage universal respect for and observance of human rights and fundamental freedoms for all, without distinction as to race, sex, language or religion,

Considering that the Universal Declaration of Human Rights and the International Covenants on Human Rights proclaim the principles of nondiscrimination and equality before the law and the right to freedom of thought, conscience, religion and belief,

Considering that the disregard and infringement of human rights and fundamental freedoms, in particular of the right to freedom of thought, conscience, religion or whatever belief, have brought, directly or indirectly, wars and great suffering to mankind, especially where they serve as a means of foreign interference in the internal affairs of other States and amount to kindling hatred between people and nations,

Considering that religion or belief, for anyone who professes either, is one of the fundamental elements in his conception of life and that freedom of religion or belief should be fully respected and guaranteed,

Considering that it is essential to promote understanding, tolerance and respect in matters relating to freedom of religion and belief and to ensure that the use of religion or belief for ends inconsistent with the Charter, other relevant instruments of the United Nations and the purposes and principles of the present Declaration is inadmissible,

Convinced that freedom of religion and belief should also contribute to the attainment of the goals of world peace, social justice and friendship among peoples and to the elimination of ideologies or practices of colonialism and racial discrimination,

Noting with satisfaction the adoption of several, and the coming into force of some, conventions, under the aegis of the United Nations and of the specialized agencies, for the elimination of various forms of discrimination,

Concerned by manifestations of intolerance and by the existence of discrimination in matters of religion or belief still in evidence in some areas of the world,

Resolved to adopt all necessary measures for the speedy elimination of such intolerance in all its forms and manifestations and to prevent and combat discrimination on the grounds of religion or belief,

Proclaims this Declaration on the Elimination of All Forms of Intolerance and of Discrimination Based on Religion or Belief:

Article 1

1. Everyone shall have the right to freedom of thought, conscience and religion. This right shall include freedom to have a religion or whatever belief of his choice, and freedom, either individually or in community with others and in public or private, to manifest his religion or belief in worship, observance, practice and teaching.

2. No one shall be subject to coercion which would impair his freedom to have a religion or belief of his choice.

3. Freedom to manifest one's religion or beliefs may be subject only to such limitations as are prescribed by law and are necessary to protect public safety, order, health or morals or the fundamental rights and freedoms of others.

Article 2

1. No one shall be subject to discrimination by any State, institution, group of persons or person on the grounds of religion or other beliefs. . . .

Article 3

Discrimination between human beings on the grounds of religion or belief constitutes an affront to human dignity and a disavowal of the principles of the Charter of the United Nations, and shall be condemned as a violation of the human rights and fundamental freedoms proclaimed in the Universal Declaration of Human Rights and enunciated in detail in the International Covenants on Human Rights, and as an obstacle to friendly and peaceful relations between nations.

Article 4

1. All States shall take effective measures to prevent and eliminate

discrimination on the grounds of religion or belief in the recognition, exercise and enjoyment of human rights and fundamental freedoms in all fields of civil, economic, political, social and cultural life.

2. All States shall make all efforts to enact or rescind legislation where necessary to prohibit any such discrimination, and to take all appropriate measures to combat intolerance on the grounds of religion or other beliefs in this matter.

Article 5

1. The parents or, as the case may be, the legal guardians of the child have the right to organize the life within the family in accordance with their religion or belief and bearing in mind the moral education in which they believe the child should be brought up.

2. Every child shall enjoy the right to have access to education in the matter of religion or belief in accordance with the wishes of his parents or, as the case may be, legal guardians, and shall not be compelled to receive teaching on religion or belief against the wishes of his parents or legal guardians, the best interests of the child being the guiding principle.

3. The child shall be protected from any form of discrimination on the grounds of religion or belief. He shall be brought up in a spirit of understanding, tolerance, friendship among peoples, peace and universal brotherhood, respect for freedom of religion or belief of others, and in full consciousness that his energy and talents should be devoted to the service of his fellow men. . . .

Article 7

The rights and freedoms set forth in the present Declaration shall be accorded in national legislations in such a manner that everyone shall be able to avail himself of such rights and freedoms in practice.

SOURCE: Reprinted in Joel D. Beversluis, *A SourceBook for Earth's Community of Religions*. Grand Rapids, MI, and New York: CoNexus Press and Global Education Associates, 1995, pp. 167–9

Ground Rules for Interfaith Dialogue
by Leonard Swidler

Serious attempts to explore differences and similarities between religions may require a certain mindset. Professor Leonard Swidler, Christian theologian, editor of The Journal of Ecumenical Studies, *and a veteran of many interfaith conferences, proposes some basic ground rules to facilitate such dialogues.*

Dialogue of course is conversation between two or more persons with differing views, the primary purpose of which is for each participant to learn from the other so that both can change and grow. . . .

But that is not what dialogue is. Dialogue is *not* debate. In dialogue each partner must listen to the other as openly and sympathetically as possible, in an attempt to understand the other's position as precisely and, as it were, as much from within, as possible. Such an attitude automatically includes the assumption that if at any point we might find the partner's position persuasive, we—our integrity being at stake—would have to change. . . .

The following are some basic ground rules of interreligious, interideological dialogue that must be observed if dialogue is actually to take place. These are not theoretical rules given from "on high," but ones that have been learned from hard experience.

First Rule: *The primary purpose of dialogue is to learn—that is, to change and grow in the perception and understanding of reality, and then to act accordingly.* We come to dialogue that we might learn, change, and grow, not that we might induce change in the *other*, as one hopes to do in debate—a hope realized in inverse proportion to the frequency and ferocity with which debate is entered into. On the other hand, because in dialogue *all* partners come with the intention of learning and changing themselves, one's partner in fact will also change. Thus the intended goal of debate, and much more, is accomplished far more effectively by dialogue.

Second Rule: *Interreligious, ideological dialogue must be a two-sided project— within each religious or ideological community, and between religious or ideological communities.* Because of the "corporate" nature of interreligious, interideological dialogue, and because the primary goal of dialogue is that each partner learn and change, it is also necessary that each participant enter into dialogue not only with partners across a faith line—Catholics with Protestants, for example—but also with coreligionists, with fellow Catholics or fellow Protestants, to share with them the fruits of interreligious dialogue. Only thus can the whole community eventually learn and change, moving toward an ever more perceptive insight into reality.

Third Rule: *Each participant must come to the dialogue with complete honesty and sincerity.* It should be made clear in what direction the major and minor thrusts of the tradition move, what the future shifts might be, and, if necessary, where the participants have difficulties with their own traditions. No false fronts have any place in dialogue.

Conversely, *each participant must assume complete honesty and sincerity in the other partners.* Not only will the absence of sincerity prevent dialogue from happening, the absence of the assumption of one's partners' sincerity will do so as well. In brief: no trust, no dialogue.

Fourth Rule: *In interreligious, interideological dialogue, we must not compare our ideals with our partner's practice,* but rather our ideas with our partner's ideals, our practice with our partner's practice.

Fifth Rule: *All participants must define themselves.* Only the Jew, for example, can define from the inside what it means to be a Jew. The rest can only describe what it looks like from the outside. Moreover, because dialogue is a dynamic medium, as Jewish participants learn, they will change and hence continually deepen, expand, and modify their self-definition as Jews—being careful to remain in continual dialogue with fellow Jews. Thus it is mandatory that all dialogue partners define what it means to be an authentic member of their own tradition.

Conversely, *the interpreted must be able to recognize themselves in the interpretation.* This is the golden rule of interreligious, interideological hermeneutics.[1]... For the sake of understanding, dialogue participants will naturally attempt to express for themselves what they think is the meaning of the partners' statements; the partners must be able to recognize themselves in that expression....

Sixth Rule: *Each participant must come to the dialogue with no hard-and-fast assumptions as to points of disagreement.* Rather, each partner should not only listen to the other partner with openness and sympathy, but also attempt to agree with the dialogue partner as far as possible, while still maintaining integrity with one's own tradition. Where one absolutely can agree no further without violating personal integrity, precisely there is the real point of disagreement—which most often turns out to be different from the point of disagreement assumed ahead of time.

Seventh Rule: *Dialogue can take place only between equals.* ... Both must come to learn from each other. Therefore, if, for example, the Muslim views Hinduism as inferior, or if the Hindu views Islam as inferior, there will be no dialogue. If authentic interreligious, interideological dialogue between Muslims and Hindus is to take place, then both the Muslim and the Hindu must come mainly to learn from each other; only then it will be "equal with equal."

Eighth Rule: *Dialogue can take place only on the basis of mutual trust.* Although interreligious, interideological dialogue must occur with some kind of "corporate" dimension—that is, the participants must be involved as members of a religious or ideological community—for instance, as Marxists or Taoists—it is also fundamentally true that it is only *persons* who can enter into dialogue. But a dialogue among persons can be built only on personal trust. Hence it is wise not to tackle the most difficult problems in the beginning, but rather to approach first those issues most likely to provide some common ground, thereby establishing the basis of human trust. Then, gradually, as this personal trust deepens and expands, the more thorny matters can be undertaken. Thus, just as in learning we move from the known to the unknown, so in dialogue we proceed from commonly held matters—which, given our mutual ignorance resulting from centuries of hostility, will take us quite some time to discover fully—to discuss matters of disagreement.

Ninth Rule: *Persons entering into interreligious, interideological dialogue must be at least minimally self-critical of both themselves and their own religious or*

---

[1] Hermeneutics—the branch of knowledge dealing with interpretation of scripture.

ideological tradition. A lack of such self-criticism implies that one's own tradition already has all the correct answers. Such an attitude makes dialogue not only unnecessary, but even impossible, because we enter into dialogue primarily so that *we* can learn—which obviously is impossible if our tradition has never made a misstep, if it has all the right answers. To be sure, in interreligious, interideological dialogue one must stand within a religious or ideological tradition with integrity and conviction, but such integrity and conviction must include not exclude healthy self-criticism. Without it there can be no dialogue—and, indeed, no integrity.

Tenth Rule: *Each participant eventually must attempt to experience the partner's religion or ideology "from within."* A religion or ideology is not merely something of the head, but also of the spirit, heart, and "whole being," individual and communal. John Dunne here speaks of "passing over" into another's religious or ideological experience and then coming back enlightened, broadened, and deepened.

SOURCE: Leonard Swidler, "Interreligious and Interideological Dialogue: The Matrix for All Systematic Reflection Today," in Leonard Swidler, ed. *Toward a Universal Theology of Religion.* Maryknoll, NY: Orbis, 1988, pp. 6, 13–16

Celebration of all religions

Beyond the level of comparing different religions in a spirit of mutual tolerance, is it possible that people from different religions can enter into the spiritual experiences of others on a deeper level?

Can We Share in Others' Spiritual Traditions?
by Rev. Marcus Braybrooke

The Reverend Marcus Braybrooke is Chairman of the International Interfaith Centre in Oxford, England, and is one of the longtime leaders of the interfaith movement.

The life of faith is nourished in a particular faith community. Such a community has its beliefs, its symbols, its pattern of worship, its expected behavior. These are interwoven and cannot easily be unraveled. There is a particularity about the life of faith. To what extent are we able to enter into another tradition's spiritual experience or do we impose our own meaning on it? This is partly a question of understanding the other at depth but also of whether another's spiritual occasion can become for us an encounter with the Divine. . . .

Dr. Jonathan Sacks[2] says: "A multicultural mind can use Zen for inwardness, Hassidic tales for humour, liberation theology for politics, and

---

[2] Dr Jonathan Sacks—Chief Rabbi of Great Britain.

nature mysticism for environmental concern. But that is a little like gluing together slices of da Vinci, Rembrandt, Van Gogh, and Picasso and declaring the result a composite of the best in western art."

Each religious tradition has its own integrity and I am not suggesting such pasting together. But if we have been shaped by and treasure Western music, may we not also learn to appreciate the beauties of Indian music? Indeed there are now musical works which draw upon both traditions. Can we not admire both the great Gothic cathedrals of Western Europe and the mosques of India? I believe that just as we can come to speak a language that is not our native tongue or appreciate a culture that is not our own, so we can to some extent enter the spiritual life of another faith community. Because this is the heart of the religious life, it is the most vital aspect of interreligious fellowship, even if it is the most sensitive. Here we begin to appreciate the other in the depths of his or her spirituality.

"Take off your shoes, for the place where you are standing is holy ground." God's words to Moses are a warning to all who approach the sanctuary of another faith. There is much that we shall not understand: the sacred language, the mythology, the music, the age-old gestures and ritual movements. Yet if we believe in the Oneness of God and the unity of the human family, then despite all the splendid difference and variety, there is "the selfsame aching" for God in every human heart. The attempt to enter sympathetically into the spiritual life of other traditions is a vital contribution to human unity, for such meeting is at the deepest level of our being.

It may be also that not only do we begin to appreciate the other's spirituality, but that our own also is enriched. While our regular spiritual diet will continue to be that of our faith community, it will be deepened by our discoveries, just as many peoples' traditional meals have been added to by dishes from overseas. There are some who draw from several spiritual traditions, but do not count themselves members of any particular faith community—some call themselves seekers or even universalists. . . .

Whatever our background and approach, there are moments when the gift of togetherness blinds us to our labels. . . . In some interfaith services that I have attended or helped to arrange there has been an experience of oneness felt by almost everyone present. At one service, held at Christ Church, Bath, we invited the readers to select a passage from their tradition about forgiveness and reconciliation. These were not texts from sacred writings but stories which told of recent experiences. As we listened together, the sources of the stories did not matter, for their messages spoke to us all. . . .

Interfaith worship attracts strong opposition because it is the most powerful symbolic expression of the interfaith vision. . . . Interfaith worship is not a substitute for the regular life of prayer and worship of a particular faith community, but it is a powerful symbolic reminder of our unity in the presence of the Holy One. In the Bible, all people are said to be descended from common ancestors, namely Adam and Eve. If we are to live together in one world, we need to recognize that we are one family, children of One God.

SOURCE: Marcus Braybrooke, *Faith and Interfaith in a Global Age*. Grand Rapids, MI, and Oxford: CoNexus Press and Braybrooke Press, 1998, pp. 114–19

God Will Break All the Barriers!
by Baba Virsa Singh

His Holiness Baba Virsa Singh is a revered teacher from Sikh tradition. Under his inspiration, celebrations of the major holy days of all religions have long been held in his communities in India and the United States, known as Gobind Sadan. As Sikhs, Hindus, Muslims, and Christians gathered on December 28, 1996 at his community outside New Delhi to joyously celebrate the birthdays of both Jesus and Guru Gobind Singh, His Holiness made the following prophetic statement.

One day, when Gobind Sadan was facing many problems, I was sitting on a sofa, feeling very serene and joyous. My mind was neither asleep nor awake. Great rays of light awoke me and in a vision drew my attention to this very place where we are sitting. Jesus was standing right here [a place near the dairy where now a statue of Jesus has been erected], with his arms outspread. Speaking as loud as thunder, he said, "Blesssss!" His voice seemed to echo through the cosmos. For an hour and a quarter, Jesus kept blessing and speaking about the things which were weighing on my mind. Just by his words, they were all resolved.

Even before that, I did not think that Jesus was separate from other prophets. Whatever slight sectarian boundary that existed in my mind was completely demolished then. It was not a matter of faith or pride on my part. It was by his wish that I saw him standing here in vision. I fully believe that after this happened, indescribable blessings came to Gobind Sadan.

These spiritual Powers are not only for one country, one community, one fortified institution. I feel that they are meant to bring enlightenment to the whole cosmos. Their light spreads everywhere. Our attempts to divide the Light into different countries and sects have caused us great trouble. The Light cannot be broken into pieces. It is everyone's right to celebrate whenever the holy day of any prophet, messiah, or messenger of God occurs. It is our right to welcome them in all places. I feel that if we all mold our minds like this, the light of the prophets will manifest in everyone's minds, throughout the world.

Guru Gobind Singh said, "Listen everyone, for I speak the truth: Only those who have deeply loved God have realized God." What is God? Love. Guru Gobind Singh, who called God his Father, said, "My Father is spreading light throughout the cosmos, giving blessings to the entire Creation." Jesus likewise said, "If you want to see the Power of my Father, the Creation of my Father, look at the flowers, the rivers, the trees, the animals. There is no place where my Father's light is not doing its work of blessing."

At present, our problem is that we take the name of religion without having faith in religion. Love is one, truth is one, and God is one. Then why are there divisions? If a person speaks ill of one messenger and praises another, he can never receive enlightenment. We must believe that light appeared when they came, that they were bestowing light, and that their light is here even today.

Today you yourself may be feeling inexplicable happiness, inexplicable peace. Why? Because we have been celebrating both Jesus's birthday and Guru Gobind Singh's birthday. Our feeling is that we have been moving through light all day, with light falling all around us. My firm faith is that God has filled each one with love, each to his own mind's capacity for love. Those who have come here have learned something new: that Jesus has come to a gurdwara [Sikh temple]. What is a gurdwara? The house of God. And Jesus is His son; he must come to his house. And we are loving him— what else?

Don't go near people who are critical of such things, for they are far from the Light. All of us should come beneath the Light. When you shall see one Form in all the prophets, your mind's tendency to hate will turn into kindness. Your mind will rise above the tendency to create boundaries.

I can say from full inner wisdom that these boundaries will be broken, that all these barriers will be removed, because God wants it so. He has been looking at these barriers, confined within these boundaries for a very long time, and now He feels, "I can no longer live within these boundaries." God wants to enjoy Himself, and God wants you to enjoy yourselves. Now you will see: God will break all these forts. We will all be happy, for then His blessings will fall upon us all. When a person breaks out of confinement, he breathes fresh air and moves freely through nature. When he remains in confinement, he feels suffocated.

We have been in confinement for a long time, but God now wants to break the barriers. At last He will now manifest His Light. I have full faith that the minds of the whole world will change. The public will be happy, but the religious authorities may experience some difficulties. They may be disappointed with God: "We were enjoying ourselves—What have You done now? We have concealed You until now, but now You are in the open." God will laugh: "I waited for a very long time, but you did not allow Me to come out of the boundaries, so now I am going to manifest Myself." He will say, "Let the Light go forth! Such a long time has passed while you 'authorities' were keeping a curtain between the Light and the people. . . ."

I pray, "Oh God, please make Your priests understand, for they have become very rigid and exclusive. You are the King of the Spirit. Please refresh their minds and make them understand. The public is very good; they will follow whatever they are told." Today our prayer has reached God, and now He will send a bit of His Love to His priests. He can make them understand through their dreams, through visions. We leave it to God to decide how to make them understand, but He will surely do so.

Today is a day of great happiness, of great blessings of great mercy. I have never spoken like this in the past, but today He has said, "Speak!" and I have done so. Today is a day of great celebration. It is a day for dancing. All of you dance!

SOURCE: His Holiness Baba Virsa Singh, "God will Break All the Barriers!" Talk given on 18 December 1996, at Gobind Sadan, New Delhi

REVIEW QUESTIONS

1   Find and list quotations from the religions you have studied this term that would support Interfaith unity.
2   Find and list quotations from the religions you have studied this term that would reject Interfaith unity.
3   What role is the United Nations taking in the Interfaith movement?
4   How is the word "dialogue" being used in this discussion?
5   What are the most persuasive arguments that all religions are ultimately one? Name texts and authors who present these arguments.
6   From your studies this term, what are the strongest arguments that each religion is distinct and cannot easily join an interfaith movement?
7   Do you think that religious believers can ever relinquish beliefs that their faith is the absolutely true and the exclusively valid revelation of divinity? How?
8   If you were charged with organizing an Interfaith meeting, what ground rules for discussion would you propose?
9   Write a persuasive speech that you would give to an Interfaith gathering.

INFORMATION RESOURCES

Braybrooke, Marcus, *Pilgrimage of Hope: One Hundred Years of Global Interfaith Dialogue.* New York: Crossroad, 1992.

Council for a Parliament for the World's Religions, <www.cpwr.org/index.html.>

"Dialogue," in *The Oxford Dictionary of World Religions,* ed. John Bowker. Oxford: Oxford University Press, 1997.

Ecumenical and Interfaith Links, <www.rci.rutgers.edu/~religion/links/groups. html#Ecumen>.

Gobind Sadan, <www.gobindsadan.org>.

Institute for World Spirituality, <www.worldspirit.org>.

Interfaith Center of New York, <www.interfaithcenter.com>.

International Interfaith Centre UK, <www.interfaith-center.org>.

LITERARY ACKNOWLEDGMENTS

For permission to publish copyright material in this book grateful acknowledgment is made to the following:

Chapter 1: The Religious Response: **Beacon Press**: From *Interpreting the Sacred* by William E. Paden (Beacon Press, 1992), © 1992 by William E. Paden; **David L. Miller:** From *The New Polytheism* by David L. Miller (Harper & Row, 1974); **International Publishers Inc.**: From *On Religion* by Karl Marx and Frederick Engels (Foreign Languages Publishing House, 1955); **Penguin Putnam Inc.**: "The Gay Science" from *The Portable Nietzsche*, edited and translated by Walter Kaufmann (Viking, 1994), translation copyright 1954 by The Viking Press, renewed © 1982 by Viking Penguin Inc.; **Princeton University Press:** From *The Hero with a Thousand Faces* by Joseph Campbell (Princeton University Press, 1949; second edition, 1968), © 1949 by Bollingen Foundation Inc.; **Princeton University Press:** From *The Archetypes and the Collective Unconscious* by C. G. Jung (Princeton University Press, 1968), © 1959 by Bollingen Foundation Inc.; **Rabbi Fritz A. Rothschild:** From *Between God and Man: An Interpretation of Judaism*, edited by Fritz A. Rothschild (1959; revised edition, Simon & Schuster, 1998); **Routledge Inc.:** From *The Near-Death Experience*, edited by Lee Bailey and Jenny Yates (Routledge, 1996).

Chapter 2: Indigenous Sacred Ways: **Bert Gunn:** From *Nahui Mitl: The Journey of the Four Arrows* by Tlakaelel (Kalpulli Chaplin); **Paragon House:** "Flowers in the Garden: The Role of Women in African Religion" by John Mbiti, from *African Traditional Religions in Contemporary Society*, edited by Jacob Olupona (Paragon House, 1991); **University of Nebraska Press:** From *The Sixth Grandfather: Black Elk's Teachings Given to John G. Neihardt* by John G. Neihardt, edited by Raymond J. DeMallie (University of Nebraska Press, 1984), © 1984 by the University of Nebraska Press.

Chapter 3: Hinduism: **A. P. Watt Ltd.** on behalf of Michael B. Yeats and Banares Hindu University: From *The Ten Principal Upanishads* by Shree Purohit Swami and W. B. Yeats (Faber, 1937; Rupa & Co., 1992); **Bharatiya Vidya Bhavan:** From *Ramayana* by C. Rajagopalachari (Bharatiya Vidya Bhavan, 1990); **Columbia University Press** via Copyright Clearance Center Inc.: From *Sources of Indian Tradition:* Volume I, edited by William Theodore de Bary (Columbia University Press, 1958); **Columbia University Press** via Copyright Clearance Center Inc.: From *Sources of Indian Tradition:* Volume II, edited by V. D. Savarkar (Columbia University Press, 1988); **Motila Banarsidass:** From *The Hymns of the Rigveda*, translated by Ralph T. H. Griffith (Motilal Banarsidass, 1976, 1986); **Motilal Banarsidass:** From *The Siva Purana*, translated and annotated by a board of scholars (Motilal Banarsidass, 1990); **Motilal Banarsidass:** From *The Devotional Poems of Mirabai*, translated by A. J. Alston (Motilal Banarsidass, 1980); **Navajivan Trust:** From *The Message of Mahatma Gandhi* by Mahatma Gandhi, edited by U.S. Mohan Rao (Publications Division, Ministry of Information & Broadcasting, Government of India, 1968); **The Times of India:** From "Pilgrims' Progress" by Swami Agnivesh (April 2, 1999).

Chapter 4: Jainism: **Columbia University Press** via Copyright Clearance Center Inc.: From *Sources of Indian Tradition:* Volume 1, edited by William Theodore de Bary (Columbia University Press, 1958); **Indian Books Center:** From *The Unknown Pilgrims: The Voice of the Sadhvis* by N. Shanta, translated by Mary Rogers (Sri Satguru Publications, 1985; 1997); **Jain Vishva Bharati:** From *Acharya Tulsi: Fifty Years of Selfless Dedication* by Acharya Tulsi (Jain Vishva Bharati, 1985); **Motilal Banarsidass:** "The Five Great Vows", Akaranga Sutra, Book II, Lecture 15, translated by Herman Jacobi, from *Sacred Books of the East*, Vol. XXII, edited by F. Max Muller (Oxford University Press, 1884; reprinted Motilal Banarsidass, 1964).

Chapter 5: Buddhism: **Grove/Atlantic Inc.:** From *Bankei Zen. Translations from the Record of Bankei* by Peter Haskel (Grove Press, 1984); **Jean Latz Griffin:** From "Buddhism Comes Home" by Jean Latz Griffin, from *Common Boundary* (January/February 1999); **Motilal Banarsidass:** From *Buddhacarita* by Asvagosha, translated by E. H. Johnston (Motilal Banarsidass, 1984); **Office of His Holiness The Dalai Lama and Paljor Publications:** From *Love, Kindness, and Universal Responsibility* by Tenzin Gyatso, The Fourteenth Dalai Lama (Paljor Publications); **Oxford University Press Inc.:** From *The Dhammapada* by John Ross Carter and Mahinda Palihawadana (Oxford University Press, 1987), translation © 1987 by Oxford University Press Inc.; **Parallax Press**: From *Being Peace* by Thich Nhat Hanh (Parallax

Press, Berkeley, 1987); **State University of New York Press**: From *Engaged Buddhism* by Christopher S. Queen and Sallie B. King (SUNY PRESS, 1996), © 1996, State University of New York. All rights reserved.

Chapter 6: Confucianism: **Princeton University Press:** From *A Source Book in Chinese Philosophy*, translated and compiled by Wing-Tsit Chan (Princeton University Press, 1991), © 1963, renewed 1991 by Princeton University Press; **Princeton University Press:** From "Ta Chuan: The Great Commentary" from *The Book of Changes*, translated by Richard Wilhelm, rendered into English by Cary F. Baynes (Princeton University Press/Bollingen Foundation, 1950, 1967), © 1967, renewed 1977 by Princeton University Press; **Xinzhong Yao:** From "Confucianism and its Modern Values: Confucian moral, educational, and spiritual heritages revisited" from *Journal of Beliefs & Values: Studies in Religion & Education*, Vol. 20, no. 1 (Carfax Publishing, 1999).

Chapter 7: Taoism: **Celestial Arts:** From *Embrace Tiger, Return to Mountain: The Essence of Tai Ji* by Chungliang Al Huang (Celestial Arts, Berkeley, 1988, revised edition), © 1973, 1987, 1997 by Chungliang Al Huang; **John Murray (Publishers) Ltd:** From *The Book of Lieh-tzu*, translated by A. C. Graham (John Murray, 1960); **State University of New York Press:** From "Awakening to Perfection" by Zhang Boduan, from *The Taoist Experience: An Anthology*, edited by Livia Kohn (SUNY Press, 1993), © 1993, State University of New York. All rights reserved; **University of California Press:** From *The Yellow Emperor's Classic of Internal Medicine* by Ilza Veith (University of California Press, 1972), © 1947, 1975 Ilza Veith.

Chapter 8: Judaism: **Balkin Agency Inc.:** From *The Legends of the Baal-Shem* by Martin Buber, translated by Maurice Friedman (Schocken Books, 1969); **KTAV Publishing House:** From *Passover Haggadah* by Rabbi Nathan Goldberg (KTAV Publishing House; revised edition, 1993); **Schocken Books**, a division of Random House Inc.: From *On Being a Jewish Feminist* by Susannah Heschel (Schocken Books, 1983), © 1983 by Schocken Books; **Simon & Schuster Inc.:** From *I and Thou* by Martin Buber, translated by Ronald Gregor Smith (Scribner, 1958), translation © 1958 by Charles Scribner's Sons.

Chapter 9: Christianity: **Augsburg Fortress Publishers:** From *Models of God* by Sallie McFague (Fortress Press, 1987) © 1987 Fortress Press; **Hodder & Stoughton:** From *Hildegard*, edited by Robert Van de Weyer (Hodder & Stoughton, 1997); **Orbis Books:** "Not Development, but Liberation" from *A Theology of Liberation: History, Politics, and Salvation* by Gustavo Guttierez (Orbis, 1988).

Chapter 10: Islam: **Ruth Mas:** "Women and Islam". Courtesy Ruth Mas, Center for the Study of Religion at the University of Toronto.

Chapter 11: Sikhism: **Gobind Sadan Institute and Surendra Nath:** From *Jaap Sahib of Guru Gobind Singh*, translated by Shri Surendra Nath (Gobind Sadan, 1996).

Chapter 12: New Religious Movements: **Bahá 'i Publishing Trust:** From *Gleanings from the Writings of Bahá'u 'lláh*, translated by Shoghi Effendi (Bahá 'i Publishing Trust, 1996), copyright 1939, 1952, © 1976 by the National Spiritual Assembly of the Bahá 'is of the United States. **Foundation for a Course in Miracles**, 1275 Tennanah Lake Road, Roscoe, NY 12776 USA: from *A Course in Miracles*, © 1975, 1992; **State University of New York Press:** From *When Prophets Die: The Postcharismatic Fate of New Religious Movements*, edited by Timothy Miller (SUNY Press, 1991) © 1991, State University of New York. All rights reserved; **Syndications Today:** From "Transcendental Meditation Today" by Hemant Kumar, from *India Today PLUS* (Fourth Quarter, 1998); **Watch Tower Bible and Tract Society of New York, Inc.:** From *Life in a Peaceful New World* (April, 1999), © 1987, 1994 Watch Tower Bible and Tract Society of Pennsylvania.

Chapter 13: The Interfaith Movement: **Orbis Books:** From "Interreligious and Interideological Dialogue" by Leonard Swidler, from *Towards a Universal Theology of Religion*, edited by Leonard Swidler (Orbis, 1988), © 1987 by Leonard Swidler.

Every effort has been made to trace or contact all copyright holders. The publishers would be pleased to rectify any omissions brought to their notice at the earliest opportunity.

INDEX